SERMONS

FOR THE PEOPLE.

BY

F. D. HUNTINGTON, D.D.,

PREACHER TO THE UNIVERSITY, AND PLUMMER PROFESSOR OF CHRISTIAN MORALS IN THE COLLEGE, AT CAMBRIDGE.

FIFTH EDITION.

BOSTON:

CROSBY, NICHOLS, AND COMPANY.

CINCINNATI:

GEORGE S. BLANCHARD.

1858.

CAMBRIDGE:
STEREOTYPED AND PRINTED BY METCALF AND COMPANY.

If I were to say, in the familiar phrase, that these Sermons were "prepared in the ordinary course of the ministry," and for the most part at an earlier period of it, and "with no view to their publication," I should thus show no cause why they should now be deliberately printed. If I were to record my sense of their manifold and large defects, I should but appear to be pronouncing myself, in advance, as wise as the critics. Let me only remark, therefore, that they have been both written and printed, because I thoroughly believe the things affirmed in them to be true, and have hoped that other persons might be willing to meditate upon them with me.

The title given to the book will probably suggest all that needs to be said of the principle that has governed the selection of subjects and the style of their treatment. One topic, the Reconciliation in Christ, though by no means neglected here, has a less extended and less complete presentation, because of a desire to discuss it separately, more at large, and more at leisure, than is possible now. Without bringing forward any personal claim to the attention of considerable numbers of "the people," I am earnestly desirous to render a little service to some of those who are not much in the habit of reading discourses prepared for the pulpit. Were I to give to this title a more special and local application, by emphasizing the definite article, I should not exaggerate my feeling of unmingled and unmeasured gratitude and love towards my former congregation, — a People that must always be to me, in a signification that stands alone, THE PEOPLE, — a People that I tried for thirteen years to help, whose harmony, energy, and fidelity made my work delightful, and whose constant kindness I cannot repay, save by these unworthy acknowledgments, and by an attachment that will never be changed.

F. D. H.

CAMBRIDGE, MAY 1, 1856.

CONTENTS.

SERMON IX.

SERMON X.

SERMON XI.

SERMON XII.

SERMON XIII.

SERMON XIV.

SERMON XV.

SERMON XVI.

SERMON XVII.

SERMON XVIII.

SERMON XIX.

SERMON XX.

SERMON XXI.

SERMON XXII.

SERMON XXIII.

SERMON XXIV.

SERMON XXV.

SERMON XXVI.

SERMONS.

SERMON I.

OUR CHRISTIAN FAITH A REALITY.

VERILY, VERILY, I SAY UNTO THEE, WE SPEAK THAT WE DO KNOW, AND TESTIFY THAT WE HAVE SEEN. — John iii. 11.

It seems, at first, but a very moderate claim to set up for the alleged truths of our religion, to ask that they be respected as realities. But a second thought will notice that this demand covers the whole ground. Admit that these grand affirmations are authentic, — that God is a real Father and really a Sovereign, while each personal soul — yours and mine — is his child and his subject; admit that spiritual separation from him is the most terrible of disasters, and is to be healed at any cost; admit that Jesus is really the Christ, who achieves that reconciliation, coming forth out of God, and taking up the whole experience of man; admit that for a Divine law broken, which was the real emergency, Divine Love condescending, with a Gospel for its voice and a sacrifice for its pledge, is the real relief; admit, once more, that a righteous life is really the fulfilment of human destiny, and that such a life reaching on and expanded into the life eternal is the real and personal immortality, — and you have granted the whole conclusion. For the very terms of the statement imply something beyond intellectual assent. Something beyond is certainly wanted. Such is the frailty of the connection between an abstract conviction and a vital practice, between a concession of the understanding and a grasp of the affections, that history affords scarcely a more common spectacle than an ineffectual creed. But the term I take to characterize the subject implies another element. When we say that we have come to *realize* a doctrine, we mean that, somehow, that doctrine has been wrought into the roots of our life. It has passed from a proposition accepted into an influence that actuates. Instead of lying stored away among undenied but unprized facts, never brought out for use, it enters in among cordial and controlling interests, goes into the pulses of the blood, and the changes of pain and joy. This *realizing* of Christ's truth takes place only when the truth in question emerges from the nebulous haze of conjecture into clear, sharp light, — takes hold of feeling, and is taken hold of by faith, — is transfigured from a dull guess into a radiant assurance; when religion rises among the solid verities of existence, a thing not to be put by, nor gone around, nor reasoned away, nor even let alone, but to besiege the heart with that solemn and immediate Presence whose word is, "Behold I stand at the door and knock," — to appear face to face before the whole roused and wakeful vision of our inward nature, and insist on being owned and obeyed.

Precisely this is what appears to be most needed now, and among us, for the true efficiency of religion. Speculative unbelief is not very formidable. The technical objections long ago lost the flavor of originality, and were always rather the afterthought and apology of a sceptical state, than the logical producers of it. The quarrel of Reason with Revelation, under the umpireship of just interpretation, is almost spent. The doubt that is constitutional has little to say; the doubt that is earnest commonly labors and groans its painful way to the light; and the doubt that is the offspring of a crude and conceited intellectual ambition is calmly rebuked by riper studies, outgrown with a loftier dignity of thought, and put off with childish things. But is that enough? Have we reached, or are we nearing, the victory of faith then? Is not passive insensibility often as tough an obstruction as positive denial, and unconcern as hopeless morally as opposition? We can hardly afford to boast that sophistry has not deluded us, if indifference has stupefied us. How long will it take for Christianity to rise to the throne of the world, and command its practical energies, where it meets only with the lifeless allowance, that the objections have been duly considered, and found, on the whole, not to be valid? For our religion is neither a dogma nor a theory, a thesis nor an hypothesis, a category nor a dream. It is a spiritual power. It is a personal presence. It is a governing genius of life. It is a comforter of actual sorrows. It is a quickener to every noble work. It is the world's best builder and planter and legislator and reformer. It is not a stranger to be scrutinized, but a friend to be loved, because it has first loved us. It is not a guest to be entertained, but a leader to be followed; not a secret to be found out, for its very face is a revelation; not a clever and promising applicant for a place, which thrift may turn to account or vanity display, for it speaks in the name of the Lord; not an institution that can expire by limitation, nor a form that grows old, nor a ceremony that can give up the ghost and still keep on its feet, but an everlasting and ever-living law, "vital in every part"; not a policy that can be shaped, but a principle that, by its own formative and irresistible spirit, shapeth all things. It is a reality; and, if a reality at all, then a reality that can say, "Thou shalt, and thou shalt not"; "Come unto me and I will give you rest"; "Whosoever believeth in me passes from death unto life"; "We speak that we do know, and we testify that we have seen."

I invite you to notice, then, some of the few central facts in the Christian faith, that authenticate its claim as a religion of realities. Start with the idea of God;— the *idea* of him, I say, which is a fact of our own humanity. Start, that is, on the ground of personal experience; for, if anything is real, it must be the home-scenery of your own breast. The common arguments, from the necessary notion of the Infinite, from the universality of worship in all tribes and times of the globe, I pass by. Christianity does not create the idea of God, but finds it extant. In taking the being of God for granted, it simply places itself on the basis of natural reality, — a reality affirmed by the consenting feelings and philosophies of the nations, — East and West, North and South, agreeing to pronounce atheism a monstrosity. But what concerns us here is, how Christianity deals with this sacred instinct, and proceeds to nourish and satisfy it. I say, it is after the manner of reality, unfolding real relations between this Infinite One and us, filling real wants by its revelations. "Whom, therefore, ye ignorantly worship, him declare I unto you," said not only Paul to the Athenians, but Messiah to the world. It is a real authority that speaks. This Jesus, who says to the representative Pharisee of the old Judaism that comes creeping and hungry to him by night, "We speak that we do know, and we testify that we have seen," is the ever-living Immanuel that left the glory he had with the Father before the world was to manifest that Father, one with the Ancient of Days, the same yesterday, to-day, and for ever. When he opens his lips, the style is real, because the spirit is sincere. The message is cordial, because the motive is love. There is reality in the very attitudes and occasions: for he sits down weary by a Samaritan well, in a summer noon, and talks of the worships of ages with the woman that comes to draw water; he points, as he walks on, to the sparrows that the Heavenly Father feeds; he stoops and plucks a lily, and shows it clothed of God in a glory passing the imperial splendors of Solomon.

Then there is reality in the substance of his doctrine. "God is a spirit": with that simple announcement vanish old idolatries that materialized the gods, and mythologies that multiplied them, emptying the Pantheon as no Constans or Urban could, and prostrating the altars of pagan profanation. "The Lord of the servants cometh and reckoneth with them; small and great shall stand before him; there is a right hand and a left; he divideth the sheep from the goats; whatsoever a man soweth, he shall reap": how real this makes his judgment, and how genuine his justice! But what is perhaps more special in the Christian teaching about God than anything beside, is its tender disclosures of his nearness, and his condescension to our lowliness. He is no God of distant skies, of enthroned pomp, of royal reserve, but to believing hearts close as the air and intimate as the light of day. Nothing so small but it partakes of his majesty; nothing so obscure but it publishes his paternity.

"Teach us that not a leaf can grow,
Till life from thee within it flow;
That not a grain of dust can be,
O Fount of Being, save by thee!"

This morning's waking was the touch of his hand. Last week's plan of life or study was looked down upon with his sympathizing notice. This worship is engaging his compassion. When you left your home the other day, your heart devised your way, but the Lord did really direct your steps. When you prayed that God would keep those you left there, your prayer was verily heard, and, whether by granting or denying, it will be God himself that answers you, — the personal, listening, loving God. No God that is hid away in heartless laws, or prisoned in Pantheistic ice, but the friendly God of each separate soul now, as of the elders and prophets, — of John and James, of Peter and Simeon, of Mary Magdalen and Jairus's daughter. Judæa did not exhaust his love. He is the God of these houses, and streets, and schools, as well; of our parents' solicitude, of our children's happiness, of our own frail feet. The Christian's God is a reality. No reality on earth so real!

Out of this opens the true doctrine of human intercourse with this God, or Prayer. It sweeps away the artificial notions and mechanical customs that have grown up around this most natural of the soul's acts, and restores it to its just simplicity. What is natural, if not that a child should speak to his parent, dependent weakness to sustaining power, the needy subject to the gracious king, — speak his wants, his gratitude, his trust, his hope, — speak in the common language that earnest feeling always chooses and always finds; should ask for what none else than this God can give; tell him the truth because there is a privilege in telling it? And this is prayer. It is a reality, then. It is something yearned for, and something satisfying. So speaks the world's best experience, ever since man has breathed upon it, and looked up from it to the pitying heavens. And this is what Christ and the New Testament teach about prayer: make it real; keep it fresh, simple, true, and then it will be fervent and constant. Fall under no torpid routine in it. The only safeguard for reverence in the service is to realize what it is. There is one error of worshipping God as if he needed anything we can bring; and another more common error of pretending to worship him without really believing he will grant us what we ask. To pretend to supplicate things we do not really desire, but only things that we suspect we ought to desire, — or things that we have heard others ask for, and therefore coldly conclude it is proper we should ask for, — is not prayer. It may be speculation. It may be imitation. It may be self-excitation. But it is not prayer. It is hearsay. It is traditional mummery. It is a hollow and ghastly affectation, which murders faith within, and degrades it abroad. Christ brings back the doctrine of prayer to reality: "Ask, and ye shall receive." It is all in these five words. And five homely words out of the heart are better than prolonged and polished ascriptions on a thoughtless tongue. Prayer for the least things, the commonest things, the really wished-for things, intercessions for others beloved, as little children ask what they know they shall receive, or what they know a Love wiser than their own will deny! This was the temper of those brave devotions that went up through the morning air of the Church, and have been renewed ever since where trial has kept faith clear, or the searching Spirit has touched the soul; such prayer as heroic and lofty-minded men have found to be the best of joys, — no weakness of sentiment, no refuge of fear, no hypocrite's trick, but precisely the manliest, the most rational, the maturest, the sublimest act of man.

Co-ordinate with this open-hearted and loyal communion with Heaven is the love of man, another of the Christian realities. Here again Christianity does not create the sensibility, or the faculty, but out of it weaves the bond of spiritual brotherhood. In the handling and training of that social instinct, what would be the brightest tokens of reality that any teaching could give? Undoubtedly, that it should stimulate fellowship by the healthiest motive, regulate it by the wisest law, and direct it to the purest object. Those conditions are satisfied in the New Testament. It inspires, it organizes, it consecrates charity. Its motive is disinterested mercy, of which its central and crucified Form is lifted up, the incarnate example. Its law is a broad and far-seeing equity, saving it from wronging one class by righting another, from destroying without constructing. Its object is the personal relief, the universal liberation, and the spiritual rectitude of every soul, and thus the preparation of a righteous society, or church, which is the coming of the heavenly kingdom on earth. In all this process, in every step, reform, advance, does not the action come straight home to us as the very necessity of history, prophecy, aspiration? Yet this, and only this, is the philanthropy of Christ. All wanting from this is short-coming from the Gospel standard. All added to this comes of mortal mixtures. To publish calls to honorable labor in the kennels of starvation; to equalize work and wages for the least protected workman and workwoman; to open roads to self-respect from every home in the land; to encourage defeated and despairing energies; to bring celestial pity and gentle words into those dismal dens where a false civilization has too long caged its insane or outcast children; to break the bonds of old oppression and let the oppressed go free; to measure labor, not by the traditions of prejudice and pride, or the outside form of the business, but by the spirit of the workman, and so to make all lawful toil of impartial estimation; to ward off cold and hunger from penniless infancy and age; — all this is of the very substance — is it not the glorious reality? — of our Christian faith, in its action on the mutual life of men.

Turning from the social to the private offices of Christianity, we find the self-witnessing proofs of genuineness equally bright. For here we encounter the only satisfactory interpretation of what may be called the natural admiration and yearning towards an ideal moral perfection. It is only in very inferior natures that this sensibility to exalted goodness is utterly depraved, and its frequent dulness on the one hand is hardly a more palpable stupidity than the denial of its existence on the other. Baseness itself secretly confesses the beauty of magnanimity. A guilty life rarely wipes out the last trace of childish loyalty to the right and good and true. The story of triumphant fidelity, of an incorruptible conscience, of purity coming out white from her walk through foul intriguings as if "a thousand liveried angels lackeyed her," — this is the perpetual charm of literature, the undertone of drama and epic, and the unconscious challenge of every people under the sun; — while with all select souls, the tantalizing disparity between the aspiring aim and the lagging performance, is the tragic element that, except for the Gospel, so often throws over our life the sickening suspicion of total failure after all. So real is the passion for the Best. How does the Gospel justify it? First, by pronouncing its hearty benediction on these native aspirations, as the very divine seal set on humanity,—its pledge of kinship with heaven, the silent prophecy and infallible foreshining, however baffled for the present, of a life to come,—a "light lighting every man that cometh into the world." By encouraging them: "Why, even of yourselves, judge ye not what is right?" By furnishing them nutriment and a discipline, to ripen their vigor, and make them strong leaders towards a goodness unattained: "forgetting the things that are behind, reaching forth unto those that are before." By holding ever up, before us, one in whom all their promises are realized,—realized,—a veritable instance of immaculate sanctity and symmetrical virtue, taking our infirmities, yet "the master-light of all our seeing," "tempted in all points like as we are, yet without sin." And finally by giving them an hereafter where they shall mature into open vision and into calm and balanced power,—thought running unrestricted into deed,—aspiration playing, through some finer spiritual organization, into direct achievement,—and believers who now see through a glass darkly, and know but in part, shall see face to face, and know even as they are known;—the sad reality of our nature met, fulfilled, satisfied, in the animating reality of faith, by him who is the Resurrection and the Life!

Not less does the New Testament fit the varieties of human consciousness and experience in its great doctrine of a ruling choice determining character. It does divide the world into two sorts of persons, by the inexorable line of that voluntary consecration. Every life has a preponderating bias, — a characteristic motive. If our weak insight fails to read these hidden qualities accurately in others, it is only because our function is not that of critics on one another, but of stewards answerable for ourselves. Of course Christianity does not stultify itself by denying the mixtures of disposition, or disallowing the gradations of virtue and vice. But it fixes a limit where those mixtures no longer confuse. There is one differencing point — and it is the point of motive — where the world's people and God's people divide. There is a mark where living for self-gratification, whether sensual or intellectual, ends, and living for Christ and his righteousness takes its place; where self-will ceases to be the controlling force, and religious submission or consecrated principle begins to be. There may not be, there will not be, spotless holiness on one side, nor unmitigated and demoniacal depravity on the other. But there is a divergence as wide apart in its issues as heaven and hell. On one side, notions, feelings, acts, which might otherwise seem to be neutral, take a taint of evil from an ungodly bias of the life. On the other side, actions and feelings which might otherwise be indifferent are stamped as good, because the ruling affection, the radical intention of life is right, or Christian. So neutrality ends, and every least thing has one of two contradictory, characteristic qualities. And so regeneration is both a philosophical and a Christian fact. "Ye cannot serve God and mammon." If the Lord be God, follow him; and if Baal, then follow him. Except ye be born again, out of the negative natural life into the positive and spiritual, ye cannot enter into the kingdom of Heaven. Christianity confirms common sense. Just as the world says of you, "He is a sound, true man, through and through," — or, " He is a false, hollow man at the core," — the Bible replies with a scene of judgment where there is a right hand and a left, and by saying, " I know mine own; no man can pluck them out of my hand"; " Between Dives the glutton, and Abraham's bosom, there is a great gulf fixed"; and " Choose ye this day whom ye will serve."

But there is one reality in human nature darker and more fearful. That law and guide of life I spoke of, so real in its uncompromising command, — so benignant in its protection of our waywardness, has been broken, — is broken every day. Those soaring aspirations that beckoned us to Heaven are shamefully trailed in the dust. Or even if the choice has been fixed aright, still the law is holy, just, and good, for it is the will of that Infinite Purity before which angels veil their faces, while the saintliest life ever transfigured by trial or refined by the fire of martyrdom is not clean. Yet there is no concession in that august command. "Thou shalt, and thou shalt not," sounds on from age to age, as if obedience were expected to be. Without speculating on a problem so vast, the question gathers close home to the breast, and grows intensely personal, Where am I, and what is for me? I am daily disgraced by these earthly appetites and small desires, these petty captivities to temper and vile surrenders to sense. I am weak, and worse than weak. I am frail and offending and guilty. The meanness of ingratitude to my best Benefactor aggravates the iniquity of transgression. By speech, by thoughts, by imagination, by things undone that I ought to have done, by openings of blessed opportunity neglected, by stationary capacities and languid zeal and cold affections, I am condemned and lost. I look up at the splendor above the stars, the holiness of God, and it is both too dazzling and too far. Who shall deliver me from this death?

Christ shall deliver thee. He has come for that, — to seek and save the lost, because his Father so loved the world. And somehow, in ways that I will not be presumptuous enough to try to shut up into my definitions nor measure by my dogmas, — by his life, teachings, death, resurrection, intercession, all contributing ineffably to complete a redemption that no creed can comprehend, nor critic analyze, — he brings the wandering will back, the prodigal spirit home. The stern handwriting of ordinances is blotted out. Whoso believeth in him cannot perish, but is passed from death unto life, — eternal life. This is all. Ingenuity can add no supplement to that. Theologians can make it no plainer. Sects may fasten on this or that special feature of the redemption, and shape their systems accordingly; but it is *the whole* that redeems. The heart of the world has accepted the reconciling mystery, and will not let the divine reality go. "This only I know," said the believing, wondering, trembling blind man when his eyes were opened, — "this only, whereas I was blind, now I see." This only I need to know; the faith that saves is the faith that inspires, — the faith of practice, working by love, proved by charity, triumphing in integrity, constant unto death, making the Christian ever more and more like the Master, more true to man, humbler before God. For if any man have not the spirit of Christ, he is none of his. We have reached the supreme reality, characterizing the Gospel, crowning the cross, satisfying the soul.

From these slight and obvious suggestions, putting forward only what is plainest and most familiar, infer, my friends, what you see I have been attempting to open, of the reality of our Christian religion. In its ministry to the deep cravings of simple, honest hearts; in its marvellous adaptation to the pain and gladness, to the fear and hope, to the frost and the fire, of our inexplicable humanity; in its unpretending address to our common habits, speaking the language of life and wearing the look of nature; in its boundless relief for a boundless difficulty; in its expanding and exhaustless fulness for all glowing souls, — it is the reality of realities. I had almost said, it is the one only reality of which all visible being is but the unsubstantial shadow. It is the closest, dearest, most undeniable, most human, and divinest fact given us to feel. Religion is all of this, or it is nothing. Its claim is valid altogether, genuine from core to surface, or else it is counterfeit, metal and mould alike. The pulpit is grounded on this foundation, or it is grounded nowhere. It stands, not to repeat dead ceremonies, nor to mutter magical incantations, nor to echo heartless traditions, but to reproclaim and reaffirm verities that enter in among throbbing hearts, yearning souls, and beat with all the solemn and joyful pulses of life. It is the dispensation of God, the highest law of man, the determiner of destiny, the master-thing in thought, and study, and action, — a reality for the lowly and the exalted, for illiterate and learned, for the slave and the sage, hidden how often from the wise and prudent, but revealed evermore unto the childlike heart. I ask you to honor the ministry of Christ for Christ's sake, and to heed it for your own, — to honor the office as a reality, spite of the ever-present and ever-palpable proofs of the infirmities of the administration, — to heed the cause, notwithstanding the poverty of the plea. For here it shall not be otherwise than it has been from the beginning, — that the weakness of God is mightier than man, and the foolishness of God is wiser than man.

Brethren, in the first conflict between the Gentile darkness and the Christian light, Paganism condescended to offer Christianity a respectable place in the temple of its idols. The poor Galileans knew their poverty; but, shelterless and few and friendless as they were, they were too rich for that proud patronage. They turned away. They took up staff and scrip; they tied on their sandals, and journeyed forth. Christ went with them. Out of weakness they were made strong. They went up to Rome, the world's centre and strong-hold, as prisoners, and took it as conquerors. They quenched the violence of fire, stopped the mouths of lions, waxed valiant in fight, put to flight the armies of the aliens. They led captivity captive. They looked on the Pretorian eagles and were not afraid, — for the Spirit had descended like a dove. They did not tremble at crosses, for they bore a cross for their standard, and its banner over them was love. They turned from prudent philosophies to the eager heart of man. They preached, they lived, they died, they rose again, for a reality. They spake that they did know; they testified that they had seen. And unto the end, when all things shall be surrendered up to the Father, the ministry that avails must be the ministry of their Christ, and of their sincerity, — of their reality of faith, as the substance of things hoped for, the evidence of things not seen.

SERMON II.

REALITY IN RELIGIOUS MANIFESTATIONS.

SIMPLICITY AND GODLY SINCERITY. — 2 Cor. i. 12.

I TAKE these words out from their connection, and present them alone, because the rest of the passage is less suited to my purpose. It is enough to notice that the Apostle mentions these qualities as attributes of the genuine Christian. He thinks the whole Gospel he is set to preach and defend is more likely to get a hearing from the world's common sense, and to lodge itself in the world's convictions, for being presented in the spirit and manner of those traits. Whatever may be his own infirmities and short-comings, he rejoices in the consciousness that he has been honest. Gifts and accomplishments aside, he can say without immodesty that he and his associates have at least this legitimate claim to confidence, — the testimony of a good conscience that in simplicity and godly sincerity they have had their conversation in the world. Had it been otherwise, the planting of the Church might have taken damage from their obliquity, and the tardy triumph of the Christian ideas might be chargeable upon the messengers. Such congratulation is not pride, but Christian dignity; not self-laudation, but self-respect, which is the opposite of self-laudation; not boasting, but gratitude to the grace of God.

You will readily recall those aspects of the Christian faith which offer it to us as the Supreme Reality. Real in the positive and eternal objects it reveals; real in determining our relations to that Original and Infinite Spirit, diffused through all things, creating all, sustaining all, the ground of all life, and thought, and act, and hope; real in the style of its address, the tone of its appeal, and its whole bearing toward our humanity; real in its express adaptations of supply and satisfaction to personal and universal wants of human nature; and real in the palpable ends it proposes, as righteousness, charity, beneficence, for earth and heaven, — Christianity cannot be more viciously misunderstood or foolishly maltreated, than when it is thrust out of the circle of solid interests, and held at the arm's length of suspicion. The Church is a vital, natural, rational, precisely because it is a divine organization. It has its roots in God's miracles precisely because of the depth and intensity of man's need of it. Its fibres are all intertwined with the fibres of human breasts. The cover is not going to be taken off, some time, to show us an ingenious contrivance of mechanical wires, springs, and pulleys, for working up stupendous stage-effects of Christian impression and Christian history. The tapestry is not going to open, and terrify us with some ghostly apparition. The sun is not going to rise and scatter these sacramental hosts, like airy armies of morning mist and cloud. We stand on substance, or there is no substance, and the universe itself is spectral.

To this way of welcoming the divine message, there are unquestionably hinderances, partly clinging to the weaker or worse side of human nature, and partly a factitious result of theologic mismanagement. One of these hinderances is the invisibleness of the objects of faith, though I suppose the prominence of this cause for religious indifference has been popularly overrated. It would be a sufficient answer to it, that the things most valued, and clung to, and suffered for by men, are not commonly things that can be seen or measured. The sacred ties of friendship are not fastened by the senses. Would you allow me to say, Your friend is nothing but his body? You never saw the national fame for whose unsullied purity you would die, nor touched nor tasted that fidelity of love whose defence writes half the tragedies of literature. Money itself, the very symbol of material value, is rated — by any but the most sottish cupidity — less for itself than for the imponderable deference, admiration, self-complacency, independence, which it is thought able to buy. In fact, so far from the invisible repelling interest, there is no charm so bewitching as a new theory of its mysteries. The superstition that will pry behind its veil, or listen for its vaguest noises, is one of the most permanent and most absorbing passions of the race. Still, with a portion of mankind, and, in certain materialistic moods, with very many, a degree of dimness does probably invest spiritual things from their being unembodied; what is seen crowds what is not seen out of thought, and finally out of faith; heaven remains an abstraction simply because its gates are shut to the senses.

Another unrealizing influence strikes religion, from the oppressive disparity between the magnitude of the concerns and the infirmity of the treatment. Reverence fades out, wonder is tamed down, faith is frittered away, with the familiar belittlement of themes vast as infinity, by unworthy hands. The Gospel has to be repeated by stammering tongues. Promises that of themselves should thrill all souls with ecstasies of hope, are pronounced in our flat, insipid speech. Warnings more tender and awful than a mother's entreaty are uttered in tones that routine and repetition have rendered thin and dry. The wisdom of the All-wise has for its advocates frail judgments, dull insight, and men of like passions with the rest. Shall it never be learned that treasure is none the less treasure because it is in earthen vessels? In other matters, the enthusiasm of a close, personal interest is not deadened by a dull declamation. A science is hardly held responsible for the eloquence of a lecturer, nor does a tempting speculation go by default if the story of it happens to be brought across the continent by a poor specimen of a man. To make Christianity depend on the power of its preachers, or the skill of theologians, is at once to measure absolute beauty, truth, and good by mortal competency, and to stimulate the pulpit with a spur as foreign from Gospel simplicity as it is insulting to the authority of God. The function of a clergy is not the audacious one of representing the Majesty of Heaven, but to plead generously with the reluctance of men; not to dole out God's compassion by the petty dimensions of their intelligence, but to be unpretending heralds of a Christ who makes their weakness his strength, and even the foolishness of preaching the wisdom of God unto salvation.

It aggravates this unreality, that there is so imperfect an adjustment, in the Christian mind, of the relations between the spiritual world and our present life. By a twofold error, the object of religion has first been represented as personal happiness, and then that happiness has been located in an arbitrary future, not beginning till death rids us of bodies. A selfish salvation, with mechanical conditions! In this sharp-cut division of earth and heaven an artificial antagonism is created, not between good and evil, or sin and holiness, which are the actual opposites, but between two epochs in a chronological succession, the grave being the partition line. Heaven is wages to be waited for, instead of a nobler play of the disinterested life already begun. Two worlds from the same perfect Hand are put into contrary sides of the scale, and hatred of one of them is made a passport to the other. At once unspiritualizing the motives to piety, and indiscriminately condemning the present, the doctrine repels all natural confidence. Shallow minds recoil from a representation which they instinctively feel to be false, and seek a wretched refuge in unconcern. Add to this, sometimes, a technical phraseology, putting the moving and blessed facts of righteousness and redemption into language which either to educated tastes or to unsophisticated common sense sounds like both a provincialism in letters and an affectation of theology, and you have another explanation why these transcendent realities look unreal to so many eyes. This may be no excuse for blunders that study would correct; but it is an instructive admonition to direct, simple, every-day speech in dealing with things so supremely real.

After all, however, there does remain a vast, conscious indifference to Christian truth, from sheer and guilty impatience of its control. These realities are purposely thrown into obscurity, because they interfere with indulgence, cross ambition, yoke the passions, chastise temper. They not only ask that we should allow the spiritual world an inert place in our belief, as we might a new planet or botanic species, but they enter as a prohibition and a compulsion. There must be irksome self-denial. This Gospel is something more than an entertaining comer at the table of literary hospitality; it erects itself into a master of the house; and lo! every appetite and lust must obey it on penalty of a judgment. The mouth of slander must be stopped. The jealous competition must relax. The profanity must be renounced. The stubborn, atheistic knees must bend. The arrogant will must cry out of the dust, "Not as I will, but as Thou wilt, for Thou alone art holy." So the struggle begins. Depravity fights this benignant master. Rebel passions reject that heavenly coercion Still, the Eternal Voice cannot be put by. What, then if the coward spirit should feign ignorance, and, by keeping the ineffable glory at a distance, gradually make it as unreal as sin could desire? Let these bright rebukers fade from me, and be dim! Is there no magic that can turn substance into shadow? no chemistry that can transmute facts to phantasms? It appears again, what I said before, that to realize the Christian facts would be to take up the Christian consecration, and enter on the life. Christianity wants nothing so much as a steady look at it, out of honest, seeing eyes.

The question next before us, then, concerns the manner of operation and manifestation of this Christian power, in the lives of its believers, and the conversation of its teachers. The law here appears to be clearly enough pronounced, by the nature of the power itself. A spiritual principle and fact, the very essence and inmost soul of real life, Christianity must be offended and weakened by any other than a look and tone and temper of reality in its expression. After its first supernatural incarnation, its agents are men. The organs of its movement are human faculties. Then its action ought to be according to the natural working of human powers in their right or normal play. The Christianity that is meant to be developed on earth, beautifying its life and blessing its affections, is not an abstract thing, nor an angelic thing, but a human thing: human, that is, in the sense of acting through human conditions in free harmony with the best human forces, though superhuman in its source and sanctions, as in fact humanity itself is: so that the correspondence holds throughout. The kind of Christian action and Christian speech wanted for the best exhibition of Christian truth, is that where the word and the deed just follow and obey the meaning of the soul; where the feeling or conviction of the truth exactly measures, spaces, and shapes the outward profession; where the disciple holds it an equal infidelity to pretend to more or to less faith than he possesses; where the spirit of zeal just occupies, fills up, and animates the body of appearance; where, in fact, the expression is not nicely regulated by a conscious and special reference to its external effect, as being exemplary, but by a certain spontaneous and irresistible impulse of a holy purpose in the breast. The bearing of a religious man, that is, must be the bearing of a man *with religion in him and actuating him;* religion, not as a supplement to his manhood, but infused all through it, hallowing and animating it; religion, not taken on, but circulating within; not worn, but informing; not borrowed, but breathed forth; "simplicity and godly sincerity."

To this Christian reality of living there are two principal opponents: hypocrisy on one side, and indifference on the other. Each needs to be a little analyzed and illustrated.

Hypocrisy, as respects Christian qualities, is the general name we give to the disposition that aims to appear better than it is. The hypocrite seeks the credit of qualities which he not only does not possess, but knows he does not possess: it is a conscious deception. To complete the idea of hypocrisy, there must be a reference to some selfish advantage, as custom for a trader, or votes for a politician, or fame for a scholar. The pretention is not only fraudulent, but the fraud of meanness, — the grossest of all forms of insincerity; — "the lie," as Bacon says, "that sinketh in." The intensity of Christ's disgust at this temper may be gathered, as from the whole spirit of his teaching, so especially from the vivid rebukes he gave it in the Hebrew Pharisees. The common instincts of honor accord with the Bible in declaring it the guiltiest of all sins that are not crimes. It is the most fatal enemy that Religion has to confront, and tearing off its mask is her most unwelcome task. Yet superficial critics persist in making her chargeable for the very insults it heaps upon her.

On the same side of reality, or departing from it in the same direction, as professing more faith than there really is, we find a lifeless formalism. In the former case, Christian vitality had no existence, and the semblance of it was a pure fabrication. Here it lived once, but has gone into decay, and the semblance of it is the surviving shape, when the life has gone out. It is to the credit of human nature that this sin, if more frequent, is less enormous. Yet there is no calculating its practical mischiefs, especially in repelling from the Christian ranks the sympathies and confidence of the young. For, notwithstanding its aberrations, the soul retains this trait of native nobility, that it will knowingly trust none but true men.

There are two branches of this trespass upon reality: excess of ceremony and excess of dogma.

Like all the great practical interests, religion clothes itself in a dress or form, — institutional customs, modes of worship, ordinances. So long as we inherit forms, and have in our natures an element to which visible ceremonies appeal, this tendency will not be eradicated, though it is constantly being modified. The real argument for religious forms is found in all civilized usages, — such as the general arrangement of houses, uniformity of fashions in clothing, tokens of recognition, familiar phrases of salutation, the manners of hospitality. Variety amounts to modifying the form, never to abolishing it, — those sects which have started with the idea of abolishing it generally ending in a more rigid formality than the rest. Yet at this very point lies a constant peril to "simplicity and godly sincerity." Church history shows a perpetual struggle to keep an honest balance between the spirit to be expressed and the form expressing it, — the faith of the heart and the fashion of the institution. Whenever this proportion is lost, the disorder that we call formality begins. Observance overlays feelings. The faith is not vigorous enough to inform and carry off the institution. The temple is too big for the divinity. Instead of the grace of nature, you have the awkwardness of imitation; instead of speech, mummery; instead of expression, grimace; instead of gesture, beating the air. Either there must be an accession of fresh feeling within, to reinvigorate the old form, or else the old form must be abated, or changed, to suit the changed feeling, or buried for decency's sake. Somehow, at any rate, the man will not enact what he does not believe. That is the one wrong that kills reality and kills respect.

To expect to revive a declining faith merely by multiplying ceremonies, is as hopeless as to multiply pumps in a dry well, or to try to restore the dead by more garments. The life to refill these empty veins must come from another source. It must come, by prayer, from the Spirit of God. No preservation of the dried shell of the cistern will cheat nature into thinking there is a fountain beneath. "Simplicity and godly sincerity" require that every ceremonial observance should be so adjusted as to convey the real feeling, and no more, — the real faith, and not an artificial faith or a faith such as may have been felt once. The ceremony was meant for the symbol of a real conviction. When we substitute it for the conviction, and let that drop out, going coldly and mechanically through the genuflexion or the manipulation, we destroy reality, and enter on a mocking falsehood. Yet it is just when men find their interest failing, and are alarmed at it, that they are tempted to redouble their assiduity at the ceremony.

A corresponding loss of soul, and sacrifice of reality, take place in respect to creeds, or statements of belief. Too much ceremony is acting more than we believe: too much dogma is affirming more than we believe. In each case, the expression outruns the sentiment. The salt has lost its savor. No heartless eloquence ever yet stole the secret of a sincere conviction. The reason that the first period when faith is declining, and before it has yet gone over to worldliness or sensuality, is generally marked by a multiplication of dogmatic articles, or definitions, is that the inward consciousness of want alarms the conscience, and the intellect goes to work to supply the deficiency. Theologians grow sensitive, exacting, and controversial. An age of dogmatism is, therefore, an age of morbid self-consciousness, when the understanding is trying to do the heart's neglected business.

The common and offensive form in which these unrealities of religious profession appear is cant. The source of all cant seems to be an attempt to speak and act certain things, which the narrow and perverted mind has decided should be the proper utterance of religious emotion, — but with the emotion left out. The best that can be said of it is, that it is not always hypocrisy, but sometimes only stupidity. Of course it is totally inconsistent with spirituality, which is always fresh, always vital, always real. No soul that has been touched with the simple majesty of the Sermon on the Mount, that has sat at the feet of the truthful Jesus, that takes its spiritual draughts from that fountain of which if a man drink he shall never thirst again, can consent to affront the eternal veracity by offering as a plea for piety, or a prayer to the Father, a hollow phrase, a sanctimonious manner, a technical expostulation, a language caught from the ancient lips of faith, but emptied of all its living significance, and dwindled now into the drivel of make-believe. As soon could a son ask for his lost mother in the pompous and stilted terms that memory has learned from some printed dialogue. Let learned unbelief, let sneering scepticism, let ingenious and sophistical infidelity, accumulate all their arguments upon my child's unfortified intelligence, rather than that this paralyzing cant of an unfelt devotion should creep with its slow poison into the reverence and earnestness of his soul. Paul's justification of his apostleship, "I believed, and therefore have I spoken," is the only decent pretext for any preaching or any prayer. "Simplicity and godly sincerity."

Godly sincerity. The other danger to reality in a religious life and conversation, besides that of its not being religiously real, is that it will not be really religious. If there is one false tendency to pretend to more faith than is felt, there is another, not to let feeling have its free and natural way. If some men speak more than is honest of religion, others have no religion to speak honestly of; and the one class is as far from *godly* sincerity as the other. Never imagine that a diluted, indifferent, half-worldly character is a more genuine or more conciliating sort of character than one that is decidedly, thoroughly, and zealously Christian. If that is the opinion of men of the world, as they are called, then men of the world do not know the world they are of. There is no fascination on earth like that of disinterested and steady enthusiasm. Every class of men will pay it at least a secret homage. When you would win the confidence and interest of thoughtless persons to the Christian life, do not introduce them to professed disciples, who keep their Christianity as far as possible in the background of their daily interests, and have practised the art of living so near the boundary of righteousness as to fraternize with the levities and ambiguities and sharp practices outside. You might better hope to engage a young man's interest in knowledge by being a little ignorant, or in work by being a little idle, or in philosophy by being a little foolish, than try to make him respect religion by meeting him half-way and being a little irreligious. I think there is a deep, silent loyalty in most men's hearts for that inspired maxim, — "Whatsoever thy hand findeth to do, do it with thy might." Even in the most careless breast I suspect there is a notion which might express itself something like this: "No; I am not, I frankly confess it, on Christian ground; I hope I shall be; I know I ought to be; but whenever I am, it shall be a Christianity that is thorough, that is definite, that is positive, that is in earnest; I want that or no religion at all; no lukewarm, sluggish vacillation between God and Mammon; I would rather be Mammon's altogether, and know my master: and wherever I see an earnest, consistent, whole-hearted Christian, there I find the mightiest argument for the Gospel." So it is that godly sincerity becomes a silent missionary everywhere, and converts more hearts to Christ than all loud and loquacious temporizers and compromisers with the passions and fashions of the world.

For two reasons, my friends, — for our own soundness of heart, and for the recommendation of the Gospel to others, — we want a type of Christian character that is simple in its spirituality, and real in all its manifestation. Nothing is surer to consume the health and vigor of the soul, than the constant acting of an unfelt part, — like the pretender, on the one hand, or the constant denier of his holiest aspirations, the unrepenting worldling, on the other. There is a reflex influence from every tone and gesture of insincerity, which strikes back and debilitates the moral energies. Utter what you do not believe, and you will have less and less capacity for believing anything. Pretend what you do not feel, and feeling will die out. The retribution is dreadful, and sure, and works by an inevitable law. Or if you stifle the religious life that really wakes and rises within you, denying it air and light, you forfeit no less the blessing of the candid and sincere.

Then a ministry unquestionably gains power, just in the degree it drops factitious methods and weapons, and abides by the simple instruments of genuine convictions.

We all know the narcotizing tendency of official repetition. Pray for the preacher, then, that he may be delivered from its lethargy. God will never suffer it to be irresistible. Remember that it is in the power of any audience, by a responsive and wakeful assistance, to neutralize it, and almost to compel from their minister the heartiness they prize. Besides, you yourselves are, in some sense, to be ministers of heavenly truth. For Christ or against him all of you are living, speaking, acting, every day. Does the immortal cause take hinderance from your falsity, or furtherance from the reality of your righteousness?

The exigencies of the Church, the mixtures of sects, the progress of theology, all point out the style of life that is wanted now, to gain, for the ideas and the spirit of our common faith, a fair and cordial reception. It is a life that flows evermore from the divine spring of a living and personal communion with the Father, and goes to help every brother, and to bless every neighbor; that, while it is hid with Christ in God, walks among men with the tenderness and dignity of the Son of Man; that asks no deference for its profession, but professes simply because it cannot help telling its trust, owning its gratitude, honoring the Master; that by open and solemn reverence for the times and places of God's worship obeys the manliest of instincts, and by consecration to the Church confesses the inmost obligation of conscience; that finds an exercise for its Christian principle in all the companies, associations, resorts, employments, of the world, and a temple for its praise in every scene of joy; that brings an added grace to all the innocent amenities and hopes of youth, and sets a more splendid crown on the saintly head of age; that sanctifies society and kneels in the closet; that hallows study and guards homes, and is not afraid to show its sacred spirit of justice and moderation in places of sinless amusement; and that everywhere bears with it this meek, brave testimony, that by "simplicity and godly sincerity" it has had its conversation in the world.

God has graciously relieved us of all concern about the special shape our Christian life shall put on, that we may be the more undivided in our care for its spirit. Have the soul of goodness, and it will fashion its own form, hour by hour. The best profession of righteousness is being righteous. The best form of godliness is the form most naturally taken by the power thereof. The best temper of church or clergy is "simplicity and godly sincerity." The best bearing for a believer, making confession of his faith, is the bearing with which he comes out of the closet of a lowly and solemn communion with his God. The best posture of dignity is the attitude that yields most friendly service to needy men. The transcendent and majestic posture of the Son of God was when he leaned to wash his followers' feet.

When this last, most spiritual, and most evangelical reformation comes, Christianity will have gone out from cloisters, from creeds, from clerical confinements, into the open field and broad experience of the people and the age. But it will never be by breaking the strictness of its commands, nor lowering the standard of its holiness. For there is no entrance within the gates of a holier Future, save the new and living way which Christ hath consecrated; nor is there any other name than His given under heaven among men, whereby labor or learning, wisdom or simplicity, rich or poor, can be saved.

SERMON III.

ASKING AND RECEIVING.

ASK, AND IT SHALL BE GIVEN YOU.—Matt. vii. 7.

SIMPLE words, but covering the deepest facts in our life! Consider how much they imply:—the being of God; the dependence of man; a communion, or intercourse, between their spirits; a feeling of want on the part of man; a faith, with him, that God can fill that want; and the absolute truth, independent on his notions, that God is able to fill it, out of his infinitude. These are certainly great facts. They are as impressive to a rational intellect by their grandeur, as they are affecting to the heart by their tenderness. They are at once majestic ideas and comforting promises.

I have sought in the New Testament for my present use some expression that should not only contain an injunction to pray, as a duty, but should offer a motive, also, turning it into a privilege. This is precisely the significance brought out by the turn of the text's language. "Ask, and it shall be given you," conveys a reason that moves the affections, as well as a precept issued to our will. "Ask," which is bare command, borrows persuasion, and so couples with itself a new force, from the assurance, "It shall be given you." This is the form, I suspect, which the doctrine of Prayer takes oftenest, in the minds of those that really feel what it is. They are less conscious of being constrained by a sense that they *ought* to pray, than by a feeling that that is the way of gaining what they crave. The authority that prompts the service is not external, but within. And when they would draw their companions into the same devout habit, they are more anxious to illustrate it as a satisfaction than as an obligation.

This Discourse will aim to exhibit not so much the entire compass of the subject as certain specific and salient points in it, — some of them of the nature of difficulties, — which, as having engaged themselves with some interest in one experience, may be fairly supposed to have a practical value to more than one. Even of a spiritual exercise so permanent among men as prayer, it is true that it presents different phases and questions at different times, according to the genius of that period, the mental fashions of the day, and the tendencies of religious speculation. Whatever affects devotion, affects the prime power, the root, and cardinal element of religion itself.

In the study of any subject that deserves to be studied at all, we wish to go to competent and authentic sources of knowledge. These sources, in respect to spiritual intercourse between the soul and God, must be two, — biblical authority, and experience. Each of these interprets the other. If they both agree, they produce a double certainty of conviction, so far forth. Whatever exceptions reason might take to the report of either one alone, they are so beautifully fitted to complete and confirm each other, that reason cannot reject their united testimony, without becoming unreason. Outside of these two, we cannot expect much light. Abstract reasoning cannot inform us reliably about prayer, because prayer is an act eminently and essentially personal; it is an act lying aside from the province of abstractions, between two persons, and involves all along personal attributes, relations, and emotions. On the other hand, mere mortal insight is an incompetent teacher here, because one of the parties necessary to this high commerce is above Nature, the very centre and impersonation of the Supernatural. So far as that part of prayer is concerned which relates to the feeling of want in us, natural insight suffices as an expounder; but the moment we look over, to inquire about the answer, — what ground we have for confidence that we shall be answered at all, who is to answer, and on what conditions the answer is gained, — simple intuition leaves us in the dark. Experience and Scripture combined, then, exactly meet our case, — sufficient guides. Experience suits the personal character of prayer, — satisfying the heart as to the actual interchange of feeling in it. Revelation lays open the supernatural secret, — telling us explicitly of the God we pray to, how to worship him, and how infallible the guaranty, that, if we ask believing, we shall receive.

It may be inquired, of what use experience can be in teaching us the nature and privilege of praying, when the presumption is that the practice has not been begun, and the very object of the knowledge sought is to establish the habit by which experience comes. The reply is twofold. In the first place, by the effect of testimony, one person's experience is carried over and made good for another. One devout soul, bearing simple and earnest witness what it has received by asking, reporting, with tokens of voice and manner too sincere to be mistaken, the actual peace and strength God has sent it, will inevitably act, as by a kind of holy contagion, on the consciousness of others, kindling at least a transient flush of sympathy, quickening, often, a deeper faith, and initiating possibly some young or impressible spirit into the heavenly life. Herein lies the pious efficacy of much religious biography, modest relations of experience, and the friendship of faithful men. They cast private joys into a commonwealth of hope, and multiply one real believer's prayers into the thanksgivings and supplications of a Church.

In the second place, the act of praying, as fast as it is encouraged, is found to fit itself in, by a remarkable and beautiful harmony, with all our better moods, and all higher states of the soul. In other words, the experience of prayer, even in its feebler beginnings, is suited to all other moral experience, and so seems to gain confirmations from every purer feeling we are conscious of. When any soul truly asks God for a spiritual gift, — truly, I say, that is, with those dispositions of heart that are indispensable to such an act, humility and trust, — not only is it thereby better prepared to renew this particular act of prayer, but all its Christian traits are strengthened at the same moment. Purity becomes more transparent, forbearance more patient, charity more catholic, uprightness more inflexible, conscience more vigilant. Such a divine provision has God made to tempt the least stirring of devout inclinations on, — to comfort the disciple's earliest resolution, and to lead his hesitating feet forward into the steadiness and serenity of sainthood. Of course the consciousness of such inward blessings will be faint, according to the dimness of an undisciplined faculty; but a delicate perception will discern them, and an honest perseverance will bring them to maturity. A fact of such large and striking effects, so uniform as to become a law of our constitution, rewarding the first real petition with the germs of many reformations and the budding of a cluster of graces, justifies us, I think, in saying that prayer is enjoined and supported by human experience.

You will observe that this view discards the maxim, which some creeds have dogmatically pronounced, that it is a sin for a man to pray till he is sure he is already in a state of grace; discards it, at least, unless it be granted that the very impulse he feels to ask God's help is evidence that he is already in a state of grace. It cannot be wise, not evangelical, not promotive of healthy effort, to draw these bars of forbidding iron across the avenue to the mercy-seat. The moment man or child feels one earnest impulse lifting his desire heavenward, that is the providential moment for him to cry, "Our Father," and pour out his heart's emotion to the last drop, whether of penitence, thanksgiving, or anxiety. The Father never rebuffs such eager confidence. To deny that holy yearning, to bid it wait, and cautiously examine, inspect, and analyze itself to see if it is fit, is only to throw a door open to chilling doubts and altered moods. It is to refuse a divine call. It is to wrong the soul's friendliest angel. It is quenching the Holy Spirit. How are we, weak children of vanity, ever to be thoroughly renewed, except we entreat the "Spirit that helpeth our infirmities"? Shall we despise the means, expecting to leap miraculously to the end? Shall we wait, before asking, for that elevated frame of the soul, which only asking obtains? Let no such sophistry of perverted theologies, and inverted reason, betray us. You would not deem it wise, nor filial, to postpone begging your injured mother's forgiveness, after the penitent thought had once waked in your breast, till your mended life had quite recompensed for your disobedience, or till her love had overcome your sullen reluctance by violence. Confession first, peace afterwards. You will not "ask" too soon, — if you must "ask" before it is given. The instant for thee to enter into thy closet is when the first thrill of repentant sorrow or holy faith shoots down from above, to make the soul mindful of its immortal destiny, and its account.

I have spoken of praying as an act between two persons, man and God. If we adhere to such language as is used in the text, — or to the representation, exactly according with this, that runs through the whole Bible, — we shall wonder, probably, that any other philosophy of prayer should have ever come into vogue in Christendom, than what stands out so plainly in this simple statement. Asking, on the one side, and giving, in answer to that asking, on the other, would seem to be nearly as unmistakable an account of a direct transaction as speech is capable of composing. Especially would it appear to stand clear of all possible ambiguity, when we remember that the whole Revelation, from end to end of its records, offers no hint of any different theory; that it was precisely in this spirit, and with this understanding, that every biblical believer prayed, from Adam in Eden to John in Patmos; — Abraham, Isaac, and Jacob, all patriarchs speaking to Jehovah, and answered by Him; Moses, Samuel, Elijah, and the whole line of valiant, praying prophets; David, whose devotions have been the common language of worship through both dispensations, and bear to-day fresher marks of perpetuity than when his own tears fell upon the lines he wrote, — whose petitions were accounted worthy to be taken upon the lips of the Redeemer himself amidst the tortures of the crucifixion; the disciples, the mother, evangelists, apostles, — all, with undivided agreement, asking the Father for what their soul craved, and receiving at God's invisible hand, immediately, blessings, that, but for such asking, could not have been bestowed. Not a doubt hangs over a phrase of the narrative. The witnesses are explicit. There are placed before us two parties. One is just as literally and exactly a person as the other; the divine side of the mutual transaction involving precisely the same attributes of personality as the human, — no hint to the contrary; and — mark especially — the fact of conscious request and conscious compliance every way as distinct — the difference between faith and sense being of course granted — as if a hand were visibly stretched out on one side open, and were visibly filled from the other.

Now, if the biblical authority did not settle this truth in exactly this form, falling back on experience some of us certainly would have facts to produce, which, however they might affect sceptics, must, for us, for ever place the literal doctrine of asking and receiving beyond all misgiving, as the only possible theory of prayer.

Yet into such labyrinths of confusion, and such mazes of perplexity, has theological thinking brought itself, that a stark rejection of this doctrine is no very rare phenomenon in modern theology, so called. Prayer, instead of that distinct, specific, blessed thing, — an asking for the sake of receiving, — finding its clear and touching image in the daily beauty saluting all our eyes of the confiding and hearkening communion between child and parent, — instead of this, it is — what shall we say? or rather, what do some men *not* say it is? — a convenient name for almost any reputable deed or any innocent state: prayer is want; prayer is well-doing or well-wishing; a good life is prayer: to work morally is to pray; to have a general sense of subjection to the Infinite, is to pray. There is no enumerating these loose, rhetorical, paradoxical, and superficial definitions. The only radical feature in which they are all agreed, is in shading off prayer into some other thing that is not prayer, and *should* have another name; in confounding things that differ; in destroying that one essential ingredient without which no prayer can be, — an asking on the part of man for a granting on the part of God.

There is one abuse of the term, however, that takes a different shade, and lurks under specious pretences. It is this, — that what we call prayer is nothing but a mode of self-excitation. We are exhorted to take the attitudes, and use all forms and words of prayer, — just as if what the act pretends were really true, and there were literally a God to hear and answer, only because it has been found on experiment that this is a successful way of stirring us up to do better. We exert ourselves more, and so are more blessed by Nature, who loves to see her children toil. We are refreshed by making our supplications to Heaven, only so far as we impose on ourselves the trick of asking of a God what man is just as competent to give himself. It might seem to be enough, with single-minded persons, to explode this heresy, that it inextricably involves a duplicity, — such a one as to implicate our veneration and profane worship, — insulting the God that we only approach in a rhetorical device, and pretend to pray to for effect. I say nothing of the impossibility of a soul's elevating itself above itself, with no *purchase* outside of itself. The moral objection is enough. The error only illustrates the working of a philosophy that cuts itself loose from the New Testament. "Ask, and it shall be given you." It is enough for us to pray as Jesus prayed. This entangles us in no subtleties, and freezes us with no negations. It takes us straight to our Father, with no misgiving that he veritably hears what we pray. This places the object of our religious confidence beyond ourselves, and so clears us of that besetting sin of egotism, which is as destructive of church life as it is of nobleness of character and personal piety. It centres faith outside this narrow region of self, — even our better self, — and gives assurance and comfort, "which only he that feels it knows," by hanging every circumstance of life, the most minute or most afflicting, on the direct and immediate word of our Lord, in whose spirit we are embosomed, in whose foresight our little plans are lost, in whose hand we are only instruments, moved hither and thither as he will. This Christianizes our prayers; for it makes them with their answers that veritable communion, that literal asking and receiving between the soul and God, which is as strictly personal as the petition of any child and the answer of any parent, — a precious praying, — real praying, — the Bible's praying.

At this point another question has been sometimes started: How such specific answers to prayer can comport with the regularity of Providence and the government of the world by appointed laws. Unquestionably this is one of the deep secrets passing our limited knowledge, and belonging to the Infinite Mind. It is no deeper, nor harder to reconcile, than a hundred other facts in the Divine economy, which yet we must admit, or deny sense and faith both: such, for example, as the fact that we are all free to choose how we shall act, and yet are completely bound in the hands of Omnipotence; that God is almighty and all-good, and yet leaves his children liberty to do wrong. These are transcendent mysteries, simply because they are the doings of a transcendent Being, — God. In the end, we shall find, I suppose, that there is no more contradiction between a fixed order of laws and special answers to our asking, than there is between a general household arrangement for their children's good, on the part of earthly parents, and their daily favors granted in answer to particular requests. Through all this stable and mighty system of irreversible decrees, — laws of growth and decay, summer and winter, evening and morning, centripetal and centrifugal forces, regimen and health, cause and consequence, — there plays for ever the silent presence of God, the unrestricted action of God's free will. So has he built the world, and organized its constitution. The balance of these two forces — Law and Liberty — is the wonder of the universe, the supernal sign set upon it. Before we pray, he is Love itself; yet he hears the prayer, and sends a blessing that could not have come without. The uniform shelter of laws that we can rely upon in our every-day business is merciful; and so are those direct, impressive tokens of his listening spirit, which make a part of the experience of devout souls that no reasoning can take away.

This care extends to the least particle of creation, — to the windings of a worm, as much as to the circle of a planet; to the eyeball of a fly, as much as to the splendor of the sun; to your lowly path each morning from street to street, as much as to the august pilgrimage of Arcturus along the "streets of stars," or to the rise and fall of empires, the battle that captures an old fortress, or the reformation that liberates nations. Believing this, I can no more hesitate to ask a Divine direction for the details of my common life, than for the salvation of my soul. Indeed, do we not know that the *salvation* of the soul is nothing else than the *safety* of the soul, and so that it is bound up inextricably with these very familiar incidents, — their effects upon the soul, and, in turn, the soul's use of them, determining its salvation or its perdition? What companions I shall be thrown among, what tasks I shall have brought me to do, what difficulties I shall have to encounter, what misunderstandings and consequent alienations I shall be rescued from, what words I shall be inwardly prompted to speak, what temptations I may be spared each time I go out of my house or return to it, — these, and all the class of events they belong to, are the very material out of which salvation or ruin is wrought; and so they are fit subjects of prayer. They are things wherein God answers. For over the motions of heart and mind — others as well as my own — he holds an unceasing control. And if you watch the history of almost any hour, you will see many junctures in it where two ways parted before you, and the choice was more with God than yourself. In this spirit, and with this faith, a Christian will find no difficulty in asking for earthly good. If he does it regarding its moral connections and influences on character, it is lawful, reverent prayer; such prayer as was often on the lips of righteous men of old, and had signal answers; such prayer — for life, health, rain, fruitful seasons — as James enjoins, citing Elijah as an example.

The *mode* of the answer rests with God. If he sees it will strengthen faith, and, taking all bearings into view, fulfil his will, he may answer it directly, according to the form of the request. If he sees that this would encourage worldly-mindedness, or hinder any of his broader purposes, he will send a secret response into the heart. One thing we may always know beforehand; if the earthly advantage holds a higher place in our desires than spiritual purity or God's truth, it is no prayer of faith, and carries in its own nature the forewarning, that, even for our own sake, we must be denied.

This leads in the last great feature of the present Doctrine of Devotion. Every asking that expects to receive must be an asking with submission, — willing to wait long before receiving, — willing to be utterly refused. For along with every act of such communion goes this attendant truth, never to be forgotten, — that it is mortal weakness, ignorance, and imperfection communing with everlasting Power, boundless Knowledge, perfect Holiness. No doubt, " Lord, I believe, help thou mine unbelief," is a right, and often our most becoming supplication; and some confession must be implied in every worship. But unless we can feel, while we are asking, that we could cheerfully give up the things we ask for, at God's command, I suppose we are not in the true attitude of prayer. This must be that spirit of believing, or faith, that Christ refers to, where he says, " Whatsoever ye ask *believing*, ye shall receive." Thomas à Kempis, who seems to have entered farther into the inmost shrine of devotion than any writer since the Apostle John, has this passage: — " Let this be the language of all thy requests: 'Lord, if it be pleasing to thee, may this be granted, or that withheld; but if thou knowest it will conduce not to the health of my soul, remove far from me my desire. Give me what thou wilt, and in what measure, and at what time. Place me where thou wilt, and freely dispose of me in all things. Do thou lead and turn me whithersoever thou pleasest.' For," he adds, "every desire that appeareth to man to be right and good, is not born from heaven; and it is difficult always to determine truly whether the desire is prompted by the good spirit of God, or thy own selfish spirit." I have known devout persons to stand year after year, in utter wonder that their prayers, so reasonable in appearance, brought no visible return; yet the faith that came at last out of that trial and proving, in a furnace seven times hotter than fire, "more precious than gold that perisheth," finally justified such patience by its splendor.

For, even while we wait, through all the breathings of our aspiration, from the first hesitating, stammering whisper of entreaty, on to the last strong syllable of praise when faith triumphs over the failing flesh, — prayer is ever, moment by moment, its own sufficing recompense. Its words do react on your soul like a benediction. Its every struggle is a consolation, and every sigh is peace. It puts the world under your feet. It makes all things yours, while ye are Christ's and Christ is God's. The spirit comes back from its seasons of converse with God, into the strife of the world, its interior face radiant with a veil of glory like that Moses wore when he came down from the mount. Every calamity is disenabled to agitate, and every cross to terrify you. You say, with the brave serenity of Paul: "What can separate me from this unspeakable joy? Shall tribulation, or famine, or sword? Shall loss of goods, or pain, or bereavement by death? Nay, in all these things we are more than conquerors!" The very intellectual interest that will be shed over a life where this mutual interacting of prayer and fulfilment so stimulates the soul, rewards the understanding, while a far profounder and holier satisfaction descends into, illumines, and inspires the heart.

Not for ourselves alone are these heavenly gifts attainable, but by one for another. Intercession, — that too often neglected privilege of prayer, even among those who have learned the Christian lessons, — intercession, it is the divinest gift of friendship. By its celestial ministry, conquering all distances, the thoughts of separated spirits meet, in God. When patient love, in its reserve or its baffled hope, can do no more, it can ask on all it loves the love of Christ. When ingratitude makes self-sacrifice itself helpless, and repulses all tenderness with malignant hate, or unconcern almost as torturing, Prayer can still watch, and guard, and supplicate, and weep; and God counts its tears. Mothers for their erring sons; sisters for their falling brothers; companions for each other; believing children for worldly fathers; all souls for all souls, — prayer is their sure refuge, the one office of affection and faith that no indifference can deny.

In the lives of the Fathers there is an account of Abbot Lucius. To a company of young men that were boasting how they prayed continually, but never worked, he said: "Not so; for if you never work, then, while you eat and sleep, you neither work nor pray. I will show you how you may pray continually. I am not ashamed to labor with my hands; and while I work, I send forth still, between, some short petitions to my gracious God. When I have some quantity of finished work, I give away about a third thereof to the poor. And now, these poor men praying for me while I eat or sleep, through them I pray without ceasing."

Over every day's life, let us write the twofold inscription, — "Not slothful in business"; and "Continuing instant in prayer."

SERMON IV.

THE SOUL'S SEARCH.

SEEK, AND YE SHALL FIND.—Matt. vii. 7.

An intelligent criticism has often pointed it out as one of the secrets of moral impression, as well as of rhetorical effect, that the true power of eloquence may be almost as strikingly displayed in what is omitted from a discourse as in its contents. That is to say, an orator may accomplish his persuasion as well by knowing what to leave out as what to put in. Of course, this skill presupposes a wise acquaintance with the structure of language, and its relations to thought, a delicate perception of the laws of association, and the knowledge how to make what *is* said suggest that richer part of wisdom which must for ever remain unsaid. But whatever we may think of the maxim as a judgment on the art of expression, it certainly refers to a great and yet a simple fact in our spiritual economy. It might be shown, I think, that there are omissions in the New Testament more spiritually significant than any speech out of it. An example occurs in this passage. The Son of God says to the world, "Seek, and ye shall find." He does not there tell us what we are to seek. It is enough that he urges us, with such condensed concern, to seek,—for we shall find. What the *object* of this ceaseless and infinite quest shall be, — so far as the immediate language goes, — is left sublimely unuttered. In this case, as in many of the utterances that break the most solemn pauses, and declare the grandest truths, the unmentioned thing is the supreme thing. Precisely because there is but one word that can fill the blank, no word is needed.

Observe now how impressive the inevitable inference. It is like saying that the one true search of man can have but one object, — God. What it is to find God, we may try to state in different forms of words. But they must all have one meaning. To live daily under the conscious inspiration and guidance of his Spirit, is to find him. To believe in Christ, provided that belief embraces practice as well as faith, and engages the affections as well as the intellect, — which it must do if it is living and sincere, — this is to find God; because God is in Christ. To keep a conscious harmony of one's own will with God's will, so as to gain spiritual liberty, patient submission, is to find him. To blend justice and mercy toward man with prayer; is to find him. To live so that the ruling aim, or uppermost purpose, shall be under the constant control of the principles of Christianity, is to find him. To be spiritually-minded, and so discern spiritual things, is to find him. Of course, then, to be really *seeking* any of these things, — which, after all, are essentially the same thing, — is to seek God.

But in the fact that Jesus does not specify in words what we are to seek, we may find this truth hidden; namely, that if you once fairly bring yourself to the inquiry what you shall seek, with a resolve to seek it, you can come to but one reasonable answer. There is only one aim large enough, and noble enough, to satisfy your soul's hunger, when you make a fair, free, deliberate decision. I believe that, if we could all see how we choose, when we hesitate between God and Mammon, we must choose aright; especially if the choice is made before a corrupt habit has hardened the wrong growth, and stiffened the twist of sin into a permanent deformity, and partially crippled the will. Really and reasonably to choose, will be to choose for eternal life over the loss of it. That glorious necessity God has wrought into the very texture of our being, — a bright and everlasting witness of his own truth. Otherwise, reason is a mockery, the invitations of Heaven are a dismal satire on our helplessness, and our very nature is a fallacy.

What shall we conclude, then, looking at mankind as they are, but that many of them have not fairly chosen? When you see a life whose inmost motive is clearly selfishness, and whose whole face is stripped of every impress of the sense of spiritual obligation, you may safely say that life has never passed under any experience that deserved to be called a choice. No doubt it has a direction, and a motion. So has every vessel that floats adrift. We live on waters that are never at a dead calm. If we neither sail nor row, we are driven. But such a man either follows the current that the world's fashion has set, or is the plaything of gusty appetites. He has not grasped the helm in the hand of a strong, individual, and morally independent will, conquering at once the tide of social example and the caprices of his own passion. He has not lifted his look to the immortal lights that burn fixed and serene in the sky, and laid his course by their heavenly admonition. Who shall measure the guilt of that wretched refusal to choose?

Some kinds of election such men have undoubtedly made. They have chosen, perhaps, which one of the many modes of self-enrichment or self-gratification they will take. They have chosen the path and the scene of their property-search, or their pleasure-search. They have chosen whether they will be rich by one set of tools or another, — by dry goods, or hard-ware, or jewelry, or stocks, — by a hammer and chisel, or a plough. They have chosen whether they will be famous at the bar, or in the medical faculty, or in a pulpit, or in Congress. They have chosen whether they will get gain in New York or Boston, San Francisco or Calcutta. Have they chosen between self-service and God's service? Have they chosen whether their property shall be got according to the New Testament, or according to the Satanic text-book of expediency? Have they chosen whether their chief pleasure shall be that of a luxurious table and the pride of a handsome establishment, or the pleasure of blessing their fellows and feeling the beat of a satisfied heart? Have they chosen whether, by whatever instruments, in whatever city or village or country, through whatever calling, with fortune or without, admired or neglected, courted or despised, they will be brave for the right, and carry out of the world a conscience undefiled? In one phrase, have they chosen — have you chosen — between the servile obedience to interests that all terminate in earthly comfort, and the nobility of a character upright before all men, bending with humble devotion only before God, rich in good works, a disciple of Christ? Is there one among us all that hesitates an instant which he ought to choose, if he choose at all? How true is it, then, that where our spiritual safety is perilled, it is not so much that we do not come to the true life when our faces have once been turned to seek for it, as that we do not turn them to seek for it! The one primary, fundamental, underlying question is the question we have left unsettled. Seek, really seek, and ye shall find.

Christian faith is the most appropriate action of the soul; and the way of a righteous life, as it is thrown open by the Son of God, is the answer of Heaven to the soul's wants. Now if this be true; if the heart of man wants the Gospel as much as the body wants food, and is the organ of holy feeling; if the spiritual atmosphere of religious belief and principle is as exactly and beautifully fitted to our inward life, as the outward air is to the lungs, or light to the eye; and if every irreligious person is out of nature, disordered and disorderly, a morbid and abnormal creature, till he stands in reconciliation with his Maker, — then the seeking for the way must be the foremost concern of all health-desiring and rational souls. How to find and keep it is the simple question, beside which all the decoration and ambition of our material estate, all dress and bargaining, all opulence and office, even all learning and accomplishments of the mind, are humbled into secondary things.

I said secondary. I ought to use some stronger word. The distinction is more than one of degrees. The alternative between a life taking its law from Heaven and a life taking its law from any of the forms of self-interest, — ranging as these forms do over all grades of guilt and shame, from the beastly sensuality that eats and drinks and lusts, all the more reckless to-day because its to-morrow looks so ghastly, on to the passion for power and splendor which is the "last infirmity of noble minds," but none the less ungodly because it is the last, — this alternative is always the simple one between piety and atheism. We cannot keep a deity that shall simply wait on our table, or whisper to us beforehand the favorable chances of a speculation. There are no wages, whether occasional attendance at a sanctuary, or any other professions, that can suborn Providence into a skilful steward and butler, or an intelligent foreign correspondent to keep you advised of commercial prospects. God must have the heart or nothing, — and have its direct loyalty and love, or none that is accepted. He looks in to see which way the inmost spirit kneels, — and not Sunday only, but all days, — whether towards the Father of Righteousness, or some idol of the popular admiration. He lifts the folds that are plaited so cunningly over our inmost selves, and judges what that inner rule is by which we refuse or accept bribes from the hand of man or woman, by which we do or scorn to do an unclean deed. So that, in reality, the difference between seeking God, and seeking him not, is something more than a relative or comparative difference. It is absolute and decisive. It supposes a distinct centre of attraction, and so another sort of life; what the New Testament calls a "new man." You may ascend from the flattest plain to the adjoining hill, from the hill to the loftier table-land, from that to the proud range that puts its snowy shoulder against the arch of blue, and up still from that to the solitary and imperial peak that seems to soar quite *through* the sky, but still you remain a citizen of the earth, and your climbing feet are held fast by the old gravitation. It is not till you spring over to another planet that you are clear of the sublunary imprisonment, and become an inhabitant of the heavens. Now God is willing that our home should be on this world; places are nothing; he even offers to send heaven down to us. But the heart must confess to an attraction from beyond the little globe of self. We "cast anchor upwards." "No man ever went to heaven whose heart was not there before him." If we would "find" the life eternal, we must "seek" something better than the best kind of material good.

All our life is a search. We are a race of seekers. The eyes planted in the front of the head are a symbol of our inquisitive constitution. With some of us the aim is consciously taken, is clear, is fixed, and embraces, in one, the perfecting of character and the glory of God. These, call them by whatever name, of whatever sect or no sect, of whatever nation or rank, are the men that God loves and honors. They are the saints, modern or ancient; as good if they walk our streets to-day, as if they held sweet counsel with Fénelon in Cambray, or knelt with St. Cecilia, or wept with Paul on the shore at Miletus. And because they find the Christ the only way unto the Father, they are the true Church of the living Lord. All of us, I hope, have been privileged to know such.

Then there are others who seek nothing so noble, nothing so generous, nothing so holy. They seek how much they can call their own, by whatever means, — of how much benefit they can hold a monopoly, from how large a place in God's universe they can keep other men off, and how much envy they can rouse in rivals and neighbors. These have never mastered their baser and greedier instincts, and so have never known the divine joy of being blessed for their benefactions, and have never tasted of the peace that passeth understanding. Very often God punishes us, by letting us have what we seek. And so such persons seem to succeed. Men of that stamp are affluent and respected; or rather, the accessories, under which the man is concealed, are respected. It requires a spiritual judgment to uncover their emptiness, and show how real ruin is compatible with apparent success.

There are none, I suppose, who can be said literally to seek nothing; but there are those — and these, too, you have seen — who come so near to that, that no man, looking on, can guess what it is they seek. The aims are so minute and so variable as not to be easily detected, — one thing this morning, another this evening, all trifling, and all ineffectual. Find what the magnet is that draws each one on, and you have discovered his character. His supreme desire fixes his value. To know what he seeks is to know what manner of man he is, better than by knowing in what way he seeks it: just as you can judge a traveller's destination better by seeing which way his face is set, than by observing his mode of conveyance.

To the seekers of mere material and selfish comfort, one serious consideration is presented by the progress of history. That kind of search is sinking. Every new day that breaks into the sky degrades it; both because new lights are stationed about it, in our educational and industrial wakefulness, to show its shame, and because the practical tendencies of the time force upon materialism a more and more hard and sottish character. In more imaginative periods, romance threw about idolatry at least the graces of fancy, and made it poetical. Now it is either shrewd or stolid. It is the idolatry of the arithmetic, the stock-list, and the palate; not of fable and heroism. The noblest element has vanished. It is bare gluttony. If you are going to worship the animal, then return to the inventions of Egyptian and Grecian genius, — "the fair humanities of old religion." Give us back at least the simplicity of feticism *with* its sensuality. Rebuild the Pantheon. Relight the fires on Pagan altars. Repeople the woods with dryads, and the waters with nymphs. Anything, rather than the gross surfeit of appetite, and the clinking creed of dollars! And if you cannot do that, take it as a sober hint that God's providence does not mean to have materialists in the world at all. Seek something worthier of your humanity. Seek a larger and purer spirit from the Father, who grants such gifts by his Son, and ye shall find.

In the text there is a task enjoined, and there is a promise published. The task is for man; the promise is from God.

The task is for man. Seeking is a labor. We are cast upon our faculties. Faith itself is not passive. Why is that pearl of great price, a Christian character, concealed behind so many counterfeits that glitter, and perplexities that hinder, if not to stimulate our zeal in seeking it? Self-denial is a part of that search. So is drudgery, familiar as our own hands. So is patience under contradiction, and the crucifixion of pride. If a young man asks me how he shall be a Christian in the midst of the sorceries of politics, the temptations of merchandise, and the profligacy of convivial manners, and yet is not willing to brace himself against the reproof or ridicule of his elders and the blandishments of seducing companions, to begin every day with Bible and prayer, and even to persevere through loss of income, I only remind him of another young man who had it said to him, "How hardly shall they that have riches enter into the kingdom of Heaven," because he was not equal to the sacrifice. And if a distressed spirit in woman, scourged by the pain of doubt, or entreated by the Holy

Spirit, inquires for the way of life, and yet will not bend her vanity or her self-reliance lowly at her Redeemer's feet, I remind her of the sister that was more careful and troubled to display her hospitality to Jesus, than to give up all, and put her heart into the Saviour's hand, and sit satisfied with his love. These do not truly seek, and cannot find.

The promise is from God. Seek, and ye *shall* find. Was a Divine promise ever broken or forgotten? There is a secret misgiving, or uncertainty, whether a thorough consecration, a righteous character, will bring the peace, or strength, or glory, which the Almighty has engaged it shall. I believe Christian people themselves do not duly weigh the affront of distrusting God's pledges. We deem it an insult to doubt man's word, yet discredit the Unchangeable's. The loss is double. We dwarf the proportions of our own goodness. We alienate the blessing that falls only on believers. So seek eternal life, then, as those that know they shall find it.

You know the ways and the helps of this seeking. They are fixed and definite as the rules for any human attainment. They are studious and self-examining meditation, the exclusion from the heart of conflicting affections, a daily intimacy, through the record, with the perfect Christ and the whole body of Revelation, prayers as punctual as the sun, the dashing away of that one dear dark idol which stands between almost every heart and the light of Heaven, and the faithful applying of the spirit of holiness given straight from God to one district after another of the practical territory of experience. Was there ever one who so sought, and did not find?

Do not say the object of this infinite and immortal search is vague or obscure; and that you do not know what to seek, because the precept does not define it. As well say you do not know where the upward look of the pleading and weeping eye of the Magdalen is directed, because the Master's form is not painted on the canvas above her head. As well wonder why the name of the Unnamable, to whom the vast dome is reared, and whose silent praise every arch and pillar speaks, is not stamped in gilded letters on the front of St. Peter's. There are meanings at once so plain and so august, that to encase them in syllables is to belittle their dignity. The design of the whole framework of your human being is as evidently God's worship, as that of the cathedral. Know ye not that ye are the temple of God? And yet what proportion of the souls passing forward to man's estate and dangers and duties in this Christian community, what proportion of the young men that enter Christian sanctuaries, have seized on the grand purpose so manifestly held out to them? have taken a religious stand, — I do not say before men, but before themselves, — and so determined their lives towards the glorious end? The question is not put querulously, nor as from a pulpit's formality, but as from one erring man to his fellows, in a common need of strength. Character, spirituality, righteousness, is the end. Christ is the way. "Seek, and ye shall find."

There is something in this inspiriting call for every stage of our spiritual progress. The youngest child that hears me is not too young to be a seeker under Christ, for Christ took younger children into his arms. The maturest manhood or saintliest womanhood among you ought to be seeking still, and for ever seeking, — because the best are weak, truth is boundless, and the highest soul stands at an infinite remove from God. They that have not yet steadfastly set their faces as though they would go up higher, are encouraged and solicited. They that have gone some way are bidden to press on. They that have mastered the worst enemies are cheered forward to be more than conquerors through Him who hath loved them, — whose face they have beheld, whose breath they have felt. Nor is it said to one of them more than to another, "Seek, and ye shall find."

From all the fountains of religious feeling, whose living waters leap as if an angel troubled them, — from all trees of wise thought, whose leaves are for the healing of the nations, — from all the lights in the starry heavens of the elder time, the ages of faith, — from the spirits about us, on the right and the left, purer and calmer than our own, and shaming our uncertain steps, — from our own failures and mortifications, — from prayer and communion, from Bible and Providence, from Church and life, — above all, direct from that mighty and loving heart of Jesus, out of which flows the spirit without measure, — let us continually and faithfully seek, — seek summit above summit of gracious attainment, — seek depth below depth of God's unfathomable love. So shall we not lose the way, and miss our Father's house, nor come halting and maimed there, but erect and healthful souls, save as we are bended in gratitude at the mercy that forgives, in penitence for the sins to be forgiven, and in reverence at the vision of Him who makes his people whole.

SERMON V.

THE SOUL'S CORONATION.

THE LIFE IS MORE THAN MEAT. — Luke xii. 23.
YOUR REASONABLE SERVICE. — Rom. xii. 1.

I HAVE drawn the two members of the text together, out of their separate places in the New Testament, as they proceeded from the lips of Jesus and the pen of Paul, because the precise thought by which I wish to direct my discourse is more clearly brought out by their combination than by any single passage. The compound force of the two phrases is this: to keep the claims and the interests of the spiritual nature in us paramount over all other claims and all other interests, is to act according to the strictest rule of what is reasonable.

Paramount, for in the divine economy of our constitution there is unquestionably an order of preferments. No human society has ever adjusted its ranks, nor any government allotted its privileges, according to that heavenly gradation, because no legislature has ever fully copied its principle, and no community has embodied its spirit. But God has distributed creation in a series of ascending honors. Christianity, his interpreter, tells us how they range and where they culminate. That uncrowned and often unacknowledged king, the human soul, stands nevertheless the native and hereditary sovereign of our mortal estate. We may rob it of its titles; we may trample its royalty under the feet of our passions; we may fill its throne with those vile usurpers, our sensual desires; yet through all abuses, through ages of treachery and malfeasance, the soul waits, pleading its inborn majesty, asserting its divine pedigree, appealing to its parentage in God, showing its inalienable and immortal right to rule, and expecting its final coronation. "The life is more than meat." Through the inspiration of the spirit, the seat of this life is the soul. There is the centre of all movement, the spring of power, the point of intense concern. All greatness proceeds thence. All well-directed anxieties converge thither. Blind as we become to the magnificent fact, whatever interests agitate markets and families and states, — whatever influences play through street, shop, congress, the academy and college, no less than the Church, — terminate at last in the soul. For that, in the original design, however we as individuals pervert or come short of it, the farmer's tillage rears and reaps the summer's grain on all the quiet meadows and slopes; for that the arms of labor swing in ten thousand workshops; for that the printing-press is worked and types are cast; for that, at last, if the Sermon on the Mount is true, the lily blossoms and the sparrow flies. Institutions are founded, whether their founders remember it or not, statute-books are written, cities are built, new countries are colonized, factories occupy the streams, exploring expeditions animate the commercial map of the world, for the soul. It is not, after all, for the fortunes that are made, the fabrics woven, the speed attained, the money multiplied, the world's-fairs exhibited. These are only means to an end;

and that end is man's spiritual education. By far the deepest question you can ask respecting any of these mighty agencies is, What kind of souls is it helping to rear? what sort of characters is it fashioning? Is it leaving men with a larger or leaner humanity, with a purer or weaker piety? And the most momentous question any individual can put to himself, respecting all these forms of outward activity and acquisition, is the old evangelical and personal one, — "What shall it profit a man, though he gain the whole world and lose his soul?" "The life is more than meat."

I need not tell you how apt the immediate operators of all this vast enterprise are to forget its real import. In their eagerness to keep the machinery in motion, and to harvest its tangible rewards, they overlook its grandest purpose. The men who flatter themselves they manage these gigantic forces, fail, how often! to discern the final object of such a splendid apparatus. They practically invert the true saying; they act as if the meat were more than the life. Colonizers of Melbourne and San Francisco fancy the only office of those gates to golden palaces is to open avenues for worldly ambition to stride through more ambitiously; while God would make them theatres for the development, hereafter, of nobler specimens of moral beauty. Some man of science comes among us and expounds the mysteries of Arctic navigation. Avaricious eyes see nothing in this penetrating of Polar oceans but an enlargement of the sphere of traffic, or a new facility for transportation; but Providence is only getting the earth ready, from pole to pole, for the discipline of righteous men and the triumph of Christian truth. So the individual merchant may think only of the luxury of riches, and the politician only of the emoluments of office; but none the less, under all their selfish schemes, live on the everlasting will and sublime design of Almighty God. In every wonderful discovery of the age, the deepest wonder is the part it is yet to be made to play in redeeming the earth from wrong and purifying it from sin. The brains that contrive, as well as the capital that equips and the governments that organize, these forth-putting expeditions which pry into all the territory and treasure of the globe, are only servants of a vaster Power behind them, — the pages and messengers, the waiting-men and operatives, of the Eternal Providence that will have mankind for his own. The end of all this labor and thought is to bring men's souls into harmony with God, through their resemblance to Christ. One day, as sure as that Saviour's prophecy that his kingdom shall come, this human soul shall appear in its renewed glory, in a perfected humanity, and enter in and take possession of the heritage which all this selfish enterprise and this material civilization have unconsciously prepared, "building better than they knew."

Meantime what we, humble toilsmen at our several obscure posts, need to do to make us faithful servants of this reformation, is to take back our eyes from this wide prospect, and find out how the same great law — that spiritual life deserves more study, effort, and prayer, with every one of us, than all external interests — is to be applied to our personal convictions; how the deep saying of the Saviour, "The life is more than meat," is to be so wrought into our daily habits, that we shall feel a spiritual regeneration, a heart thoroughly consecrated to the holiness in Christ, to be our "reasonable service."

Enter, therefore, into a brief analysis of your own composition; see if a fair analogy between the general conduct and management of our life in relation to other great interests and religion will not hold us to keep our spiritual redemption a vital and the foremost concern. If you make even a moderate examination of the original contents or faculties of your nature, regarding them simply as facts, or in the light of science, you will not deny that you presently come upon two capacities, one a capacity for distinguishing between right and wrong, or a conscience, and the other a capacity for distinguishing between man and God, or finite and infinite, that is, a capacity for piety. You find these organs in your nature: a moral sense, or a capacity for knowing and choosing between the right and the wrong; and a religious sense, or a capacity for adoring and worshipping God. And if you admit the existence of these capacities at all, none of you that is sane will deny that they are inherently, and are instinctively felt to be, the highest and noblest of all your capacities. One of them implies a law of obligation towards men, and supposes unlimited measures of justice, charity, and purity, in all the forms of a beautiful and blameless morality. The other implies a law of obligation towards God, and supposes unlimited measures of dependence, devout love, and holy aspiration in all the sanctities of piety. Observe, I appeal only to consciousness. I say nothing yet of attainments; of use or abuse of these capacities. But if there is any person that does not confess to these things as simple facts existing in his nature, I do not reach his case, and cannot expect his sympathy.

Given these capacities, then, for Christian duty and for prayer, and granting that a certain essential elevation or superiority belongs to them, our next point is, that every capacity has connected with it a want, pushing out into some expression of desire and an effort for gratification. These wants organize themselves, and work towards their several objects systematically. The body wants sustenance, — food for its mouth, clothing for its exposure, a shelter from the storms and sun. Hence agriculture, fisheries, manufactures, and commerce. The mind wants knowledge. Hence schools, universities, printing-presses, libraries. Taste wants beauty, — not only clothing, but handsome clothing, — not only a shelter, but a house of fair proportions, inviting furniture, and pictured walls. Hence the arts of design, disposing form and color. The heart wants objects to repose in, and affections responsive to its own. Hence marriage and home. And so, leaving out religion, we have society as it is, — the apparatus and furnishings of a civilized state. Human wants have found their natural expression, and taken shape in institutions. All these institutions are vital, and of universal interest, so long as the wants that organized them are real wants.

But why leave out religion? The capacities and the wants for that, we have seen, are planted in human nature, as much as the others. Conscience wants an upright life; faith wants worship and communion with God; penitence, aching with remorse, wants a Saviour. Hence there must be, to preserve the analogy, a culture of these, to keep them alive, to enlarge their power, and to gratify them. An institution for that culture will be a Church.

See, now, the conclusions to which the argument thus far has conducted us. 1. By our original constitution, by the very nature with which we are all alike born, we are just as distinctly required to recognize and worship God and obey his commands, as we are required to supply our physical necessities, improve our minds, or cherish affectionate relations with parents or children, neighbors or friends, husband or wife. 2. Christ's Church, which is the great nursery and bond of these spiritual obligations, has just as clear claims on the personal respect and personal membership of every one of you, as business or schools or family; and, in a community like ours, a man or woman standing aloof from the consistent and thorough practice of Christian morality and Christian piety ought to be just as singular and anomalous and reproachable an object, as a person that should refuse to learn to read, or to get food for his hunger, or to love his kindred. 3. The instinctive feeling I have alluded to, which I suppose is common to most of us, that there is a certain superior nobleness and sacredness belonging to our religious emotions, challenges in their behalf a devotion more constant, a more cheerful and uniform exercise, than the instinct for bodily sustenance, for intellectual cultivation, or for domestic joy. "The life is more than meat."

Are you prepared to bring your individual lives, one by one, and compare them with this demand of your natures, — this law of your God? Or will you point to any error in the reasoning which compels us to the result?

This, however, does not by any means complete a fair representation of the case. I need not feel the least hesitation in asking you to admit, that, on independent grounds, a Christian life, including both righteousness and prayer, brings higher claims to bear on your heart than any one, or all, of those other interests to which it sustains this analogy.

In the first place, religion, embracing both its branches, is a spirit, and such a spirit, that, while it keeps its own province sacred, it is capable of being infused into all these other departments and interests of life, helping, strengthening, brightening, and blessing every one. Agriculture and commerce nourish and equip the body; but while they do it, a spiritual life in the laborers and merchants, instead of hindering, furthers them. While they are busy in the field and the market, Christianity may make as beautiful manifestations of itself in their upright toil, as in conventicle or council-room. Religion is an invisible angel, standing by them at their posts of daily sacrifice, encouraging them. It puts the light of another world into their eyes. It puts a manly serenity upon their features. It charms away the worst anxieties, compunction, and despair. In a wide reach, and the long trial, industry thrives better, and material prosperity is more stable, in Christian hands, than in the hands of men who love themselves better than God, and will not review their weekly weights and measures by the balances of the sanctuary. So, in turn, the body is wanted for, and serves, the mind and the taste. But religion honors the body. The New Testament has the most precise directions for its lawful uses and healthful management. You remember the Apostle's striking language, asking veneration for it as the temple of God. Coming up a step higher, the mind and the taste are necessary to furnish an elevated tone to household experience. But at this hour of history, no thinking person need be told, that. if religion belongs anywhere, it belongs in the school-house and the state-house, in newspapers and books, and in the parlor, chambers, and kitchen of a Christian's dwelling. Conscience and faith go into everything. Higher than all, like fountains in the sky, they send their sweet nourishment down into all the ridges and furrows of our employments; they penetrate every pore of humanity; for, like those words of Jesus which give them point and power, they are spirit and they are life. They are greater, infinitely, than the earthly labors they bless. "The life is more than meat."

Again, the spiritual life asks of you a more intense and regular concern than any other interest, because it not only penetrates all other interests, but outlives them. It is the interest, and the only interest, that cleaves to your immortality. Signs are continually appearing across the scenery of material activity which foreshadow its decay. All that is permanent about these buildings, pursuits, possessions, is the influence they leave on character as they vanish; that is fresh as ever, when the world has withered and dropped off. The most patent feature in every death-chamber is, that it is a final leave-taking between the man and his property, — not only his hands, and lungs, and feet, but his investments, his business, his relationships to the world. You will not wish me to enlarge on reflections so familiar as those that distinguish between transient goods and the eternity of the soul. The difficulty, I suspect, is not that any of us denies this contrast, but that we fail to realize it, because in order to realize it we need the very faith which it is presented to produce. It takes a spiritual vision to see that nothing but what is invisible is indestructible. Only truth, love, purity, spiritual affections, and spiritual attainments, survive that fire which shall try every man's work, of what sort it is. The soul is holier than the scene and the instruments amidst which it is trained, because it has an everlasting consciousness, responsibility, judgment. "The life is more than meat," because the one cannot abdicate the august birthright of its immortality, and the other sinks into corruption by a necessity of its nature. It is not written of our reputation, our trade, or our estate, but of our souls, that they shall "all stand before the judgment-seat of God."

Still another and the most impressive of witnesses to the superior claims over body, intellect, or friendship of the religious nature God has planted in us, is the special revelation that has broken through the order of history, to put into the world a fresh conviction of the fact. The incarnation of Divine Holiness in Christ, — what a miraculous attestation it is to the transcendent value of the spiritual life! Man had forgotten his Maker. Sin had distorted his constitution. Passion had perverted his reason. Indulgence had weakened his will. Self-love had bewildered his conscience. What went under the name of his religion was a ghost of dead ceremonies, kept on exhibition by traditions of the Past, — not a living reality, giving a vital communion with a present God. The Law had shed its virtue, and gone barren; and the world, when God thus manifested himself for its renovation, was only a type of every unrenovated, irreligious heart. What has happened for no other department of human welfare took place for the lost soul. The mediatorship of Christ breathed a new vitality into these torpid capacities of conscience and faith. By his person and his Gospel, by death and resurrection, this Messiah, this Immanuel, this Son of God, quickened these slumbering powers. God so loved the world. Is not the life, then, — the life for which Christ died, — more than meat? Gethsemane, Calvary, the cross, — they stand for ever, before the ages, mighty tokens of the soul's worth. That spectacle of infinite compassion, changing the face of the world, by first changing the heart of man, is proof enough how awful the issue is between spiritual life and spiritual death. It restored Religion to its throne, and planted a Church for its nurture, against which the gates of hell shall not finally prevail.

The Church, then, in a right understanding of it, — for I am not using the word in any technical or theological sense, — is at once a divine institution, in that it is the perpetuated body of Christ and witness of his redeeming power; and it is also a practical manifestation of whatever spiritual life resides among us. It is the appointed means for unfolding and nourishing our capacities for morality and for piety. It is a nursery of goodness. It is a school for the conscience. It is an oratory for prayer. It is the soul's house, collecting, protecting, cherishing, multiplying, spiritual life. This is what the Church is by intention, — the ideal Church, — the Church of God's design. It is an organization for giving practical efficacy and triumphant power to the deepest truth we know; namely, that life is more than meat; the soul too precious to be bartered for the world. But come, then, into the Church as it is. Come, that is, into the region of men's spiritual purposes and doings as they are, — into that department of their life which they call religion. What do we see? Life? interest? energy? reality? Pass in there from the streets of travel and the shops of merchandise. Is there life before you like the eager, throbbing intensity of life you leave behind you? Pass in there from the halls of legislation and political debate. Is there interest in duty and worship like the interest in the problems of public economy and the questions of party success? Pass in there from the school-house and the university. Is there energy spent on forming righteous characters like the energy that beams in the faces and animates the ambition of students and their teachers? Pass in there from the joyous groups of kindred in their homes. Is there reality like the reality of the love and games, the sympathy and talk, the fellowship and fervor, of families and wedlock, of parental devotion and filial gratitude?

Why not? Is it not a reasonable service? Where is the fallacy in the argument? What is the falsehood in the New Testament? Was the Saviour mistaken, when he declared the supremacy of spiritual interests, — said it would be profitable to sell all the world beside for the soul, — and bade men seek the kingdom of Heaven and its righteousness *first?* Were the Apostles exaggerated in their zeal? Is sin a matter of small concern to us, when God cannot look upon the slightest stain of it without abhorrence? Is spiritual ruin less dreadful to us than it was to the immaculate Lord who was crucified to save us from it? Is repentance an indifferent matter, when veery prophet Heaven has ever sent has made it the burden of his message? Why then do spiritual concerns languish and dwindle beside the strong activities of business, the onward march of learning, the vital forces of the world?

It must be because the lower nature has overborne the higher. Conscience and faith are absorbed and quenched by appetite and ambition. The carnal life enslaves the spiritual. In the noise and pressure of our weekly gain-getting and gayety, we lose our perception of the true proportions and objects of our being. We exchange our immortality for a fortune, our Saviour for pieces of silver, and prize the inmost and eternal life less than the body, its raiment and its meat.

Here, then, is the inevitable conclusion we are brought to, looking straight on from our starting-point. What is wanted is to restore the spiritual life to the sovereignty God has designed for it; to recrown the soul and make it master of the flesh; to estimate it as God estimates it; to seek its regeneration as He did who laid down his life for its sake, and declared, that except a man be thus born again, he cannot see the kingdom of Heaven.

What shall reawaken the sleeping heart? What shall restore the alienated estate? What shall lift men into the honor they were designed for, — persuade them that to be Christians is nobler than to be capitalists? What shall subordinate comfort to character, exalt the spiritual capacities over the fleshly, and give back to the soul its lost throne?

The question is personal, and not abstract. It is to be answered by each for himself, and not by public demonstrations, nor any voting in assemblies. We must take it home with us into a private meditation. Self-examination must furnish the key to it. What shall it profit *me* — is the searching word — if I gain the world and lose *my* soul? Will *that* be a rèasonable service? And then, remembering the weakness of your best resolves, and casting off your pride of will, like the blind man at the road-side, lift your arms in patient trust to Christ, saying, "Lord, that mine eyes might be opened, that I might see these spiritual realities as they are, and apprehend the way whereby thou canst lead me to immortal peace."

There must be personal effort. There must be personal energy. There must be watching and prayer. There must be a roused, a diligent, an urgent seeking, — as much more earnest, profound, systematic, and persevering than all our worldly enterprise, as the life is more than meat. It is your reasonable service. The kingdom of Heaven comes not into any breast by accident, by sloth, by unconcern.

Riches must begin in the feeling of poverty. And the vilest poverty is that of the rich man who fancies he has need of nothing. Poor and blind and miserable, the heart must feel itself, before it can possess itself of all things by reconciliation to God. And man is never so destitute as when his outward opulence and comfort mock an empty, aching breast. All that is external and material is never really possessed, till it is made to serve the soul, which is independent of its favors. Learn to look on the splendor of your physical prosperity as only the fading raiment of your spiritual substance. Not the garments, not the meat, not the skill, nor the pleasure, but the life they strengthen and discipline for eternity! Then, gaining or losing, you are rich; living or dying, you are immortal. Believe this: believe in the Christ who revealed and established it. All things are yours the moment you are Christ's. That will be the soul's coronation. For to be faithful unto the body's death, is to put on the crown of an undying life.

SERMON VI.

HOMEWARD STEPS.

FOR YE WERE AS SHEEP GOING ASTRAY; BUT ARE NOW RETURNED UNTO THE SHEPHERD AND BISHOP OF YOUR SOULS. —1 Peter ii. 25.

It is a common habit, both of the popular mind and of the pulpit, to look at Christian truth by fragments, rather than as a whole. We take it up in its parts, get interested in special aspects of it as they are presented by passing events or a personal experience, give our attention to its duties or its doctrines, one by one, without special regard to order or system. Even when we consider our religion as a practical power, working on the heart, turning it from darkness to light, and leading it along all the way of change and growth from sin to holiness, we are not very apt to bring the whole process under our view at once, so as to take in the full sweep of that sublime renewal at a single glance. We fail to observe the connection of one step with another, marking the beautiful continuity and the consistent progress from the beginning to the end.

Such modes of inquiry are to some extent inevitable. For, with our narrow reach of vision and our fallible reason, when we have proudly compacted our scheme and adjusted its harmony, the Holy Spirit is very apt to show us that his powers for converting the world are too large and too free for our comprehension, and that his path to the sinning heart transcends our poor contrivances. Besides, the way I spoke of has its advantages. A true and vital religion has so much to do with variable emotions, is so much a thing of the heart, partakes necessarily so much of the ever-shifting nature of life itself, that perhaps we treat it as profitably when we seize vigorously on the vivid points it presents to our faith and practice, one at a time, in the path of Providence, as if we stopped in cooler blood to arrange our notions into a very formal and rigid system. For it is one of the undoubted lessons of history, that what a theology gains by the anatomical precision of its framework, it often loses in life-blood, healthy lungs, and freedom of motion.

But, on the other hand, there is a positive good to be gained by occasionally taking the less familiar course; by laying the whole field under a single rapid survey, looking along the complete line of advance, and seeing how the soul is conducted on, under its Divine Guide, from the far country to its Father's house. To gather up, in this way, the principal points of a Christian experience, and to present them together in an outline of spiritual biography, is what I now propose. Such a statement must be in some sense a confession of faith, a doctrine of salvation; only it is presented to you, not in the abstract language and forbidding formulas of a scholastic theology, but in an actual and living history, such as may belong to any one of you. So your own heart, answering as far as it goes along, will either sanction or rectify the representation.

I first sum up these successive stages, through which Christ leads his followers, under the several terms that represent them, taken in their order. They are the Need, the Difficulty, the Warning, the Relief, the Application of the Relief, the Fruit, and the Result.

1. What is the Need? It is the need of feeling one's self in friendship with God. As respects our religious nature and prospects, that is the one radical, universal, undermost necessity. If you look deliberately down into your own heart, and think, you will find that, provided only you could feel confident that you and God were agreed, were desiring the same things, were working towards the same objects, were in a certain divine partnership, were mutually pledged to one another, and had one heart, mind, and will, then you would be perfectly safe and happy. You would be at peace. Nothing could harm and nothing could greatly terrify you. Let any possibility happen, this Almighty Friend would instantly come to your rescue. You could bear any sorrow, and any pain, and any mortal uncertainty. With that assurance, you would know, that, even if you were to commit an occasional sin, this perfect Friend, so wise, so affectionate, so gracious, would understand, would pity, would forgive. Heaven and earth might combine against you, temptation and trial, poverty and disease, desertion and death, tempest and earthquake,—you know you could stand untroubled and secure. Why? Because you are on the side of the Eternal Builder and Ruler of all, who will yet bring out order, beauty, sunshine, through the earth and sky.

This, then, is the soul's one great need. Men have different names for it. Ask one, and he will say, "Reconciliation"; another, "Harmony with the Infinite"; another will call it a "Hope," and another a "Faith," and another a "New Heart," and another "Religion" in general. Some persons will not allow that they need any such thing. This is only because they have not yet looked far enough into themselves to be conscious of what they do want, or else their pride will not let them confess. It stands to reason, it stands to common sense, it stands to Scripture, — no logic and no folly can get away from it, — the first want of a created spirit is to be on friendly terms with its Creator, child with Father, man with God. I say nothing yet of the difficulty of reaching that assurance, nor how it is done. But it is the want; and there will be uneasiness, there will be secret restlessness, there will be inward tossing and trouble, till it is had. Friendship, or reconciliation, with God: it was what Paul needed, with all his Pharisaic propriety and excellent education, when he went to Damascus. It was what Peter and Cornelius, what the jailer and Magdalen, what the prodigal son and the fallen woman needed. Profligate Augustine with his scholarship, profane John Newton in his hammock on shipboard, the accomplished, blameless Chalmers, needed it; all men, however upright, without piety, and all women amiable without consecration, — all among us that have it not, — need it. Thousands need it who only know, miserably enough, that they need something; thousands more, whom some appetite or vanity is robbing of their peace, who are trying desperately to live without it; unsatisfied hearts in this church, empty hearts all around it, and aching hearts over the whole earth, — this is their Need.

2. What is the Difficulty? The difficulty, of course, is having something in us that is opposite to God, some-

thing that does not assimilate with his holiness, something that refuses to harmonize with his love, and that therefore keeps us apart from him. In other words, the difficulty is sin. If there were no sin, our natures would stand naturally and constantly in accord with his, because he made man, — made man to resemble himself, made man after his own likeness and pleasure. Unless, then, something had come in to create a separation, we should dwell in the bosom of his favor from our birth.

Drop out, entirely, the question how this sin got in; it is there. The problem of its origin is one with which our present practical discussion has no concern. Theories on that point are as thick in the Church as withered leaves in a forest path in October, and often as dry. Two facts are enough: one is, that sin is actually found in every one of us, from the moment he wakes to consciousness, that is, the moment he knows that he exists at all; the other is, that it is to be got rid of, or its burden is, by personal effort. It is inside of us, an internal disease, and not on the surface. It is of the heart, and not of the hands and feet. It belongs to character before it belongs to conduct, or else it would never seriously estrange us from God. It is a vitiated state of the spiritual system and its circulations. It is bad blood in the veins of the soul. Its forms are manifold; it breaks out into avarice, lust, temper, falsehood, slander, vanity, selfishness, profanity, — the whole brood of vices, crimes, impieties, worldlinesses. But they all have one organic root in the heart. They press and goad us, they beset us in society and solitude, they follow after and irritate and corrupt us. And just so far as they master us, they drag us apart from God. Just as far as we yield to them, we lose sight of him, and the blessed feeling of friendship which is our need. The difficulty is sin.

3. What is the Warning? It is the law. That is God's voice, telling us when we are out of his friendship; in other words, telling us what this sin is. The law is what shows us the eternal distinction between being on God's side and being against him; that is, between the right and the wrong. How many voices this law has! It speaks from Sinai, from Jerusalem, from the Mount of Olives, from Calvary. It speaks from dwelling-houses among us where passion has darkened every window with a curtain of shame; from the dishonest merchant's disgrace; from the death-scene of the debauchee; from the funeral of the early victim of fashionable pleasure. It whispers through our secret fears of punishment; it makes a dramatic exhibition in our trembling nerves; it turns our sick-bed into a pulpit; it sends those shrieks that are rather felt than heard through the soul's remorse. Wherever law is violated, there law is reproclaimed. The Bible is its prolonged and solemn cry. It is written out all over the world. Sun and darkness are its light and shade. In every man and woman and child it finds some hearing, because it finds a conscience. If we ever start the treacherous inquiry whether we cannot be friends with God, and get the benefits of his favor, without renouncing our sin, — whether we cannot be one with him without giving up what is opposite and hateful to him, — this law rebukes our presumption. It is our warning. It never temporizes nor parleys. It offers no compromise and no postponement. It requires perfect obedience, immaculate purity, undeviating justice. There is no provision in it for anything but penalty and suffering upon the violator. It is clear as the sunbeam, sure as gravitation, terribly sincere. "This do, and thou shalt live." "Do that, and die."

Another attribute of law, making it yet more intensely a warning, is that it constantly keeps in advance of our performance, and yet condemns us for not keeping up with it. With the august and awful splendor of its purity, it frowns upon our pollution, shames our inconsistencies, threatens our guilt. The farther we go in complying with its demands, the keener our sense of its perfection grows; the higher the standard rises, the clearer the command sounds, and the more hopeless our self-disgust and our agony become. There is no satisfaction there. Just in proportion as we come consciously under law, and *law alone*, we are wretched. It is warning, and nothing but warning. Paul's wondrous spiritual insight saw that; and so he says, in his energetic phrase, that sin comes by the law; the strength of sin is the law; when the commandment came, sin revived. That is, by the law, the rule of right, comes a knowledge of transgression. No law, no violation of law, — and so no accusing conscience. And the more law, that is, the more clearly you see the command, the more sin. This is logical; and it is experimental. When you have fathomed the spiritual argument in the first eight chapters to the Romans, you have learned the profoundest lesson of personal and practical wisdom you are likely to find in the present life. The difficulty with our prevailing style of religion lies precisely here. We are legalists, and not children of grace; we are Jews, and not Christians; in fact, though not in form, we take after Moses, and not Jesus. We think to be saved simply by performances, by moral regularity, by following a rule of decency, by correct habits, by a respectable deportment. And certainly we must try with all our might to keep the law, or else we are not fit for grace, and have no promise of forgiveness. But unless we have something beyond and after law, it is plain we are only warned.

4. With such a Need, such a Difficulty, and such a Warning, it is not strange that we look for a Relief. What is that Relief? What must it be, by the very conditions of the case? In the first place, whatever it is, it must come forth out of God himself. The offended one must forgive. The harmony our sin has destroyed cannot be restored by the act of one party. Reconciliation can come only from the Infinite and Unchangeable Will restoring us, mercy and justice both being kept inviolate. Then the Relief must be a living person. No dead expiation, nor mercantile bargain, can heal that deadly and moral alienation. There must be personal affections, personal influence, personal mediation. It must be a person *like us*, as well as *from God*, — of human sensibility, as well as of divine authority and power. All the plenitude of God's wisdom and truth and love must be there, and all the sacrifice and suffering and temptation of humanity. There must be a perfect life, revealing and incarnating the divine. There must be a death, melting, moving, redeeming, by a transcendent sacrifice. You turn from the image in the mind to the historic reality, and behold! Jesus of Nazareth. He is the relief. You listen, and a voice out of heaven, over his head, "This is my beloved Son; whoso believeth in him shall not perish, but have eternal life." You listen again, and a voice at his side, "Behold the Lamb of God that taketh away the sin of the world." You listen again, and in his *own* voice, "Come unto me"; "The Son quickeneth whom he will"; "Whosoever liveth and believeth in me shall never die"; "All that the Father hath are mine." Here is an answer to the Need.

Here is a way out of the Difficulty. Here is peace after the Warning. The words spoken are the Father's words. For reconciliation he is the Reconciler. To save sinners this Saviour came into the world. To satisfy, and supersede, and fulfil the Law, he brings a living Gospel. The Spirit of the Lord is upon him, because he preaches that Gospel to the poor, and opens prison-doors, and lets in light upon dungeons, and unfastens chains, and anoints the fretted limbs. And this Saviour is not only making intercession for his Church to-day, in the heavens, being ascended into that glory which he had with the Father before the world was, but he is literally and personally present in the midst of his Church, fulfilling his own promise, the life of every believer's heart; not a dead Christ, but a living; not a departed Redeemer, but keeping personal relations with his own who love him. What infinite inspiration in that faith! In the great conflict, where victory is immortal life, our Leader watches us.

There is a touching fact related in history of a Highland chief, of the noble house of M'Gregor, who fell wounded at the battle of Preston Pans. Seeing their chief fall, it is said, the clan wavered, and gave the enemy an advantage. The old chieftain, beholding this, raised himself up on his elbow, while the blood gushed in streams from his wounds, and cried aloud: "I am not dead, my children; I am looking at you to see you do your duty." These words revived the sinking courage of his brave Highlanders. "There was a charm in the fact that they still fought under the eye of their chief. It roused them to put forth their mightiest energies, and they did all that human strength could do, to stem and turn the dreadful tide of battle.

Now they do it to win a corruptible crown, but we an incorruptible. When our strength falters, or confidence wavers, the Prince of Peace, with no vengeance but love only in his voice, says to us also: "I am not dead, my children, though my blood has once been shed for you. Lo! I am with you alway, even unto the end of the world." Law is melted in love. Instead of commandments graved on tables of stone, we have a cross whose blood is mercy. We are no longer under law, but grace. Christ is the Relief, our Redeemer.

5. What is the Application of this Relief? I ask again, How does a child "apply" his mother's love? He opens his heart and lets the blessed influence stream in. How does the young man, struggling with a hard fortune, in a crowd of strangers, "apply" the good-will of the generous benefactor who offers him sympathy and counsel and credit? He stretches out his confidence, and welcomes the timely friendship that saves him. These are fair illustrations. All our spiritual affections are under one law. If we would have the benefits of Christ's divine mediation and ministry cleave to our hearts, and regenerate our natures, and build us up into strong and noble and beautiful characters, we must, first of all, throw open our breasts to him. We must believe on him. We must trust in him. We must drop our doubts of his own promises. The grand condition of being saved is, after all, simple willingness to be saved. We have not to go after a Saviour, nor to invent one by our ingenuity, nor to purchase one by our performances, nor to propitiate one by persuasion, but simply to receive one who waits, to unbar the heart's door where he stands even now and knocks, to let him freely in.

"Let not justice make you linger,
Nor of fitness idly dream;
All the fitness he requireth
Is to feel your need of him."

We must sit at his feet, not to criticise his claims, but to listen; not to speculate, but to be renewed; not to use the scale and dividers of a metaphysic or dogmatic scheme upon him, but to adore the blessed mystery, to drink in his spirit, to catch the heavenly sympathy of his love, to yield ourselves up to his inspiring and moulding touch, to bend the knee, and lay our heads in his bosom, and so be ready to rise up daily to do his work, and press on after him into his kingdom. That is, the application of the Relief is Faith. Again and again the Apostle said, "Believe on the Lord Jesus Christ, and thou shalt be saved." Believe, that is, not with the brain, but with the heart, — with that kind of faith in which love is a larger element than intellect, and trust is more than assent. This is the faith that completes the whole work of regeneration. It carries penitence deeper down among the springs of feeling. It heightens the blush of shame at living a selfish and worldly life, because it is so alien to the disinterested and devout temper of the Master. It makes the new life a reality, because it founds it in the deepest motives. It changes the whole inner man. It works by love. It enters the invisible, and dwells in the secret tabernacle of a most holy joy.

And so it is commonly found that the beginning of a real and right religious life is a penitent and humble renunciation of self, — self-will, self-confidence, self-guidance, self-love. Only he that thus humbleth himself shall be exalted. Before we can lay hold on the Master's hand, we must let go money, dress, wine-cups, worldly honors. Before we are lifted up, we must be cast down. A young artist at Rome went down into the vast, dark Catacombs alone, to copy some of the designs on the tablets of the sepulchres. After he had groped his way through many intricate and winding passages, led on by the fascination of his discoveries, suddenly his lamp went out. Not a ray of light penetrated those subterranean acres. It was the blackness of darkness. In increasing terror, he felt his stumbling way among the labyrinths of tombs and dead men's bones, not knowing whether he was nearing the outlet or receding from it. At last, faint with effort, choked with dust, and in an agony of despair, he gave up all reliance, and fell prostrate to the ground to die. But as he fell, his hand accidentally grasped the thread which had been placed as a clew to the pilgrim; hope revived; and he regained the open air and the day. How often it happens, that some distress or misfortune, some nearness to the tomb almost as literal as his, must create in us the feeling of utter helplessness first, before we are ready to lean with faith on our Guide. When we renounce ourselves, we seize the clew; and then we rise, in the energy of a new-born and confident hope, and work steadfastly on into the light.

6. What is the Fruit? It is righteousness. Infallibly and invariably, it is righteousness. If that fruit does not grow, some one of the previous links in the line of causes has been left out. The penitence was not sincere. The reform was not true. The faith was not genuine. By their fruits ye shall know them. Not righteousness always in one style of its manifestations. It may be in a tradesman's bargains, or a mechanic's jobs; in a scholar's simplicity, or a clerk's fidelity. It may be in a forbearing disposition, where there are daily provocations; it may be in magnanimity toward a mean com-

petitor; it may be on a couch of slow and patient suffering, where needed energies are crippled, and a dependent family are left unprovided for. But it is none the less righteousness in one case than the other,—as dear to God, as resplendent to the spiritual eyesight of angels. It has equally glorious exhibitions in the statesman that carries an incorrupt breast through the lobbies of a state-house or through the bribes of the capitol, and in the woman that sways with patient justice the perplexing politics of the nursery, or is daring enough to resist the tyranny of fashion. It is in the politician that refuses to mortgage his conscience to the Devil, and in the freeman that cannot be hired by office, nor persuaded by sophistry, to make his brother-man a slave. It is in the preachers that reverence their message more than their salaries, and in parishes that keep a soul as well as a sanctuary. The lustre of a saintly heart needs no artificial reflectors to enhance its glory. It is splendid by its own original radiance. That panoply of sacred principle that lets no arrow of the adversary through any joint of its harness is the Christian's every-day garment. Every Christian cause is stronger for his hand and his tongue. No tempter is cunning enough to wring a scandal from his behavior. No neighbor shall hesitate on which side, in the grand division of the world, to reckon him. He is committed frankly. He is pledged irrevocably. He is consecrated manfully. If he is Christ's man, there is no situation, nor turn, nor emergency, where Christ is not honored in his life. And that because the Master's spirit is in him.

Christianity patronizes no system of half-education. It asks a form of manhood embodying every natural idea that philosophy has propounded, genius represented, or history disciplined. It is no ally of a stationary intelligence, nor of a sluggish will, nor of a timid heart. Growth is its law, — growth in wisdom and growth in love. It is not satisfied, therefore, with conversion, but is quite as exacting of sanctification, bidding the convert forget the elements and go on to perfection. Christianity wants to build after the pattern of a divine beauty, a symmetry without blemish, and a wholeness without defect. It is itself incarnated in a living example of that completeness. It has a welcome for every contribution of science, only requiring that science shall remember its ministerial office, not exalting its telescopes and crucibles into an apparatus of will-worship, displacing dependence and redemption. It has nothing but contempt for that complacent, Pharisaic-style of piety, which fancies its only needed work is done when it has just grazed the gates of hell by sliding into a lazy church; which identifies entering the ark of the covenant with escaping from the vineyards of brave toil, and goes shuffling and dozing through a life that vibrates between formalities on Sunday and intense vitalities all the week, — alive in the shop and caucus, but asleep at church; — character all the while rotting away under those obscene inconsistencies, a cowardly conscience and a voluble confession, — a brain boiling with the plots of politics or the bargains of trade, and a heart hard as the nether millstone to all the sufferings of humanity; — a prayerless life, or else a lifeless prayer.

The Need does not tend more directly to the Difficulty; sin is not more certainly assailed by the Warning; the Law does not more naturally waken the longing for the Relief; Christ does not more gladly enter in where faith applies for him, than faith itself acts its noble energy forth into righteousness, works by love, bears the Fruit of philanthropy, integrity, patience, temperance, emancipation, brotherly-kindness, charity.

7. What is the Result? Let the noble and animating words of Paul answer: "But now, being made free from sin, and become servants to God, ye have your fruit unto holiness, and the end, *everlasting life.*" Everlasting life is the result. The soul has reached its period of victory. From the far country, through these seven stages, it has travelled back, till it has come home,—home,—O word of unspeakable and unexhausted meaning! The door of the Father's house was open, and it has entered in. To hear that sentence of forgiving welcome,—as if all the sighs of a parent's anxious and agonized affection were suddenly melted into one musical and joyous anthem of thanksgiving,—"This my son was dead, and is alive again; he was lost, and is found,"—to hear that from the Father's lips is heaven enough. After conflict, there is peace. Now is "the rest that remaineth for the people of God." This is life eternal. Henceforth, there shall be labor, indeed, because labor is the best satisfaction of a spiritual being. There shall be trial, because only by trial come strength and progress, which are the very honors of our immortality. But it shall be labor no longer outside the kingdom of Heaven. It is labor in the Master's society, labor under the encouragements of his friendship, labor with the crown on the head, and the seal in the forehead, and the reconciliation in the heart. Faithful continuance in well-doing, not *for the sake* of the reward, but for the brave relish of fidelity's own sake, has brought the disciple to his Lord; and when he looks up, behold! glory and honor and immortality are the spiritual trophies that adorn his dwelling.

Thus falls the sweet benediction of the Apostle: "Ye were as sheep going astray; but are now returned unto the Shepherd and Bishop of your souls." Have I drawn, with any traces of truth, the homeward steps of a human soul, — its need of reconciliation, its difficulty in its inward sin, its warning from a law so unbending and so pure as to be dreadful, its divine deliverance in the appointed Reconciler, its reception of his inspiring and renewing and redeeming spirit by a penitent and lowly faith, its fruit in a humane and holy life, its end in its salvation?

Homeward steps: without these can we ever see our home? Is there any encouragement, anywhere, to think we can have an answer to the momentary impulse which sometimes says, "Let me die the death of the righteous!" if we have not tried to live the life of the righteous? When Stephen, first of martyrs, falling bruised and bloody under the stones hurled by Jewish bigotry, exclaimed in rapture, "Lord Jesus, receive my spirit!" was the image of his Lord an unfamiliar vision, or the thought of meeting him a new suggestion? The last words of the mother of John Wesley to her family were, "Children, as soon as I am released, sing a psalm of praise to God"; could that be the farewell of a spirit to which psalms of praise were strange before? Could any tongue not familiar with the language of Christian hope say what Philip Doddridge said: "Let me be thankful that, though God loves my departed child too well to permit it to return to me, he will, erelong, bring me to my child?" As Owen, the author of the "Meditations on the Glory of Christ," lay dying, he said to a brother-believer, "The long-wished-for day has come at last, when I shall see that glory in another manner than I have ever done or was capable of doing in this world." Does that sound like the speech of a faith extemporized for the occasion? Margaret Wilson, "a young martyr of eighteen," in the reign of James II., fastened by her persecutors to a stake in the bay at low water, to be drowned by the rising tide, repeated in a clear, full voice the twenty-third Psalm, and then, as the water choked her, added, after Stephen, "Lord Jesus, receive my spirit." Could that tone of triumph have sounded over the waves, if the steadfastness of a long and patient confession had not inspired her lips?

In some one of these seven stages of spiritual pilgrimage every soul among us is found to-day; for beneath alienation from God there is no lower depravity, and above eternal life and love there is no more perfect holiness or joy. Which one of us shall be too cowardly or too careless to bring the wholesome questions personally home: At which point am I? Which way do my steps tend? Is my journey towards the far country, or towards my Father's house? Or do I stand weak, irresolute, and despicable, looking now this way, and now that, halting between husks with the swine, and the honors of glory everlasting? Shall I go farther astray, or shall I return, a grateful penitent, to the Shepherd and Bishop of souls?

SERMON VII.

HOLINESS TO THE LORD.

AND THOU SHALT MAKE A PLATE OF PURE GOLD, AND GRAVE UPON IT, LIKE THE ENGRAVINGS OF A SIGNET, HOLINESS TO THE LORD. — Exod. xxviii. 36.

FIRST, an examination of the word Holiness, and its meaning; then the question, how holiness, the spiritual element in character, is gained, — or what is the law of its growth; and thirdly, the question where it is to be exercised, — or what is the law of its manifestation.

How much meaning, after all our abuses of it, clings to one of these old biblical words! We pervert it, we make false applications of it, we mix it in with the deceptions of our current speech, we let it slip into our practice of that terrible social dishonesty which makes so much of our fashionable conversation what an observing satirist once described all language to be, — a contrivance for concealing our thoughts; and yet, in spite of so many frauds and forgeries upon it, we never wholly sift out the original value. And there are some words which are slower to be vulgarized by these familiarities than others, retaining an awfulness which forbids their desecration, almost like a sanctuary, or a mother's Bible, or a dead child's memory. One of these words is *holiness*. That term carries with it a strict and solitary individuality. Let us keep it, the more reverently and affectionately, for that reason. If any unnatural and artificial associations have crept up about it, by formal usage, let us take it back out of the vocabulary of cant, into the property of common sense. If it sounds somewhat vague and indefinite, let us try to fix upon it an exacter definition. It has a signification altogether its own. We are not likely to hear it where its real sense is wholly out of the speaker's thoughts. Indeed, it is rather remarkable how many men's lips there are that never can speak it. What special and sacred grandeur lingers in it, appealing to a fine instinct even in very thoughtless minds, forbidding them to pronounce it? We all know some men and women by whom it would startle us to hear this word *holiness* deliberately uttered, and who would themselves find a kind of embarrassment in forcing it from their lips. Is this because there is a certain spiritual quality suggested by it which is foreign from their characters, and a shade of religious conviction, to which nothing in their habit of life and feeling answers?

Preparatory to a fresh appreciation of the power and the beauty of holiness, we certainly want a clear understanding of the thing.

Holiness, then, in the first place, is not to be confounded with virtue. Nor is any disparagement cast upon virtue by affirming this distinction. They are names of two things, not one and the same. They do not express the same quality in character. They rest on different capacities in human nature, — virtue on the conscience, holiness on faith. They are fed from different fountains, — virtue from moral principle, holiness from communion with God in Christ. They may be guided by different directors; virtue depending more on self-will, as is intimated in the classical origin of the word, where it expressed the special characteristic of the Roman mind, which was a certain honorable, proud high-mindedness, but Pagan and not Christian, and where it was nearly synonymous with valor, or such fidelity as depends on personal courage. Holiness, on the other hand, implies a *subjection* of self-will, and the presence of those spiritual attributes, like humility, forgiveness, and religious submission, which are peculiar to Christianity. Holiness *requires* virtue, as one of its ingredients; no man can be holy without being virtuous. But virtue, on the contrary, is often found, temporarily and in individuals, dissociated from holiness; an ordinary congregation embraces two or three times as many virtuous hearts as holy ones. You can mark this distinction among professions not theological. Wherever an individual comes whose life is under the influence of daily communion with his God, you feel that there is a signet on his character, differing from that of the best man whose conduct acknowledges no higher principle than a correct morality; and most of us, I presume, would readily agree that the former character is of the nobler stamp. Before his conversion, there is no evidence that Paul was not rigidly, even Pharisaically, virtuous. But he did not ascend into the purer dignity of holiness, till the voice and the light from heaven unsealed his spiritual eyesight, and converted him to Christ. His conscience was scrupulous, but not sanctified, and so it let him persecute and hate Christians. Simon Magus, for anything that appears to the contrary, may have been a virtuous citizen of Samaria; yet he thought the gift of the Holy Spirit could be purchased with money, and had to learn from Peter that he needed repentance and prayers for forgiveness before he could have part or lot in holiness, because his heart was not right in the sight of God. This, I suppose, was the distinction in the Apostle's mind, when he said that for a righteous, correct, or virtuous man, one would scarcely volunteer to die; while for a good or holy man, — so much more impressive and affecting is that type of character, — some would even dare to die. Holiness to the Lord is not complacency towards men.

Do not suspect me of exalting Paul at the expense of James, — nor of pleading for religion by the poor trick of undervaluing morality. I think Christ's Church will never return to that error. What I claim for the spiritual principle is that it is the natural root, and in a wide reach, and the long run, the only infallible supporter, of the moral principle. If I wanted to convert a pagan people to virtue, I would first try to rouse in them some vital sense of God. And in behalf of that method, I would be as willing to pledge philosophy as the Gospel. As fast as our nominal Christendom loses its hold on God, by faith, it is preparing the final downfall of its good morals. Holiness is the essential root. Virtue is the essential fruit.

The same discrimination ought to be made, only more sharply, between all those negative epithets whereby we describe persons that avoid trespasses against the conventional rules of honesty, or against the common canons of respectability, on one side, and holiness on the other. It is an offence against the Eternal Spirit, to confound these mixtures of prudence, self-esteem, worldly sagacity, natural benevolence, or refined Epicureanism, or even moral innocence, with that spiritual affection which is as real and as positive and as practical as any of them, diviner than any, and which comes only by devout communion with the spirit God gives through his Son, creating a new life. We ought not to be long in learning that it is a very insufficient tribute we pay to the finished life of a companion, when we can only say over his grave, that he paid his debts, provided well for his family, and escaped disgrace. If we lived in a community of Calmuc Tartars, or had received our notions of character under Arabs and brigands, this would be a legitimate title to distinction. But what an equivocal comment on all our Christian civilization, if by this time it has only educated us up to the point of eulogizing, as signal examples of a right life, men that have not cheated, nor robbed, nor broken their marriage vows, nor abused their lips by lying and profanity! Brethren, Providence has called us children of a purer light. It becomes us to be awake to it. Our funeral honors, and our admirations of the living, ought to be graduated by a stricter scale. A nation that has been turning over the leaves of the New Testament, writing commentaries, establishing Sunday schools, organizing Bible societies, supporting churches, for two hundred years and more, with no religious disabilities to compromise its progress, ought to have marched beyond the childishness of rating its saints by the standard of social decency, and of canonizing honesty. Honesty is no mean thing, and not too common; but because the *rudiments* of Christian character are noble, is that a reason why we should linger in the rudiments for ever, and not press forward, perfecting holiness in the fear of God? "These ought ye to have done, and not to leave the other undone." The whole aim of Christ's teachings is to carry up the purposes and lives of his disciples, above the legal virtue of Jews and Pharisees, to that spiritual purity which is the express product of repentance, prayer, and faith. "God hath called us to holiness."

Holiness, then, is that attribute which is the very crown of all the culture of humanity; for it carries the soul up nearest to the everlasting Fountain of wisdom, power, goodness, from which it came. It enters in only where repentance opens the way, and spiritual renewal puts the heart into wholesome relations with the Divine will. It is the peculiar gift for which the world stands indebted to revelation, and it is multiplied just in proportion as the heart is formed into the likeness of Christ's. It is the summit of manhood, but no less the grace of God. It is achieved by effort, because your free-will must use the means that secure it; and it is equally the benignant inspiration of that Father who hears every patient petition. It belongs to that statesman, and only that one, who worships in his closet before he ascends the tribunal, and who feels the hall of legislation, as often as he enters it, to be a fore-court of the heavenly audience-chamber, whose foundations are justice and judgment; it belongs to that magistrate, and only that one, who is made fit to govern or to judge by personal consecration to the Master, who will reckon for his stewardship by immaculate statutes; to that merchant, and only that one, who holds a daily commerce with the Almighty Author of just balances and the Avenger of wrong, and whose trading-house, with its least transactions, lies consciously open to the inspection of the undeceived Accountant; to that laborer, and only that one, who labors for the meat that perisheth with less zeal than for that which endureth unto everlasting life; to that woman, and only to her, whose morning devotions dedicate the house she keeps as a domestic temple, and who, remembering that favor is deceitful and beauty vain, prizes no favor like His who was the friend of Mary and Martha, nor any beauty like the beauty of holiness.

My second inquiry asks how holiness, the spiritual element in character, is gained. Not by enchantments. Not by mystical openings that pour it into the passive soul, as summer showers fill lifeless cisterns. Not by constitutional predispositions; for it fits every organization, and is impartially designed for every experience. Not by strange, anomalous, interior spasms, that set aside all the regular action of our powers, and jerk the heart into conversion hysterically. It is as much conformed to regular methods as any accomplishment or enterprise in the world. It is as beautifully reducible to order and fixed conditions, as the mastery of a science or the planting of a colony. Holiness is subject to Law, both in its birth and its growth.

And the first principle of that spiritual economy is this: it must be taken up as an *express*, *specific* work. Holiness, I say, — nay, God says, — must be a special object. It is very essential, as the progress of the subject will remind us presently, to diffuse it, when we have it, into all parts of our life; but the first purpose is to get it, to know what it is that we may get it, and not so to mix it confusedly with mere proprieties of behavior and amiabilities of temper, that we shall imagine we have kept all that holy law which is exceeding broad when we have only washed the outside of our conventional cups and platters, or swept up and down the aisles of a church covered with invisible phylacteries, — phylacteries which will some day show, under hotter trial, just as the fire brings out the characters of an invisible ink. The young man who has not begun to take into special and particular concern the discipline of his character into holiness, has left out the chief element in his being, and has laid his plans for living, forgetting his inmost life. Holiness presents that side of us which joins on upon eternity, opens into heaven, and makes us kindred to God. It is not to be had without an aim, a purpose, a steady looking and striving to that end. It never was obtained by a few desultory snatches of sober reflection, hastily dismissed, — a few vague impressions, in churches or cemeteries, — a few intermittent demonstrations in the way of a charity collection, after-dinner good-nature, or summer-evening philosophy. It must be treated like an interest, a pursuit, a profession. It is the great livelihood of your heart. It is the vocation of your soul. It is the practical handicraft of your inner man. It must be begun, followed, and never ended. Resolve, deliberation, continuous effort, are its motor powers. All your members are its flexile instruments. The Bible is its text-book. Morning, evening, noon, all the circling hours, are its periods of exercise. Prayer is its rehearsal. God answering is its Teacher. Christ is its Pattern. Special, express, intentional, must the striving after holiness be, in order to secure it, like every glorious consummation in the world's history, like every solid triumph in individual advancement.

And then this crowning grace and central strength of character must be sought by a *direct process*. Astronomy is not learned by probing down among the soils and rocks of the planet we occupy. Chemistry is not mastered by studying trigonometry. Painting is not learned by handling a chisel. Men aspiring to excellence in mechanics do not go to sea; nor do sailors take their apprenticeship in a smithery. Yet there seems to be a common conceit, that, by hard following after all manner of material success and welfare, the spiritual nature in us will grow strong and beautiful. Now, for spiritual attainments there are spiritual faculties; just as for mechanical attainments there are mechanical faculties, and for success in acquisition, acquisitive faculties. Nothing need be said of their rank; for if you admit their existence at all, you must grant their supremacy. But they are to be waked and opened. They await nurture and expansion. Do not come to the recognition and training of them by any sidelong indirection, nor imagine it impossible. Do not suppose your love of God will grow, because you are faithful to your counting-room. Do not think your feeble reverence for the Everlasting Right and Good will strengthen, because you excel in your art, or take a premium for mechanism or horticulture, or foresee next month's market. Do not hope for the peace unspeakable which passeth knowledge and dwells in the meek and contrite spirit, by merely dealing about as fairly as your neighbors, and paying what the law says you owe. Rise to loftier designs. Remember, spiritual things are spiritually discerned. Answers to prayer cannot be had without being prayed for. Faith will not increase, unless you provide for faith's exercise. You will not enter into fellowship with Christ Jesus, except you seek his society. You will not behold the kingdom of Heaven, unless you direct your eye, and fix it there. And it is the universal maxim of all manly and candid seeking, to go straight to the very object you would gain. By the same rule only is the new man created in holiness.

Still another means of forming this highest grace

upon character, is to place ourselves in contact with the providential instruments that foster it, — those divine helps that favor it. It was on the high-priest's frontlet, — the plate of pure gold before his mitre, surmounting all his holy garments, the splendid investiture of his office, the robe and ephod, the girdle, the Urim and Thummim, the onyx-stones whereon the names of the twelve tribes were written, — it was over all these, that the august inscription was graven, like the engravings of a signet, Holiness to the Lord. According to that Levitic ritual, the priest passing away prefigured the ever-living Messiah, and the furniture of his sacerdotal function symbolized the simpler and grander forms of the Christian Church. For every peculiar organized work there is wanted a system of means. Culture implies a *cultus;* education, a school; agriculture, a seed-time and harvest, as well as a soil and sun; chemistry, a laboratory; literature, a library; moral experience, a moral discipline. So the spiritual life wants certain appointments, ordinances, to be the outlines of an institution where it shall get nurture. God has not mocked the soul with a false aspiration. As we have our being under the two grand external conditions of time and space, he has carved a monument and a treasury out of each, for the replenishing of our fidelity; a holy day, and a holy place, through which the Holy Spirit may multiply holiness in us. A supernatural philosophy, adapting the framework of our worship to our worshipping necessities! The Church, with its simple ceremonies, its Sabbath and Sanctuary, its Baptism and Communion, meeting the soul's unperverted wants, is the house built for the new man, as convenient and genial to his regenerate life as the dwelling that welcomes the new-born child, and shelters the natural one. These venerable, permanent ordinances are like fixed channels, through which our Lord has poured his selectest influences down the field of the world. If we, workers in the vineyard, would receive the gift, drink of that water of life which slakes the immortal thirst, we must come where the channel runs, reach out our hand to the stream, touch and taste at the brink. Specific means for a specific result. The Church organizes our spiritual life, drills its desultory habits, systematizes its irregular impulses, turns it into peace, order, efficiency. Without conscious vitality in themselves, its observances act through laws of association and impression wrought into the fibre of our being, so as to enkindle that life in the believer. Their influence depends on two things, — a cordial, receptive heart, and a faithful use. Nothing in themselves, they are clothed with power by the spiritual reaction they stimulate in our souls. Holiness is of the spirit; but these are God's way, and suited to our constitution, of making the spirit holier.

I have mentioned a third question, lying in the path of my subject: — Where is this Holiness to be exercised? The fountain being replenished by the pouring out of the Holy Spirit, in answer to our seekings and our struggles, Christ's holiness is to be reproduced in us, and sent forth again to bless the world. And so there is a law of its manifestation. Indeed, the exercise or practice of holiness, as I have intimated, is a chief means of its reduplication. To use what we possess is the surest way of being enriched with more; for unto him that hath shall be given; and the best preparation for right living to-morrow, is to live rightly to-day.

Holiness was meant, our New Testament tells us, for every-day use. It is home-made and home-worn. Its exercise hardens the bone, and strengthens the muscle, in the body of character. Holiness is religion shining. It is the candle lighted, and not hid under a bushel, but lighting the house. It is religious principle put into motion. It is the love of God sent forth into circulation, on the feet, and with the hands, of love to man. It is faith gone to work. It is charity coined into actions, and devotion breathing benedictions on human suffering, while it goes up in intercessions to the Father of all pity. Prayers that show no answers in better lives are not true prayers. We took some pains at the outset to see that holiness is not to be confounded with mere kind and correct behaving, since the love of God is not to be obscured in the love of man, and morality without piety has lost its root; but also with the qualification, which we must now revive and keep before us, that, of these two forces in the Christian life, both are indispensable. Of religion without holiness — or the spurious pretence current under that name — the world has seen enough; it has more than once made society, with all its reforms, go backward; it has sharpened the spear of the scorner, and sealed the sceptic's unbelief. It has hidden the Church from the market. It has gone to the conference and the communion-table, as to a sacred wardrobe, where badges are borrowed to cloak the iniquities of trade. It has said to many an outcast and oppressed class, "Stand by thyself; the Master's feast is for me, and not for you." It has thinned the ranks of open disciples, and treacherously offered to objectors the vantage-ground of honesty. My friends, get faith, and then use it. Gain holiness, and wear it. Pray; and watch while you pray. Keep the Sabbath; keep it so carefully that it shall keep you all the week, — a mutual friendship.

Come to the church; come to carry the church back with you, not in its professions nor its external credit, but its interior substance, into a consistent holiness.

Constant, then, but earnest, — even, but laborious, — familiar, but positive, — and universal, but also decided, — must that manifestation of holiness be, if it is to bear the tests of Christ's inspection.

Holiness to the Lord! where is that inscription to be stamped now? Not on the vestments of any Levitical order; not on plates of sacerdotal gold, worn upon the forehead. Priest and Levite have passed by. The Jewish tabernacle has expanded into that world-wide brotherhood, where whosoever doeth righteousness is accepted. Morning has risen into day. Are we children of that day? For form, we have spirit; for Gerizim and Zion, our common scenery. The ministry of Aaron is ended. His ephod, with its gold, and blue, and purple, and scarlet, and fine twined linen, and cunning work, has faded and dropped. The curious girdle, and its chains of wreathen gold, are broken. The breastplate of judgment that lay against his heart, and its fourfold row of triple jewels, — of sardius, topaz, and carbuncle, — of emerald, sapphire, and diamond, — of ligure, agate, and amethyst, — of beryl, onyx, and jasper, — has been crushed and lost. The pomegranates are cast aside like untimely fruit. The golden bells are silent. Even the mitre, with its sacred signet, and the grace of the fashion of it, has perished. All the outward glory and beauty of that Hebrew worship which the Lord commanded Moses has vanished into the eternal splendors of the Gospel, and been fulfilled in Christ. What teaching has it left? What other than this? — that we are to engrave *our* "Holiness to the Lord," first on the heart, and then on all that the heart goes out into, through the brain and the hand: on the plates of gold our age of enterprise is drawing up from mines and beating into currency; on bales of merchandise and books of account; on the tools and bench of every handicraft; on your weights and measures; on pen and plough and pulpit; on the door-posts of your houses, and the utensils of your table, and the walls of your chambers; on cradle and playthings and school-books; on the locomotives of enterprise, and the bells of the horses, and the ships of navigation; on music-halls and libraries; on galleries of art, and the lyceum desk; on all of man's inventing and building, all of his using and enjoying; for all these are trusts in a stewardship, for which the Lord of the servants reckoneth.

Brethren, it is written that, while our fathers according to the flesh have corrected us after their pleasure, God chastens us for our profit, — and for what, but that we might be partakers of his own holiness? The transcendent privileges of sorrow! It is for you and me to consider, whether this peculiar trait in a Christian character is losing anything of its primary honor; whether, in the deserved esteem rendered to upright and philanthropic men, to useful and benevolent women, Christians themselves are letting the higher order of holy men and holy women cease and be forgotten. If holiness is gradually lost in civil accomplishments, be sure God will finally be forgotten in his creature. Then human reputation is supplanting the divine favor. Comfort is usurping the throne of faith. Humanity is losing its grandeur. Introductions to the court of fashion will be preferred before the penitence that kneels at the foot of the cross. Certificates of office and inventories of wealth will be dearer possessions than the secret witnessings of the spirit.

9*

The old sentence out of Heaven, "Except ye repent, ye perish," will be rendered into the softer invitation of the Tempter, — "Soul, take thine ease; much goods and many years are heaven enough."

Such tendencies it is our part to resist, by a personal correction of our hearts. Personal motives enough plead for it, — motives that lie closest to the conscience: personal immortality and personal peace. For now, says the Apostle, when ye are made "free from sin, and become servants to God, ye have your fruit unto holiness, and the end, everlasting life." "Without holiness, no man shall see the Lord."

And now, may God himself make you to increase and abound in love toward all men, to the end he may stablish your hearts unblamably in holiness, at the coming of our Lord Jesus Christ!

SERMON VIII.

SATAN TRANSFORMED.

FOR SATAN HIMSELF IS TRANSFORMED INTO AN ANGEL OF LIGHT. — 2 Cor. xi. 14.

I SHALL best open my subject by two Scriptural examples, which both define and illustrate it.

Early in the night before the crucifixion, Jesus has retired from the chamber of the Last Supper in Jerusalem to a lonely spot on the Mount of Olives, with a few of his followers. His prophetic mind foresees the awful scenes of the next day, — scenes in which he is himself to be the victim and the sufferer. It is impossible that some feeling of desolation should not come over the spirit even of the Son of Man, in such an hour and with such a prospect. His sense of loneliness is only made deeper by knowing that one of his chosen disciples is at that very moment betraying him, and that before morning another, and one of the trustiest and most ardent of them all, shall disown him. The touching words of one of the old prophets of his nation come solemnly to his mind, and, as the night-wind of the mountain moans by the anxious group, he repeats them, with a calm voice, aloud: "All ye shall be offended because of me this night; for it is written, I will smite the Shepherd, and the sheep shall be scattered." The pathos of this mournful quotation affects the quick sensibilities of the affectionate, impulsive Peter, and he breaks out into an impassioned and confident pledge of devotion: "Though all men shall be offended because of thee, yet will I never be offended." Jesus replies, in the same sad but serene and premonitory tone: "This night, before the cock-crowing announces another day, thou shalt deny me thrice." Peter returns a warmer and intenser affirmation: "Though I should die with thee, yet will I not deny thee."

So far the temptation has not tried Peter. The shameful sin he is about to commit has only been put before him in words. He is appalled at its enormity; recoils from it; and, if it should only *come* to him in that open, direct way, that undisguised shape, he would be able to say firmly, "Get thee behind me," and cling faithfully to his Master. But the real temptation when it comes does not come openly, directly; it almost never comes so. It comes to him when he is off his guard, comes obliquely, comes under another name, comes in a maid-servant's impertinence irritating his pride, and in the taunts of the by-standers insulting his honor. And thus it masters him. The crime that looked so hateful in its own features he embraces in its thin disguise. The tempter came obliquely; and he is false to the beloved Christ he was ready to die for. Cursing and swearing crowned the guilt of his perfidy; and while the day was breaking in the sky, the bitter tears of his remorse were falling on the pavement of the palace.

There is a parallel instance in one of the old Syrian kings. When Hazael was only an officer in King Benhadad's court, the Prophet Elisha one day wept before him. And when Hazael asked, "Why weepeth my lord?" "Because I know," answered the prophet, "the evil that thou wilt hereafter do unto the children of Israel," — and proceeded to picture before him the pillage, the slaughter, the burnings, the murders, and all the savage cruelties the young man should be guilty of, when he should sit on Benhadad's throne. Hazael is shocked at this bald statement of his future crimes, and exclaims, "Is thy servant a dog, that he should do these inhuman things?" Time ran on; temptation began to put on its various disguises; it came in the fascinating forms of the love of power, empire, splendor, royal authority, national honor, military prowess, — came, that is, circuitously; and in the historic sequel we find Hazael with the blood of murder on his hands, and the oppressor's infamy upon his grave.

We shall do quite well to personify the forces of sin and the seductive influences of temptation under the concrete term, Satan. So long as we all know what we mean, so long as we understand perfectly that this kingdom of darkness and the prince of it, this "Devil and his angels," are all carried about within the unholy heart, it will be quite as true to the fact, as much according to the analogies of all forcible language, to say Satan, as to use certain abstract words standing for vague tendencies and general qualities.

But we need a new theory of Satan, more profound and more penetrating than the old fables of nursery tradition give us; more in accordance with the spiritual insight gained under our Christian culture. This power of evil that besets us, this compound force of passion and materialism, selfishness and appetite, an unhallowed ambition and an unspiritual flesh, is not a *less* fearful, but a much more terrible, because a more cunning adversary, than the old imagery represented it. It was but a shallow device, and showed a very inadequate conception of devilish art, to represent Satan a hideous and repulsive figure, with frightful marks to be recognized by, with a beastly foot to certify his track, and all concentrated malignities on his distorted features. Why, men would run from such ugliness by instinct; and if this were the type of evil, it could never come near enough to tempt us. Our virtue would be safe against a seducer that inspired nothing but disgust. In the real Satan, we must look for a shrewder cunning, a more subtle diplomacy, a more politic disguise. Whatever he may have been to the superstitious fears of ruder ages, to try the temper of the nineteenth century he takes on the address of a courtier, the self-possession of a man of the world, the royal dignity of a prince, the beauty of a seraph, and the manners of a gentleman. If you meet him now, — and meet him you certainly will to-morrow and to-day, — he will be transformed into an angel of light. And as with Peter and Hazael, so with you and me, it is the policy of the tempter to steal upon us by degrees, little by little, and by roundabout approaches, till we are taken in his net.

Except he is utterly lost from decency, and abandoned to the infernal passions, which very few even of bad men are, a man will not set up an atrocious aim before his own eyes, and move straight towards it. He must partly conceal his wrong purpose, even from himself. He must find an honest name to associate with his dishonest dealings, even in his own habits of thinking about them, or else, in some careless moment, he will betray his secret to the acquaintances he is practising upon. He must tamper a little with his own conscience, and half convince himself that the evil in him can bear some favorable construction, or he will not be able to put on the saintly look to impose on the world about him with. The treacherous demon in him will peer out through his guilty eyes, or tremble in his lying tongue, or give some public advertisement of itself by the twitch of his agitated muscles. For God has so made all the parts of this human creature to sympathize together, that when the spirit in us sins, the body over it is shaken; when the inward law is violated, the material vesture is disturbed. A pallid face reveals the corruption of the heart; tremulous nerves, like magnetic wires, convey abroad the swift exposure of the criminal intent;—just as sympathetic earthquakes undulated through the solid frame of the world when ingratitude crucified its Redeemer;—just as when Eve reached forth her hand to the fatal fruit in Eden, and plucked and ate,

> "Earth felt the wound, and Nature from her seat,
> Sighing through all her works, gave signs of woe,
> That all was lost."

It is not enough, then, for the success of bad intentions, that they deceive the surrounding public; they must to some extent, and first, deceive the breast that harbors them. It is the understood condition of all stage effect. The skilful actor must lose himself in the character he assumes. The appointments and the costume of the theatre must beguile his own imagination, till, in the magic of their transforming power, even his own identity loses its reality, and he is no longer himself, but the Richard or Shylock or Iago that he personates. Without this he will forget his part, the charm of the illusion vanishes, and all the pains and the splendors of the posture-master and the scene-shifter are reduced to plain deal-boards and plaster and gas and paint. The kingdom of iniquity would never make its way in the world one inch farther forward, if the wrong-doers that swell its ranks did not first deceive themselves. Men do not plunge into infamy for infamy's sake. They must have a pretext, and go sideways to perdition. We are not a race of diabolic fiends, seeking hell; but we are a race of assailable and tempted mortals, by our careless yieldings to the sorceries of appetite turned away from Heaven.

The peculiarity of temptation that I would fix your thoughts upon now is the indirectness of it, — the circumventing policy by which it conducts us to shoals of shame, and into a vortex of tempests, while we are all the while flattering ourselves that we are making a prosperous voyage.

Come down, then, below the plane of action to the subterranean springs of action, — below superficial behavior to the primitive stratum of motive, — below appearances put on, to the living soul that a man is.

When a man begins to sin, he begins with something of the original simplicity and sensibility of his nature. Accordingly, whatever the wrong he is about to do, he does not go about it as being wrong; he tries first to give it some color of right. He must throw over it some pretext or apology to make it tolerable to the unperverted part of his moral sense. He must fasten to it some excusing title, make out for it some sort of claim to respect, and thus provide a palliation to that conscience in him which would revolt at it if it stood before him as naked guilt. By a succession of such artifices we are led on, step by step and little by little, to degrees of sin which would have shocked us if we had seen their full enormity from the beginning. Few men follow sin as sin; and yet how many follow it. Fewer still leap into the depths of degradation or crime by one plunge; but they are not few that are degraded, and that are criminal. The Bible account of the Fall in paradise gives us a key to the whole secret of the way and the power of temptation. Sin besieged the human heart, and carried it, and made its fatal entrance into the world, not *as sin*, but as the means to the knowledge of good and evil: Satan transformed into an angel of light.

For want of an unscrupulous and a hardened conscience, to set clearly before him the low aim he is following, the transgressor seeks out one a little more honorable which it will do to avow. Thus, by living always below his profession rather than above it, his professions themselves will come down to the miry level of a besotted worldliness. What is best in him is not set up as his rule and his law, — his best knowledge, purest conceptions, loftiest visions of goodness, most spiritual aspirations, — but only something that is not quite the worst. And by this means he surely comes to the worst at last. He is tempted down by a circuitous process. He is dragged down through a series of moral obliquities, as by a winding staircase, and, for want of a steady principle and an upward faith, he drops at last, through the gyrations of his self-deception, into perdition.

The young merchant, that has not a thoroughly Christian purpose to govern him, tells you he would become a prosperous capitalist that he may dispense public benefits; but he ends with being a wealthy miser. The law-student will aim at the bench, he says, for the sake of vindicating justice and elevating jurisprudence, or at the senate for the purifying of legislation; and he becomes a pettifogger in law, or a turncoat in politics. The young physician's triple sign points to a votary who ponders the enlargement of medical science and the deliverance of mortality from its disorders; but as he grows older, he grows rich on a bigoted opposition to all therapeutical reforms, and traffics in the fears and superstition and ignorance of the miserable. The crafty excuse under which preachers are tempted to keep back salutary truth, to prophesy smooth things, to lay private plots for reputation, and to condescend to cowardly and humiliating arts, is that they may increase their influence, — forgetting to ask how much influence so got is worth, — forgetting that God will not let the merit of any good end be carried over to lend a sanction to the unrighteous means.

Satan does not march his victim up to face perdition point-blank. He leads him to it by easy stages, and through a labyrinth that shows no danger. Round and round go those circling currents of the Northern Sea that swallow the ship; and by the same winding coil goes the spiritual decline that ends in spiritual death. It is gayety, not the grave, that youth is seeking, when it steps inside the circle of forbidden pleasure. It is for social cheer, for good-companionship, because he would not be morose, because he would scatter his despondency, that the drunkard drinks damnation, not for damnation's sake. It is to pay his debt, the gambler urges, that he plays, — to pay one debt that he forfeits all his credit. The first falsehood of a practised liar may have been told to save a friend's reputation, — a generous motive he thinks: Satan transformed into an angel of light! A worldly life is begun for the more decent uses that wealth may be put to; but it is followed afterwards in servitude to that unscrupulous task-master, avarice.

How much idleness that is full of guilt, under the plausible apology of husbanding our strength! The sluggard will save himself for future labor, he says; and in the very economy of his purpose acquires a lazy habit that drains all the strength out of his sinews. When envy would detract from a rival, it puts itself into the chair of impartial criticism. When prejudice would stab a blameless character, it pretends to be indignant at hypocrisy. Many a man and many a woman have been thought righteously opposed to sin, when they were only maliciously opposed to some particular sinner. Spite against an erring brother or sister was the feeling. Zeal against vice was the cloak put over it. Jealousy or revenge is the motive; but it borrows a mask of morality. Out of the general maxim that books make us wise, an unwholesome and prurient imagination fabricates a flimsy apology for reading flimsier profligacy. A patriotic pretence of loyalty to good government covers over the vulgar lampoon, the chicanery of the caucus, the systematic detraction of the party newspaper. Satan is transformed into an angel of light. Truth is compromised, from the slavish fear of losing office or custom or popularity, — and it is called prudence. The luxurious aristocrat embroiders his estates with unpaid toil, wrung from the muscles of his starving tenants or slaves, and pleads allegiance to the ancient usage of his ancestors. The thief explains his stealing by the hunger of his children. Murder itself disclaims all thirst for blood: it was revenge for insult; it was desperation; it was a paroxysm of wounded pride, or of ungoverned anger. If a man fears that reform will disturb his comfort, or interrupt his immoral traffic, he would have you believe he is a stanch conservatist on principle. But if he can realize private profits out of a new movement, he first makes a merit of radicalism. "When I the most strictly and religiously confess myself," said Montaigne, "I find that the best virtue I have has in it some tincture of vice; and I am afraid that Plato, in his purest virtue, if he had listened and laid his ear close to himself, would have heard some jarring sound of human mixture."

Be sure that the attack of temptation is most apt to be oblique, not open and direct. It destroys our moral foothold by a sidelong onset on our principles. When the Russian troops were retreating across a frozen lake before Napoleon's army, Bonaparte stationed his artillery on a neighboring elevation, and ordered them to fire on the ice and break it up, and thus engulf the enemy's regiments. The guns were levelled and discharged, but the balls glanced and rolled on the ice without breaking it. Suddenly one of his colonels thought to elevate his howitzers and fire into the air. The momentum of the descending projectiles, a falling shower of iron and lead, shattered the ice, and sent down the host into the waters of the lake. It is not the only instance in which the arts of war have followed precisely the arts of the Devil. It is by the oblique shot of our tempters that

> "The meanest foe of all the train
> Has thousands and ten thousands slain."

Satan never plays a bold game. He wins by not showing his worst at first, by concealing his tricks, transformed into an angel of light. It takes a great deal of effort to put us thoroughly on our guard against his wiles; but when it is done, it is worth the pains.

Tempting men imitate their great leader and prototype. They never go directly and openly to their object. If they would bend you from your integrity, they will flatter your self-respect by holding out to you a moral inducement. If they would corrupt your purity, they insinuate the poison through some appeal to your better affections. If they would weaken the holy restraints that gird in, with their blessed zone, the innocence of childhood, they will urge some sly argument to an honorable pride, or else to a friendly sympathy, or else to a praiseworthy love of independence; and the first battery that has been plied against many a boy's virtue has been the cunning caution that bade him not be afraid of his elders. They may say, as Milton makes the Archfiend say, sitting like a cormorant on a tree that overlooked the sinless Eden and the yet innocent inmates, deceiving even his own black heart:

> "Should I at your harmless innocence
> Melt, as I do, yet public reason just,
> Honor and empire with revenge enlarged
> By conquering this new world compels me now
> To do what else, though damned, I should abhor."

Theologians can cover their sectarian misrepresentations with the plea of "zeal for the cause," and controversialists baptize their bigotry with language of Holy Writ wrested from its meaning.

> "The Devil can cite Scripture for his purpose. . . . . .
> O what a goodly outside falsehood hath!"

Says the Apostle Paul: "If Satan himself is transformed into an angel of light, it is no great thing if his ministers also be transformed as the ministers of righteousness, — whose end shall be according to their works."

Unrighteous souls are like performers at a masquerade; only all the costumes are chosen out of the wardrobe of religion, while all the living figures under them are disciples of Belial. Every iniquity that is done under the sun would be glad to furnish itself out of the haberdashery of respectable appearances. No apostle of holiness ever lived, perhaps, but has had his likeness taken, his deportment mimicked, and his features copied by hypocrisy, to palm off depravity with. Every noble look and gesture of heroic virtue has been mocked by villany and shame.

> "There is no vice so simple but assumes
> Some mark of virtue on its outward parts."

For Satan transforms himself into an angel of light.

And now, if it shall be allowed to stand for our excusing, that temptation came to us circuitously, veiled with the mask of virtue, then history has recorded few crimes that can be condemned. The business of our moral vigilance, and the test of our moral strength, is to penetrate the delusion, to tear off the mask, to recognize Satan even through his transformations. We should know our tempters as the sure instincts of innocent hearts know hypocrites, "through the disguise they wear." Perhaps no tyrant, traitor, debauchee, or robber ever lived, who chose depravity for its own sake, or loved sin for its ugliness. If we are to be exculpated because temptation is cunning, oblique, crafty, then Herod was innocent, and Judas has been harshly judged; Nero is an injured man; Benedict Arnold has been misrepresented; and Jeffries and Rochester were rather sinned against than sinning. All our sins creep on us under concealment, creep on us circuitously. Our first lesson of resistance is to learn that Satan is a deceiver, transforms himself, looks an angel.

Ever since the first mother gave her ear to the serpent,

his approach to his victim has been "with tract oblique"; "in circling spires, fold above fold, sidelong he works his way."

It is so on the rough pavements of our modern cities, in these dusty streets, in the homely warehouse and the familiar dwelling, as much as among the hyacinths and asphodels of Paradise.

This assembly! where are your temptations? You sit in God's house, with no signs of peril; you will go to your homes, as you came up from them, with no alarms of danger ringing in your affrighted ears. Where are your temptations? Not marching down your streets, a bannered host, with trumpets to proclaim their siege, and with warlike notes of preparation. Virtue's victories would then be comparatively easy. But your temptations hover about you in wary ambush. They are not in great emergencies, heralded by horrid threatenings, but in the little things of your daily life, and hidden under unsuspected appearances. They lurk in the luxuries on which you repose; in the pillows of comfort on which you lay your thoughtless heads; in the emulation where you mistake the pride of excelling for the love of wisdom, and superiority for scholarship; in the common labor where the world gambles for your soul; in the merchandise where you are offered gain for falsehood; in the social fellowship where criminality corrupts under the name of cordiality; in the flatteries of your beauty, or your talents, or your disposition, which borrow the silver tones of friendship, and sound so like them that you listen; in the familiar pleasures that make the feet of the hours so swift, and the earth so satisfying, that you feel no need of heaven. Here are your tempters. They are disguised; they take circuitous paths; they carry gifts in their hands, and place crowns on your heads; they are clothed like angels of light.

Examine yourselves. You are put upon your self-scrutiny. To know your enemy is half the battle.

Examine yourselves. "But ourselves only?" do you say? "Shall we not go and watch Satan's kingdom, and the gates whence his legions issue, as well?" No; yourselves, watch yourselves only. For the kingdom of hell, as well as the kingdom of heaven, is within us. All the mischief is there, its origin there, its power there, its fatal result there. There Satan's seat is. No harm can come nigh you, but through the gate of your own yielding heart, set open by your own perverted will.

SERMON IX.

FOUR APOSTLES.

THERE ARE DIVERSITIES OF GIFTS, BUT THE SAME SPIRIT. AND THERE ARE DIFFERENCES OF ADMINISTRATIONS, BUT THE SAME LORD. — 1 Cor. xii. 4, 5.

It seems to be a method of the Divine Economy to bring out the complete circle of Truth by a variety of characters. Christianity is not so disobliging a system, that it requires of all its disciples that they have one temperament; not so angular, that it must mould every constitution into one fixed shape, and condemn all our differences from one another as departures from itself. On the contrary, it rejoices in diversity, grafts its heavenly spirit on constitutions the most contrasted, and uses the peculiarities that distinguish one good man from another as only a more copious language for illustrating its illimitable doctrine.

Just as God shows the world the fulness of his great historical ideas, and pushes forward the plans of his providence, by bringing upon the grand theatre a multiplicity of nations, each marked by its own national characteristics; just as he supplies a defect in one by an abundance in another, corrects the excesses of a past age by the antagonistic tendencies of the next, and sets off the traits of this country to balance the opposite traits of that; just as he appoints Judæa to represent reverence, Athens intelligence, and Rome law, counteracts tropical luxury by Northern simplicity, quickens Italian indolence by Scandinavian enterprise, outweighs the dreamy Oriental mysticism by the practical genius of the West, opens industrious America to atone for military Europe, and checks Ultramontane sentiment by Saxon logic, thus combining an educational apparatus of many climates and a normal school of many kingdoms to teach the lesson of universal wisdom;—so does he convey that higher and diviner gift, the religion of his Son, which is finally to conquer, penetrate, and outlive them all, through many forms of living example, and many kinds of statement corresponding.

After Christ, the Gospel was not planted on earth by one man, but by several men. And these several men were not alike altogether. There were striking contrasts between them, and this did not happen by accident. The more minds, and the more unlike each other, chosen as channels for putting the new life into human society, the more certain was that life to gain access to all classes, lay hold of different sets of thoughts and feelings, and act broadly on the consciousness and convictions of the whole. It exemplifies the inexhaustible richness and depth, as well as the wonderful flexibility of Christian truth, I think, that its Apostles bore so slight resemblance to each other. Perhaps we shall find reason to regard it as a cause for personal gratitude.

Out of the thirteen men that acted as Christian Apostles, there were four, the most active, the most conspicuous, and the most efficient in founding the Church. I select these four — Peter, Paul, James, and John — as representing respectively four prominent qualities in a well-proportioned disciple, four branches of individual character, as well as four classes of persons. The points that I would have fasten your attention especially are these: 1. That, while these four teachers were stamped emphatically with Christ's doctrine, so that the faith of a true believer was their first distinction, rising above and subordinating all their separate peculiarities, yet that the Christian life took in each of them a distinctive form and color, modified by their several organizations, so that, though holiness was the supreme principle and end with every one, it wore a peculiar aspect in each; 2. That the combination of these four presented Christianity in its wholeness, blending their personal diversities in a comprehensive unity; and 3. That, by a personal imitation of what was paramount in each, and adjusting together the elements of character they represent, we may approach to something like a symmetrical life.

I. First appears Peter, ardent, impetuous, vehement Peter. Neither the most effectual nor the most attractive type of discipleship will be manifest, without a good allowance of his fervor. A character where that quality predominates is liable to glaring faults; because the energy of the impulsive nature may act with equal force in any direction, and unless principle and judgment sustain the proportion, there will be plenty of follies to be ashamed of, and hasty sins to be atoned for by remorse. Considering, too, that Simon Peter was summoned to follow his Master when he was already somewhat advanced in years, it is not singular — indeed, unless we suppose a miracle to have been wrought to transform him, it would have been quite singular otherwise — that some of the faults incident to that sort of temperament, faults that his old religion had not disciplined into restraint, should be often reappearing to dishonor his profession. Accordingly we find, in tracing his career, that his zeal was mixed with many inconsistencies. Inconstancy compromised his ardor; temper lurked in close alliance with his impetuosity; and violence of speech was a mortifying appendage to his vehemence. But Christ saw that he had in him the noble material of a vital and victorious apostleship, and it is most interesting for us to see how the benignant spirit of the new faith worked upon him, till it finally purged out the old bitter leaven, refashioned him into a self-commanding as well as an eager champion, and at last made him first and foremost of the twelve companions of his Lord. It was a long battle, however, as it must be with many a Peter-like disposition among us, between spontaneous activity and calm control. Standing by the sea-side, at his business as a fisherman, he was one of the first that Jesus called to come with him; and there at the very outset, ready as ever after, he did not hesitate an instant to leave his nets bleaching on the sand, abandoning his property and his home, for the uncertain fortunes of a leader that had not where to lay his head. It was he that cried out in an abundance of self-confidence almost childish, when he saw Jesus walking on the waves, "Let me come to thee on the water," but the next moment, by a revulsion as rapid, screamed, "Lord, save me, for I sink." It was he that, when Christ asked sorrowfully, seeing some disaffected adherents forsaking him, "Will ye also go away?" broke out into that passionate pledge of devotion, "Lord, to whom shall we go? we believe and are sure that thou art the Son of God." It was he that, another time, answered so promptly to the question, "Whom say ye that I am?" — "Thou art the Christ, Son of the living God." It was he that interrupted that serene and majestic prophecy, "The Son of Man must go up to Jerusalem, suffer, and be killed," with his impatient protest, "Far be it from thee, Lord," and had to be rebuked for his worldly ambition. It was Peter — it could not have been any other, and we should have known it to be he if no name were given — that rejected the menial service whereby the condescending Redeemer symbolized the humility of his religion, and exclaimed, "Thou shalt never wash my feet"; but the next moment, at the touching reproof, "If I wash thee not, thou hast no part with me," sprang to the opposite extreme, and was ready for any amount of superfluous submission, begging, "Lord, not my feet only, but my hands and my head." With fortitude enough to draw his sword and smite the high-priest's servant at the arrest, he yet fell asleep from fatigue amidst the solemnities of the garden, and could not watch one hour when the traitor was leading on the officers. Above all, you will remember that most flagrant proof of his unregulated impulses, when, after all the privileges of his earlier and constant intimacy with the beloved Messiah, — after having been admitted to the confidence of sharing his dwelling at Capernaum, — having been one of the three favored friends permitted to be present at the raising of Jairus's daughter, when all others were shut out, and to witness the glory of the Mount of Transfiguration, and to share in the awful hour at Gethsemane, — having been put forward to speak on every occasion for the Twelve as their acknowledged head, and having resolutely promised, "Though all men should be offended because of thee, yet will I never be offended," —

he three times declared, when stung by insult and ridicule, "I know not the man." And yet, so far as subsequent fidelity, both in intensity and perseverance, *could* atone, he washed out the stain of these sad disgraces, by deeds as well as tears. When that burning, fiery spirit once took the steady poise of principle, it wrought out splendid triumphs of virtue; it pierced the Gentile idolatries with an impassioned eloquence that turned them from Jupiter and Diana to the living God, from pride and sensuality to repentance and immortality. It quickened this brave Apostle, till he shook the Eastern world; made him the first to spring down into the empty tomb out of which his Lord had risen, and first to proclaim the resurrection among the living; plunged him into the sea to greet Jesus at his reappearance in the body; brought three thousand converts into the Church by a single speech at Pentecost; enabled him to sleep calmly as an infant between the two soldiers and under the double chain in the prison; braced him to that magnificent assertion of the everlasting truth of a Law higher than any of man's making, when, standing arraigned for speaking the truth, before high-priest and rulers, he said firmly, "Whether it be right to hearken unto you more than unto God, judge ye"; and, at last, inspired him with that characteristic courage that prompted him, as the traditions tell, to request at his execution that he might be crucified with the head downwards, because he deserved to die in greater agony than the Saviour that he had once denied. His Epistles overflow with the same zealous devotion. Did not his fervor finally justify, then, the title given him by one who knew what was in him, — Peter, — Cephas, — a rock, — the rock on which he should build his Church?

Peter was an enthusiast. He was much else besides,

but pre-eminently he was that. In the culture of our spiritual life, and the exercise of it, both, we need this Petrine element. We want the glow, the warmth, the flame, of this energetic, fervent, resistless zeal. No individual heart, nor any system of theology, will have vital power without it. Selfish frigidity and worldly indifference are its enemies. If we grow cold, we shall freeze; if we grow torpid, we shall go to sleep. Doubtless, we are liable to the same errors in it that the Apostle was. Such errors are in private places as in public. If we had known Peter in his house, we should probably have overheard him retorting angrily to his housemate, or giving some unreasonable indulgence to Petronica, his daughter. The place is nothing, and does not much vary the temptation. To guide the impulse, wherever you are, by carefulness; to steady the wayward transport of feeling, at home or abroad, by sober meditation; to hallow the hot enthusiasm by the sanctities of prayer; — this is the task of all of you that have Peter's ardent temperament, and would share his moral victory.

II. And to that very end, we must call in a new element, the element that had its peculiar impersonation in Peter's fellow-Apostle, Paul. A Greek by birth and a Jew by ancestral blood, a Pharisee, by education, of the strictest sect, and a Christian by one of the most wonderful of conversions, he was a man to understand both the Judaism he was to pull down and the Gospel he was to build up and spread abroad. His fierce natural temper made him a fearfully alert persecutor, under the Sanhedrim, and his elegant literary culture fitted him to dispute powerfully with Greek sophists at Mars' Hill. Whether as Jew or Christian, he believed with all his soul. The same earnestness of conviction, strength of will, and vitality of allegiance, went into his Judaism and his Christianity; for after the straitest sect he lived a Pharisee, and yet was not disobedient to the heavenly vision of the light above the brightness of the sun. He was a man to look on with cool consent at Stephen's martyrdom, before he heard the voice from heaven; and after the Word, like a two-edged sword, had pierced the joints and marrow of his spirit, to accuse himself as the chief of sinners, and cry, "O wretched man that I am! what I would not, that I do; who shall deliver me from the body of this death?" His strong passions made all his religious experience vivid as the lightning, and his comprehensive intellect made his eloquence reverberate like the thunder. His moods were various, but all intense. He could with equal skill sport satire with the Corinthians, or foil such dignitaries as Agrippa and Felix with his polished rhetoric, or smite Elymas the sorcerer and the backsliders at Galatia with the battle-axe of his indignation. Too rapid in his style to balance an antithesis, or limit a parenthesis, or modulate his sentences, he forgets all the rules of composition in the thing to be said. He was resolute enough to withstand Barnabas, his associate, to the face, in a question of principle, yet tender enough to restore Eutychus and comfort afflicted women; a man to confound equally the Jews who required a sign, and the idolaters that sought after worldly wisdom; a man to spend three years in Arabia to prove whether the inspiration was genuine, and its pulse healthy; a man to sing praises at midnight in a jail, and, when an earthquake opened the walls, calmly to tell the jailer to do himself no harm, for he had not availed himself of his liberty; and then to preach Christ there to the frightened keepers, and the next day, when the magistrates were troubled at their illegal arrest, to stand upon his dignity, and refuse to go out till he had humiliated them by compelling them to come and beseech him to go; a man that could tell, and tell without complaining, but with a light heart and in a cheerful tone, of stripes and stonings, shipwrecks and perils by the wilderness, of robbers and false brethren, of watchings and nakedness, of escaping by a basket from a window, of hunger and thirst and weariness daily, glorying in his tribulations, — could tell also of visions and revelations in the third heavens, of joy unspeakable, and the peace that passeth understanding.

The secret of all this steadfastness of spirit was faith in God, — Paul's leading doctrine. He had known the tossings and wrestlings of a sinful nature, and pictures them in his terrible description of the warfare between the lusts and the spirit. "Chief of sinners" was the dark background that contrasted the radiant mercy of the cross. He had tried legal righteousness, or keeping the letter of the law, and found no man living could keep it inviolate; there was no satisfaction there. Like all men since of very deep and intense moral experience, — and such always find themselves interpreted and satisfied only by Paul, — he came out at last upon the ground of acceptance on account of faith in Christ, and entire giving up of the soul to the free mercy of God; — the only permanent ground for Christian theology to rest upon.

Here, then, for the second element of Christian character, with Paul as its exemplar, is faith, a belief, resident, in his case, in a mind of such logical acuteness and dialectical address, as could shape it into a system for the understanding, and reason it into the convictions of the churches by his argumentation. Something to believe, — something definite, — this is the Pauline contribution to Christian completeness. Its grandest effect is seen in himself; but in humbler degrees it may work results of inconceivable greatness and blessedness in us. It gives steadiness to fervor and permanence to a Peter's impulsiveness. It was by its uplifting power that Paul could break forth into those triumphant strains, ringing like sublime anthems down through all history to this hour. Listen to two or three whose lyric modulations show a poet's nature throbbing under the logician's armor: "And now I go bound in the spirit unto Jerusalem, not knowing the things that shall befall me there, save that the Holy Ghost witnesseth in every city, saying that bonds and afflictions abide me. But none of these things move me; neither count I my life dear unto myself, so that I might finish my course with joy." "For I am now ready to be offered, and the time of my departure is at hand. I have fought a good fight, finished my course, kept the faith: henceforth there is laid up for me a crown of righteousness, which the Lord shall give me at that day." "For I am persuaded that neither death nor life, nor angels, nor principalities, nor powers, nor things present, nor things to come, nor height, nor depth, nor any other creature, shall be able to separate us from the love of God." "This corruptible must put on incorruption; this mortal must put on immortality. Thanks be to God, who giveth us the victory through our Lord Jesus Christ."

III. This doctrine of faith, however, so dear to Paul, is capable of being urged to an extreme; or rather, though faith itself cannot possibly be too abundant, we may hold a particular notion of it in such disproportion as to exclude another element, quite as necessary. We begin to feel that we must call in an apostle of works, practical righteousness, an external life of integrity and charity, to keep the balance even; but before we call, he has already come. James, a near kinsman of Jesus, a man upright from his youth, of irreproachable manners and respected character, even before the new splendor of the Gospel standard broke upon him, was that Apostle. James was the representative of the right life, as Paul was of the right mind; and so consistently did he exemplify in his person the doctrine he preached in his ministry and wrote in his Epistle, that he received from his acquaintances the noble title James the Just. Not very much is said of him in the narratives, but, as often happens with silent men, a great deal was done by him. He clung to a quiet, straight path in his ministry at Jerusalem. Believing that usefulness is the best test of piety, he was content to be unostentatiously useful. Some honors, to be sure, could not be kept away from so trustworthy a mind, however modest. He was chosen moderator of the first Christian Council, convened at Jerusalem to consider the question whether Gentile converts should be admitted to equal privileges in the Church with converts of Jewish education, and without circumcision. He summed up the merits of the case in a short speech, which, curiously enough, contains in its brief compass a clear assertion of his cherished idea that a right line of life is of more consequence than any form. There is a tradition, that he was so spotless in conduct that he was suffered to enter the Holy of holies in the temple, where none but the high-priest entered. And as his death at the hands of his persecutors took place just before the destruction of Jerusalem, the Jews used to refer the ruin of their city to the vengeance of Heaven for the slaughter of so holy a saint. Doubtless James, from his correct habits, was shocked at the occasional sins of Peter, and perhaps he was not quite satisfied with the sharp reasonings and metaphysical theology of Paul. His single brief letter, full of concise, epigrammatic expressions, runs in a direction not to controvert Paul's, but to provide for a want Paul's left open. Whether or not it was designed, as some of the ancients thought, to be a reply to Paul, it is at any rate an admirable sequel. It is a plea, in language, for the noble righteousness of action that distinguished his character. Paul had said, and truly, "Ye are saved by faith." James added, "Show me thy faith without thy works, and I will show thee my faith by my works." This is the burden of his doctrine, — not works independent of faith, not mere external morality, not dry, legal obedience, with no moisture and no root, — but works as expressing faith, manifesting it, its natural fruit, and in turn re-acting upon it, to confirm and multiply it. Paul bids us believe and we shall be saved; James says "Amen" to this, but reminds us, that, if we deal justly, and follow conscience, and show mercy to the poor, and keep the law, we shall find our faith increasing thereby, and without these is no salvation. Paul says, "Faith cometh by hearing"; James exhorts, "Be ye doers of the word, and not hearers only," and goes on to explain, that mere careless hearing will no more change a man, than looking in a glass and going away to forget the image. Paul passes a glorious eulogy upon charity; James explains what charity is, and is not, insisting that merely to say to the hungry and naked, "Go along and be warmed and fed," is no charity, just as a faith which lies inoperative in the outward letter, — letting the man cheat, or deceive, or oppress, or practise dishonest politics, or play the hypocrite in his daily business while he professes it, is a dead faith. Paul proclaims the immortal truth, lying, as I believe, at the very heart of the Gospel, "By God's grace are ye saved, and that not of yourselves; it is free gift." James accepts this declaration, but urges us to remember that the spirit must have a body; that God's free grace is granted only on conditions, and may be detected by certain signs; and that where it really has a vital seat within, it will inevitably bud and blossom into the pure and undefiled religion, which visits the fatherless and widows in their affliction, and keeps itself unspotted from the world.

Here, then, we have morality. James is a teacher of ethics. We are to obey the commandments, as well as feel and believe. Alone, this legal righteousness will be hard, barren, and Jewish. Doing things only because they are commanded, is not inspiring, and does not bring peace. It needs the infusion of Peter's animating impulse, and Paul's vivid reliance on God; needs Peter's warm blood, and Paul's unshaken confidence. These will yield vitality and earnest persistency. We have then ardor, conviction, and morality; but one thing is wanting yet, and that is love. We get, by these three, zeal, faith, and works, but not yet perfect peace.

IV. We must summon, therefore, a fourth witness; and he is at hand in the person of John, — John, whose love for Jesus earned for him the epithet, unequalled in all the honors and dignities of the world's nobilities, "the Beloved Disciple," — gentle, affectionate, contemplative, seraphic John. We have already seen him very near the Saviour, on more than one occasion of unusual solemnity, in private, tender fellowship. It was he who leaned his head on Jesus's bosom at the Supper; he who received from the lips quivering on the cross that dying charge, "Behold thy mother," — and thenceforth took Mary to his own home; he that first believed, out of the fulness of his trusting heart, after the stone was rolled from the sepulchre; he that, with Peter, wrought the merciful miracle, and healed the lame man at the gate of the temple named Beautiful, and made it more worthy the name by that beautiful compassion; he that, in the infirmity of extreme age, when his voice could utter no more, stretched out his hands, every Sabbath morning, over the assembly, and said that simple precept, — the rich substance of many longer sermons, — "Little children, love one another." His Gospel and his Epistles are constant breathings of spiritual aspiration and benignant charity. His Gospel, so unlike the other three, relates few incidents, but gives us more of Christ's devout meditations and lofty discourses. It opens with the mystical passage on the Logos, or Word made flesh; gives the midnight conversation, couched in terms that seem to borrow mystery from the shaded scene, with Nicodemus, on the New Birth; repeats all that symbolical language of Jesus, since become so precious to spiritual minds in his Church, where he describes himself and his truth under the analogy of Light, Life, Living Bread, a Fountain of Water, and pictures sin under the strong figures of Darkness and Death. It is from John that we have the divine prayer of Jesus before his agony; the mystical words about the soul that is born of God and dwells in God; the whole unfathomable doctrine of oneness with the Father and the Son; the touching account of the raising of Lazarus at Bethany; that blessed chapter of consolation, known so well to every Christian heart that ever suffered by pain or by bereavement, beginning, "Let not your heart be troubled"; all the pathos that pervades the sorrowful record of what took place before the crucifixion; and the full reports, so overflowing with the fond memories of Christian grief, of what was spoken after the resurrection. His main Epistle is almost a repetition of these few comprehensive thoughts: God is love; beloved, now are we the sons of God; love one another; walk in the light of life; every man hath the witness in himself; the light lighting every man that cometh into the world.

In one word, John is the Apostle of spirituality. He goes, for evidence, proof, satisfaction, within, into the breast; not, like Paul, with dialectics and metaphysics, but with simple love. His wisdom is of the heart; his faith is less of belief than trust; less by argument than by intuition. His view of Christianity was introspective and subjective, in the terms of philosophy; but he was no rationalist; for with all his soul he loved a supernatural Christ; and his doctrine was as simple as a child's thanksgiving. No Apostle seems to have clung with such reverential affection to the person of Jesus. His faith is all bound up in that personal attachment. For him there was not, as for any of us there cannot be, any Christianity without the Jesus of Nazareth, any institutional, or philosophical, or intellectual Gospel, without the Son of Mary crucified and ascended, gone from the Bethlehem stable to the right hand of his Father.

John, then, completes the full Apostolic manifestation of Christian character. He is the fourth of that united quaternion that show us what we ought to be. He adds to Peter's fervor, and Paul's belief, and James's morality, his own affection. He is a reconciler, and brings in that crowning and harmonizing element of love without which zeal and faith and conscience are all wanting. The churches blessed with his living superintendence were scattered over Lesser Asia. Let us see to it that over all churches, this our church, and over every heart, broods the benignant blessing of his heavenly spirit. His countenance has been portrayed by the arts as radiant with inspiration. Let the beauty of his gentleness shine in our lives. " His thoughts," says Jerome, one of the old Fathers, " mounted, like an eagle, to the very throne of God." It is not too much to believe, that, if we commit ourselves cordially to their guidance, they well bear our souls up, on their wings, to the same heaven.

Here, then, let us rest. You need no lengthened application of so suggestive a subject. Peter, Paul, James, John: the zealot, the believer, the moralist, the spiritualist; Impulse, Conviction, Law, and Love; will, intellect, conscience, affection; a good disposition, a clear faith, a right life, a pure heart. These are the constituents of the perfect man.

I said these qualities are not found alone, nor without some admixture of all the rest, in the several Apostles that exemplify them; nor is any of them held as by adverse title against the others. Every one shares, in some less degree, in the ruling peculiarity of his companions. I speak only of the trait that predominates in each, and the symmetry that comes by the mutual counterbalancing of their defects.

Peter's vacillation is offset by Paul's steadfastness; James's regularity, by Peter's impulsiveness; John's mysticism, by James's common sense; Paul's logical understanding, by John's affectionate heart.

We should go to Peter for animation, to Paul for a creed, to James for rules of behavior, to John for peace. Peter supplies hope; Paul, steadfastness; James, self-control; John, sensibility.

In your own lives, take something excellent from each. Whether your natural temperament be Petrine or Pauline, Jacobean or Johannean, copy what is imitable in all. Blend their virtues and graces together. Count it high honor to share largely in the attainments of any one, — but better still to gain generous proportions by following so many. Strive to expand your obedience, and stretch, by ever loftier examples, your aspiration. Quicken zeal, strengthen faith, enlarge beneficence, and deepen love. Rejoice that the Christian standard is so high, is infinite, is unattainable here; yet struggle none the less to rise to it hereafter. Above all, labor, and watch, and pray, that, looking to Him who is greater than Apostles, and Head over all churches, you may be changed into the same image, finding the fulness of the measure of the stature of Christ. For though "there are differences of administrations, there is the same Lord."

SERMON X.

ACCEPTANCE OF THE HEART.

SHE HATH DONE WHAT SHE COULD. — Mark xiv. 8.

IN many aspects of it, I regard this simple sentence as one of the most encouraging expressions that fell from our Lord's lips. It was uttered in defence of a woman who ventured to approach the Messiah under the unceremonious impulse of affection, destitute, so far as we know, of any recommendation from family circumstance or social distinction, but urged solely by an irresistible longing to do something, however humble or irregular, in behalf of this divine friend, who has gained the unutterable, enthusiastic devotion of her soul. Had she brought those badges of high position which are so potent to hush the criticism and rouse the admiration of the multitude, had she come bearing the recognized authority of some official alliance or lordly husband's estate, we should have heard no complaints of the waste of the ointment that she poured on the venerated head. Still, the inherent grace and beauty of the act forbade any direct reproof; and so jealousy meanly suggests that the precious perfume might have been better sold, the price given to the poor, and this woman have rendered her demonstrations of gratitude in some more "practical" or active way. The answer of Jesus not only rebukes the littleness which these censures betrayed, but it instructively vindicates the woman's cordial, unstudied sacrifice, and not hers only, but the offerings of humble loyalty and silent love to him in all time and over all the earth. "Let her alone: why trouble ye her? She hath wrought a good work on me. She hath done what she could. Wheresoever this Gospel shall be preached throughout the whole world, this that she hath done shall be told for a memorial of her." It is the acceptance, by the Son of God, of lowly and retiring goodness. It is the legitimation and approval of all hearty gifts to the Master, by the Master's voice. It is the eternal benediction of the Gospel on despised fidelity and neglected love.

I proceed to mention some of the bearings of this significant saying, which show it to be full of encouragement, and full of instruction.

I. The first of these is, that it so plainly and powerfully asserts the superior worth of the heart's feeling over any outward acts. The implication of Christ's language certainly is, that, so far as *doing* went, this woman had but small title to consideration. If she were to be judged by visible achievements, by showy enterprises, by notable charities or literary fame, her life might be called a failure. Nothing in the way of performances marked her out for pre-eminence. But "she had done what she could." That alone made her preeminent. The very form of the expression implies that, in one sense, she had done but little. Yet that little was enough. It was a test of her sincerity. It said distinctly that she was in earnest. The costliness of her gift in proportion to her means, while it was nothing to

Him she would honor, was a guaranty that she was not trifling. In fact, by a more correct rendering of the original, the Greek word translated here "very precious" would read simply "pure" or "unadulterated" spikenard, — not "costly." Had it been far less than it was, and had it been all she could bring, his blessing would have been the same. For mind, he does not say, "Stop, consider, this alabaster-box really cost a good deal of money; it could not have been bought for less than three hundred denarii." No; but he says, "She hath done what she could"; that is, she hath demonstrated the deep and tender attachment of her soul. She believes on her Lord. She loves the Saviour for his holiness, his mercy, his divine benignity. One penny's worth, if it is only the utmost that self-denial can do, is as good for that as ten thousand shekels. Did he not declare as much, in what he said of the two mites that the poor widow cast into the temple-treasury? Nay, did he not equally accept, and bless with the same favor, another woman, poorer and frailer still, who had nothing to give him but tears and kisses for his feet? The whole spiritual meaning of gifts consists in the disposition of the giver. Distinctions of weight and measure, standards of currency, tables of value, rates of exchange, calculations of outlay, color, material, and shape, vanish before that simple and royal touchstone in the breast. It is felt to be so, even in the presents of human friendship; and spiritual sincerity does not pass for less in the eyes of Him who searches and sees the heart, than with us.

Had the question been between actions and professions, Christ's decision would have been different. Here is a point of constant mistake. Professions and feelings are not equivalent. As compared with professions, good deeds are put into ever-lustrous eminence, both by their solid quality, and by that grand refutation of all talking hypocrisy and ceremonial cant, from the mouth of the Judge himself, "Not every one that saith unto me, 'Lord, Lord,' shall enter into the kingdom of Heaven, but he that doeth the will of my Father." We cannot be wrong — if there is such a thing as truth in God's universe, we must be right — in esteeming one palpable and ponderable action in Christ's name before a library of dogmatic *credos*, subscription to the straitest ecclesiastical vows, or the handsomest adjustment of the mantle of public conformity. If we must have one without the other, an acre of statements must be let go rather than an ounce of life. This, however, is not the alternative put before us in this homage of the Hebrew woman. Christ's eye falls, not on the box of ointment, as if to weigh its pretension or spell out some article of a Rabbinical creed graven on its cover, but it falls on Mary's secret, inmost soul. That being sound, all is sound. She believes, she trusts, she loves; therefore "she hath done what she could." Out of that deep and rooted affection all manner of obedient fruits must grow, in time, as surely as love is the willing servant of the beloved.

And here opens upon us a great spiritual truth, of the utmost practical importance. Nothing is more common than to hear this among the private confessions of earnest and self-distrustful persons, wishing they could feel themselves accepted before God: "There is so little that I have done, so little that I can do. My station restricts me, my weakness disables me. I look round on others, and they are busy and useful, earning gratitude or fame. But I am hemmed in by four narrow walls, or by narrower circumstances. Is the difficulty in them or in me? I seem to have done no more this year than the last, and to gain nothing in achievement as I go on. Regarding either the disinterested Saviour as my example, or his toiling followers even, I am certainly an unprofitable servant." Now, supposing this to be sincere, — and we must have had a barren experience if we do not know it often is, — what such a disciple needs for encouragement is obviously the very doctrine of the text. "She hath done what she could"; and the one thing most momentous, most central, most decisive of all that can be done, — she hath believed in her Lord. There is no station, no fortune, no bashfulness of nature, no timidity of nerve, no obscurity of condition, where that is not possible, and where the joy and glory of the reward thereof may not arise and shine. Helpless invalids, reserved women, servants under command, young members of worldly and unsympathizing families, may all trust in their Divine Friend with patient submission, love him with constant devotion, commune with him in sincere desires for his excellence, and they can try for ever to preserve and illustrate his gentle and serene and disinterested spirit. If they do this, they ought to know that they are *his*, to dismiss despondency, to rely on his promises, to count themselves committed and accepted friends of his household and his heart. They shall, one day, if they keep that temper and purpose, hear him say, "These also have done what they could." If the New Testament holds forth one clear doctrine, it is that character before God is determined by the state of the affections and the bent of the will. Where these incline selfward or earthward, all is weak and wrong.

You have not done what you could. A righteous life is not an accidental appendage to a good heart, but an inevitable consequence or outflow of it. Christ and his Apostles understood man's profoundest nature when they made it their constant answer to the question, "What shall I do to be saved, or to win eternal life?"—"Believe on the Lord Jesus Christ with all thine heart"; for they knew this was what each and all *could* do,—what would prompt every other needful work of righteousness. Do we need a simpler, more spiritual, or more invigorating revelation?

II. Again, the words I have used for my text bestow a blessing on the feeling of personal affection towards Christ. This was what this woman had shown; it was all that she had shown. She had not yet gone abroad into public duties; we do not read that she had visited the needy, or joined in any public measure for the forwarding of any Christian cause. All this she was sure to do, just so fast and so far as social occasions, her own powers, and other providential conditions, would permit; for she could not love Christ without loving the whole cause for which he lived, the whole Church of which he is the Head, and the whole world for which he died. But, thus far, it was enough to know that she could give everything for the Divine Being in whom all these movements and reformations centre. There are times when the particular must make way and give place to the general. The Messiah says, very strikingly, and in this connection: "The poor ye have always with you, and whensoever ye will, ye may do them good; but me," in the body, "ye have not always. She is come aforehand to anoint my body to the burying. She hath wrought a good work on me." "Her gift," he seems to add, "is an unconscious embalming before my agony. These most sacred impulses of divine reverence are greater than any common almsgivings. Let each have its due. Whoso loveth me will love my poor, and serve them in the time and place. Let the heart be fastened personally on me as a living Redeemer, and Christian duties will soon fall into their order, and abound."

The wisdom of the plan of the mediation, in thus giving intensity and personality to our religious affections, just suits itself to our natural wants. You are familiar with precisely the feeling that drove this woman to bring her box of ointment, provided you have ever had that mingled sense of gratitude and love toward a person which made you long, above all things, to find out some way of serving him, and made it a positive pain to be denied that privilege. Such are the reality and the supremacy of personal relationships and bonds. A religion that did not provide ample room for their exercise, by showing us the Divine perfection under human conditions, would lack as much a practical hold on human sympathies, as it would a philosophical adaptation to the exigencies of the moral problem.

III. Further, Christ's words of defence for the woman against the disaffected by-standers affirm, for true goodness, a complete independence of place. It is a familiar maxim, among Christian didactics, that acceptance with God is as possible in small fortunes, or limited reputations, as where power carries with it a commensurate influence, and the object of many popular regards is supposed to be a favorite with Heaven. And yet, so much is our judgment controlled by appearances, that we are constantly falling back under the old fallacy. This plain saying of Jesus strikes every illusion away. "She hath done what she could." How much is covered by that "could," we do not inquire. Not more, probably, than lies in the power of every one of us at this moment. Yet it was enough. Then neither is there one of us that is excusable from the full requirement of Christ's word, nor is there one to whom the whole infinite wealth of his favor is not offered.

I confess that I sometimes distrust the effect of frequent references to those persons who have been led into places of large and prominent usefulness, in any walk of philanthropy. As instances of signal energy, self-sacrifice, and constancy, they stand as noble examples of what humanity may accomplish. And, as I believe the admiration of even distant greatness to be a wholesome emotion, I thank God for such illustrious heroes and martyrs. But we misuse them greatly if we ever allow ourselves to feel that theirs is the only true way of being great, and that, because we cannot serve God or man in some such famous mode, we will retire from the field. That is sheer unbelief. We ought to know that the sentence, "She hath done what she could," is just as sufficient and adequate for the ablest as the most infirm; that it is enough for such as Elizabeth Fry, Hannah More, and Madame Adorna, and no more than enough for the unlettered woman carried out from an obscure lane last week, having died in the joy of her Lord, and her name never seen in printed letters, perhaps, till it was enrolled in the record of the dead. When I read a description of Kaiserswerth, near Düsseldorf on the Rhine, — of that vast establishment of Christian mercy, with its hospital, insane asylum, Magdalen retreat, charity schools, and institutions for training the most scientific nurses and accomplished teachers, graduating superintendents for the humane houses of both Europe and America, and a few miles away another building for the rest and refreshment of those that have been worn down by the fatigues of these voluntary labors of love, — when I see how, throughout, charity has been systematized by skill, and benevolence perfected by perseverance, and then behold the benefits flowing forth to be extended and multiplied, in ever enlarging proportions, over the whole sick and suffering and groaning earth, — I am as much abashed and humbled before this devoted Pastor Fleidner, whose active spirit and benevolent genius have called up all this busy and organized kingdom of Good-Samaritanism about him to glorify the age, as I suppose my sisters are before the beautiful and accomplished baroness who has laid down youth, rank, and wealth as an offering to sorrow and disease; or before the high-born, gifted, and admired English girl* who came to Kaiserswerth as a pupil, and then reproduced the same wonders of consolation and healing for sick and destitute governesses, — not amidst the rural quiet and sweet verdure of her own paternal home in Hampshire, but in a dismal street in London. Yet we ought all to remember that these too only did what they could; that, if we do that, God's honors are impartial; that if we do not that, then ours is indeed the shame of the short-coming. And when we follow this last-mentioned minister of angelic mercy on the horrid and bloody path of war to the banks of the Bosphorus, and read how, in the hospital of Scutari,

"Through miles of pallets, thickly laid
With sickness in its foulest guise,
And pain, in forms to have dismayed
Man's science-hardened eyes,

---

* Florence Nightingale.

A woman, fragile, pale, and tall,
Upon her saintly work doth move,
Fair or not fair, who knows ? but all
Follow her face with love," —

while I bow with reverent confession before this transcendent realized vision of celestial pity, I still believe we ought not to forget that God may have, that he asks, that he requires of us that there *shall be*, servants of his love as self-denying, as heroic, as resolute, of whom hospital never knew and poetry never sang, right here in these homely houses and these prosaic streets. For the hour will come when every soul that hath done what that soul could, shall be seen on the right hand of the throne of God.

IV. Again, Christ's encomium on the affectionate Mary announces the great principle, that ability is the measure of responsibility. No soul is tasked beyond its power. God's commandment never passes the line of a possible obedience, and so never goes over from justice to tyranny. But what we fail, through inability, to render in actual work, he mercifully permits us, through Christ, to make up in those penitent and self-renouncing affections, which gain forgiveness, and open the way of reconciliation. If any one dreams this is a lax or easy rule, let him only ask himself, in a still and thoughtful hour, Have I done what I could ? Has my service to the Master reached the full measure of the powers and gifts, the capacities of affection and the opportunities of well-doing, with which my Master has intrusted me ?

This language of the Saviour most naturally associates itself with the closing up of life's great account. Of how many among us, when that trial-hour comes, with all its retrospections and searching examinations, can those glorious words be spoken? We cannot recall nor judge the dead. They are in the hands of the All-Just. But we can speak to one another as yet living. How many of us are so striving righteously, and watching soberly, and praying earnestly, that this shall be the just and consoling eulogy, — They have done what they could? The busy man of affairs, the successful one, the disap pointed and losing one, the young adventurer, the older and long trusted and finally unfortunate one, — those that have prospered by others' industry, and those that have been ruined by others' crimes, — has each one of them done what he could? The wife or mother whose very name is sacred, because the sacred office of forming character is her perpetual duty, the lonely woman that has only her own heart to discipline, the young girl that has so few cares for herself that God requires many of her for the less-favored, — has each done what she could? The bereaved parent, the desolate widow suddenly summoned to take up the dreary and dreadful burden of solitary suffering, — has each done what she could? is each one doing what she can? Christ draws near to us, and repeats the question. He turns and puts it, with twofold solemnity and sadness, to those that leave him and pass away. To all that sit at his feet and follow in his steps in the spirit of her who poured the fragrant offering on his head, he is ready to speak the same benediction with his infinite love, — hiding in it the sure promise of life everlasting.

I said we cannot adjudge the deservings of the departed. But we can guard ourselves against those hallucinations of mortal glory, and all those artificial illusions, which are so apt to cheat our souls, and obscure the plain truth we have been meditating. There goes to his august repose, enveloped in imperial pomps, the ruler of the world's mightiest, vastest empire. Fifty-seven millions of human souls, embracing nine different races of men, with a million soldiers, drew their daily breath subject to his direct and despotic will; but not all of so many millions could add one single breath to his prostrate lungs. Eight millions of square miles of territory were yesterday ruled by his word; now he needs not eight feet, out of it all. The guns of massive fortresses on the huge ramparts that guard widely divided waters made a continent tremble in their volleying answers to his edicts, and the haughtiest noblemen of the world bent at his smile or frown. Common cabinets and kings were perplexed and afraid at the cunning of his brain, as boys are of their master, and the armies of the strongest governments, after his own, felt the globe to be a more conquerable and practicable domain, the moment they knew he was dead. But he is dead. And neither the millions of acres nor men, the fortresses nor the fears, the armies nor the brain, shall make it a whit easier, but harder rather, for his single soul — when it goes alone, disrobed of crown and purple, into the presence of the King of kings whose right it is to reign — to answer that simple question, Hast thou done for me — ah! for me — what thou couldst? Canst thou stand with the lowly and powerless woman who crept with the box of ointment to her Redeemer's feet, and who shall have the story of that act of love told for a memorial of her wherever the everlasting Gospel is preached, when the history of Cossack and Czar shall be dim as that of princes before the flood, and on to the end of time?

But here, close by us, falls asleep a meek, patient girl, — a faithful sister, an obedient daughter, a mild and friendly counsellor of a few children that she knew, ruler of none on earth but her own patient spirit, and thereby made greater than he that taketh a city, or prevents its being taken. She too dies, and no anxious hemispheres dispute about the report, nor do kingdoms mourn nor cowardly assemblies clap their hands, when the report is confirmed. And in the day when the secrets of all hearts shall be revealed, our only question is, which of these two shall be found nearest to Him who sitteth on the one throne, and shall wear the crown which is a crown of life.

There seem to be three thoughts that offer themselves to us, to be carried away as the practical substance of the subject.

One is, that this saying of Jesus is dangerously perverted and shamefully abused, if we take it as excusing us from the utmost effort in well-doing, and a laborious progress in Christ's service. The whole tone of our New Testament religion is searching and high. It allows no laxities, and no apologies. It is satisfied with nothing less than entire consecration. The piety it asks is both active and ardent, warm and constant, ever burning and ever advancing. It summons into the Master's service every power, every energy, every affection, every hour of life. The very words of the text imply a strict and comprehensive judgment. For which one of us could truly say to-day, I have done what I could?

The second practical lesson is, that, in order to serve Christ acceptably, we have not to revolutionize our lot, nor to seek other conditions than those Providence supplies. The place is nothing; the heart is all. Chambers of patient invalids, beds of submissive sickness, obscurity, weakness, baffled plans, — a thousand nameless limitations of faculty, of opportunity, of property, — all these are witnesses of silent but victorious faith. In all of them God is glorified, for in all of them his will is done. Out of all of them gates open into heaven and the joy of the Lord. Mercifully the Father has appointed many ways in which we may walk toward his face, and run on his errands. Work is the way for strength; lying still is the way for infirmity, if only there are trust and prayer in both. There is some instruction in a picture I have read of, which represents the lives of twin-brothers diverging from the cradle. One, by study, becomes a learned and skilful physician, reaching great riches and honors by ministering to the sick. The other has no talent for books, and no memory, and so no science; he becomes a poor, strolling musician, but spends his days in consoling, by his lute, sufferings that are beyond all medicine. The brothers are shown meeting at the close of their career. The vagrant is sick and worn out, and the brother prescribes for him out of his learning, and gathers ingenious compounds for his relief; but meantime, he to whom God gave another gift touches his instrument for the solace of the great man's shattered nerves, and heals his benefactor's disordered spirit.

Finally, there is no service thoroughly right which does not directly acknowledge and honor the Saviour. The heart's offering to him is the beginning of all righteousness. He who knoweth our frame has ordained that our spiritual life shall grow strong and earnest, just in proportion as our personal affections and faith centre in the living Saviour, who manifests the Father unto the world. We must touch his garment, sit at his feet, lean upon his cross. So we are made. We may wonder at the way, but we adore it, in our deeper experience, none the less. The want of nature our Redeemer blessedly supplies. There is no other name given among men whereby we can be saved. And it is they who do what they can out of love for him that have the joy of hearing, in his own voice, "Thy faith hath saved thee; go in peace."

SERMON XI.

WOMAN'S POSITION.

YET IS SHE THY COMPANION. — Mal. ii. 14.

THE main proposition is, that, for the wrongs and disadvantages of woman's present social and civil condition, Christianity offers the only true relief.

Recent measures and discussions have so put upon this topic a new aspect, and surrounded it with new associations, that it can hardly be opened, even in a sermon, without some reference to their tendency. I shall advert to these the more willingly, because they involve considerations that lie directly in the course of our inquiry. A statement of the main principles affecting them can be compressed into a brief compass.

The problem of modern speculation, in regard to woman, is to define and secure her rights. Rights imply wrongs: a reform implies abuses. The allegation is, that, hitherto, civilized society has abridged woman's freedom, restricted her faculties, and doubted her capacity. The charge — with the outward demonstrations, such as conventions and treatises, through which it manifests itself — has this significance, that it discovers a spreading conviction in the minds of the people, that woman is not yet fulfilling her whole work in the social economy; which

13*

I hold to be a very interesting fact, worthy of much consideration. But it also takes an unfortunate form; because, not content with asserting her legitimate prerogatives, and challenging a fair field for their exercise, it attaches an unphilosophical importance to certain outward and subordinate particulars; lodging the difficulty where it does not belong, and confusedly mixing together a hostile demand, on the part of women, for being what men are, with a righteous aspiration for making themselves what women were intended to be.

After all, the question resolves itself into one of intention and constitution. Were man and woman designed by creation for the same kinds of service, endowed with the same mental aptitudes, and fitted for the same species of success and distinction? or were they not? If the history of their formation teaches anything; if the facts laid open by daily experience prove anything; if organization reveals anything; if that law of the Divine operations, by which different contrivances imply a variety of purposes, establishes anything, — they were not.

If, now, we proceed to ask, what the grand mental or moral distinction is, and what the peculiar endowments of each are, we find ourselves obliged to speak only in very general terms; for the attributes in which they differ are shaded off into other attributes in which they are alike. Every woman possesses many mental characteristics in common with man; every man has some feminine traits. Employ any classification of the powers of the mind you please, and you find every faculty represented in both man and woman, — understanding and will, consciousness and perception, abstraction and imagination, love and hate, fear and fortitude, desire and aversion; for they are both human. Nature makes "a female Newton and a male siren." The difference, then, must be in the differing degrees and proportions in which these faculties are mixed. One combination of them, so commonly found as to form a rule, constitutes the interior character of one sex; another combination, of another. Now, the real relative *rights* of each of the sexes are settled, when each enjoys an opportunity of unfolding and exercising its *own peculiar* character, whichever it may be, *suffering no obstruction or interference from the other.*

Bearing in mind this explanation, it may be asserted, without offence, that the *distinguishing* faculty of man is mental concentration; that of woman, moral impulse. Woman is the representative of affection; man, of thought. Woman carries her strength in her heart; man, in his head. Neither one monopolizes the special department; but, by eminence, he is intellect, — she is love.

What is the reason some of us are not quite satisfied, in woman's behalf, with this discrimination? Simply because so many of us — men and women both — still labor under the old unchristian heresy, that the heart is inferior to the head, and that a strong intellect is more to be honored than a good spirit. But for this heathenish mistake, woman would ascend instantly into her rightful superiority in the scale of human dignities.

The mistake appears first in the unprincipled vanity of man. He stands, with his stout arms and executive will, and says superciliously to the woman: "It is enough for you to be good: leave power to me. Content yourself with your moral dominion; practise your humble virtues as you are bid; and I will rule the world as I please. Keep my house; mend my clothes; cook my food; see that I am comfortable; and give me a quiet life. Be thankful that your obscure situation does not expose you to the fierce temptations that beset my more splendid career; and accept a slave's security as an offset for the slave's humiliation." This man allows her moral pre-eminence; but he teaches her, and flatters himself, that far above this pre-eminence towers that ability of his own which makes money, speeches, or reputation. It is the same selfish arrogance that prompted the great Greek tragedian to say, in one of his chief productions, "Better a thousand women should persish, than that one man should cease to see the light." Traces of the same contemptible feeling are seen in the literature of later ages, especially in periods of corrupt morals and general scepticism, as well as in the patronizing manners with which vile men fawn on women, with base flatteries, in their presence, and sneer at their virtue, or exult over the scandals of their frailty, with one another. We have not yet quite attained even to that rudimentary truth, that "women are not born merely that men might not be lonely, but are in themselves possessors of immortal souls."

The same mistake appears in ambitious woman herself, when, instead of accepting this her glorious distinction, and wearing it as the unrivalled honor, she longs impatiently for some more pompous but ignobler fame. The reason she feels herself insulted by the theory, that man represents the head, and she the heart, — as if some advantage were thereby referred to man, — is because she is not yet thoroughly a Christian; is not willing to acknowledge that the heart is greater, nobler, wiser than the head, goodness than mere intellect, love than logic, purity than eloquence, holy living than able reasoning. She lingers still under the old barbarous error which sets

Napoleon above Howard, Byron over Wesley, Mary Wolstonecraft over Sarah Martin, and a wicked orator over a working saint. Herein we are all still stumbling among the elements, disloyal to that Gospel which is a dispensation to the affections. It is a delusion — lodged so deep in human judgments that it will be the last to be dispossessed by the triumphant banners of the cross — that the strong brain is nobler than the meek and lowly spirit; that they who "seek after a sign," or "require wisdom," and not the "pure in heart," "shall see God." Woman commits the same error, when, in the choice of her models for imitation from her own sex, she prefers the brilliancy of Madame de Stael to the calm excellence of Elizabeth Hamilton; envies Lady Blessington, or even Madame Dudevant, above Mrs. Barbauld; and, in her heart, would rather have Jenny Lind Goldschmidt's fame, genius, and admiration, than her charity. Still more grossly does she err — because she then ruins her self-respect and her social and moral independence — when she shows it to be, or suffers it to be, the first doctrine of her practical catechism, that the chief end of woman is to be married to a man.

Is it nothing for woman to remember, when her sex is made the type and tabernacle of Love, that we have ascribed the loftiest glory even to the Almighty Father when we have said that his name is Love? Is it nothing to her that her place in society and her powers in the world correspond to her character? that while she shares with man, in honorable and often equal measure, certainly in these modern times, every intellectual privilege, literary accomplishment, and public function, — authorship, the chair of science, the throne of state, — she yet has a realm all her own, sacred to her peculiar ministry, where she reigns by a still diviner right? Is it nothing that it is her face which first bends over the breathing child, looks into his eyes, welcomes him to life, steadies his uncertain feet until they walk firmly on the planet? Suppose man were the natural enemy of woman; consider that from his birth, for the first ten years of his life, he is put into her hands, with scarcely a reservation or exception, to be impressed, moulded, fashioned into what she will, — so that, if he were born a wild tiger, her benignity would have its opportunity to tame him; consider that it has been historically demonstrated that scarcely a single hero, reformer, statesman, saint, or sage, has ever come to influence or adorn his age, from Jacob to Washington, who was not reared by a remarkable mother that shaped his mind; and then ask whether it is not equal folly for woman to claim the *name* of power, and for man to deny her the *possession.*

The genius of controversy never evoked from the "vasty deep" of free discussion a more infelicitous spirit, nor achieved a more unprofitable issue, than when it opened the unnatural question of the comparative merits of the sexes; and for the reason, that the whole design and constitution of their being, the law of their mutual relation, and the primitive providential distinction in their respective functions, make every such comparison an impertinence. The first record of God's creative act — "male and female created he them" — ought to have foreclosed for ever this worse than fratricidal strife. Whichever way the controversy should be decided, the decision would be wrong. Comparative merits of man and woman! There are no terms in which such a comparison can be drawn. You might as well inquire which of any two of the great essential elements of existence, or laws of matter, or faculties of mind, could best be spared; you might as well ask, respecting any of those grand dualities between which the sublime order of nature is poised, and unity is preserved, which member of the equation is most important; you might as well debate the *comparative merits* of spring and autumn, of morning and evening, of oxygen and hydrogen, of the bones and the blood, of memory and hope, of the centripetal and centrifugal attractions. Each holds its title by the ordaining of a divine plan; and the displacement of either from its sphere would be a resolution of the whole system into chaos. The whole controversy is a monstrous absurdity, conceived in a miserable jealousy, prosecuted by an insane insurrection against good manners, and sure to end in nothing but a profane putting asunder of what God has married together. "Yet she is thy companion."

But the question forces itself back, whether, in the civilization of the past, woman has found a fair and equal chance for the development of the powers God has intrusted peculiarly to her, as man has found for the development of those granted peculiarly to him. Manifestly she has not. And here we find the special dignity conferred upon her by Christianity; here appears her chief indebtedness to Christ. Just as fast as that new spiritual ministry has made itself felt on human institutions, her real rights have been recognized. So it will be more and more: as the day of Christian sunlight broadens, the horizon of her appropriate duties will expand. Nor is there any danger, so long as religion guides her progress, that there will be any confusion of claims, or crossing of lines, between her loftier offices and the humbler and rougher tasks of her muscular companion, — man.

In the pagan antiquity, woman was hopelessly degraded by polygamy, as she still is under the Oriental barbarisms, and in savage society generally. A rigorous seclusion, dictated by jealous passions, shuts her in from all free opportunities of ennobling influence and all the dignity of usefulness. The imperious will of her despotic lord imprisons her spirit, as the harem does her body. And it must be confessed that, in some of our houses in Christendom, the spirit of these gross wrongs, if not their form, is renewed by selfish and vulgar husbands, who would rather find in their wives a toy for idle hours, an animal pleasure, or a pride from the admiration they command in assemblies, than an impulse to their own intellects, a benignant influence drawing them out of their worldliness, or a guardian to their virtue. These are the houses where Christianity may be a name, but has not come in renewing power. The inmates are Turks or Hindoos still.

It is true, in some of the more refined of the old nations of the East, a few examples appeared where woman escaped these restrictions on her freedom. Plato, in his "Divine Dialogues," introduces a maxim, which, by implication, renders a worthy tribute to woman, to the effect, that whatever was most excellent in the state must always begin at the fireside. But too often, like Aspasia, Sappho, Helen, and Cleopatra, she gained both her liberty and her celebrity at the expense of her modesty. The alternative lay between obscurity and effrontery. The rare names that stand altogether above reproach in the ancient literature — names that classical veneration repeats with enthusiasm till to-day — were generally the ideal creations of some poet's or artist's fancy, rather than actual women dwelling in flesh and blood. In the Roman empire, as in the Greek oligarchy, when woman emerged from her state of abject servitude, it was only to take a share in the impure ceremonies and dances of an idolatrous worship, and thus to pass forth upon the theatre of a voluptuous publicity. The heathen religions had no word to raise woman to her true equality with man; and, by consequence, the woman and the man and the religions must needs sink together into destruction.

The introduction of Christianity formed the grand epoch in the condition of woman. But even Christian ideas did not spring full-grown into history; and so the elevation of female character to its true rank has been gradual. How it was originally regarded, by the pure spirit of the New Testament, certainly admits no doubt. The spiritual insight of Jesus saw that the readiest and clearest reception of his heavenly doctrine was in the heart of woman. With what dignified tenderness he always saluted her! The hospitalities of the sisters at Bethany; the tears and ointment of Mary Magdalen; the dying looks and immortal blessings bestowed on those that were "last at the cross, and earliest at the grave"; the honorable offices of charitable ministration assigned to females in the Apostolic Church, — all these were only fit proofs of the estimation in which that Saviour held woman, who was to be, down through all future ages, the unfailing refuge of her spirit, the companion of her solitude, the rest of her weariness, the compassionator of her frailty, the comforter of her pain. By its indestructible reverence for the virgin mother of our Lord, the Christian Church has not only woven into its sentiments a new idea of woman, but it has done something to cancel the contempt that was thrown upon her in the person of Eve, the seduced of Satan. If woman was the first in the world to sin, it was on her breast also that its Redeemer was nourished; and Bethlehem has atoned for Eden. Abating its superstitious excesses, the homage paid to the Madonna is a consecration of womanhood quite becoming a religion that displaced paganism, and condemns sensuality.

Since the primitive age of the Church, however, the condition of woman has shared in the slow progress of religious ideas generally. Civilization has never more than partially realized Christianity. But the advance has been steady. The greatest hinderance it has experienced was in an institution which superficial judgments have often instanced as promoting it, — the chivalry of the Middle Ages. The honor paid by knight-errantry to woman was a false honor. The hollow complaisance of the courtier covered a low style of morals; and the romance of chivalry was rather the flattering gallantry of passion, than an honest and substantial recognition of woman's actual worth. It is this chivalry that has too much given law and fashion to the relation of the sexes ever since, — substituting the forms of effeminate courtesy for sterling respect, and bringing in that foolish style of manners where women are fawned upon with empty compliments and polite nothings, instead of being frankly met with intelligence, good sense, and genuine deference.

The next great impulse was given to female culture when the Saxon element began to be felt in history, and out of the old German forests came forth those stanch hearts and heroic hands that were thenceforth to rule the destinies of Christendom. They were true respecters of woman. They were the first people that, independently of Christianity, rendered to her her natural rights. They made her a companion, a counsellor, a confidante, — not a servant, a mistress, nor a doll. And when Christianity came and grafted its heavenly spirit on that noble stock, new examples began to be witnessed of female capacity and character. The Church was never, indeed, without its female saints and heroines; though only a few names, like those of Theresa, Catharine Adorna, Madame Guyon, and Joan of Arc, have travelled down to us from the Catholic ages. Protestantism has its higher illustrations of dauntless courage, genius, and piety, in letters, art, and philanthropy, from such as Lady Russell and Hannah More, Dorothy Dix and Elizabeth Fry, Frederika Bremer and Hannah Adams, Harriet Newell and Mary Ware. It is unquestionable, that loftier and more abundant examples of high-hearted womanhood are living to-day, than in any hour of history before.

Accordingly, as we should expect, there is hardly a walk of public or private life where female talent is not heartily honored, and does not command its deserved success. The fine arts, the sciences, classical learning, social reform, philosophy, education, empire, — all are represented at this day by accomplished women. Do they suffer detriment, or loss of influence, because they are women? Is Mrs. Somerville, or Miss Mitchell, less esteemed among the scientific minds of the age for her sex? Does not the whole British kingdom learn a heightened regard for woman from the womanly character it beholds in its queen? Is there a department of knowledge from which woman is now, by our modern systems of education, shut out? Must it not be very soon true that her power shall be proportioned to her energy, and her influence be measured only by her merit? Probably the larger proportion of scholarship and public enterprise will still be with men, — the providential constitution of the sexes justifies that expectation; but when exceptions appear, the demand of Christian liberty is, that they be welcomed, recognized, and rewarded.

Some disabilities, however, still accrue to woman, especially in respect to property, and just payment for her labor. Tasks that she is fully competent to every way, public opinion and false custom will not let her do, cruelly telling her she shall sooner starve; and for work that she actually does as well and as rapidly as her companion, man, she receives only a quarter of his wages; both of which are wrongs that Christianity rebukes as clearly as it does slavery or defalcation, and wrongs that Christian men must speedily remedy, or else cease to be Christians, and well-nigh cease to be men. Already they are partly remedied, in countries otherwise less advanced than our own, by protection granted to woman in employments that sustain her independence and shield her virtue.

A darker wrong yet is strangely done to woman by that obstinate and most unrighteous judgment of men, which, not satisfied that she should sustain all the severer agonies that attend the perpetuating of the race, insists on extending a vile toleration to the wretch who ruins her virtue and robs her of her peace, passing over his "deep damnation" as a venial thing; while it mercilessly dooms and casts off the Magdalens, barring every gate against their return to purity.

What, then, briefly, in respect to woman's social position amongst us, *as it is*, — her rights and her power, — are her own immediate duties, and those of man in her behalf?

First, of man's. Let him learn to be grateful to woman for this undoubted achievement of her sex, that it is she — she far more than he, and she too often in despite of him — who has kept Christendom from lapsing back into barbarism, — kept mercy and truth from being utterly overborne by those two greedy monsters, money and war. Let him be grateful for this, that almost every great soul that has led forward or lifted up the race has been furnished for each noble deed, and inspired with each patriotic and holy aspiration, by the retiring fortitude of some Spartan, or more than Spartan, — some Christian mother. Moses, the deliverer of his people, drawn out of the Nile by the king's daughter, some one has hinted, is only a symbol of the way that woman's better instincts always outwit the tyrannical diplomacy of man. Let him cheerfully remember, that, though the sinewy sex achieves enterprises on public theatres, it is the nerve and sensibility of the other that arm the mind and inflame the soul in secret. "A man discovered America; but a woman equipped the voyage." So everywhere: man executes the performance; but woman trains the man. Every effectual person, leaving his mark on the world, is but another Columbus, for whose furnishing some Isabella, in the form of his mother, lays down her jewelry, her vanities, her comfort.

Above all, let not men practise on woman the perpetual and shameful falsehood of pretending admiration and acting contempt. Let them not exhaust their kindness in adorning her person, and ask in return the humiliation of her soul. Let them not assent to her every opinion, as if she were not strong enough to maintain it against opposition; nor yet manufacture opinion for her, and force it on to her lips by dictation. Let them not crucify her emotions, nor ridicule her frailty, nor crush her individuality, nor insult her dependence, nor play off mean jests upon her honor in convivial companies, nor bandy unclean doubts of her, as a wretched substitute for wit, nor whisper vulgar suspicions of her purity, which, as compared with their own, is like the immaculate whiteness of angels. Let them remember, that for the ghastly spectacle of her blasted chastity they are answerable. Let them multiply her social advantages, enhance her dignity, minister to her intelligence, and, by manly gentleness, be the champions of her genius, the friends of her fortunes, and the equals, if they can, of her heart. And if any man is tempted to that meanest of unmanly tricks, — making a woman his wife that he may buy for himself, by a husband's name, riches or social standing or popular favor, — let him take the spirited advice of a true woman-poet to Prince Albert at his wedding: —

> "Esteem that wedded hand less dear for sceptre than for ring;
> And hold her uncrowned womanhood to be the royal thing."

Be the husband the "head of the wife," not as despot or voluptuary, but in that holier headship signified by the Apostle, as Christ is the Head of his Church. "Yet is she thy companion."

And, finally, of woman's duties for herself. For the wrongs that remain to her position, and the disabilities that man's too selfish and partially Christianized nature has not yet removed, let her not, in the name of all that is lovely and all that is skilful, go to separatist conventions, nor to the platform, nor to novel schemes of political economy or social re-organization; but to that moral tribunal, where she is as sure to win her cause at last as the sunlight is to compel a summer. Let her take up and wield the spiritual sovereignty that is her everlasting birthright. Let her understand — what so few of her sex have been willing to learn to this hour — the power lodged in her whole spirit and voice and look and action for or against the kingdom of Heaven. Let her be content with the possession and exercise of power, in all its higher forms, without that appendage which unhallowed pride is for ever insisting on, — the *name* of it. Let her unfold every nobler faculty that our imperfect social state invites; and then be sure that the social state will ripen into more perfect humanities, and full justice come at last. Let her be the brave domestic advocate of every virtue, the silent but effectual reformer of every vice, the unflinching destroyer of falsehood, the generous patroness of intelligence, the watcher by slandered innocence, the guardian of childhood, the minister of Heaven to home, the guide of orphans, the sister of the poor, the disciple of Christ's holy Church. On Jesus of Nazareth, — all fails except for this, — on the Saviour's heart, let her rest her unchangeable and unassailable hope, her unquestioning trust, her unconquerable love.

For then shall man and woman be fellow-helpers to the truth; marriage, the pure sacrament of a spiritual faith; and families on earth, humbler branches of the great family of heaven.

SERMON XII.

THE CHRISTIAN WOMAN.

WHOSE ADORNING, LET IT NOT BE THAT OUTWARD ADORNING OF PLAITING THE HAIR, AND OF WEARING OF GOLD, OR OF PUTTING ON OF APPAREL; BUT LET IT BE THE HIDDEN MAN OF THE HEART, IN THAT WHICH IS NOT CORRUPTIBLE, EVEN THE ORNAMENT OF A MEEK AND QUIET SPIRIT, WHICH IS IN THE SIGHT OF GOD OF GREAT PRICE. FOR AFTER THIS MANNER, IN THE OLD TIME, THE HOLY WOMEN ALSO, WHO TRUSTED IN GOD, ADORNED THEMSELVES. — 1 Peter iii. 3 – 5.

THE views presented in the preceding Discourse on the social and moral position of women lead on to some further contemplation of her character as matured and enriched by Christ. My doctrine will be that woman can realize her proper ministry only as she is inspired by Christian faith, and that she can find the solace so sorely needed by her discipline only as she enthrones the religion of the Son of Mary as the supreme principle of her life.

Let our thoughts be guided by this twofold proposition: — 1. For the unfolding of woman's character, and the balancing of her spirit, Christianity supplies the only sufficient impulse and guide. 2. Christianity exhibits no more perfect illustration or achievement than in the completed proportions of her spiritual life. Let us follow her through the three principal stages in the solemn career of her womanhood, to see how helpless she is in every one, except she leans on Jesus, the friend of Mary and Martha.

The first epoch of trial in woman's life begins when the period of education ceases. It encompasses a reserved, but always an intense, and sometimes a tragic experience. Hitherto, except in cases of rare misfortune and bleak exposure, her home, parents, and that shield of childhood's innocence which no serpent and no demon dare assail, have sheltered her. Now she steps forth, if not into the fierceness of public temptation, at least into the path of solitary and secret struggles, — bitternesses of spirit which pride and modesty both press back unspoken into the enduring but inexperienced heart.

I envy not that man's sensibility, nor do I credit his manliness, who treats these things as only the flimsy sentimentalities of a girlish fancy. I think there are gathered into those few years that intervene between the busy hours of the school-room and the sober cares of the family terrible conflicts of the moral nature, questions of duty, tossings of conscience, weariness of patience, quenchings of the spirit, buffetings and resurrections of holy aspiration, of a meaning deep and solemn enough to impress any earnest mind.

It is a period of dependence, in the first place, with most women; and who does not know that trials lie hid in that word "dependence"? — dependence on parents, to be sure, often, not always, — but still not the less irksome for that, if the woman, with a consciousness of strength, sees the parent worn and anxious with excess of labor; or if, with willingness for effort which her position or social prejudice forbids, she sees her every want met only by reluctant and grudged supplies. It is a period of uncertainty; for it looks straight out upon all those contingencies that determine her future lot, — a lot for which she is not so much to lead or choose as to wait and weigh the perils of being chosen, or to learn the calm fortitude that conquers neglect with dignity. It is a period of highly-wrought sensibility. The emotions have swelled, from the babbling brook that kept its quiet way within the banks of youth, into the rushing river of impetuous passion. Opening vistas of gayety bewilder the eye. Overhanging shadows of disappointment alarm the soul. Sanguine expectations welcoming joy, and apprehensive instincts portending danger, divide the day and brood over the night. It is a period of comparative irresponsibleness; and who shall say that irresponsibleness is a blessing, when we know so well how occupation dispels morbid introspections, and how daily strain upon the muscles fortifies timid and tremulous nerves?

I cannot agree with those superficial observers who see in the life of early womanhood no more than a careless pastime, where nothing is so easy as to be happy, or read in its noiseless exterior an infallible sign of perfect peace within. Oh! peace within! It is not there; but whence is it to come? Must it be a stranger for ever to that agitated heart? Must woman endure and strive and suffer, treading the wine-press of that comfortless solicitude, or that weary and discontented round of unmeaning trifles which is a still heavier curse, alone? Must she walk that perilous way, withstanding flattery, bearing neglect, curbing complaint, bracing the nerves, masking tempests of feeling under an unchanged face, sifting sincerity from falsehood in the speech of men, and mastering gloomy meditations by voluntary activities, alone? Alone it must be in many cases, as respects the fulness of any mortal sympathy; but not *so* alone, if she will have faith, as to exclude a companionship mightier and more blessed than the mortal. For such as she is, Christ died; for such as she is, the Mediator lives; for just that perplexed spirit Jesus says, "Come unto me, thou weary and heavy-laden! Let not your heart be troubled. This way, daughter! Be of good comfort." For many a one who has not sinned as the weeping Mary sinned, but has sinned with the secret sin of the thoughts, and has sorrowed penitentially, or has feared lest sin should overtake her suddenly, and so has been ready to wash her Master's feet with tears, he is saying still, "Thy faith hath saved thee: go in peace."

It is not true, I think, of any other condition of human discipline, more than of this one, that nothing short of a personal acquaintance with Christian trust can satisfy its wants. Two other and different resources, indeed, the young woman has; and we need not wander far to search for proofs how often she tries their value. They are her womanly pride, and the excitements of society. The one *will* help her, so far as to a stubborn silence, a stoic strength, such as lurks often in the fragile feminine frame, which hides pain, but does not smother it, and disguises trouble with levity, but never consoles it. The other — social excitement — *defers* the hour of grief, but, while it puts it off, is gathering up additional material to intensify its visitation when it returns. At last, it dissipates self-respect, turns simplicity into affectation, and benumbs the moral sense. Whether these are satisfying comforters, is a question not for argument, but for testimony alone. Summon your evidence; for you know where it is to be found. Perhaps you are witnesses yourselves, and need only to call Memory to the stand, before the examinations of Conscience.

What will Christianity do? It concentrates the aimless and restless purposes of woman on the one grand object of a personal acceptance with God. It takes off the load, which no human spirit can bear and be cheerful, by its promise of forgiveness for what is lacking, and by its encouraging assurance, that, when once the life is consecrated to God, no single act or thought of good can fail of fruit in the spiritual harvests of eternity. It offers her what the mind of youth more than anything else craves, — a friendship at once unchangeable and trustworthy as the heavens; and so it opens the gates of the city of God straight into her closet of prayer, and, when the world looks most inhospitable, shows her friendly angels ascending with her supplications, and descending with counsel and compassion, between her Bethel and her Father. It gives her that inward gift which none can see but by possessing it, and which had its best description when it was said of it, by Him who knew its power, that it "passeth all understanding." More than this Christianity does for her. It provides for that sad deficiency in so many women's lives, — the want of some specific aim for undirected energies. No poet nor tragedian nor artist has yet depicted the misery that comes of the cruel divorce between the active spirit of many a woman and its appropriate work. Religion leads her to her task, — the white field that her soft but resolute hand can reap. It not only quickens her to a new fidelity, in all the homely ministrations of the house where she lives, towards brothers and sisters, parents and servants; it opens to her the lowly door of poverty; it draws her, by cords stronger than steel, to the unclad orphan, and the bedside of sick wretchedness; it stimulates her invention, it exhausts her economy, it plies her fingers, it inspires her intercessions, for the instruction of poor children's ignorance, and the redemption of their despair. By a beautiful feature in the moral economy of the Church, no less than of nature, the mercies of life are assigned pre-eminently to female enterprise; and, if Protestantism does not deserve to be converted back to Rome, the pity of her daughters will outwatch and outlabor the splendid benefactions of the Sisters of Charity.

Another task still Christianity solemnly charges upon woman in her youth. It bids her by every separate obligation of her discipleship, be true to immaculate virtue, in her intercourse with companions, and in the bestowment of her favor. It not only surrounds her own person with the "sun-clad armor" of chastity and temperance and truth, but it commands her to exact the decencies of morality from every acquaintance, of either sex, that she honors with her intimacy.

Would to God that some angel from his own right hand would reveal to her the power she controls for the redemption of those horrible vices that defile and intoxicate the land! for then she might take up her benignant ministry as an apostle of holiness, persuading the tempted by her unbending principle, as well as bearing her own profession incorruptibly. Not that I would have young women trespass over the line of a most delicate propriety, in the hope of winning young men from dissipation by compromise or complaisance; for I have had proofs too painful how the kindness of that generous benevolence may be outwitted and betrayed by the cowardly cunning of the voluptuary. But woman should awe vice everywhere by the sternness of her disapproval, and the unmistakableness of her language.

Learn, women, as the Master beseeches you, that a divine trust is committed to you, in your example and your very smiles, for which God will call you into judgment. Know, as I know, that a trifling remark, falling from woman's thoughtless tongue in the whirl of some animating assembly, — extending her allowance to excess, treating sensuality as a venial error, or ridiculing strict virtue as a puritanical scruple, — has been the feather's weight that turned the scale of a man's wavering character to infamy. Know, as I know, that your sober rebuke may carry the power of many sermons to the heart, and rescue a soul half lost, making you ministers of the cross. There is a record in the Hebrew history of a young maiden taken captive from the land of Israel, and made a servant in the house of Naaman, the illustrious captain of the king's host. The great man was smitten with leprosy, and could get no cure. The girl had courage to stand up against all the ridicule and obloquy of her despised religion. She dared to be true to the God of her fathers, and to the prophets she had been taught from infancy to revere. She persisted in saying, "Would God my master were with the prophet that is in Samaria! for he would recover him of his leprosy." At last, her faith conquered the Syrian's haughty prejudice; and he went down to Elisha, washed in the Jordan, and was clean. There are leprosies on men's souls; and by the mouth of other maids than the Jewish captive, if they are as brave and dutiful to God as she, the simple word may be uttered that heals them.

It is time to advance to a later stage of the Christian woman's experience. If her moral power is so decisive at the time when life has devolved upon her the fewest responsibilities, and neither age nor station has vested in her any adventitious authority, that even then she stands in her private place either as a preacher of righteousness or an emissary of the Tempter, it is only more commanding yet when she has taken up the complicated relations of marriage, and assumed the spiritual governance of that lesser church, that sacred seminary, — the family. At the height of her influence, both domestic and social, she then acts at once through the living medium of an individual example, and through the manifold ties of her position, for the blessing, or the fatal misleading, of many. I say again, nothing but the piety of the New Testament can suffice for her high calling.

The chief enemies to her Christian simplicity — and thus to the symmetry of her own character, as well as the integrity of her influence — are social ambition, an appetite for admiration, the passion for indiscriminate excitement, and, in other constitutions, a dull servitude to the routine of mechanical tasks.

1. By social ambition, I mean the vulgar appetite for those external distinctions, which are even more dangerous to woman than to man, because of the inherent, natural aristocracy of her nature. A wife or mother, who suffers it to be her supreme exertion to rise in the public consideration, has already parted with that artless sincerity which is the chief grace of her womanhood. It is inevitable, then, that she should be always bringing the most tender sanctities of life into market, — reducing the charm of honest courtesy into a financial convenience, and making a brokerage of hospitalities. Mechanics and merchants, whom thrift would have elevated into legitimate prosperity at last, are led into ruinous extravagance

by this poor slavery to names, appearances, and outsides. Not culture, nor the real mental nor moral advantage of better associates, not solid gain of mind or heart, but a nominal superiority, pride of place, successful competition with neighbors, — these are the rank shoots of social ambition. Growing refinements and elegances *are* honors, so far as they are modest badges of growing diligence. Any other "getting up in the world" is not getting nearer to heaven. Low tricks and transparent artifices are Ambition's awkward tools. Falsehood is too often its ally; and a spirit alien from that of the Gospel is its instigation.

2. Appetite for admiration. Could some searching census register the number of those who are kept aloof from the love of God by this foolish vanity alone, should we dare to look into the swelling catalogue? Could some magic reflection be added to mirrors, so that, while they show back the adjustment of garments, they should also reveal the emptiness of the soul, what dismal disclosures would startle the sleeping conscience! How slow pride is to learn that every accumulation of useless finery upon the person bears an exact proportion to the poverty of character beneath it! When the true Christian standard of dress and furnishing shall be confessed, these wasteful outlays on gaudy colors and superfluous ornaments will be blushed for as indecencies. God in his justice cannot be satisfied while the grand charities and philanthropies of his kingdom languish, and the treasuries of ostentation are so full. Honesty stands aghast, economy is laughed to scorn, Christian humility is insulted, the Gospel is denied, by dresses that almost every Christian assembly tolerates. The reformation of these abuses belongs peculiarly to woman, "whose adorning,

let it not be that outward adorning of plaiting the hair, and of wearing of gold, or of putting on of apparel; but let it be the hidden nature of the heart, in that which is not corruptible, even the ornament of a meek and quiet spirit, which is in the sight of God of great price. For after this manner, in the old time, the holy women, who trusted in God, adorned themselves."

3. Passion for indiscriminate excitement. What hold has religion taken of that mind which never rests in its insatiable craving for some public spectacle, — is never satisfied except when it is preparing for some scene of social display, or exulting over its conquests? What place in that distracted and disordered heart for Religion to breathe the first whisper of her tranquil benediction? what place for the patient exercises of self-examination, for communion with God, for the prayer that asks "the calm retreat, the silent shade"? There is no noble type of womanhood that does not wear serenity upon its forehead.

4. On the other hand, in constitutions of an opposite inclination, female life is apt to degenerate, if not inspired by religion, into a tame routine of narrow domestic cares, dwarfing the spirit to its own contracted limitations. The very nature of woman requires animation for its health. Religion, with its infinite mysteries, its deep and stirring experience, its boundless duties, offers that needed stimulus, — offers it to the obscurest and the lowliest. At her call, the whole army of martyrs, and the glorious company of Apostles, pass by. The veil is lifted from Judæa, peopled with miracles. The Prophets repeat for her their majestic visions, and David chants to her his undying songs. Heaven opens the leaves of its shining portals, the angels are singing over Bethlehem, the Magi kneel

with Mary, and our Lord is seen blessing the women that hide their eyes at Calvary. These are the scenes, and these the voices, that animate the Christian woman's meditation; and, when she passes from them into the gayeties of the world, it is like coming down from the high mountains of transfiguration, and from among the lamps of heaven, into the lurid glare of some playhouse pit. Imaginative, dreaming, musing, mystical woman! Christianity, after all, is thy most satisfying friend.

The Christian wife and mother is a Christian in the spirit by which she orders her household and nurtures her offspring. Too many mothers make their first request for their sons that of the mother of Zebedee's children, — that they may sit on thrones of wealth and power. What wonder if those sons are worldlings, are hypocrites, are criminals? Too many train up their daughters with no loftier aim than to be beautiful brides, or the centres of meretricious observation at summer watering-places, or to value a husband by his income, or not to be over-nice in their judgment of men, because they are not expected to be virtuous like women. Infamous effrontery towards God! And thus are reared, generation by generation, those successive ranks of artificial and perverted things called "women of the world," — women that might figure without disgrace at the court of a profligate Louis or a shameless Charles, where disgrace is annihilated by making corruption the fashion; women that are fit for no other career than in the unprincipled saloons of the Paris of the last century; women who have passed that pagan sentiment into a Christian adoption, that "mothers are sad when daughters are born."

Not such — O very far from such as she! — is the mother that has sat, with the sisters of Bethany, at the feet of Jesus; that has entered into devout communion with the Redeemer in his Church; that has made her quiet dwelling fragrant with the odors of the prayers of saints. *She* stands in her household, the priestess of an immortal faith, the reconciler of human love with the divine; *she* moves among sons and daughters, folding the hands of infancy in prayer, joining the hands of all in fellowship, opening them in charity, and pointing with her own to heaven.

> "*She* can so impress
> With quietness and beauty, and so feed
> With lofty thoughts, that neither evil tongues,
> Rash judgments, nor the sneers of selfish men,
> Nor greetings where no kindness is, nor all
> The dreary intercourse of daily life,
> Shall e'er prevail against us, or disturb
> Our cheerful faith, that all which we behold
> Is full of blessings."

And thus I have come, finally, to what may be briefly established, — that Christianity exhibits no more perfect achievement than in the completed character of a spiritual womanhood; for, passing on one stage later yet, we find the united result of a life's discipline and a heavenly faith in the Christian woman's old age. Providence has not withheld that confirmation of the power and beauty of religion from our eyes. We feel new confidence in truth, new love for goodness, new zeal for duty, new trust in God, new gratitude to Christ, when we look on her ripened holiness; and, as her strength faints before the power of decay, behold the crown of immortality descending almost visibly upon her head! The recollection of her former activities blends with the hallowed hope of her renewed energies in the immaterial body, with which she shall be clothed upon from heaven. The thanksgivings of the poor that she has blessed, the tears of orphans that she has led, the tributes of the sick that she has visited, the perfume of the charities she has scattered, throng up to make the fading light of her evening tranquil. She is a mother to her children after they cease to be children ; she is a matron in the Church, because the Church has been strengthened by her blameless walk. Every good cause of humanity is encouraged by her prayers, sent up from a shaded chamber, because those prayers have had no contradiction in her deeds. The heart of her husband trusts in her. Her children rise up every morning to call her blessed. In her tongue is the law of kindness. Strength and honor are her clothing. Like the holy women of old time, her ornament is a meek and quiet spirit. And she shall rejoice with what exceeding joy, when heart and tongue fail, at the right hand of God!

I cannot so well finish this account of a Christian woman as by repeating the following touching, simple, sorrowful memorial of his wife, written by one of the statesmen of England — Sir James Mackintosh — in a private letter to a friend. "She was a woman," he writes, "who, by the tender management of my weaknesses, gradually corrected the most pernicious of them. She became prudent from affection; and, though of the most generous nature, she was taught frugality and economy by her love for me. During the most critical period of my life, she preserved order in my affairs, from the care of which she relieved me. She gently reclaimed me from dissipation, she propped my weak and irresolute nature, she urged my indolence to all the exertions that have been useful or creditable to me, and she was perpetually at hand to admonish my heedlessness and improvidence. To her I owe whatever I am, — to her whatever I shall be. In her solicitude for my interest, she never for a moment forgot my character. Her feelings were warm and impetuous; but she was placable, tender, and constant. Such was she whom I have lost; and I have lost her when a knowledge of her worth had refined my youthful love into friendship, before age had deprived it of much of its original ardor. I seek relief, and I find it, in the consolatory opinion, that a benevolent Wisdom inflicts the chastisement, as well as bestows the enjoyment, of human life; that superintending Goodness will one day enliven the darkness which surrounds our nature and hangs over our prospects; that this dreary and wretched life is not the whole of man; that a being capable of such proficiency in science and virtue is not like the beasts that perish; that there is a dwelling-place prepared for the spirits of the just; that the ways of God will yet be vindicated to man."

SERMON XIII.

THE LAW OF THE HOUSE.

THUS SAITH THE LORD, SET THINE HOUSE IN ORDER; FOR THOU SHALT DIE, AND NOT LIVE. — Isa. xxxviii. 1.

As Religion asks only the simplest array of circumstance to demonstrate her sublimest principles; only the little sphere of an obscure fortune to round out all her majestic orbit of duty; only the common people as spectators, to unroll the splendid constellation of her promises; and only the humblest foothold in the heart, to bear all that heart's affections with her into the highest heaven, — so she requires only the plainest language to declare her most searching doctrines.

The ordinary meaning of the word *Economy*, which makes it apply to mere prudence in pecuniary expenditure, or a judicious handling of the financial resources of living, is only the secondary, not the original, import of the term, as appears by a reference to its Greek derivation. Restore its primary signification, and it instantly stretches out to embrace far more than worldly thrift, more than honesty, more than philosophy. It gathers up and condenses the whole religious obligation and responsibility of one great department of our life. We may preach the whole Gospel of Christ, to the household, through the suggestions of that simple word *Economy*. For it signifies, literally, the Law of the House; the ordering of man's whole domestic existence; the inauguration of the Divine Will over his dwelling. To the soul surrounded by its natural, human relationships, the command out of the mouth of God is, "Set thy house in order": obey this spiritual economy.

The subject I set before you is The Law of the House. And the discourse will proceed through these three positions:—1. That the house is a divine institution; 2. That every family has its law of family life,—its ruling principle or passion; 3. That only one law, and that promulgated in Christ, can comprehend, meet, and satisfy the household, in a spiritual economy.

Out of the Romish Church, which claims special revelations of divine authority for every ordinance it enjoins, we have scarcely any terms to define exactly what an ordinance is. The Protestant identifies a religious ordinance by finding, upon its origin, its preservation, and its uses in the world, wonderful marks of a heavenly design.

I. Judged by these rules, the Family is an ordinance of God. It draws its credentials from the parental appointment in Eden. Its solemn ceremony of installation was the crowning act of creation. No other institution, whether surviving now or perished in the past, can show such an antiquity. The records of it are the first syllables of written history, and the faintest stammerings of tradition. It runs up, beyond Assyrian or Chaldean empires, and the founding of Palmyra, to the tents on the plains of Shinar. The first breathing of its spirit was the simplicity of patriarchs. It began while the earliest beams of the world's twilight were shooting up into a sky whose stars no tongue had yet called by their names, — over an unpeopled world. Was not its origin, then, divine?

And is not the preservation of the family as clearly stamped with God's purpose as its origin? How marvellously that institution of the House survives revolutions! How tenaciously, everywhere, it clings in the web of human events! How obstinately, under all conditions, it justifies its right to be! You might as soon find by chemical analysis, and pluck out with your finger, the living principle of a growing cedar, as eradicate from society the indestructible tendency it has to throw itself out into families. Subdue that tendency in one place, and it will break out in another. An empire may rot, a nation may be wasted, a city may be sacked; but, as if some immortal element quickened it, this hallowed institution of the household lives on; refuses to be destroyed. Surely there have been changes enough on this convulsed, decaying, and ensanguined earth, to shake out of its place any form of life God does not mean shall stand. But the house is just as sure, after a Macedonian or a Mexican dynasty has fallen, as before. That little charmed circle of parents and children stands against all the destructions of time, more secure than any army clad in steel. You may scatter mankind like the Hebrew tribes; but straightway they will group themselves, and be found in families. You may bury Nineveh, or strangle Herculaneum, or starve Babylon, or burn Warsaw; but the family you cannot dispossess, nor batter down, nor drown with water, nor burn with fire. The advancing growths of civilization only vary its form; they do not affect its substance. The tents of shepherds vanish; but more stable dwellings take their places. The bamboo hut of the Indian, and the European mansion, each holds its family. Agricultural communities build their separate houses of wood, and commercial in blocks of wood or stone, but not dispersion nor agglomeration can blur over the lines that divide the invisible or spiritual house from its neighbor. Is not its preservation, then, divine?

Its uses, — with equal distinctness, with what bright tokens, with what emphatic demonstrations, do they speak of the home as God's appointment! Where lie the clearest proofs of a heavenly watchfulness over our heads, if not in the shelters where we lay those heads at night? Consider what securities home affections bind about tempted virtue; how the man of business carries a zone of moral purity woven about him by the caresses of children, from his house to the market-place; how the false or fraudulent purpose, half conceived in the counting-room, is rebuked and put to shame by the innocence that gazes into his eyes and clings about his neck when he goes home and shuts the door on the world at night. Consider what a hinderance household love interposes, to stay the straying feet of dissipation; what a triple shield it holds up against the sins of prodigality, indulgence, or dishonor! Consider that, with most of us, whatever impulses of generosity visit the soul, whatever prayers we breathe, whatever holy vows of religious consecration we pledge, whatever aspiring resolves we form, are apt to spring up within the sacred enclosures of the house! Consider how the mere memory of that spot, with all its precious endearments, goes forth with the traveller, sails with the sailor, keeps vigils over the exposed heart among the perils of the foreign city, sweetens the feverish dreams and softens the pain of the sufferer in the sickly climate, and, by calling his love homeward, calls his faith to Heaven! Consider that the discipline of disease, the purification of bereavement, the tears of mourners, are all elements in the sanctity of home; that closets of devotion are parts of the architecture of the house; that Bibles are opened on its tables; that the eyes of new-born children open, and their first breaths are drawn, in its chambers; and that the dead body is borne out of its doors; — how fast do the gathering proofs accumulate, that the human dwelling is a sanctuary of the Most High!

Whoever builds its walls, God hallows them for his temple. That outward house is but the visible pattern of the interior edifice; and of that spiritual structure God has laid the foundation, and sprung the arches, and commanded the economy. The family is surely his ordinance.

Who doubts it? Do you doubt it, because the daily on-going of domestic life is so often commonplace, so often vulgar, so often selfish, and tedious, and ill-tempered, and vicious? or because some disgusting disclosure of conjugal faithlessness, shamelessly reported abroad from the proper privacy of courts of justice, sickens all honest sensibilities, and makes us half ashamed that we are men and women ourselves?

I reply, that, in the analogies of its constitution, we may regard every family as only a smaller commonwealth, or a more complicated individual, or an undisciplined church. God has *ordained* it, as he has ordained the state, the individual, and the Church. But he has not, in one case more than in the others, fixed, by absolute or arbitrary rule, the form that the institution shall put on. He leaves the body, into which the life shall be developed, to be shaped by the shifting conditions of time, circumstance, culture, temperament. Just as the empire at Rome, the oligarchy at Athens, the chieftainship of the Cherokees, and the republic of the United States, are all alike divine powers in the world, — not because they are empire and oligarchy, despotism or democracy, but simply because they are all government, that is, organized order, for each given people, — so the family may be a very different institution, in kind, in Siam, in Turkey, or in New England; but in each country it is an institution, and God recognizes it as sacred. It is the best representative of the idea of family to be had of that nation in that age. It is suffered to stand, not as the best abstract or absolute form of family, but because there is now none better. The prime intention of it is only very imperfectly embodied in the historical fact; the particular example, savage or Turkish or English, may be a poor expression of the original and universal idea of family, as it lay in the Creative Mind. Still, man must accept it into his respect, as God accepts it into his providential method, not for what it lacks, but for what it contains; not because it is everything it might be, but in spite of what it is not. If the Almighty Justice could take into the system by which he works out the destinies of the race, such corrupt societies as Corinth and Carthage, such tyrants as Cæsar Borgia and Herod, such princes as Louis XIV. and Henry VIII., man is bound by every moral law to reverence this appointment of the household for the germ of truth it holds in its bosom, — though in any given case it should be outwardly as unsound as the shell that falls off from the springing corn.

Do you ask why, then, if God meant the family to be

regarded as a sacred institution, he has not kept it sacred from degradation and abuse, I refer you to the simple fact, — obvious certainly if not intelligible to us, — that he has admitted into the problem of all our life another element besides his own almightiness, namely, man's free will; that is, allowing a certain amount of interference from human perversity, short-sightedness, and depravity. And these disturbing influences have thrust themselves in to mar the beauty and debase the virtue of the house, as they have to pollute every region, business, and faculty. "The trail of the serpent is over them all." We might as well ask why the sacred trust of government has been suffered to fall into bloody and rapacious hands, — why the Church has sometimes reeked with corruption, and its sacraments have been dispensed by perjury, blasphemy, and sensuality, — as hesitate to hold the family an ordinance of God, because all the heavenly graces are not grouped together to adorn every dwelling. Heaven's benignant design has suffered postponement from our choosing evil over good; and certainly we who have introduced the mischiefs of disorder should not be forward to censure what our own folly has spoiled.

So much for the first point, — that the house is a divine appointment. And the rule of practice drawn thus far is, that the more we reverence it for that divine ordaining, the more we shall see God in its daily aspect, and strive to set it into his order.

II. My next position is that every family has its law of family life, — its ruling principle or passion. Its individual members may differ very widely from each other in disposition or character. The same house may hold a quick-tempered brother and an even-tempered sister; a thoughtful husband and a worldly wife; a conscientious parent and a headstrong child; yet you will discover running through them all a certain family character, a spirit of the house, pervading all and modifying each. Just as a general physical resemblance, mixed up with many diversities of feature and manner, marks them as of one blood, so a uniform tone of the dwelling pierces through all that is peculiar to the person. This characteristic something, giving moral complexion to the whole, we may call the Law of the House. It is made up of the moral convictions, purposes of life, habits of domestic intercourse, and degrees of culture, common to all. The law of a feudal castle was stately supremacy; of a Puritan's dwelling, devout decorum; of a modern Jew's, avarice; of a South-Sea-Islander's, indolent luxury; of an Algerine's, plunder; of a frontier huntsman's, hardy adventure. So within our own social system: the law of one house is personal display; of another, money; of another, animal comfort; of another, social ambition; of another, unceasing mutual irritation, where each man is an overreaching Esau; of another, petty anxieties, where every woman is a troubled Martha; of another, intellectual improvement; of another, affectionate attentions; of another still, religious duty. And there are some families — Heaven forbear with them! — in which the only law of the house seems to be that the lodgers there shall be in it as little as possible; the problem of every morning being where to spend the evening, — the dreaded curse being the necessity of spending it at home, and home itself sunk into a compound contrivance of dormitory and eating-room. If each one finds it difficult to understand its own ruling trait, it will easily be satisfied of the quality of its neighbors. And it is among the habits of our familiar conversation to specify certain moral attributes as pertaining to certain families, speaking of them collectively.

Observe, too, that this general spirit of the household life is really a more powerful element in it than any special plan or work. Being permanent, it gives a right or wrong character to that multitude of little actions which hardly have much moral significance of their own, and it makes every deed we do more virtuous, or more sinful, by putting into it so much of a good spirit or a bad. This supreme Law of the House bears the same relation to ordinary domestic transactions that political science recognizes between what Lord Bacon called the law of laws, that is, the universal principles by which all governments, however framed, should act for the benefit of the people, and those laws pertaining to a particular state, discriminating as to its several departments, regulating judicial, legislative, and executive functions. It will predominate, in the long run, over all occasional impulses, all the affairs of the day. It is the great controlling influence, determining the spiritual standing of the family. It is the law of the family life.

Observe, also, that no inmate of your house is too inexperienced to have this influence stealing in upon him, moulding his future manhood. The law of the house works itself into the circulations and fibres of every growing branch. The youngest child in the circle is watching your face, committing your tones and motions to memory, taking your most unconscious language for a lesson, and laying up the careless revelations of your frivolity or your piety for future imitation. If he sees that all your familiar arrangements are made to redound to your selfish enjoyment, at the cost of others' welfare, why should he not turn out a self-seeker, — disagreeable and wretched? If he sees that you make worship and conscience subordinate to a bargain, or a pleasure-party, what is to hinder him from growing up into a dishonest speculator or a dissolute prodigal? If, on the other hand, he beholds in your daily example some noble evidence of a devotion to God, and fidelity to right, which shape all your transactions into an offering of religion, then, unless some very cruel seduction besets him from abroad, he is a candidate for a Christian maturity.

This, then, is the second point established, — that there is always a spirit of the house, or law of the family, of one kind or another, blessing or cursing, — forming character, day by day, for salvation or perdition. The practical reflection is, what tremendous consequences to every soul hang on the decision, whether this law is a ruling passion or a ruling principle.

III. But another truth is to come, — a truth to which these preceding ones are but preparatory steps. There is only one law, after all, which can meet, satisfy, and redeem a family of God's children. Without this, whatever desire or purpose takes ascendency, there is no durable order, there is no established peace, there is no spiritual fellowship. I wish to deny no facts, even though, by being misplaced or exaggerated, they may mislead and betray. Admit all that the utmost sophistry, pleading the cause of flesh and the Devil, can pretend. Wealth will do something for you; a library will do something; increasing profits in merchandise, increasing dividends on stocks, a salary that more than covers your expenditure, — verily they that seek these as the supreme good have their reward! Does it satisfy, then, the hunger of an aspiring soul? Does it meet the craving of your soberest, which are your truest, hours? Does it even realize that dim and vague ideal with which you started on your course? Unless you let the friendly authority of the Son of God, who knew all that is in the heart and died to save it from sorrow, answer for you, you must answer for yourself by the fearful process of trying the experiment. Try it; and if you do not die before it is done, you will infallibly admit at last, with a satiated heart and a broken spirit, what you refuse to believe at a Saviour's invitation!

You have seen manhood and womanhood begin their household life, with no deeper purpose than the accidental pleasure of the day; no preparation of faith for any other than times of prosperity or health; no consecration to the God of death and life, of sick-chambers, of the dull waste of hope, and disappointed fortunes, and parting clasps of the hand at death-beds. But neither I, nor you, nor any human witness, ever saw that a life so begun, and lived through on that low level, was felt to answer the high ends for which life was given. There was a certain fading away, year by year, of the meaning that was hid in honest vows; a tragic dying out of all luminous and satisfying thoughts. There will be some low under-note of warning in all endearments and all gladness; some hollow sound in mirth; some sudden drooping of spirits at the end of the feast; some dimness on the fine gold, — wages that enterprise has earned, or prizes that bold ventures have drawn. There will be a dreary look sometimes on the costly furnishings. Curiosities of art and ingenuity will mock the empty spirit. A father's praise will not be a father's blessing; a mother's glance of pride will not be a mother's holy prayer; the brother's departure to other lands will leave no consoling presence of faith to commend him to the God of oceans and of storms; the innocence of the sister will be the charm of earth rather than the benediction of Heaven; and the child's promise, a foreshadowing of honors here, instead of immortality hereafter. Even the sanguine affection that gives the marriage-pledge cannot keep its beauty, its purity, or its power, unless prayers to Heaven relight its decaying flame. The faith of heart in heart will fail, at last, without faith in God. Except you "set your house in order" by the religion of Christ, you throw it open to an inevitable anarchy of passions.

"Set thine house in order," by the faith of the Redeemer who died for thee, by the holy vigilance of a prayerful mind, by enthroning over your every action reverence for Almighty God. Nothing else will bring that order in. However the outward economy may flourish, the omnipotence of Heaven is pledged, that in the spiritual house no order can be, but discord rather, and confusion, and every evil thing, save by faith.

Set thy house in order by a religious faith. Parents, without Christian hearts, not tasting, nor even praying to taste, regeneration for themselves, offer substitutes. There can be no substitute. It is not in the power of irreligious ingenuity to devise one. It is not in the justice or the mercy of God to accept one. Some parents you have known, and some such there are, possibly, amongst you, who seem to have strangely imagined they can live out the remainder of ungodly lives with impunity, if they will atone for their own worldliness by affording their children a good moral education. "Our sons and daughters," they say, "shall learn prayer and holiness; have us excused." God has no relief for thee, under that profane inconsistency. He calls thee, evasive father or timid mother, thee alone, and by thyself, thou wicked and slothful servant, to give thy own soul to him. Set thy house in order; and that the order may come, establish that spiritual economy, where religion is law, first in thy own penitent soul. Order shall not be, except it is Heaven's order; and of that, self-renunciation is the foremost condition. Sunday-schools to lead thy little ones to Heaven! evening-hymns listened to heartlessly by their pillows! an occasional sigh, of mock humility, that they may come out well at last! these are not the gates of safety on which you are to depend. Come out well at last? What right have you to hope they shall ever come out into paths of righteousness, where they shall never see your own feet leading the way?

Set thy house in this order of devotion. It may cost sacrifice and struggle; it must cost repentance, humiliation, breaking up of vicious alliances, abandonment of unrighteous gains; it may cost you the "dread laugh of the world" to bend your knees to your Maker. Does the Eternal Voice say any the less solemnly, "Set thy house in order"? Are there exceptions for your indifference? Are the mandates of eternity to be suspended, are the twelve legions of angels to be perplexed with wonder, are the instant counsels of the God of heaven to be adjourned, for your unyielding pride? Mock not thyself, nor thy Maker, with the decencies of refinement, purchased into thy house with money, with all the accomplishments of many languages and sciences, with elegances of hospitality, and dignity of breeding, and even the correctness of an external prudence hallowed by no trust in the Christ of Calvary, — by crowding these things — O mournful, desperate attempt! — into the empty throne where the love of God alone in Christ Jesus should be!

Set thy house in the spiritual order. Hang its walls with nobler pictures than art ever brought to adorn Vatican or Escurial, — with the living beauty of holy deeds. Arrange in its spiritual economy, each in its own appointed place, charities that shall make its air genial, solid virtues of integrity and faith to be its foundation-stones, graces of forbearance and meekness and gentleness to embellish it, hopes of immortality to light it, and peace which comes of trust to fill it with fragrant incense. As there never yet was order without law, nor law without authority, nor authority without a supreme or ruling head, — so in the household, as in the soul's single life, there can be no setting in order, unless Christ's cross is lifted up in the midst of it.

There is another clause of the text which I have not repeated; and how soberly does it admonish us, that any other order than this I have described Providence must some day disturb, — breaking in upon the visible circle with what a desolating hand! "Thus saith the Lord, Set thine house in order; for thou shalt die, and not live." Order in the outward family, — in the perpetual array of sons and daughters, offspring and parents, — does Scripture bid you seek for this? Eyes blinded and burnt by scalding tears, for sudden and bitter bereavements, will weep yet again and again, as they wander over the broken group that gathers now at their side, searching for some vanished form. And the mourners are ready to cry, "O tantalizing expectation, that we should ever see *that* order restored, and the beloved ranks of manly strength, or maidenly bloom, or childish grace, refilled!" Patience; for it cannot be. But if the other order is unbroken, — if Faith waits in it with her heavenward look, and Hope with her strong anchor, and Resignation, saying,

"Thy will be done," — then the vacancies of the earthly house shall be supplied again in the heavenly; the departed shall come back to the places that knew them before, in tabernacles not made with hands; the order of Christian affections here shall be a type of the perfect order of the new family in the skies.

"Thou shalt die, and not live." We cannot see before us. No hand can tear one leaf from the sealed book where the recording angel has written against all our names the day of our great change. A veil shuts close down before our eyes on the very spot where we stand. This year, or another; yourself first, or one you love better than yourself; by slow decline, or swift destruction: these are secrets. But there is no dimness over the command that points us to the open way of life; no uncertainty in the immortal promise, "Set thy house in order"; and then, though "absent from the body," thou shalt be present with "the Father of Jesus Christ, our Lord, of whom the whole family, in heaven and earth, is named."

SERMON XIV.

CHILDREN, — HOW TO BE RECEIVED.

WHOSOEVER SHALL RECEIVE THIS CHILD IN MY NAME, RECEIVETH ME. — Luke ix. 48.

IT sometimes seems to be understood that Christ, in these words, means merely to commend childlike qualities, — like moral simplicity, guilelessness, trust, affectionateness. We have independent proofs enough that all these traits engaged Christ's personal interest, and are enjoined by the whole spirit of his religion on every disciple. Wherever the divine light really shines, these pure qualities will open their beauty and fragrance to the air, as gracefully as the first wild-flowers obey the solicitings of the sunshine in spring. Undoubtedly, as Jesus elsewhere says, whoever will not receive the kingdom of Heaven with this simple, unaffected childlikeness, this heart of unquestioning faith, this subordination of intellectual pride and personal ambition to spontaneous Christian love, cannot enter therein.

But here the statement is different. We are told what it is to *receive* a little child. The Master instructs us how to greet new-born souls on their entrance into life, with what feelings to take them into our arms, what estimate to put on their immortal capacity, and with what grand purpose to educate them. All this he includes in the precept, that we "receive them in his name." Could the sacred and profound and peculiar duty which Christendom owes to its offspring be more comprehensively declared? How can we be said to receive children in the name of Christ? Plainly enough, it is not by lavishing upon them a sentimental admiration, or an indulgent fondness; it is not by making them the materials of a thoughtless amusement; it is not by rejoicing over them with a selfish sort of pride, as the heirs of our property or the upholders of our worldly reputation; it is not by carelessness of their spiritual training and neglect of their souls. On the contrary, it is by regarding them as the lawful inheritors of Christ's spiritual promises, — as the intended members of his Church, and imitators of his life, and partakers of his redemption, — as the appointed subjects of baptism, of prayer, and of inward renewal, — as being born, each one, to yield the world a Christian character, and thus as being profanely and terribly wronged whenever an irreligious indifference cheats them of this immortal portion. This, Christ would teach us, is to receive children in his name. This is to take them for what they are; solemnly to take them into our hands, as out of the hand of God, and while clasping them to our breasts with natural human love, to look reverently up to their higher Father, and lift consecrating petitions that they may be saved in the life everlasting. Do this, and you will have no occasion to run in search of a visible empire, or outward honors. You may cease contending with one another, ambitious disciples, about high places in the government, and turn your emulation into a more domestic realm. Do this, parents, and the kingdom of Heaven will come in the natural way, handed down from parent to child in the blood and all the hereditary influences of believing generations, spreading and gaining power with all the growth and progress of the race. Do this, fathers and mothers, and instead of prostituting your energies to base contentions after the prizes of fortune or reputation, you will find your dignity and reward in developing imperishable graces in your children's hearts. Instead of honoring earthly princedoms, or an aristocracy of wealth, you will honor the Divine image in the lowliest infant. To symbolize this spiritual truth, the Divine Redeemer himself became a child; he passed to the glory of his mediatorship and the right hand of the Father through the swaddling-clothes that all humanity must wear; he entered into the complete experience of the race by being a babe in a cradle; the sages knelt at the manger; intellect bowed to spirituality. And now, to this day, whatever Christian parent, out of a living and supreme faith in Christ, recognizes the sanctity of a child's life, and diligently trains him up to be a disciple, receives that child in the name of Christ, and gives the surest evidence that he has received Christ himself. He helps to fulfil the final and inspiring prediction with which the prophet of the old dispensation ushered in and described the new, — that the hearts of the fathers should be turned to the children, and the hearts of the children to their fathers.

Let me ask you to look at some of the popular habits of regarding children, — yourselves judging how prevalent they may be, — and contrast them with what it would be to receive them in the name of Christ.

One class of parents receive the little child in the name of money. You may think the charge of such a revolting profanation a harsh one to bring against any members of a respectable community. Would that all who are prompt to repel it in language were as scrupulous to disown it practically! But look underneath words and the resentments of a false sensibility, to facts. If there are any among you who oftenest think of your children in connection with property, either through the inquiry how much they will cost or how much they will hereafter come to possess; if there are any who make the foremost pleasure in your children to consist in arraying them in the costly fineries of an extravagant expenditure, pampering your own vanity by sending them forth to the gazers of the streets, decked in the badges of a weak display, using the poor body as a dumb frame whereon to spread forth your own fopperies, and initiating their waking senses into the accursed thirst for show that fevers all our public manners; or if there are any who, by positive example or indirect suggestion, breed in your children the pernicious notion that what we live for as we grow up is to be richer than our neighbors, — then you do, in reality, receive the little child in the name of money. Merchandise is made of his mind and his heart. The same effect is produced, in a different way, if, by a penurious temper, you so misproportion your outlay as to pinch the nobler and more generous impulses in your children, thus inculcating parsimony as a lesson. I do not deny that a certain impulsive affection may be mixed with this shameful abuse. That affection may be very strong. But the tender and holy love of a Christian parentage, which God can bless, is not there. You would deem it a horrible cruelty if any father were to brand with a red-hot dollar the forehead of his boy. But you may scorch your child's spirit with the mark of a more fearful and lasting disfigurement; and that you do, whenever your conversation, your passionate eagerness for gain, or your daily practice of estimating men and things by their money-value, fixes slowly but deeply in his mind the avaricious lust that is never satisfied with getting. He will take the mould of his surroundings. The style of living that you make his daily scenery, the tone of talk that you make his common atmosphere vocal with, will reflect themselves infallibly in his future manhood. He will have a large soul, or a belittled one; he will be brave and self-poised, or a feeble driveller; he will be an independent leader of public opinion, or a miserable slave to his own interests; — in a word, he will be a nobly developed child or a spoilt one, according as you receive him in the name of Christ, or in the name of money.

Another class of parents receive the little child in the name of worldly success. By this estimation of childhood I mean something a little less sottish than the one just noticed, because it admits some less gross ingredients. To receive a child in the name of worldly success, is to be chiefly anxious for his social position and his business prospects. It is to make everything in his training bear on his thrift in trade, or, with the daughter, on her marriage with a thrifty husband. It is forgotten, that, for every man, there is a better kind of success than success in his trade, — not inconsistent with that, but, on the contrary, helping it as righteousness always strengthens prosperity, — and that for every woman there is a devout womanhood attainable, more honorable than any wedlock. The mistake I speak of is not inconsistent with the utmost pains to furnish children with a good secular education. Only every science studied must light some path to enterprise, and of all sciences calculation is the chief; every language learned must be a stepping-stone to a profitable situation; every talent must be convertible into current coin; every accomplishment must prepare the way to a paying office, or conciliate custom. No faculty like the faculty of skilful traffic or pushing for promotion. If we were stark materialists, — and nothing is more exactly adapted to degrade us into materialism, — this would be a very acceptable philosophy of life and learning, — a life without a faith, and a learning without a Bible. But the moment you look down a little way into the unsounded and infinite mysteries of your child's immortality; the moment you open the New Testament and sink back into the sober convictions which its inspired sentences reawaken in you; the moment you look around you at the ever-burning fires of trial, like disease, or natural calamity, or bereavement, which try every man's work, and see how all earthly goods turn to ashes in those fires; the moment you look forward and in solemn anticipation let the Divine word lead you, following your child, into the presence of the unchangeable realities and the certain judgment, — then you feel again how different a thing it is to receive and treat that child in the safe and life-giving name of Christ, from receiving and treating him in the name of a worldly success the most brilliant or most substantial.

Another class still, not unrepresented among us, receive the child in the name of selfish joy. In infancy, the radiant little creature is the graceful toy of idle hours. Later, he is the precious minister to a proud complacency, — the necessary image, and probably the central image, to fill out the circle of personal comfort and delight. The father comes home from the engrossments of business, he takes out his neck a moment from the yoke of traffic, and his children are the welcome instruments of his recreation. The mother watches her darling boy, or girl, with a vigilance that never flags nor cools. But there is such a thing as maternal vigilance prompted by mere human fondness, or the passion for the dear one's presence, — all holiness crushed out of it, because it is without God. You know what the grave does with that. And there is the vigilance of a Christian mother's love, more faithful unspeakably, and over that you know that death and the whole army of diseases have no power.

I know of hardly any gloomier sight in the world than one of these homes ruled by this world's temper, where this unsanctified pride in children's beauty or attainments, however strong or kind, is nothing under the sun but an extension of poor self-love, — the celestial quality, the divine element, of parental affection, perished from it; homes where the spiritual law and life in Christ find no grateful recognition, exercise no binding control; homes where everything else is done for children except that one thing without which all else is worthless, receiving them in the name of Christ; where parents gaze into the child's face only to see a reflection of their own personal satisfaction, and cling to the frail body all the more tenaciously and desperately because there is no tranquil looking forward beyond the bodily separation. Again and again I have involuntarily shuddered at one of these melancholy spectacles, — all the happiness so superficial, so fragile, so sure to be rent to pieces presently and scattered on the winds. I have seen the sad instinctive terror with which the thought, or the uttered hint, that the child might some time die, was stifled. I have seen the dreadful struggle of unbelieving love, to put aside and cover up the irresistible decrees of God. A pure and lovely child in such a house, in the arms of such a father, ought to be painted like a spotless angel held in the grasp of some cool, calculating, faithless demon of the pit. O was there no better, no more spiritual, no more Christian welcome, for that stainless heart on God's earth than this? Love is there, if so bad a counterfeit of God's best gift deserves the name; but think of the anguish that waits inevitably on unbelieving affections. The hour comes. If the dark distress of moral ruin, a wrecked conscience, does not come, that other event comes that is inexorable. No selfishness is hard enough, or firm or close enough, to ward off disorders or baffle Providence. And when it comes, God spare the anguish of the parent that is bereaved without Christ, and so sorrows without hope! To those that have never tasted the experience, these words may sound unreal; but all of you who have looked on your dead child's face, know that in that hour there are but three realities in the universe: one of these is sorrow, — and it is sorrow, utter and hopeless to all them that do not feel the other two, — God, and the eternal life brought to light in Jesus Christ our Lord.

There is another class of parents yet, — beside those that receive the child in the name of Christ, — and it is made up of those that receive him in the name of a blind fatality. That is to say, they have a general and honest enough wish that their children might be found on the side of goodness; but they fail to see that the work of putting them there is a business of their own. They have not given up the hope that their offspring may turn out well; but they leave the sacred, slow, responsible toil of *making* it turn out so untouched. They answer to your surprise with some vicious maxim about all children being obliged to go through a period of insubordination, and knowing the world, — which commonly means knowing everything that is worst in the world. They trust to accident. They hand over their own children's immortal purity and welfare, like pagans, to luck. At this terrible life-and-death encounter between a young soul and perdition, they, the parents, are only to look on! At that mortal struggle they are idle spectators! Everything else they have done, or are willing to do, for their child, everything save taking up, with ear nest and ardent purpose, his spiritual nurture and his Christian salvation. The utmost they can give besides clothes, board, spending-money, and schooling, is an occasional moral reflection, or an introduction to the minister, or a few months of irregular attendance at Sunday-school, and possibly the birthday present of a Bible with a clasp, which no example of their own encourages him to open. Systematic, patient, persisting, entreating, prayerful nurture of the undying spirit, — there is none. Yet is there one of you all that can deny that this training of the soul is infinitely the most weighty and solemn of all duties to the child? Why do you not receive him, then, in the name of Christ?

But, praise Heaven! there is another class; and there is no cause, in nature or reason, but only in our dull and sluggish hearts, why it should not come to include all the others. The Master has shown us a more excellent way. That other name, the only one under heaven whereby we can be saved, is given us. Bring the children, says the Saviour, unto me. He that receiveth them in my name, receiveth me. What, then, is included in that Christian treatment of the young, as before God and his Church?

First, that, having yourselves been joined to Christ by repentance and faith, you hold and treat them as the rightful heirs of a spiritual life in yourselves. You have more to transmit to them than your constitutional temperament, your property, and your name. When God permitted you to be parents of living children, he bound you, by a law that admits no escape, to breathe into them a higher life than that of the body or the mind, even that spiritual life whereof all make themselves partakers who heartily believe in the Son of God. And this goes out of you by other means than formal speech. Let it be in you, and it must emanate, by unconscious waves of influence, from look and voice and attitude, and all the countless and nameless tokens of parental faith. What ordained preacher has the power of a Christian mother? I have been told, that, in the wonderful and gracious experiments made in our times for kindling up a little light even in the darkness of idiocy, the first ray of intelligence that is observed to gleam across the imbecile's vacant face, and the first pulse of feeling strong enough to overmaster furious passions and arrest the wandering eyes, are commonly observed to appear when some gentle touch or tone of womanly kindness rekindles in the heart the flickering and faint impressions of a mother's tenderness. Could any proof more striking show us what lips, what countenance, whose pleadings and intercessions, ought first to dedicate the child to holiness and the Holy One? Even the old Romans, in their heathenism, had a touching superstition of holding the face of the new-born infant upward to the heavens, — signifying, by thus presenting its forehead to the stars, that it was to look above the world into celestial glories. The goddess that was supposed to preside over this aspiring ceremony was named from the word "*levare*," which means "to raise aloft." It was a superstition then.

Christianity dispels the fable and the doubt, and gives us the clear realization of that dim, pagan yearning, in a Christian baptism and training. What shall be said of those nominally Christian parents who do not discover even the heathen's sensibility, — and, with all the blessed ordinances of the Son of Mary in their sight, content with low and earthly satisfactions, refuse to their children even the Church's benediction?

Again, the spiritual obligation involved in receiving a child in the name of Christ requires that you esteem him, even in his childhood, as a sharer with yourself in a Divine covenant. He is to be sheltered under that sacred promise, reaching down from Abraham through all dispensations, by which the Heavenly Father admits the offspring of all believing and faithful disciples to the same secret privileges with their parents, — provided only they will consent. This makes the title to Christian citizenship hereditary. It rests with the voluntary consent of the child, when he is free to choose or to reject, to ratify and confirm the baptismal pledge which the parents made in his behalf; above all, it rests with the parent to follow up the sprinkling of water with daily and devout instruction in divine knowledge, — line upon line, precept upon precept. These things being insured, God is not forgetful of his promise, nor will he leave faithful servants to strive alone. Keep that promise ever before your baptized child's eyes. There will be sanctity in its encouragement and power in its restraint.

Yet further, God requires us to regard our children as an element in our judgment. We shall meet them again. Face to face we shall all stand, when the books are opened. No daysman can come in between us and the spirits that have been ripened in our care. Their souls will be required at our hands. These broken circles will have one reassembling more; and there the Judge will make that awful inquisition, from which no parental heart will be allowed to shrink back. There the questioning will be, In whose name received ye the immortal ones? In the name of money? in the name of worldly success? or of selfish joy? or of a careless unconcern? or in the name of Christ? And whosoever has received them in the name of Christ, "he," saith Christ, "hath received me"; and that sentence is his everlasting reward.

And now, do any of us ask what constitutes the true Christian fidelity of parents, and what is the method of this high duty? Let us remember to ask that question of Him who alone is the Guide. He answers it by his Word; he will answer it, even more and more clearly, to the sincerely seeking heart. These simple truths we know, and may affirm confidently.

There must be prayer. Your child must know, he must see, he must feel, that between your parent-heart and Him who is the Infinite Father of all alike, there is open and conscious communion. Till there is established, in all simplicity, this confiding and daily intercourse between the soul and Heaven, you have not received your child in the name of Christ. What was testified by one of the strong statesmen of our early American history, might be declared, in spirit, probably by nearly all the best men that have lived in Christendom. "I believe," he said, "that I should have been swept away by the flood of French infidelity, if it had not been for one thing, — the remembrance of the time when my sainted mother used to make me kneel by her bedside, taking my little hands folded in hers, and causing me to repeat the Lord's Prayer."

But the whole work, or privilege, of Christian culture for the child is by no means to be handed over to the mother. That has been too much the fashion with men. When did God excuse fathers? Where is the permission for one parent to add to the necessary hours of absence from home, at his business, an evening at the billiard-room or a Sunday in the country? In order to the full and right influence in forming the child's character into holiness, both sides are wanting; God asks the Christian father as much as the Christian mother; the Apostles adjure the father oftenest. Buxtorf tells us, the Jewish fathers held themselves responsible for the guilt of their children's sins till they were thirteen years old. In that great reckoning at which we have already glanced, the Divine voice will question with both alike; nor does the Lord say of either one alone, of woman more than man, that whosoever receiveth the child in his name, receiveth him.

Moreover, there must be regular biblical teaching. No child is received in Christ's name, that is not reverently and carefully taught Christ's Gospel. Somewhere and somehow, not by chance, not at interrupted and infrequent seasons, but patiently, and humbly, and week by week, that wonderful, most ancient and Eternal Book must be opened before him. Its sublime yet simple truths, plain to the child's understanding, its holy personages, its grand Prophets and ardent Apostles, its venerable patriarchs and its inspired children, must all pass, in their robes of light and forms of singular majesty and beauty, before him. Its psalms must be sung into his soul. Its beatitudes and commandments must be fixed in his remembrance. Its parables must engage his fancy. Its miracles must awe his wonder. Its cross, and ark, and all its sacred emblems, must people his imagination. Without that Bible, no child born among us can come to Him whom only the Bible reveals.

Then there must be a distinct Christian purpose, penetrating the household, elevating the whole spirit of the home, and evermore resisting temptation. There is a fable, in German literature, of the daughter of an Erl-king whose business it is to tempt little children away from parents and home. She comes even into the parents' presence, and there, with fair appearance and cunning disguises, she deceives them in her malignant purpose, contriving to whisper into the ear of the unsuspecting one many an artful promise of fine shows and happy plays. And thus at last she wiles away victim after victim into a dreary land, in the midst of dark and shadowy forests. Do we not all know of something answering to this crafty child-thief? Temptation is the Erlking's daughter that never dies. She tears away children from the blessed peace of their Father's house, — from virtue, from happiness, from heaven. You, parents, must be watching, or before you are aware your beloved ones will be caught and carried into the wilderness.

And finally, knowing well how little is the most our weak arms can do, and how infinite are the appointed mercies of our God, we are to bring our little ones, as we are to come ourselves, to the fountain's brink, — to the great streams of spiritual benediction and grace that flow down through the channels of the Church, — to the baptismal font, — and, if only their own free-will shall afterwards consent, to the table and love-feast of our Lord. Come first yourselves. For where the waters of purification and renewal are poured, there the forgiving voice speaks; and where strength is gained by communion, there is the entering in of a peace never known besides. "The just man" not only "walketh in his integrity"; "his children are blessed after him." May the great Shepherd gather us all, us and our little ones, the fathers, the mothers, the children, into his immortal fold; out of the far country of a wilful and worldly and alienated life, into the Church on earth, into the larger Church, the household undivided and everlasting in heaven!

SERMON XV.

ENTRANCE INTO THE CHURCH.

AND CRISPUS BELIEVED ON THE LORD, WITH ALL HIS HOUSE. — Acts xviii. 8.

THE Christian faith is shown to us, in the Acts of the Apostles, working out its first simple developments in human society. In that plain picture, we see how this new force, this divine idea, behaved itself in the world of living men, and women, and children; how it acted on them, and laid hold of them; how it took possession of them, and organized them into a peculiar institution, which has lived on ever since, — the Church. Christ's visible presence is withdrawn out of the world at his resurrection; but thenceforth he appears to mankind in the living body of his Church, which, holding in its heart and its hand his Spirit and his Word, takes the place of his physical form. And now, from this short statement I have just read about one of the first converts, in the earliest record of Church history, we catch a glimpse into the practical working of the system. It appears that persons came into the Church, not only as separate individuals, but by families. From this, as well as several other passages, we find, that when the parents, or heads of households, became Christian believers, so did their children. All were baptized together. So, in one place, we read of "the church which is in the house of Nymphas"; showing that such a group of believers, comprising parents and their children, might constitute a church of itself.* How much beauty and sanctity there would be in such a spectacle, — a church in each house, — and how mightily the world would gain in Christian order, purity, and power, if it were generally realized, you can readily imagine. It corresponds to the whole sentiment of revelation, in all the stages of its progress. The covenant made with the Patriarch was made with Abraham and *his seed after him*. Throughout the Mosaic period, children were included with their fathers in all the blessings of the elder Testament. "The promise is unto you *and your children*," is the constant doctrine through all God's messages to the Israelites. We are expressly told, that under Christ, in the New Testament, the same covenant is renewed, only expanded and deepened. Throughout, the law of descent is carefully respected. The hereditary tie is recognized. Offspring, at birth, are supposed to be bound up in the same bond of Christian privileges and helps which encircles their believing progenitors. Does our practice, in our modern churches, imply that this is our belief?

From time to time you have heard affirmed and reaffirmed this view of the birth-relation of children born of Christian parents to the Church, especially in those bearings of it which relate to the administration of the

* Irenæus, of the first age after the apostolic, referring to the administration of baptism, says: "Christ came to save all persons by himself, who by him are regenerated to God, — infants, and little ones, and children, and youths, and elder persons."

ordinances, — Baptism and the Lord's Supper. The same idea seems to have been received, with different degrees of clearness, in former periods. It was distinctly declared by many of the early theological teachers, by whom God planted his Church in New England, and it has found, more recently, a few earnest advocates; but hardly anywhere anything like a real adoption into practice, so as to present a church formed after its plan. If what I have just said be tenable, then it has these weighty and decisive testimonies, for all Christian minds, in its justification: first, the undeniable usage of the apostolic age, — the purest, because the nearest to the Master; secondly, the explicit sanction of the authority of the New Testament on the matter; and thirdly, the analogy and agreement of the Old Testament, reaching back to the primitive era, disclosing God's whole design for the saving of the world, as it opens and ripens from Abraham, or Adam rather, to Jesus of Nazareth.

My object at present is not only to remind you afresh of the important place held by this great truth in reference to your personal and domestic welfare, but to trace it out into its necessary connections with the whole position and constitution of the Church, — inquiring, with you, what the Christian Church is; how entrance is got into it; and what are its claims, functions, and privileges. Of course, I must confine myself, with a scope so wide, to compressed statements merely, leaving trains of argument and illustrations aside. I wish it might be particularly understood, that, so far from dealing with matters that have no application to any but those who are church-members already, I address myself especially to those who have taken no part in any public profession, and do not share in the communion which is the common token and privilege of members.

I. What is the Church? On the authority of the New Testament, I say it is the body of persons who believe in Jesus Christ, the Son of God, and Saviour of men, crucified and risen; and so believe in him as to be personally conscious of a supreme desire to live his spiritual life, to resemble him, and be his true redeemed disciples. This definition takes the whole qualification for church-membership out of the power of sects and external ceremonies, lodging it in the internal region of the heart, — among the affections and motives, — whence all life makes its way out into speech, profession, and conduct. Its only test, therefore, is spiritual, not formal. The definition also proposes terms that are strict, without being absurd, and reasonable, without being lax. It requires that the purpose to be a Christian, within and without, shall be supreme over all other purposes, — take precedence in every deliberate choice, and express itself in prayer and in righteousness. Love to God as manifest in Christ, and love to man as God's child, must be the ruling affections in the soul, — whether they have conformed the character perfectly to them, or not. The Church is the aggregate of these consecrated souls, aiming and longing, above all things, to live righteously; irrespective of names, of forms, of creeds, of age, of place, except so far as these affect this internal, central consecration to Christ. If there were only "two or three" such persons in the world, they would be a church, and Christ, fulfilling his promise, would be there in the midst of them. In all periods since Christ ascended, this has been the Church. It is distinct from all other bodies, —

whether scientific, civil, educational, benevolent, moral, or even religious, if they are not religious after the way and Gospel of Christ. Its boundaries, as it is embodied in actual persons, may be indistinct to man's eye, but they are plain to God's; and the definition is plain. The Church is that body of people, in whatever age or nation, of which Christ is literally and spiritually the Head. And any one particular church, here or there, is a smaller collection of such people, and so a branch of the Church Universal.

II. How, then, does any individual enter into this Church, so as to become a member of it, enjoying the privileges and incurring the responsibilities of a member? I answer, By conversion. This is for all those who have been living any time outside of the Church, — that is, without the supreme purpose I have spoken of, — without a conscious dedication to holiness, without treating Jesus Christ, in heart and life, as Lord and Master. All such must obviously be regenerated, before they can be *in* or *of* the Church. Hitherto they have been living only that natural life, whose ruling motives are mere selfish instincts, whose appetites and passions were not subjected to conscience, whose better traits were spontaneous and irregular, not having taken on the character of principle, and whose external proprieties were the result only of some form of worldly interest or policy. In all such persons, there must be a new birth of Christian conviction. There must be a sincere penitence for this sinful habit, which has disobeyed and denied God's commandment. There must be a holy heart, with prayer in it, created by regeneration and washing of the Holy Spirit. There must be a turning about from the old, false direction, which led away from Christ, to the opposite, which sets the face towards him. Whether slow or swift, — and it certainly cannot be too swift nor too early, and the earlier the easier, — this conversion is indispensable. We see many instances of it in the New Testament. In those early times, it commonly involved a change of the mind as well as of the heart; that is, a Pagan or a Jew must change the whole opinion of his head respecting religion, as well as the love and motive in his heart. His nominal and intellectual belief must undergo a revolution. Accordingly, to describe this transfer from one scheme to another, we find the terms "conversion," and "believing on the Lord Jesus Christ," used in the New Testament synonymously and interchangeably. Now there may be cases among us of the same radical and mental change as with all heathens, Jews, Mahometans. But otherwise, and where, as with most of us, there is no mental dissent from the evidences and truths of Christianity, the conversion wanted is only that of the heart, giving that up to Christ. Then the individual can clearly say, I have resolved, God's grace helping, to be a Christian disciple. And whenever that is really done, the soul truly becomes invisibly united to Christ, and so, of course, is virtually a member of his body or Church.

But souls may also come into a certain relation to Christ's Church by spiritual adoption. And all those, I maintain, are subjects for this, who are born of believing parents, or parents who are members in it. If they discover from the first no repugnance to holiness, no settled alienation from Christ, but appear to have had the renewing work of the Spirit wrought upon them in a steady and early grace, so that they seem "sanctified from the womb," they pass into Christ's Church as they pass into a self-conscious experience. By this I mean that all children so born are to be received into the arms of their parents, and treated as the sacred property of the Church. The Church lays claim to them, from the very outset, as her own. Her presumption and prayer for them is that they will walk from their childhood in newness of life. She sets the sign of that belief and hope. Properly trained up, by spiritual teaching and example, under the blessing of the Spirit, they are never to know of a time when they were not included in God's covenant of promise. Instead of being cast out, as little aliens, to run wild awhile in the world, having no part nor lot in the blessed Christian shelter and inheritance, they are to be always folded inside that security. The Church is to come forward, in the person of those parents who are its members, — the divinely and naturally appointed guardians of these young souls, — and thus press them to its own gracious bosom, and feed them on its own heavenly truth; until such time as they are old enough, by their own conscious and personal responsible act, to confirm the covenant which their parents and the Church made for them in their infancy, by openly espousing the membership. For I do not overlook the dreadful possibility, that, in the stress of temptation, and a depraved inclination, the child, even when all this has been done for him, may wander off and be a prodigal. He may viciously disown the covenant made in his behalf. He may plunge into sin, in despite of all. Then his only way back into the Church of Christ must be by conversion, as with the children of unbelievers. All I say is, that such instances ought to be prevented or diminished by wiser and more Christian notions and practices. Let the Christian parents continually speak to the young child of Church privileges, of the joy and the duty of his Christian heritage and home. Let that child have the doctrines and life of Christ faithfully instilled into his soul, by domestic instruction and family prayer. Let him be reminded of his baptismal dedication, and taught to live worthily of it. No magical, talismanic effect is thus to be wrought upon him, but a perfectly natural and simple one, standing in harmony with all other educational influences, and guaranteed also a peculiar blessing. This Christian child, like others, must have a spiritual nature and life formed upon him, in addition to his natural life. Only, this blessed boon of a new and holy heart steals in upon him gradually, by way of his parents' eyes and voice and prayers, from the very dawn of his consciousness, grows with his growth, hardens with his muscles, expands with his understanding, and matures in him as gently and regularly as any of the growths of the forest or the field; so that there shall be no period in his remembrance, when he was not moving straight on towards a ripe Christian character, and full communion in the Church. All this I place in contrast with our strange and savage habit of turning off our little ones to feed on the husks and chaff of the senses, till some dreadful wrench of sorrow, after they have grown up, possibly wakens a few of them to conviction, and drives them back, broken-spirited, from the far country where they had wandered, to their Father's house.

III. This brings me on, as the next step, to the place and the meaning of Baptism. The value of that ordinance is sufficiently attested throughout the New Testament. Christ himself, notwithstanding his divine elevation, submitted himself to it that he might fulfil all righteousness.

So early as his conversation with Nicodemus, while he was announcing the grand principles of his new kingdom, he spoke of the new birth as requiring both the Spirit and water. He enjoined its universal observance, through the Church of all nations, in his last charge to his disciples. By studying the design of it in other parts of the New Testament, we can come to only one understanding of its object. Everywhere it signified the entrance of the subject of it into the Church of Christ. It was the outward sign of that single fact, — the beginning of the Christian life. It was applied to adults and children indiscriminately; for we read of whole households baptized. Whenever any person was converted, that is, became a true believer in Christ, young or old, he was baptized; and that was the only ceremony of admission into the Church. After baptism he communed, as a matter of course. According to the convenience of climate, and the usage of the Oriental nations, this baptism was doubtless by the immersion of the whole body. But, obviously enough, what the Spirit sought, as a means of outward order and general benefit, was simply the outward application of water, and not the quantity of it.

With what understanding, then, may a Christian minister administer the rite of baptism now? I answer, it must be according to one of the three following modes: —

1. Baptism may be applied, according to the whole Scriptural doctrine I have been opening, to the children of believers in communion with Christ's Church. In that case, the ordinance is the outward sign and seal that the children, who receive it, follow the organic law of their parents, and are the rightful property of the Church. The Church comes forward, and stretches out her arms, with holy sprinkling, to claim and bless the new-born immor-

tal. The parents engage, for the offspring, the blessings of the same covenant that covers themselves. Parental love, if it is Christian, cannot do less. To refuse would really be worse than the unnaturalness of disowning them; for, in the latter case, they are only turned out of the earthly home; in the former, out of God's spiritual home, and denied the saving nurture of the Christian family. Baptism is here put, where the New Testament puts it, at the beginning of the Christian life. For, as the adult convert begins that life at his conversion, so the child of believers is presumed to begin it at his birth. Baptism signifies a faithful hope that the child will grow up a Christian, and a reverent trust that the regenerating spirit may already be descending upon him. This kind of baptism is so clearly the right kind, that we must long for the time when there shall be no occasion for any other.

2. Baptism may be applied to persons who have advanced some way into their natural life, not baptized in their childhood, and now resolved to be of Christ's Church, because they are regenerated, or Christian-minded. Here, exactly as before, the rite marks the beginning of the Christian life: only that beginning lies at a later point in the person's history. Here the act is a self-dedication, — the individual who comes into the Church thus doing for himself what no Christian parent did for him. So far, all is consistent and obvious.

3. But there is a third class. Parents who have never manifested a desire to be of Christ's Church themselves, nor openly avowed discipleship, seek to have their children baptized. When this request is granted, if the foregoing positions are sound, it must be on one of two understandings: either that these parents, though not avow-

edly church-members, are so earnestly possessed of the spirit of Christian piety and of all Christian purposes, that they are approved believers in the sight of the Great Head of the Church, and so members of the Church invisible, — which would always be the supposition most grateful to entertain; or else, where this presumption is inevitably excluded, the ceremony must be another thing, — an act of pious intention, a consecration, perhaps, not without salutary impressions, springing from a thoughtful parental regard, but not the sign of induction into Christ's body. Let this question be remembered, however: Are not parents, not being church communicants themselves, who provide baptism for their children, bound to consider very deeply whether consistency does not require them to observe, in behalf of their own souls, the same veneration for ordinances that they profess in behalf of their progeny? And how can they expect these to obey God, and belong to Christ, if they themselves do not go before in the appointed way?

IV. This brings us on to consider the place and signification of communion at the Lord's Supper. By all that has gone before, that service is not what *makes* any of us members in the Church, but it is both a privilege and a duty consequent upon such membership. The true formula would be, not, "I commune, therefore I am a church-member"; but, "I am a church-member, therefore I commune." What gives any of you a title to participate at the Supper is Christian baptism, because, as I have said, baptism is the sign of the beginning of the Christian life, whether administered in infancy in the parental covenant, or afterwards, on conviction and spiritual renewing. It follows, therefore, that all baptized persons are privileged to be candidates for full communion in the Church, whenever they will personally present their claim.

At the same time, they must personally present it. It is an act wholly within their own choice and responsibility. Such choosing is wholesome, and, for a free agent, quite necessary. A moral act done for a child cannot force or bind his liberty when he grows up. The baptismal covenant only throws about him its gracious influences, pledges the Eternal Help in his behalf, and welcomes him to the Saviour's organized body. But he must be free to live outside if he will. This view makes his alienation his own act, and casts the terrible accountability therefor on his rebellious violence, which tears him away from his home. His home, and his belongings, are within his Father's house. On the other hand, if he will, as soon as he is old enough to understand and weigh the matter for himself, come straight forward to the Master's table, he thereby recognizes, confirms, ratifies, for himself, — in fact, makes his own act, — what his Christian parents did for him. His voluntary communing is, then, precisely what some Christians call it, a confirmation.

If we had a definite and orderly system among us, as one must heartily wish on every account we had, then I suppose a plan something like this might be found at once perfectly simple and practicable, and also full of most effective and glorious fruits. In every parish, by every minister, let there be kept a record of all children baptized into the Church. Each year, at a stated and convenient time, let the minister call together, as a matter of course, but by personal and direct invitation, all such young persons, so baptized, as have, within the year preceding, reached a certain suitable age, — suppose fifteen years. Let him bring them under a brief course of friendly and religious instruction, in addition to any Sunday-school or domestic teaching, so faithfully reminding them of the parental covenant and other obligations, and renewing in this form the demand of Christ and the Church, that they come into the fold, and stand pledged for their Divine Master; and, if proper dispositions exist, at the end of such tuition, admitting them. At the same time, let him offer corresponding instruction to all unbaptized children; striving thus for their conversion, or spiritual renewing, their baptism into the Church, and their admission to the Supper. When any family pass from one parish to another, let them procure from the one they leave to the one they join, a letter, signifying not only the communicants among them, but the names and ages of the baptized children, that they may be properly taken up and nurtured in their new religious home. Who can tell what noble and vital accessions of holiness and strength the Church might gain, in such an ordering of her internal economy? What spectacle can be conceived more full of moral beauty and promise, than ranks of the young, thus early, and while they need the hallowed securities of faith most urgently, pressing straight forward into the gates of the kingdom, — this, instead of what we now too often see, the shame of our Christendom, and the sorrow of all devout hearts, namely, crowds of bewildered and neglected youths, plunging fearfully away, unguarded, into the perils and vices of the world, broken hearts, and ruined hopes, and characters lost, lost beyond recall?

If any are still disposed to inquire *why* they should commune at the Lord's Supper, a complete answer could be given only in much greater space than is now at my command. Let these simple reasons enter into your reflections, and not be dismissed till they are pondered fairly: — 1. Because God, the Maker of our frame, has so shaped and colored the whole structure of our being, that there is an exact adaptation between spiritual life and progress, and this memorial ordinance. So much is settled, by the authority of his own word, and by the vastly accumulating testimony of the millions of believers, in all the lengthening generations of the Church. The soul and the Supper of communion meet one another, and are meant for one another. 2. Jesus himself, the tenderest friend, the dying Saviour, the spotless sacrifice "for us the unjust," the divine and gentle Lord, has enjoined it, under the most impressive conditions, on all his followers that truly love him, — reason enough, to human feeling, if every other failed. 3. There is a personal satisfaction resulting from it, — a satisfaction not realized, of course, to those that have never come where it is tasted, but very real and unspeakably precious to those that have. 4. It is a testimony to the Divine cause, to God's law, and Christ's kingdom in the world; and when the two opposing forces, righteousness and sin, God and mammon, are drawn up in as sharp and bitter a warfare as they are everywhere about us yet, it is cowardly and slothful for us not to take open ground, on the Lord's side, or on Satan's. 5. And finally, it is a means, almost unsurpassed, of encouraging and multiplying holiness, — all the virtues, principles, graces, charities, that elevate society, redeem from wrong, brighten, bless, and sanctify the world. The Supper, for all who partake of it, with right preparation, in a right spirit, is a mighty quickener of goodness, a mighty guard against temptation. My friend, whoever you are, is your path so clear of danger, and your soul so strong in its own strength, that you can afford to scorn the heavenly help?

I know the current objections, — as that you are not good enough. Judged by positive attainments, no man or woman is good enough, nor pretends to be. Profession, in that case, would be arrogant and offensive presumption. But, if I understand the conditions of the Gospel, they are sincere penitence for sin, faith in the Lord Jesus Christ, and a ruling desire to lead a holy life, sustained by prayer. Here is no impracticable demand, — only a heart of love and trust and pure aspiration. If you have that, you are good enough to commune with Christ, and thus to grow better; and if you have it not, you are not fit either to live or to die.

As to its being a form: that is the made-up objection of only a few fastidious and sentimental persons, who are not thoroughly in earnest about the matter. It is a species of cant, that reappears from time to time, but never has much force. Instead of any special spirituality, the objectors to forms are commonly those that have too little spiritual life to put life into the forms God has kindly provided as a lodge for the Spirit, and so faint under them, or stumble at them, and find them meaningless, instead of vitalizing them. The only real test of fitness for communion is a cordial, deep, deliberate desire, or want, or sense of need, of the communion. "Whosoever" so desires, and "will, let him come, and take of the" bread and the "water of life freely."

Here, then, our course of thought is finished. The whole doctrine is practical and personal. To those who are not believers, it says, "Believe, be converted, turn ye, repent, cast off indifference and sin, for your own sake and your children's." To Christian parents in church-communion, it says, " Bring in your children, by baptism, into the dear Redeemer's covenant and fold, and train them up for immortal life." To the young it says, " Come, early, *before* ye are weary and heavy-laden, and have the joy, the peace, the strength, of faith and righteousness."

To all, it offers the honors of the Church, the order of a reconciled society, the beauty of holiness, and the triumphant hope of heaven.

SERMON XVI.

TRIALS OF FAITH.

THE TRYING OF YOUR FAITH. — James i. 3.

THE nature of the thoughts I am to lay before you is such, that the profit of our exercise will depend quite as much on your attention as on my speaking. To yield any satisfaction, it requires patient study and a silent heart. If this is true, in some degree, of all religious themes, it is especially true of one so purely spiritual in its character, and internal in its bearings, as the Trials of Faith.

On the other hand, we shall be assisted by the fact that our topic touches personal interests, which are immediate and universal. In one form or another, either as a pleasure or as a cross, either with a welcome or by compulsion, either in a calm mood or an agonized one, every separate soul has to come at it, and deal with it. For, at last, each person of us has to be a sufferer, has to stand a culprit at the bar of conscience, to be a prisoner behind the iron grates of pain, to hold a secret dialogue with Providence.

The forms of trial I shall bring before you are those that belong to the commonest experience. I shall endeavor to gather them into such groups that they will be clearly recognized, and yet will comprehend many varieties of situation. My arrangement will embrace three classes; trials in religious confidence, trials in human affection, and trials in earthly hope. We are to examine them in the light of the New Testament. We will seek an interpretation of them, that shall be in accordance with the whole wisdom of God, the whole order of his creation, and the divine harmony of its laws. Christ is our authority and guide; Christ the prophet, Christ himself the sufferer, — Christ tempted like as we are, without sin, — Christ taking our infirmities to lift us above them, and dying on a cross to give humanity a crown of life.

I think we shall not find a phrase that better describes the real end and purpose of our discipline in this world, than the one James has given us: "The trying of your faith."

How very different a color these words cast over our life, — over our houses and sick-beds, our tradings and marriages, our bankruptcies and funerals, — from most of those we hear, when men talk together of the chief business! Not to build strong cities and roads and factories, not to make swift passages over oceans, or up to fame, not to celebrate victories over the resistance of matter and the cunning of fellow-tradesmen, not to outwit the elements of nature or a neighbor's policy, did God put breath into our bodies, and lay the world under our feet, and arch the heavens over our head, — but to multiply and prove our faith.

It takes a great while for most of us to find it out. Some of us make out to live without believing it, and never see it till we die; but none the less it is for this we were meant to live, and but for this we should not need to die. It is for the trying of your faith that your will is suffered to be free; that limits are set to your strength; that your desires outrun your ability; that your aspiration transcends your performance; that your energy so often has to droop its tired wings, and sink back baffled; that the flesh lusteth against the spirit, and your passions chafe against your principles.

It is for the trying of your faith, that unexpected joys rise up and flock about you; that mornings of consolation break after nights of sorrow; that prosperity surprises you at the door, when you thought it was loss and poverty that knocked; that your alienated child falls on your neck a penitent; that the post whose arrival you have been dreading, awake and in troubled dreams, for weeks, brings you news that turns anxiety into thanksgiving, and starts tears from another fountain. It is for the trying of your faith, that the alarm of pain sounds through your chambers at midnight; that the cry of death comes forth from the lips of a man, on whose neck the welfare and affections of great communities had hung, — a statesman that upheld the commonwealth, a merchant that dignified commerce, a physican that healed hearts as well as frames, or a preacher whose character repronounced his sermons; for this that a consumptive paleness on the best-beloved face makes you tremble; that a broken bloodvessel throngs your brain with a thousand fears; that scarlet-fever shows its spots on your children's arms; that an Asiatic pestilence sends its gloomy heralds on from city to city across the continents; that inward admonitions point you forward to a day when all costlier garments shall be exchanged for a shroud, and strange hands shall lower your dust into a grave.

It is for the trying of your faith, that your little island of knowledge is embosomed in an ocean of mystery; that the Bible is not all plain to the understanding, nor God's voice audible when we are perplexed, nor the way-marks of duty always visible; that the brightest lamps are often quenched first; that

"the good die first,
And they whose hearts are dry as summer dust
Burn to the socket";

that moral purity is not outwardly rewarded, and righteous plans seem to fail. And, what is perhaps unlikelier to be believed than all, — it is for the trying of your faith that markets fluctuate, banks discount, iron and cotton carry your fortunes up or down, tariffs change, gold-mines are opened, crops grow or fail.

It is for this God places us in the world, schools us in it, takes us out of it. For are we not immortal? And is not the principle of our immortality, faith in the Father of our spirits, — in his Son, who manifests Him and is the way to Him, — in his spiritual truth, — in the kingdom of Heaven?

I suppose this statement of the true end of life, and of God's design with us, would be more acceptable in some quarters, if, instead of *the trying of your faith*, we were to say *the formation of your character*. There ought certainly to be no quarrel with a man who has so cleared himself of corrupt and selfish influences, as to be able to set it up as his supreme purpose to form a right character. Yet this preference of the term *character* for *faith* may possibly betray a tendency in the religious habit of the times, which would, if indulged, give narrow and one-sided proportions to the spiritual life.

Faith is the stronger word, and contains a richer meaning. Faith includes character, and also the internal principle, the motive, the germ, the secret life, out of which character grows. If we could only escape from the formal impressions connected with it, and take it on our lips, not as theologians, but for the fresh and simple feeling of every good heart which it really signifies, we should find it to express something deeper and dearer even than character. Character refers rather to what one is in his relations to others; faith, to what he is in his own heart, and thus what he *must be* to others. His character tells us how he will behave; his faith, why he behaves as he does. His character speaks for his conscience and his principles; his faith speaks for his affections, as well as his conscience, and plants his principles on the only sure foundation, — love and trust towards God, personal sympathy for Christ, a fervent communion with the Spirit. The Apostles, whose insight into the depths of spiritual truth always gave them the most exact and comprehensive language, and Jesus himself, insisted on faith in almost every discourse; but although they were continually enjoining the virtues that make up character, the word *character* does not occur in the New Testament.

Turning now to the great classes of trials I have mentioned, let us seek for some clew to the law by which they are meant to work together for our good, in strengthening this faith.

First are trials in religious confidence. I believe a great many persons sincerely desire religious satisfaction, who do not know where to go for it nor how to get it. They wish they were Christian, in the full meaning of that name, and yet do not see clearly how to proceed. They would be willing to make sacrifices; they have looked far enough into the life of fashion and pleasure to see how empty it is of all permanent rewards ; they look at the tranquil souls and serene faces of thorough and consistent disciples, and long for the same peace ; they have a general belief in the claims of revelation ; but there is a restless yearning in their breasts for something more ; and, as the days and months wear on, they are weary at making no nearer approaches to a real reconciliation and fellowship with Christ.

Let them understand, then, that this is the trying of their faith. The first condition of our attaining to any real strength of soul, is that we become fully conscious of our weakness. Before we can be made fit to receive so great a gift as the feeling of being forgiven and accepted, — safe, or saved, — it is necessary that an intense want should be created in us. Utterly discontented and homesick the prodigal must be, before he will set his face towards his father's house. There must be a mighty hunger in a man's heart, before he will gladly seize and eat of the Bread which cometh down from heaven. This is the reason, evidently, for the Saviour's beatitude, " Blessed are they that do hunger and thirst after righteousness, for *they* shall be filled." Very often we have to be kept a long time out of our inheritance, because our hearts are not in a fit state to receive it humbly and gratefully. It was to prefigure this fact of experience, beyond question, that the Saviour himself spent forty days of temptation in the wilderness before angels came and ministered unto him, and Paul tarried three years in Arabia before he could take up the responsibility of his apostleship. Now, with most of us, so short-sighted is our calculation, and so seducible is our conscience, this preparation is got by a bitter and disastrous experiment. Instead of going into the privacy

20

of religious meditation, and settling the sharp controversy between self-will and God's will, as the governing principle of life, by a wise reflection, in our youth, we insist on trying the world first. So we go round through the circle of transient interests, tasting one cup after another; dropping our manhood, and running off, wherever a siren's invitation calls us, — the senses, ambition, money, a fine estate, long life, gay society, — till, finally, discovering that every phantom cheated us, every *ignis fatuus* led us into a slough, and every metal we struck rings hollow, we creep back, and beg of God and the Church to take what folly and sin had well-nigh spoilt, mocked, and thrown away. Well, if the conversion is earnest, and the consecration sincere, the forgiving Father accepts us. But what wonder, if, before he introduces us into the full joy of believing, or the rewards of obedience, he first tries our faith? Be sure that no otherwise can we have that faithful spirit of which Christian disciples are made. You have been years wandering, unfitting yourself for spiritual peace, because out of harmony with God, who asks the supreme devotion of your soul. What right have you to expect to spring, at one bound, into the complete restoration of every abused and disordered faculty? It ought to be enough, if, your face being firmly turned towards your Father in heaven, he lifts, little by little, the veil that hides the full splendor of his presence.

Here, then, is the trying of your faith. Because you insisted on trying the world, God insists on trying you. You long for religious peace. Do you long for it enough to wait, as well as strive for it? Are ye able to drink of that cup, and be baptized with that baptism? The first lesson God has to teach you, after so much obstinate self-will, is the humiliation of your pride. What you are to learn by this discontent is, that you are not sufficient to yourself, but must look above yourself; that you cannot guide yourself, but must beseech the Spirit to guide you; that you, being finite, cannot grasp infinite things, but must let the Saviour reach up for you, show you where your uncertain hand shall lay hold on the rod and staff, and make you one with him. The two powers that this slow trying of your religious constancy is meant to develop in your soul, are humbler prayers, and a more patient feeling after, and following after, Jesus. These together are faith; and their certain end is peace.

But again; at the same time, and for the same end, faith is tried through our human affections. Have you ever seen — so as to know how dreary a spectacle it is — the trust in Heaven trampled out of a soul, instead of being strengthened, by the tortures of grief? Have you ever felt in yourself, in some moment of darkness, a passing fear that an impending sorrow would be too much for your spirit to sustain? Have you ever felt the painful and guilty doubt, whether you have been carried up to a loftier plane of life, and holier states, by your past afflictions? If you have, you will need no farther explanation of what is meant.

The first demand of the soul, under such an ordeal, is to realize that its suffering has an object. We commonly think we could endure trouble with composure, if we could only see what is to be accomplished by enduring it. Why, why is it? is the question that haunts the aching breast, and disturbs its submission. We must be content to suffer without an answer to that question. That is the trial of faith. If a full answer were to be given, there would be no room for faith. Who am I, that I should require the Infinite and Eternal One to assign me reasons for his counsel? "What I do, thou knowest not now, but thou shalt know hereafter," is explanation enough to my impatient curiosity. That is what God demands of faith to feel.

When the smart and the load of fresh afflictions are not upon us, we are able to feel it, perhaps, quite easily. But how, when the nerves are torn, and the separation has come, — when the dead body lies in the next room, and the tones of the silenced voice yet linger in our ears, and the sense of bereavement presses in through every pore of the heart? Can we realize it then?

In such particular cases of suffering, we have to fall back, I think, on some reserved fund of faith accumulated in calmer moments. On your way to your child's or your husband's burial, you are not expected to generalize, nor to reason, nor to draw philosophical deductions from a wide circle of facts. God will not be angry if you fail to see, just in that bewildered paroxysm of grief, how it is well for you to be so stricken. Yet you can say to yourself, even then, in the midst of your tears, "It *is* well; somehow it is well; it *must* be wise, and right, and merciful." That will be both the trial and the triumph of faith. And if you have noticed, looking back over your past experience, or out among your companions, that sorrow is the chief producer of human goodness on the whole, and crosses are the mightiest instruments of spiritual purity on the whole, you are held to apply that general conviction of your reason to this special instance of affliction. If it is a law that a stormy air nurses your moral vigor, you must abide by that law while the storm beats in, and the waves are high, as bravely as in sunshine and still seas.

The settled conclusion God obviously wishes us to reach and rest in, and one that he passes us through all this mixed encounter of pain and peace to establish in us, is this: that in every passage of our life there are two parties engaged, — God and ourselves. Some persons, saints, find this out early; and to them pain thenceforth loses its tormenting power. Most of us have to learn it by a long and gradual trying of our faith. A nominal belief in such a truth is common enough. But veritably to realize that God is personally present and interested in the little gettings-on of our virtue, is a rarer attainment, and needs a peculiar training. To achieve that result, the Divine methods are wonderful. He buffets and caresses. He gives and takes away. He sends now a providence signal and exceptional, and then the regularity of nature. He answers some prayers according to their request, and others by withholding the boon, but still thereby increasing submission. He twines together motives the most complicated. He keeps generous men poor, and lets the selfish and sensual gain the world. He cuts off the philanthropist, and spares the tyrant. All this, for the trying of our faith. If you accustom yourself to watching this play of the Divine purpose, you will find it, apart from your personal implication in it, one of the most fascinating of all problems. Yet how often do we complain of the crosses as evils, and snatch greedily at the comforts, as animals at their fodder!

The acknowledgment of mystery, then, the frank confession that our being is folded all about with the unknowable, our light fringed on every side with darkness, our little globe swimming in an ocean of unfathomable designs, but God guiding it on and caring for every passenger soul, — this is another end of the trying of our faith.

But there is another feeling under suffering, that furnishes another trial of faith. Each sufferer regards his own burden as peculiar; and, comparing himself with his neighbors, cannot understand the unequal distribution. A father sitting in his desolate dwelling, where no children's voices ring as they used to do, cannot discover that he deserves the scourge more than his happier friend. A young wife, that has suddenly waked out of a trance of terror over her husband's fever, only to feel the light of life all expunged, and the sun quenched, wonders why she is chosen out for the awful fate. A believing widow kneels by her only son's coffin, and cries in her despair, "What have I done, that Thou shouldst curse me thus?"

Several things might be answered; as, that fortunes are never so unequal as they seem; that, under a florid surface, prosperity often hides abysses of anguish; that the forms of sorrow have not so much to do as they seem with its amount. But these are not the answer of faith, which is, that the purpose of suffering is never to be found out by a comparison of merits among neighbors, but by considering how it draws the soul in more childlike dependence towards the Father. By this principle, the right-minded and well-meaning must be tried, quite as much as the faithless. Trials are signs of celestial favor, seals on their forehead, badges of favorites, crowns of honor. We forget that it is just as important that the good should be made better, as that the bad should be reformed. Vessels that are to be made meet for the Master's highest uses are to be refined in the furnace seven times heated. We must learn that it is a far richer blessing to be taught what the feeling of the Comforter is, and what peace comes with self-renunciation, than to go through life in any holiday dance. Just as the wise and affectionate mother shows her true maternal love more manifestly, when she causes her child to cry with disappointment by snatching him back from the candle he grasps at as a flaming toy, than when she gives him the costliest plaything; so God often shows a tenderer concern when he denies us health and riches, than when he grants them, — when he enfeebles us with disease or poverty, than when he covers us with flesh or fortune. But this also we never should discover, but for the trying of our faith.

And thus, finally, we touch the trials that come to faith by the breaking up of earthly hopes. I held the hand of a valiant man, the other day, whose body was faint with five years of pain. He looked up at me with a smile on his white, thin cheeks, and whispered very feebly: "They say this is a hard, dark world; it is no such thing. It is a bright, genial world. Christ has been in it; he is in it still." Prophet of immortality, and preacher of a victorious faith! I thought, — here is the victory that overcometh the world, for it overcometh suffering and death, the world's two cruellest tyrants. I called him valiant. He was more than valiant, for he was patient. The trying of your faith worketh patience; and patience, experience; and experience, the hope that maketh not ashamed.

I know of few gloomier spectacles than that of a man who has been put by God into a sick-room, or into the arms of some sharp calamity, to be made purer, coming out as corrupt in his tastes, as low in his aims, as eager in the chase for bubbles, as before. It is such a waste of divine privilege! A great fortune suddenly lost, by shipwreck or fire, or a convulsion in finance, or a partner's forfeited faith, is such a splendid opportunity for moral heroism as may never come again. A family that step down gracefully and sweet-temperedly from affluence to strict economies, need not go as missionaries to illustrate Christianity. How many examples have proved that it is not till the fruits of outward labors have been swept away, that the toils of the spirit can begin to rear the spiritual edifice on clean foundations! It is the trying of faith that glorifies humanity, and saves the soul.

Brethren, the truth we have pondered has a threefold bearing, according as we look towards our Lord, towards one another, or toward ourselves. We are entangled together in a chain of common feeling, all whose links are forged and welded in pain. But we are bound also, by the same chain, to the heart of the Redeemer; either to be made more wretched, one day, because our estranged and irreligious consciences cannot bear the look of his purity judging us, — or to be filled with consolation, and animated with courage, because he will judge that our suffering has disciplined us into penitence, purged us, and proved to be the trying of our faith. We talk of carving out our own fortunes, and stimulate each other to that transient emulation. There is no way we can look on one another so noble as to see rather how each is carving his fortune itself into a ladder of ascent towards spiritual perfection, making all his lot a refiner of his soul, and ever adding to that solemn wisdom of experience, by which life is directed towards its immortal end. Compared with our progress through this sublime struggle, and this deep community of trial, how poor looks all our watching of one another's wealth, and our criticism of each other's movements! Life is more than meat. Only as we help each other in that science which underlies all sciences, that practice which transcends all other labors, the knowing how to live a larger life, to breathe a nobler charity, to pray more believing prayers, to converse with God, and hold the fellowship of faith with Christ, and thus to gain the spiritual mind that was in him, — only thus are we really brethren of a Christian baptism. Be this our personal consecration; be that this day's vow. May God grant it a glorious fulfilment! For only his love can so work within us, that our discipline shall be our purification. And only the pure in heart shall see God.

SERMON XVII.

SALVATION, NOT FROM SUFFERING, BUT BY IT.

THEN SAID MARTHA UNTO JESUS, LORD, IF THOU HADST BEEN HERE, MY BROTHER HAD NOT DIED. — John xi. 21.

THE lowest view of life looks out upon it as no scene of the workings and revealings of the Divine Spirit, but only as a hostelry where every guest is to seize on so many of the good things exposed as the laws of the place allow, — to consume what the senses crave, regarding no other than sensual penalties, — to grasp the largest handful of comfort irrespective of rights or services, and to push pleasure to the utmost pitch of intensity consistent with its continuance.

Of course, this selfish hunt will take different directions, according to the ruling appetite; proceeding with some men by a cool calculation, and with others by passionate plunges of impulse. But the characteristic mark on all its phases is, that it disowns God. The whole eager race through which it strains its muscles ignores the spiritual presence. Religious accountability is an element foreign to it. Duty is a word without a meaning. Conscience is only one of the furies. Christ is a veiled figure. Stewardship is a visionary fancy. The curtain that drops over the grave is of stone, as immovable as it is impenetrable. This is paganism, only without its intellectual dreams, or its Olympus.

This system not only fails to provide for the chief *internal* necessity, namely, the native aspirations, the importunities besetting human nature with the demand for some kind of a religion, but it also fails to meet one *external* fact, which lies on the very surface of our being, and forms one of its invariable ingredients; I mean suffering. Suffering is a kind of test of all philosophies and all theories of life. It is useless to leave it out of the calculation; for, through the disorders of a mortal body, through dull discouragements, through weaknesses of the spirit, through a sensitive brain or heart, through the affections that weave families together, — through some of these inlets, it forces its way back into every lot, and will not be forgotten. Life does not really become a problem with any of us, till we taste of its bitterness. Pain, sorrow, trial, bereavement, — these are names of which no man or woman ever learns the real signification from grammar or dictionary, but only by drinking their cup in a secret experience. Whenever they come, that comfort-seeking or Epicurean plan of living collapses; utter despair sets in; cries, but no answer nor strength; and the least the agonized Epicurean can do, if he will be a heathen still, and not a Christian, is to fly to Zeno's Porch, and borrow some crumbs of frigid dignity that fall from the Stoic's table.

Ascend then a step higher. Here we find God to be acknowledged, but more through fear, which is selfish, than through devout submission. The spiritual faculty has waked, but has not become clear-sighted. Providence has returned to the world from which the sottish unbelief we were just noticing had rejected him; but the confession, " Thy will be done," is not so full and unreserved as to include the giving up of the dearest idols. A heaven is seen to overarch the earth, — but seen as yet through a glass, and darkly, because a film is on the looker's eyes. The daily dealings of the Spirit are intellectually believed in; but so much of the old earthly leaven and habit cling still to the soul, that you hesitate to yield a complete confidence; you dare to suspect that here and there some sparrow, or treasure more precious than that, *may* fall to the ground *without* your Father's notice.

This state, too, like the other, is met by suffering, the spiritual touchstone. How does it behave itself under that dread ministry? *Well,* — but not *best.* Soberly, but not serenely. Reputably, but not quite to the satisfaction of its own highest aspiration, nor of true Christian friendship. The ligaments that bind it to this world have been so long strengthening and hardening, that, when they part, a chasm seems to be left in the very core of the heart. Self has interlaced its plans and desires so cunningly with all the web of life, that some selfish preferences linger to mar the beauty of resignation, — to keep back a part of the soul's trust, and to disturb the perfect peace and joy of believing. There is the beginning of faith, — too much to be thrown away, not enough to live by. Here is a stage of religious progress, not less deserving study than any other, and needing consolations and encouragements almost as much as unconcern needs rebuke.

This, as I interpret the narrative, is precisely the state where the speaker stands, as the language of the text represents her. The Bible is a transcript of all possible experience, and has some representative for every shade of our discipline. "Lord, if thou hadst been here, my brother had not died." *There* is a mixture of the strength and the weakness of faith, — perhaps I might say, of faith and superstition. This woman believed in the power and love of her Lord; this was her true faith. But she believed that this power and love of Jesus, if they had been afforded a chance to operate at all, must necessarily have been displayed in prolonging her brother's life in the body. That was a falsity or weakness of her faith. She also seems to have supposed that the wonders of the Saviour's spirit were limited to his physical presence; not having learned yet that his spirit, and its ministry of healing love, whether to bodies or souls, is independent of all material organization or motion, and transcends the restrictions of distance or time. This Jesus immediately corrects, by saying, "Whosoever, anywhere, believeth on me, shall never die." "To whomsoever believeth on him, the Son hath power to give eternal life."

Martha, therefore, is a type of that faith, — sincere and yet imperfect, beautiful for its prompt simplicity, and yet not enlarged and disciplined into entire self-renunciation, — which believes in the Divine mercy, but continues to regard personal safety, and the outward society of kindred, as more important than the doing of God's will; which clings to, and prays for, the private privilege of clasping friends or children in the arms of flesh, more fervently than the spiritual purification, the glory of character, which may come of their removal. She represents all of us who fail of that thorough submission which rejoices more in being drawn to immortal excellence *by* suffering, than in being exempted *from* it. Out of that second state into a third and higher one — a purer and a calmer one — Christ wishes to lift her and us. That will be the state where a pure and holy soul will be felt to be of more value than any freedom from pain; where sympathy and co-operation with Christ appear a dearer privilege than the remaining of any human friend or kinsman at your side; and where acceptance into the kingdom of Heaven, which is God's favor both now and hereafter, is more to be striven for than any repose of human affections, or any satisfying of selfish desires.

Saved *by* suffering, not saved *from* it; that is the law of life revealed in Christ, — the disciple's prayer, the sufferer's consolation. Character depends on inward strength. But this strength has two conditions: it is increased only by being put forth, and it is tested only by some resistance. So, if the spiritual force, or character, in you is to be strong, it must be measured against some competition. It must enter into conflict with an antagonist. It must stand in comparison with something formidable enough to be a standard of its power.

Now, the ordinary course of a prosperous fortune furnishes no such standard. I do not deny that there are a few favored moral constitutions that will ripen into sainthood under the influence of perpetual comfort. But they are rare exceptions, if they exist; and he must be a bold presumer that will dare claim to be of their company. Suffering, then, in some of its forms, must be introduced, the appointed minister, the great assayist, to put the genuineness of faith to the proof, and purify it of its dross. What special form it shall take for each, it is for God, who knows us better than we know ourselves, to decide. Mary and Martha must see Lazarus die. Matthew must forsake all to follow his Master. Marys and Marthas must weep, the world over; the sorrows of

Bethany be revived in the homes of distant centuries and undiscovered countries, till the lengthening sisterhood of suffering clasps hands around the globe. Many Matthews, by the Atlantic and Pacific, as well as by the shore of Tiberias, must part with profits and gains for an unreserved apostleship. The most generous and beautiful children — the manliest sons and loveliest daughters — must be buried out of some families; and in others ingratitude or vice must spread a far more dreadful mourning. And because, in the mystery of God's forethought, some souls are to have tasks and stations of peculiar honor offered them in his kingdom, from these one after another of the dearest and most delicious joys must vanish, light after light be quenched, child after child droop into a sick-bed, and then into shorter breathings, and then into the infinite silence, till *all* are gone, and *all* is still. Uncongenial companionships, unreasonable tempers, unreturned affections, unrealized ideals of goodness, unforeseen calamities to property, pinching poverty, slow disorders that overcloud the spirits or tire out patience; — I need not enumerate the legions of ever-active and unwelcome ministers, abroad and busy throughout men's dwellings, never invited, yet forcing their way in, made necessary by the weakness of our faith, ordained to discipline us into independence of the world, into heirship in immortality. How many of us are yet only able, when they come, to say, at best, with Martha, "Lord, if thou *hadst been* here, — if thy goodness could have been really exercised, — these evils could not have befallen me!" Whereas we ought clearly to say, "Lord, in these very chastenings of friendly love thou *hast* been here, — not to save me *from* sufferings, but to save me spiritually through and by them ; — reconciliation is better than pleasure ; thou art ever with me ; be my only prayer, 'My Father's will be done!'"

Christ's own way of treating sufferers sustains this view. We fall into a mistake, I think, when we imagine that Jesus ever wrought those wonders, of healing disease, or restoring life to the dead, merely out of a personal pity to the sick or the mourners. Infinite as that pity was, it took a higher range, and had a diviner object, than the mere assuaging of present pain, or the prolonging of the earthly existence. Think of it. Out of the thousands who groaned and wept in Judæa while he was walking its fields, he cured but a few scores of maladies, and raised, so far as we know, only three persons that were dead to life. As mere expressions of mortal compassion, how inadequate and accidental must such instances appear! How manifest that it was to revive the world's dying faith, to gain its trust, to cure its disordered heart, that he wrought these heavenly works! It illustrates the same intention, that most of his miracles were performed in the earlier parts of his public ministry, when it was most needful to attract confidence to that new doctrine by which he was to requicken slumbering humanity. So in the case before us: very clearly it is not because he regards the removal of the sister's grief as the best service his divine friendship can render them, — nor the prolonging of their brother's life a few years, to pass through death again, as his choicest boon, — that he cries, "Lazarus, come forth!" at the gates of his grave. If that were so, he must have stayed on earth for ever, and extended his wonder-working hand over all continents, to spare mankind their calamities, instead of planting in their souls the germ and spirit of a life immortal, conquering calamity. Accordingly, when he knows that Lazarus is dead, while he is touched with tenderness toward the weeping kindred, he says plainly to his disciples, "I am glad, for your sakes, I was not there, *to the intent ye may believe.*" It was their deeper faith he sought, and through theirs the faith of all his Church. And then, just as the sublime marvel was to appear at his bidding, and the still chamber to give up its guest, he repeated to the doubting Martha, "Said I not unto thee, that *if thou wouldst believe*, thou shouldst see the glory of God?" And when he prayed to the Father, and said, "I know that thou hearest me always," he added, "Because of the people which stand by, I said it, *that they may believe that thou hast sent me.*" How manifestly the whole mercy was granted only to confirm that incomparable and eternal truth, "I am the Resurrection and the Life; whosoever believeth on me, though he were dead, yet shall he live." And now, after eighteen centuries, Jesus does not stay to revoke for us the decrees of nature,—to be a physician to our sickness, or a warder at the door to keep out death. He stays, but for a higher ministry; not to exempt us from suffering, but to conduct us through it into heavenly strength and peace; not for a physical or temporary cure, but a spiritual and final one! And so our confession ought not to be the half-faithless one, "Lord, if thou hadst been here, our friends, our children, would not have sickened and died"; but, "Lord, because thou art here, all our sicknesses, and our dying even, shall be for the raising up of our souls, and the glory of God."

Willingness to suffer for that end, — for spiritual redemption and the glory of God, — this is what we have to aspire to, and attain, under the teaching of Christ, and by that cross whereby he symbolized his whole religion, and suffered for us, thereby made perfect in his mediatorship. "Happy man," said a gay and frivolous young worldling once, when his own nerves were tortured, to a more believing and therefore more equable companion,— "happy man, to have the strength of will which can thrust its thoughts away, once and for all." "No," replied his wiser friend, "more happy are they whom God will not allow to thrust their thoughts from them till the bitter draught has done its work."

There is another class of moral experiences where the principle of this doctrine has an equally direct application,— a class not less needing its support than the bereaved, and having also frequent representatives. I mean persons who, having sincerely begun a Christian life, suffer the temptation of longing more earnestly for rest than for faithful submission. They have heard that there is joy in believing; and so they undertake to believe for the sake of the joy. They desire a comfortable and quiet mind; and this, though it is a far nobler thirst than that of the senses, is still, if it is too strong, tainted with selfishness, and wanting in faith. As there is a spiritual pride, so there is a spiritual luxury, and the appetite that lusts after it is one of the subtle enemies that beset those who have passed out of the lowest stage of conscience into the second. There is an ambition to do something as out of your own self, for the delight of approving yourself, which is nothing else than self-righteousness. The mercenary tendency to offer God your good works as a price for purchasing an allowance of self-complacency, is one that needs to be watched by sincere seekers after the liberty and nobleness of true devotion. It defeats its own end. Peace never comes in that way; nothing does but discontent and confusion. Peace comes swiftest when you seek it as an end least. Seek purity, seek renewal of heart and life, seek harmony with God, seek the society of Christ as a Saviour and Intercessor for you, and peace, in God's good time, will come of itself. How many really earnest souls of us are spoiling our work, because we will invert God's order, and, instead of seeking faith supremely, leaving comfort for an incident, go about to get comfort first, and thus miss faith and comfort both! Let us be patient. As the years wear on towards the deep sunset, we are weary at making no nearer approaches to a real reconciliation and living intimacy with our Lord. But do we long for that rest religiously enough to wait for it? Stillness is our needed sacrifice. Baffled and broken the soul must often be, before its immortal strength comes. Humiliation of pride, — an utter consciousness of infirmity, — to be kept painfully out of our inheritance, — fasting and mortified ambition, — forty days in the wilderness, — three years in Arabia, — all these are the price of conquest. Do not pray for exemption from them, but for victory by them. Homesick the prodigal must be before he will set his face towards his father's house. Except I am taught my weakness, I shall not let the Saviour reach up for me, and place my groping, uncertain hand on the eternal rock. What right have we to say, "Lord, if thou hadst been here, doubts and difficulties would not have tormented us, — our *hearts* would not have died within us," — when those doubts and difficulties are only the remaining echoes of our former disobedience? Enough if we can say, "Lord, because thou hast promised to be with us, we will bear them, and wait thy will! Not *from* this suffering, but by its purifying ministry, will we hope and beseech that we may be saved!"

Further still, if you will, you may generalize this instruction, so as to make it embrace all those many instances where the disappointed and the afflicted grieve over some of the attendant circumstances of their losses, vexing their sympathies with the superfluous doubt whether some care was not omitted, whether the fatal blow might not have been warded off! When shall we learn that God takes all the past into his secure keeping, and only disapproves the energy and despair that would knock against its closing gate? When shall we believe that even out of the sorrows we might have prevented, but did not, we may now draw a spiritual benefit *greater* than to have prevented them? Vain cry, "Lord, if thou hadst been here!" Better to receive and bless him, in whatever robes of darkness, when he comes.

The doctrine pronounces no remonstrance against sorrow; its very aim is to show the rightful place it has in maturing the loftiest fruits of character; — nor against tears; how can it, when it is in the very scene before us that we see how "Jesus wept"? It was no dainty sentimentalist, but one of the stoutest-hearted men of our Saxon blood, who wrote: "Weeping is the discharge of a big and swelling grief; and therefore, he that never had such a burden upon his heart as to give him opportunity thus to ease it, has one pleasure in this world yet to come."

> "Where sorrow 's held intrusive, and turned out,
> There wisdom will not enter, nor true power,
> Nor aught that dignifies humanity."

Paul found the secret of the wisdom that at once allows these tender alternations of human feeling, and yet subjects them to a holier faith: "They that weep should be as though they wept not; and they that rejoice, as though they rejoiced not." Because there is a life, possible to the soul through the Spirit, in which fear and mourning and suffering and death itself are swallowed up, and lost, like bubbles on some calm, deep stream.

> "'I know,' is all the mourner saith,
> 'Knowledge by suffering entereth,
> And life is perfected by death; —
>
> "'I am content to touch the brink,
> Of pain's dark goblet, and I think
> My bitter drink a wholesome drink.
>
> "'I am content to be so weak:
> Put strength into the words I speak,
> For I am strong in what I seek.
>
> "'I am content to be so bare
> Before the archers; everywhere
> My wounds being stroked by heavenly air.
>
> "'Glory to God, — to God,' he saith;
> 'Knowledge by suffering entereth,
> And life is perfected by death.'"

This, then, is the faith in which our life is to be lived, and our burdens are to be borne. And these are the steps towards that conclusion: first, that suffering is disciplinary; secondly, that, if our desires reach only after exemption from it, we pray but half-faithless prayers; and thirdly, that the true conquest and peace of faith, as well as the solution of the mystery of sorrow, lie only in our willingness to suffer, so far as it may bring us to the society and communion of our Lord. Not *from* suffering, but *through* it into life eternal, is the Christ-like longing of the believer and the Church.

It has been a saying in the German Church, "All sorrow ought to be *Heim-weh*, homesickness." Let reconciliation with the Father be *home*, — let the peace of faith, let the bosom of the Lord where the head of the beloved disciple lay, let present goodness, be home, as well as the future heaven, and in the tender and holy spirit of our religion we may adopt the aphorism. No pain that aches for immortal purity can be dreadful. No grief that strengthens your aspiration for triumph over sin, and the holiness of Christ's heart, can be a calamity. Over no falling tears and heaving sighs that wash your affections white, and put temptation under your feet, and throw open a clear and fearless communion with God, can you ever exclaim, "Lord, if thou hadst been here, these would not have befallen me"; but rather, "Be these my perpetual, solemn guests, if thereby, in this thy inward presence, and with these immortal gifts, thou, my Lord, mayest be led to draw nigh, and come to me!"

Immortal gifts! "This is the victory that overcometh the world, even your faith." There is no one of us, not the weakest, not the timidest, that may not pass through the furnace of trial, and under the shadows of death, with the song of that triumph on his lips. When a community of religious women, in Paris, during the fury of the French Revolution, which swept innocence and beauty into one destruction with crime and tyranny, were condemned to the guillotine, the youngest victims passed through the stormy streets, where terror reigned, to their execution, raising in serene voices the sublime hymn, *Veni Creator.* Never before, the listeners thought, had that anthem of majestic praise been so divinely sung, — so much as if the chant of heaven itself floated down and mingled in the melody. The celestial song did not cease when they ascended the stairs of the scaffold, and the work of butchery went on. Voice after voice had to drop from the chorus, as face after face bent under the axe; and at length one voice was heard alone sustaining the holy strain, with no faltering or cadence, even while the bloody blade fell and sealed the last martyr's testimony. Not by scaffolds, not through blood, but by silent martyrdoms, by slow sufferings, as sharp I think sometimes, and needing the heroism of patience more, must faithful spirits still walk towards God, their hands in their Master's, "Thy rod and thy staff comforting."

Submission like this binds the sisters of Lazarus to every mourner of to-day; for they all stand in the personal friendship of the risen Intercessor. Jesus came to his friend's grave and wept. O scene of unspeakable consolation under the shadow of the Mount of Olives! Shed the light, that broke there on a weeping household, into every kneeling and lamenting family among us! Unite our kindred, under the dispensation of grief, in the everlasting sympathy of one Lord and one faith, with that comforted house where Mary chose the good part, and felt safe at her Redeemer's feet! Make us also dwellers at Bethany, because Christ comes again to us; and though our brother dies, yet we know henceforth that our Redeemer liveth, and that whosoever liveth and believeth in him shall never die!

Be this our Easter thanksgiving! Be this the consolation promised to them that mourn with a disciple's trust, — the hope for the dead who died in their Lord, — the inspiration of the living who have yet to die, — that immortality is brought to light, and that, through suffering, souls may still be made perfect.

SERMON XVIII.

DIVINITY OF CHRIST.

FOR IN HIM (CHRIST) DWELLETH ALL THE FULNESS OF THE GODHEAD BODILY. — Col. ii. 9.

ALL THINGS THAT THE FATHER HATH ARE MINE. — John xvi. 15.

So long as the differences of opinion that obtain at present respecting the rank and nature of the Son of God shall continue to divide and interest those minds that think at all on religious topics, and so long as anything like the existing postures of sects and doctrines shall remain, it can hardly be unreasonable for any man to offer a careful and deliberate exposition of his belief on that subject. If we are Christians at all, Christ is the author and founder of our faith. He is the Head of that Church into which disciples gather for fellowship. The question what and who he is, to all persons of any spiritual consciousness, is vital at every point, and momentous under every aspect.

There are two prevalent apprehensions of the character and office of Jesus as Saviour of the world. One contemplates him as specially appointed to represent the perfection of humanity, meaning by humanity what we have hitherto known or conceived of the spiritual powers and possibilities in a human being. This view holds

Jesus to have been a perfect man; the completest moral example and religious genius of our race; exhibiting in his life and death the utmost that human excellence can do or be; as showing the ultimate achievement, thus far at least, of a man's virtue, love, and faith; and as having withdrawn his personal presence and power from the world at his ascension, so that the communion of his followers is not literally a communion *with him*, but is only a commemorative observance for a Teacher living on earth in the past, but retired now into the heavens.

The other view regards Christ as showing forth not only a perfect humanity, but also and primarily God himself; representing God to man, as well as man to himself; being the express image of God's person; being God in the act and character of revealing or manifesting himself, creating and saving the world; separate at no point from God's sovereignty, nor knowing, in his divinity, any limitation or abridgment from the fulness of God; exhibiting, as in God's behalf, through a union of nature with the Father not explicable to us, the Divine attributes; and reconciling alienated souls by manifesting God in his flesh. According to this doctrine, he survives in his Church to this day, and will survive, not only by influence and memory, but by the presence of his person; a distinct and everlasting person in himself, without beginning of days or end of years, the same yesterday, to-day, and for ever.

The latter of these two views appears to me not only incomparably the most benignant and precious, but to stand towards the other in the relation of truth to error; to be charged with inestimable benefits to our religious progress; to be liable to fewer theological perversions, and less dangerous abuses; and to need also that it be more distinctly asserted and impressed on our present habits of thinking, especially among the inquiring and the young.

A common form of stating the doctrine, that Christ was merely human, and of denying him a distinctive Divinity, is to say that "he was distinguished and exalted above other men, not in kind, but in degree only"; that he transcended mortals only by an excess of virtue, not by any peculiarity of being, not by any singularity of existence, not by a superhuman nature. He was purer and holier than other men; and therefore more of the Divine afflatus flowed through his life.

Against this misconstruction of the whole foundation-work of Christian doctrine, as it seems to me, — injurious, like most other religious errors, by its issues in practical piety, as well as radically mischievous to theology, comprehensively mistaking as to the very being and authority of him who is the centre, the fountain, the embodiment of whatever we have that we can call religion, — I raise a threefold objection. And I urge that objection by an appeal to the grand, threefold source, where alone we can apply for a final decision: the Word, or the New Testament writings; History, or the organic working of Christian life through the Church; and the Soul, with its best intuitions and its wants.

I should be willing, in the appeal to that first and chief of all authorities and testimonies, the New Testament, to waive every reference to the other striking passages that will appear in their natural connections as we press farther into the subject, and to rest the question on the three following explicit ones alone. Just as Jesus was opening his ministry at Jerusalem, John the Forerunner said of him these plain words: "He that cometh from heaven is above all. He whom God hath sent speaketh the words of God; *for God giveth not the Spirit by measure unto him.* He that believeth on the Son hath everlasting life; and he that believeth not the Son shall not see life." Were these words spoken of an extraordinary mortal, constituted and endowed no otherwise than as you are and I am? Almost at the same moment, Jesus was holding one of his first reported conversations with the Rabbi Nicodemus by night, where he announces some of the sublime principles of his kingdom, and the profound mystery of the second birth. And this is the well-weighed avowal by which he initiates this inquiring representative of the old religion into the great secret of the new: "God so loved the world, that he gave his only begotten Son, that whosoever believeth in him should not perish, but have everlasting life. And he that believeth not is condemned." Is this the utterance of a being who "differs from other men in degree only, but not in kind"? Many years had passed since the Saviour's crucifixion; the Gospel had been tested and tried by the terrible ordeal of the Apostolic age; and yet time enough had not passed to drift the believer away from his anchorage on the simplicity of the Master's original teaching; and then one who was able to know whereof he affirmed wrote to the reluctant converts from Judaism: "God, who at sundry times and in divers manners spake in time past unto the fathers by the Prophets, hath in these last days spoken unto us by his Son; whom he hath appointed heir of all things, by whom also he made the worlds; who, being the brightness of his glory, and the express image of his person, and upholding all things by the word of his power, when he had by himself purged our sins, sat down on the right hand of the

Majesty on high; being made so much better than the angels, as he hath obtained a more excellent name than they. For unto which of the angels said he at any time, 'Thou art my Son: this day have I begotten thee'?" Which one, then, of all the heroes, sages, saints, of any nation, commemorated by monuments, by literature, by private veneration, shall claim to be brother, in kind or in degree, of him whom even all the angels of God are commanded to worship?

But I must add here a few of the weighty declarations of Jesus himself, so grand, so comprehensive, so clear and unhesitating, so almost overwhelming in the solemn awe they awaken while we read, that to suppose them uttered by any being not divine, not an eternal dweller in the very bosom and sonship of the Father, would seem a strange infatuation. "All power is given unto me, *in heaven and on earth.*" "All things that the Father hath are mine." "Believe me, that I am in the Father, and the Father in me." "He that hath seen me, hath seen the Father." "I and my Father are one." "The Father hath committed all judgment unto the Son." "If ye shall ask anything in my name, *I will do it.*" "As the Father knoweth me, even so know I the Father." "Thy sins are forgiven thee." "I give unto them eternal life." "No man taketh my life from me; I have power to lay it down, and I have power to take it again." "No man hath ascended up to heaven, but he that came down from heaven, even the Son of Man which is in heaven." As sure as words have any meaning, these are not the words of a man. They are the words of God.

The second appeal is to Christian History, or the organic working of Christian life through the Church. Begin where you will, at any point from the least conspicuous movement of the public mind in Christendom chronicled in last evening's newspaper, up to Constantine's political conversion or Nerva's royal concession, and you will find that, whether you strike down below the surface of events, or reach out either way to trace their sequence and interdependence, the under-tide that bears all up and sweeps all along is the irresistible current of Christ's divine life. Changes with which no other change compares, revolutions for which no civil revolution can account, impulses of thought, conquests of science, growths of institutions, marches of learning and society, — all testify that a silent power was cradled in the manger at Bethlehem, which was to dwarf down the empire of Cæsars and Bonapartes into the puny dynasties of nursery games. All the growing multitudes, achievements, industry, enterprise, discoveries, wisdom, and strength of the race, lift a chant of thanksgiving that has grown louder from the first, and is swelling still, to proclaim Christ the Divine Regenerator of its destinies, the Infinite and Eternal Head over his Church.

The third appeal is to the Soul, with its intuitions and its wants. Whenever it is most deeply stirred by penitence, or strained by agony, or kindled into holy aspiration, the spiritual nature craves a more intimate communion with God than would be possible if that God had not mysteriously manifested himself in flesh; not a sovereign in the skies, but a beating and friendly bosom in Bethany. It cries out for the Christ, who, by bearing to us the pity and pardon of the Father, is Way and Truth and Life. The individual heart, when it is really agitated, whether by hope or love or pain or fear, emphasizes the promise of revelation; and the longings of the individual soul respond to the broad verdict of history.

It confesses, like Peter before the persecutors, that there is no other name under heaven, given among men, whereby it can be saved.

Objectors start other theories. It has been said, for instance, that even in our human nature there are capacities so noble, and traits so high, that we do Christ honor enough when we allow him to possess an unprecedented and complete combination of them. I believe, on the contrary, that, in the essential peculiarity of his nature, Christ is as distinct from us as the spiritual nature in us is from the perishable, as God is from man.

I acknowledge that in mere humanity there is "a nature transcendently great and sacred," a nature so surpassing the animal organization, so wonderfully superior to this chemical compound that we call the body, so far outstripping in its reach, capacity, and eternal duration, all the energy and acuteness of physical sense, so fitted to receive the impression and inspiration of God's Spirit, that it may be even said, in a certain liberal use of language, to be *kindred* to God, or, in an Apostle's vivid phrase, to be "a partaker of the *divine* nature." Thank Christ also for this very assurance,—for without him you never could have felt it,—that man is, every man is, immortal as well as mortal, a spirit as well as dust, allied to the Almighty while he is hastening to a grave. Rejoice in that great boon; and let the conscious dignity of such a conviction bear you up into a life of lofty virtue, that shall be worthy of such a heritage. And yet there is that in Jesus Christ which separates him even from this spiritual nature in humanity, distinguishes him from the best dignity in man, and exalts him above even our highest honors. There is a line drawn between his soul and our souls, not cutting us off from his perfect sympathy, not barring us from his fellowship, not veiling his face with any dimness from ours, but marking us, in our nature, as human; and him, in his nature, as divine.

We are encouraged, it is true, to call ourselves children of the Most High; but if we call ourselves so in an humble temper, remembering what sins penitence has to deplore, we shall never confound *our* filial relation with that of him who could utter the sublime and mysterious challenge both to philosophy and faith, "I and my Father are one." "Behold," says an Apostle, "now are we the sons of God." But it must be an irreverent self-conceit and a shallow insight that can mistake this thankful confession for a bold assertion of the believer's equality with him whom the Church and the Gospel unite in revering as THE SON of God, and who received that majestic anointing and seal upon his authority, when the Spirit descended visibly upon him in Jordan, and a voice said, "This is my Beloved Son; hear him." "Only-begotten Son" it is written; what means that significant word, "only-begotten," if Jesus is not a Son in some sense that we are not, and never can be, sons?

Another form taken by the argument for Christ's simple humanity is this, — that every member of the human family is capable of certain lofty spiritual exercises, is visited by holy aspirations, has a moral sense that distinguishes between right and wrong, and can form "ideas of truth, of justice, of holiness." These ideas and affections, it is argued, are God within us; because they are in harmony with his character, and it is by them that we recognize his attributes. In Christ these moral ideas were held with peculiar clearness and power; these spiritual affections moved in extraordinary purity and constancy. This fact, therefore, is held to satisfy all that language of Christ and his Apostles where he is declared to be one with God, and to exhaust the meaning of those passages that attribute to him a quite superhuman nature. He had in him more of God than we, only by as much as he gave to those ideas and affections, possible to him and us alike, a fuller development than we.

Now, this explanation is as unsatisfactory as the preceding: it grows more and more unsatisfactory, the longer I study the facts of Christ's ministry, the words spoken by him, or his effect on the world. Those facts are miraculous, or they are an imposition. Those words are an assertion of a union between Jesus and the Father altogether peculiar and distinctive and complete, or they are deceptions. That effect on the world must be accounted for by an agency behind it entirely above all other known historical motive powers; or else it is brought about by some artifice superlatively cunning, a legerdemain more incredible than miracle itself. The facts: — When I behold, through those impregnable narratives where sharp-eyed and cavilling criticism has sought and sought again, but never found, a flaw or crevice large enough to enter one splitting wedge, those compact records where the persevering batteries of unbelief, shifting their point and method of attack with every shifting current of sceptical speculation, have never opened a single breach, — behold Lazarus coming forth from his grave, the dumb speaking, the blind seeing, the shrunken hand of palsy full and flexible with the circulations of health, the stone over his own sepulchre rolled away, and doubting Thomas putting his fingers into the print of the nails, his hand into the spear-wound in the side, till he exclaims, "My Lord and my God!" — then I am compelled to recognize a present Divinity, of which no field of human history anywhere gives a token, no breath from any chamber of the past, its marvels of literature, philosophy, or enterprise, yields a whisper. The words: — When I hear him saying, not with any trace of fanatical excitement or transient enthusiasm, but with that calm authority of unmistakable truth to which all the results unite in bearing confirmation: "No man knoweth the Father, but the Son; the only-begotten Son who is in the bosom of the Father, he hath revealed him"; "Before Abraham was, I am"; "I am the resurrection and the life"; "Whosoever shall confess or deny me before men, him will I also confess or deny before my Father and his angels"; "I came forth from God"; — then, listening while he thus "speaks as man never spake," it is as impossible for me to doubt the authenticity of his speech as it would be irrational for me, admitting that, to deny that there is a proper Divinity in him that he does not share with me, and that I cannot share with him. The effect on the world: — When we have it thrust upon our convictions by every fragment of historic testimony, by even heathen Pliny and infidel Gibbon themselves, by all monuments of human progress, and by all the civilization of to-day, and all the spreading life of the Church always, that since the moment when Christ came up out of the Jordan, wet with the baptism of John, and with the glory of his heavenly consecration shining upon him, a new principle has been steadily working in the heart of human things, to transform them, new in form and in spirit, in name and in essence; — then how are we to escape believing, that, if God was in the building of the world, it was not man that by regeneration created it anew?

Choose out any of the brighter luminaries that have

poured splendor on any path of thought, or blessings on any interest of the world's welfare, —

> "Men whose great thoughts possess us like a passion, —
> Thoughts which command all coming times and minds;
> Whose names are ever on the world's broad tongue,
> Like sound upon the falling of a force;
> Men whom we build our love round, like an arch
> Of triumph, as they pass us on their way
> To glory and to immortality"; —

take the mightiest in influence, the richest in knowledge, the nimblest in genius, the purest in excellence, — Plato or Humboldt or Shakespeare or Fénelon, — and then, if your reverence will bear the shock, imagine him using any of those majestic expressions, respecting his origin and his work, which I have quoted from the lips of Jesus; and, though you had begun to doubt, you will be startled back into a sense of the real Divinity of the Redeemer. Conceive that philosopher, poet, or statesman, standing before the Eternal and Almighty Father, under the shadow of impending death, and uttering that petition in the prayer of the Lord, "And now, O Father, glorify thou me with thine own self, with the glory which I had with thee before the world was; for thou lovedst me before the foundation of the world," — you will need no other proof how far our idle speculations wander from the awful bounds of truth, when we speak of God's Messiah as in kind like men.

If our God were only an assemblage of abstract qualities; if, instead of looking to him as a personal Friend and Father, we had regarded him as only an agglomeration of impersonal attributes; or if we refined away our feeling of trustful intimacy towards him into an intellectual conception of a Causative Principle, — then the argument I have just noticed might have some force. All that would be necessary to make God manifest, either in Christ or in ourselves, would be some appearance of those qualities or attributes in us; and just in proportion to the degree in which they appeared, we should all be gods. But, if our view of God's nature and man's nature proceeds according to another philosophy than this pantheistic one, we shall presently be satisfied, that, though a man were strong, wise, just, and good, up to the full measure of the possibility of his nature, and such a pattern of all spiritual graces as should equal the Christian standard itself, yet he would be as far from participating in the essential and incomprehensible nature of the Deity as every other man; simply because his constitution is human; because, being human, he is made subject to certain limitations of ability; and because every finite being is psychologically separated by an impassable gulf from the Infinite. Christ was not so separated. He was one with the Father, in a sense and a way that we cannot be one with Him, — in a oneness which is at once the secret of the Mediatorship, the key to the Gospel, the ground and hope of our final reconciliation with both; and, moreover, it is of the "person" of God that he is "the express image." The ancient seers saw his glory. Through him Moses received his commission, —

"Light of the Prophets' learned lore!
Lord of the Patriarchs gone before!"

Our charter for the liberty of this inspiring doctrine is the whole tone pervading the New Testament, from the announcement of the Spirit to Mary the mother, — "That holy thing which shall be born of thee shall be called the Son of God; and of his kingdom there shall be no end," — down to the last benediction of the Apocalypse, in the name of "the Lord Jesus Christ." It is in the language express and general, it is in the breath and spirit, it is in the precept and the sanctions, of the whole Christian revelation. If you ask for it in a single sentence, you find it gathered up into that comprehensive declaration, "I and my Father are one," or, "No man can come unto the Father but by me." I believe, therefore, — I cannot but believe, — I am as unable as I am undesirous to doubt, — that, in regard to that deep, wide line that distinguishes the Infinite from the finite and the Divine from the human, Christ the Redeemer does not stand by his nature on the human side. I discover no way in which an estranged, lost family on earth, not knowing God by all its wisdom, and condemned by a law which it had not power or will to keep, could be raised, restored, and justified, but by one who should bring the Deity to the earth, while he lifts up man towards Deity. The Redeemer must make God manifest in the flesh, mediate between Heaven and humanity, show us the Father to move and melt the child.

There can be no half-way statement here, without a wrong to philosophy and faith both. That in Christ which is not human is God, — verily, literally, and strictly God; as truly God, and in the same sense God, as the Father is God. All the biblical language seems to me to preclude the conception of any intermediate nature. He is spoken of as man, and he is spoken of as God. That mystery is insoluble to the understanding. But this is clear: while God, to whom all things are possible, may enter into human conditions, and pass through a human experience, and thus "become man," man can in no sense become God. The difficulties in the way of receiving our Lord and Saviour as God are as nothing compared with the difficulty in receiving him as not God; nay, Faith joyfully finds that she has made them to be, not difficulties, but blessed and simple and gracious helps to holiness. For "in him dwelleth all the fulness of the Godhead bodily."

I am not unfamiliar with the several interpretations affixed to the passages cited, by those who would discharge them of the contents I have found in them, and reduce them to a consistency with the humanitarian or the Arian theory. It is doubtful, judging by experience, whether it avails much to undertake a refutation of these interpretations in detail, before the heart, by another and a surer process, is brought to an inevitable persuasion of their insufficiency. They will satisfy, till some special exigency of spiritual experience dissolves them in its potent alembic; and then they look as unengaging to the affections as they do forced and unnatural to the understanding.

If, now, any critical mind is asking what the way and method of this union between Jesus and the Father are, as if some logical difficulty there were sure to baffle my conclusion, and win a triumph over faith, let me frankly confess, that no inability of mine to make full answer embarrasses me, nor compromises my doctrine.

Into the interior relations of the Infinite One no mortal understanding can penetrate. What are the celestial adjustments of these revealed personalities; what are the modes of intercommunication between the Father and the Son; in what sense he who expressly says, with a clearness of authority that no human intelligence dares to question, that *all* power in heaven and earth are his, can yet have that power "given" to him; how he who could say, "Before Abraham was, I AM," could also say, "Of that day and that hour knoweth no man, no, not the angels which are in heaven, neither the Son, but the Father"; in what character, or referring to what office, that Lord of all, by whom the worlds were made and by whom mankind are to be judged, could declare, "My Father is greater than I"; how it could be that he who was in the beginning with God, and "was God," should yet enter a child's frame, be born of a woman, be made under the Law, pass through a mortal experience, eat and sleep, be tempted, and pray and die; in what manner it was that he who thus shows himself eternally one with the Father could voluntarily veil some things, as it were, from his own mind, and, in the wonderfulness of his condescension and the humility of his Sonship, lay aside for a time, not only "the glory that he had before the world was," but his vision of some things that the Father hath hid in his power;—these are secrets. I cannot fathom them. Let me say, I rejoice that I cannot. I gratefully adore that incomprehensible existence, — the Father in the Son and the Son in the Father. It is the life, the power, the spiritual grandeur, the one distinguishing fact and transcendent glory of the Christian faith. To me Christianity could not be without it. A God without unfathomable realities in the contents of his nature would be no God, just as a religion without mystery would be no religion. In the one case we should be orphans, as in the other we should be sceptics, faithless and forlorn.

If it be suggested that these gracious mysteries are of a character so different from other mysteries in the Divine nature and proceeding, that we ought to reject them, I find nothing in that statement that gains my assent. I find no more reason, on that ground, for rejecting them, than for rejecting the being of a self-existent God, the connection of spirit with matter, the creation of a planet, the consistency of the Almighty's power and love with the prevalence of evil. In one or another of these facts I discover what is just as difficult to my comprehension, what is just as perplexing to my intelligence, what just as much baffles my reason and contradicts my experience, as in the equally well-authenticated facts of the incarnation, or the subjection of a divine Christ to the forms and limitations of a human experience. Indeed, it would seem far more unreasonable to attempt getting clear of the difficulties by supposing Christ to be wholly human, than by supposing him to be wholly divine; because we should not only have equally grave difficulties to dispose of in the record, but others more formidable in the moral problem of the universe, the history of God's dealings with men, and the actual consequences of Christ's Mediatorship. What was wanted was a Saviour coming forth out of the Godhead, "very God of very God," at once divine in his nature and human in his sympathies, to restore, to redeem, to rescue man from himself, — to heal a fatal alienation, to put lost man and the Holy Father at one again. Who else but God manifest in human flesh was competent to this? While accomplishing it, is it very strange that he should sometimes speak of himself, in this condescending and peculiar office, as *unable* to know or to do certain things as of himself without the Father, with whom he ever dwells in perfect oneness, each in each; or that in this human sojourn he should declare himself dependent on that whole and undivided Deity, that entireness of the Godhead, from which he came forth into the world? For that also, and for all the blessed spiritual comfort, light, strength, hope, assurance, promise, salvation, it gives us, let us be humbly and most devoutly thankful. And let us look reverently up to that Lord and Redeemer who in the beginning "was God," — who left the Father's bosom for our deliverance from the law of sin and death, — who hath ascended up where he was before, — who has put it past all doubt or question that he and his Father are one, — and who with that Father reigns in consubstantial glory, ever one God, world without end.

First among the obvious, practical effects of this doctrine on the spiritual life, stands this, that it seems to be true; and, in the simple economy of God, truth always blesses, liberates, and cleanses him that holds it, by the same law that error curses, cramps, and destroys.

It stimulates our virtue, too, and our aspiration, by making us followers of a Master whom no attainments of ours can overtake, and holding up ever before us a living standard, unattainable in its loftiness, while condescending, with infinite compassion, to our finite strength. Approach him indefinitely we may in goodness; and yet the reverence of our discipleship finds nurture in this, that there is something within him that we can never compass. We must learn to dismiss it as a false feeling, that, in order to copy our Saviour's example, we must equal his dignity; that, to render him imitable, he must dwell on the level of our natures. Imitation for his holiness, but homage for his Divinity.

And, then, what encouragement is there for our trustful gratitude that we are left to no painful questioning, whether Christ's word is God's word, Christ's promises sustained by Almighty veracity, Christ's reconciling invitation pledged by the Father's power? Faith is made independent of doubt; and Hope casts her anchor fast by the pillars of heaven.

Because Christ is the brightness of God's glory, and the express image of his person, we know that our sacrament is no cold memorial, our communion no funereal pomp; but that the Master himself, as actual a person there as at the upper chamber, presides at the feast, and the very presence of his affectionate spirit welcomes us to a joyful participation.

The whole circle of Christian doctrines clusters together; — repentance, newness of life, reconciliation by the Mediator, the Saviour's Divinity, forgiveness, and acceptance with God. Let us bind them in one unbroken clasp about our hearts; live as children of the light they shed; exemplify the whole religion of him whose image, "the brightness of the Father's glory," is the centre of them all. Bear abroad his spirit, the spirit that purifies uncleanness, heals injustice, emancipates the slave, quenches strife, humbles pride, works by love, makes man the brother of man. And may his oneness with God bring our souls to his Father and ours!

The chief charm of these high views of Christ is, that they do, wherever they are welcomed into the soul, unspeakably strengthen goodness, encourage feeble resolutions, redouble zeal, enliven the Church, bless and adorn the world with the fruit of righteousness. For there is no spring to individual excellence like the feeling of the pure presence and personal intercessions of the Divine Master. There is no power to rouse and melt the sinning soul of unbelief like the condescension of that tender Redeemer, who left the glory on high, with a promise of pardon in his hand, for the bitterness of Gethsemane and the anguish of the cross. There is no glance for reverent eyes across the great fields of history so satisfying and so self-consistent, as that which beholds him, by whom it is revealed that God hath made the world and will judge all, administering the whole spiritual government of our race, from Alpha to Omega. There is no seed of noble works between man and man so fruitful as a hearty faith in the charity and the purity of the Christ who took our flesh. So it was, in the wonderful adaptations and attuning of our nature, — we know not altogether why, but we thank God it was so, — that but through him God was not to be brought to man. That is our redemption. It is the final reconciliation of Earth with Heaven. Christ is the wisdom of God, and the power of God, unto salvation, to all them that believe. We must heed both parts of John's twofold exhortation, — "Believe in the Son of God," and "love one another." And so in the blessed communion of his Church, where he dwells, looking along the line of that bright order of Revelation, — the one God, the Saviour coming forth out of the glory of his bosom, and the Comforter which Christ sendeth evermore, — we can gratefully take up the anthems of the elder time, and say: "All praise and dominion to Him that sitteth on the throne, and unto the Lamb!" "Glory be to the Father, and to the Son, and to the Holy Spirit!"

SERMON XIX.

DOCTRINE OF THE SPIRIT.

NOW THE GOD OF HOPE FILL YOU WITH ALL JOY AND PEACE IN BELIEVING, THAT YE MAY ABOUND IN HOPE, THROUGH THE POWER OF THE HOLY GHOST. — Rom. xv. 13.

It is a fact of some significance, that both the form of words which Jesus enjoined to be used in administering baptism, and the apostolic benedictions, associate the name of the Holy Spirit, or the Holy Ghost, — for the word in the original is the same, — with those of the Father and Christ. It is also noticeable, that, although the same term had been but rarely employed earlier in the Scriptures, and then evidently in a somewhat more general sense, as applicable to the ordinary influence of the Almighty energy, yet, with the opening of the Christian dispensation proper, it begins to bear a more specific and emphatic meaning; to be more copiously used as a sacred household word, very precious to the believer; and to imply, as the least thoughtful reader can see, a peculiar element of power introduced by Christ. Add to these considerations, that Paul refers four great internal states and powers of the soul — joy, peace, faith, and hope — to this creative operation, and no other reason will be wanted for a wakeful inquiry into its import. It states one of the living ideas that are indispensable to the prosperity and purity of the Church.

The true construction of a doctrine like this can only be settled by a reverential appeal to the New Testament. A proud understanding is not competent to handle it. Faith in it depends more on a teachable and worshipping heart than an ingenious brain. No man can come to Christ, except he will let the Father draw him. All spiritual truths look dim to a worldly and irreligious mind. You may pronounce the influence of the Spirit a mystery, and so reject it from your confidence; but you will find facts are mysterious, very much in proportion as they are unfamiliar. Mysteries lie all about us. You cannot take a step without planting your foot on a mystery. The passage of your voice to my hearing involves a mystery: tell me how a vibration of the air communicates one man's thoughts to the sensorium of another, and how your intelligent commerce with the world is carried on through about two pounds and a half of nervous matter in the cavity of your skull, and I might, or I might not, be able to unfold to you how the Comforter quickens the soul. "The wind bloweth where it listeth," — this was Christ's own comparison, — "and thou hearest the sound thereof; but canst not tell whence it cometh, or whither it goeth. So is every one that is born of the Spirit."

And so, to a sordid mind, never suffered to break away from the low enslavement of material interests, the whole doctrine of the Holy Spirit becomes a strange jargon, as absurd to the sensual comprehension as it is undesired by earthly affections; and the very language in which it is set forth, an unknown tongue. We might as well expect a deaf man to analyze the composition of Handel's

Oratorio of the Messiah, as that our minds, in unrenewed and unbelieving moods, should recognize the reasonableness of our being visited, or cheered, or regenerated by the Holy Ghost.

Admit this principle, and it is obvious that, to prejudge a spiritual doctrine, at the outset, by some worldly standard, is not the way of candid investigation. The very property which most distinguishes *faith* is, that it lays hold on matters which transcend all sensible demonstration. If I wait for such demonstration before I determine what to receive as truth within the circle of my beliefs, and what to debar from it, then I forsake the ground of faith at once, and come upon the ground of ocular proofs or scientific inductions; proceeding not by faith any longer, but by sight, which is a distinct principle, and a lower one. By that rule, the less faith men should have, the less religious truth there would be; the further their habits got estranged from a religious life, the less would God require of them; and, in order to escape their obligation to his law, they would only need to neglect and forget it. It is no anomaly in science, any more than in religion, for a truth to look unreasonable just to the degree that it is held off at a distance. It must be studied into, to appear intelligible; and be brought near to the heart, to appear rational. The real question, then, stands, — Is the doctrine before us addressed to our spiritual insight and our faith by the Evangelists? All our short-sighted imaginings apart, what do they teach?

The essential feature of the New Testament doctrine of the Spirit, as it appears to me, is that the coming of the Paraclete is inseparably connected with the mediatorial office of Christ; that the Holy Ghost is sent by the

Saviour in such a sense as not to be fully received till he is glorified, nor otherwise than by faith in him; and therefore that this office of the Spirit is something, by its conditions and its nature, peculiar to the ministry of redemption, not to be confounded with the ordinary effects of Divine power in nature, and least of all to be treated as only one among the vague influences found, by a poetic sentiment, a half-Pantheistic reverie, or a feeble sense of elevation or comfort, in the presence of imposing scenery, in "the light of setting suns," in the serene magnificence of midnight, in the majesty of mountains, or the blossoming of the clover, — favored by a tranquil posture of the nerves. This necessary and peculiar connection, in the Evangelical representation, of the Holy Spirit with the reconciliation of the cross, has fallen so generally out of recognition, in much preaching, as to enfeeble the force of the truth, and reduce the common notion held in some of our churches to the level of mere naturalism.

The principal passages of the Saviour's instructions, where the promise of his own continued relation to the body of his Church, and of the coming of the Holy Spirit, are contained, are the fourteenth, fifteenth, and sixteenth chapters of John. Detached entirely from one another, these passages offer difficulties. Each of them, taken separately, presents a truth of precious significance to the religious affections; but they need to be compared, collated, and held up in each other's light, in order to yield a self-consistent and complete doctrine.

Let it be remembered, that this whole discourse of Jesus was occasioned by the sorrow and the apprehensions of his disciples, because he had said to them, "I go away."* From the comforting words, "Let not your heart be troubled," throughout, it has this bearing: it aims to assure them that they shall lose none of the spiritual benefits of his presence, if only they will have faith in him as before. Scattered through it, we find these several distinct declarations:—1. Christ predicts that, in some sense, he is about to depart from the society of his followers: "I go," he says, "unto my Father." This refers, I suppose, simply to the withdrawal of his bodily presence,—the disappearance of that form of Hebrew flesh and blood, through which he had hitherto been manifested to the world, but which, if suffered to remain longer, would prove a veil † before his real and spiritual glory, and contract the universality of his religion. 2. He promises that he shall come again, and dwell constantly with them: "I will not leave you comfortless; I will come to you"; "He that hath my commandments, and keepeth them, I will manifest myself to him, and my Father will love him, and we will come unto him, and make our abode with him." This can mean nothing else than that he, the person Jesus, after his bodily departure, would yet hold conscious relations with his true Church, not visible to the fleshly eyes, but felt in the quickening energy of his Spirit, and bestowing the inward influence of his affection on the believing heart. For, 3. He speaks of these particular offices which he will perform, in the further exercise of his Messiahship: "Whatsoever ye shall ask in my name, *that will I do.*" "Without me, ye can do nothing." 4. He declares that a Comforter shall come,—a new Presence, to guide, strengthen, and assure them, in the difficulties of their

---

* John xiii. 33, 36.

† *διὰ τοῦ καταπετάσματος, τοῦτ' ἔστι, τῆς σαρκὸς αὐτοῦ.* Heb. x. 20.

ministry; and that this Comforter shall be sent to them by the Father in Christ's name: "I will pray the Father, and he shall give you another Comforter, that he may abide with you for ever, even the Spirit of Truth, — and he shall be in you"; "The Comforter, which is the Holy Ghost, whom the Father will send in my name, he shall bring all things to your remembrance, whatsoever I have said unto you." 5. He teaches that this Comforter shall also be sent by himself, though proceeding, as just shown, from the Father: "When the Comforter is come, whom I will send unto you from the Father, which proceedeth from the Father, he shall testify of me." Again: "It is expedient for you that I go away; but, if I depart, I will send the Comforter unto you." 6. This Comforter is to bring blessings equally from the Father and the Son; for says Jesus: "He shall not speak of himself; but whatsoever he shall hear, that shall he speak: he shall glorify me; for he shall receive of mine, and shall show it unto you. All things that the Father hath are mine; therefore said I that he shall take of mine, and shall show it unto you." *

From these six propositions, different in form, but capable of being so reconciled as to be one in substance, we deduce the whole doctrine on the subject. They exhaust the statement of it; and every other expression

---

* Justin Martyr speaks of the Holy Ghost as "the Power of God sent to us through Jesus Christ" (Dial. c. Tryph.), but elsewhere as one of the "host of angels." According to Origen, the Holy Ghost is "the first being, or nature, produced by God the Father, through the Son." The Latin Church did not assert the double procession from the Father and the Son till the ninth century. It was many years after the promulgation of the Constantinopolitan Creed, before the word *filioque* was inserted into it. This word, and its doctrine, made one of the five charges of heresy brought against the Western Church by Photius the Patriarch.

in the New Testament is in harmony with them. That doctrine can be no other, it seems to us, than this: that, after the body of Jesus should be removed from the Church, he should still continue to carry on the spiritual work of renewing, sanctifying, and saving souls, — which is his eternal ministry, — the Church itself thus becoming the body of his Spirit, *that* visible, but *he* indwelling, yet manifest still in the fruits of holy love and life; that, in thus acting on the spirits of believers, in answer to prayer, the Son, and the Father who sent him, are together, united in counsel and one in purpose; and that the Agent, now first distinctly revealed to men, by which they thus move and draw and change the heart, is the Holy Spirit, but also known as the Comforter, the Paraclete, the Spirit of Truth, and the Holy Ghost.

Let us now bring together, in as condensed and clear a paraphrase as possible, these scattered statements of Jesus and the Evangelist, so as to exhibit a connected exposition of the truth. "In my Father's house are many mansions; I go there to prepare a place for you. But this my absence will not separate my spirit from yours. It is expedient for you, both to try your faith by leaving you to stand alone, and to prevent my religion from being limited by my bodily presence and associations.* Yet I will not leave you wholly alone and comfortless. Let not your heart be troubled or afraid at the thought of that distressing solitude. I will come to you again invisibly, and cause my spirit to abide with you, in all your holy labors, for ever. Be encouraged: my Father also will abide with you, as he does now. Only love me, and keep my sayings, and you shall feel me with

* "Si carni carnaliter hæseritis, capaces Spiritus non eritis." — *Augustine.*

you. Pray to the Father in my name; I also will pray for you; and the Father, who is one with me, will answer you through me. Thus I will continue to bring you his blessings. No longer in this frame of flesh, but by a certain interior sense awakened in your regenerate souls,* quite as quick as the natural eye, I will manifest myself to you, — to the true disciples in my Church, hereafter, as now. But inasmuch as the mode of this manifestation is to be changed, — to be inward, and not outward, — you are to know this continued and united presence of my Father and myself, through a new Agent, — the Holy Spirit, the Comforter. He shall visit and renew you, and be your refreshing. He shall carry forward the work of salvation which I have begun in the body. Pray for the Holy Spirit. The world, that is, men of worldly tastes and gross desires, cannot understand this promise. The world receiveth not this Holy Spirit, neither knoweth him, as it has not received me hitherto, but goeth about to crucify me. That earthly and sinful temper He will reprove; convicting it of sin, showing it righteousness, and bringing it to judgment. But on *you* He will so act as to teach and inspire you, bringing to your remembrance all the things that I have said to you with this mortal tongue. So he shall testify of me. I shall indeed be with him, and so with you. By believing in the Holy Spirit, you will abide in me, in the strictest unity. Through successive generations He will build up and complete my Church. Behold, then, your privilege and your inheritance. You were just now sorrowing because I said, I must go away. But, except my body were to be crucified, you could not enjoy those

* John xiv. 19. Tholuck observes, that, "in the pregnant use of language as employed by John and Christ, ζῶ means *to lead a true life in God.*"

higher benefits that come from my resurrection. I cannot come to you in the Spirit, till my form is removed. What you cannot now understand of these mysteries, the Spirit will gradually reveal to you.* He shall take of my truth, and, little by little, age after age, show mankind the full meaning of my gospel and my redemption. It is true, my Father is the sender of this Spirit; but between my Father and me is no division of interest, or counsel, or honor. Whoever honors one of us, honors both. I said truly, therefore, that the Spirit, in showing you God's will, shows you mine; for our will is one, and our truth is one. Only believe what I have said. A little while, and ye shall not see me; for I shall be crucified, and ascend from the world. But again, a little while after, you *shall* see me by the eye of your faith, and you shall feel me, and know that I am with you, and my Father also. We will send to you together the Holy Spirit, the Comforter; and, when I thus see you again, your heart shall rejoice; and that joy no man taketh from you."

Let us next notice the harmony between this interpretation and other New Testament references to the same doctrine. In giving an account of that lofty discourse, pronounced by Jesus earlier in his ministry, when he stood, on the last and great day of the feast, and proclaimed to the world his divine invitation, "If any man thirst, let him come unto me and drink," — John puts in this parenthesis: "This spake he of the Spirit, which they that believe on him should receive; for the Holy Ghost was not yet given, [or, as the original Greek has

* "He speaks in a language best adapted to the apprehension which the disciples then possessed, as well as to the time, and topic in hand, when he speaks concerning his departure to the Father." — *Bengel.*

it, *was not yet*,*] because that Jesus was not yet glorified," that is, ascended into his heavenly glory. This shows that John regarded the gift of the Holy Spirit as conditioned on the death and ascension of Christ.

Again, as Jesus had promised the Spirit to be given at the time of his own departure, to fill the place of his bodily companionship, we should naturally expect some signal demonstration in connection with that event. Is this expectation fulfilled? "The same day" that he rose from the dead, we are told, "at evening, being the first day of the week, Jesus stood in the midst of his disciples, and said to them, Peace be unto you! and when he had said this, he breathed on them, and saith unto them, Receive ye the Holy Spirit." Furthermore, the history is taken up, immediately after his ascension, by Luke, in the "Acts of the Apostles"; and the very first sentence contains two distinct references to this doctrine of the Spirit, recalling especially the Saviour's promise that his Apostles should "be baptized with the Holy Ghost, not many days hence. Was that promise accomplished? Read the full answer in the record, just after, of that matchless wonder, the sublime outpouring and witnessing of the Spirit, on the day of Pentecost, when the Church of Christ received its visible baptism and consecration, for all time, in the tongues of fire; and Peter preached, while the multitude praised.

Passing on into the preaching of the Apostles, as they went out on their missionary work, we find their message surcharged with the burden of this great doctrine. Everywhere they preached Christ and the resurrection, and coupled with these the office of the Spirit, regenerating and sanctifying the soul. Their Epistles glow and

* οὔπω γὰρ ἦν πνεῦμα ἅγιον.

kindle with the same animating assurance. The radiance of that conviction touched with glory their sufferings by persecution, the miseries of their prison-houses, their perils by the wilderness, and the martyrdoms that crowned their good confession of the cross. "None of these things move me," cried Paul; "for the Holy Ghost is my witness." Whatever fruits of conversion and faith honored their apostleship, they described as not their own, nor of man's wisdom, but the "demonstration of the Spirit," and "with power." Three verses in the Epistle to Titus really condense the whole doctrine into one comprehensive formula: "After that the kindness and love of God toward man appeared, not by works of righteousness which we have done, but according to his mercy he saved us, by the washing of regeneration and renewing of the Holy Ghost, which he shed on us abundantly through Jesus Christ our Saviour."

It commends this construction to our cordial reception, that it meets all the variety of our different religious habits, suits itself to whatever sincere moods our shifting experience may bring, and, on whichever of the Divine agents in sustaining our moral life we fix our meditation, furnishes us a more satisfying image of each.

Some devout minds, for example, have been trained to fasten their religious reverence and affection almost exclusively on the Father. Not denying the Son, nor his offices, nor rejecting the fellowship of the Spirit, their pious thoughts turn most naturally to God as Father. It is He that dwells before their contemplation, absorbs their love, and reaches down to help and save them. For such, the doctrine, as we have presented it, offers the Holy Spirit as the gift and presence of that God, his witness, his token, one of his personal manifestations to the soul. And although, as it needs indeed to be more believed, we rob ourselves of Christian peace and power, just in proportion as we drop out of view our intimate relations to the person of Jesus; yet, as we have seen, so long as we recognize him as the Divine Saviour, he will still bestow his benediction on the heart that truly worships his Father. Did he not say to the Father, "All mine are thine, and thine are mine"? Accordingly, as if expressly to enlighten minds of the cast we have alluded to, the Holy Spirit is represented to us as the Spirit of God, — as the God that was from everlasting, and visited Moses, David, and Isaiah. Such believers will cling most fondly to that phrase in the promise, "*My Father* will love him and abide with him"; and, not forgetting that it is "in the name of the Lord Jesus," they will linger with special satisfaction on Paul's language to the Corinthians, where he says, "It is by the Spirit *of God* that we are sanctified."

Another class — and it seems to us they are apt to be Christians of a more fervent and effectual faith — find their religious life, not only originally, but constantly, dependent on the person of Christ. They want to feel the strengthening touch of his hand and the breath of his intercession. They are resolute according to the frequency with which they sit at his feet, and vigilant according as they are conscious that he is near to be wounded by their backslidings, or to rejoice personally in their moral victories; and they are constant to his Church according as they realize him to be veritably in it a leader, a friend, a reconciler. This class, then, will listen with most grateful eagerness when he tells them that he also, as well as the Father, comes in the Comforter. They bless him for the pledge, "Lo, I am with you alway, even unto the end of the world." They rejoice in the declaration, "Where two or three are gathered together in my name, there am I in the midst of them." They reassure themselves with the conviction, that, though he went away in the humiliation of the cross, he cometh again to judge the saints for evermore in glory. And the highest duty of their discipleship is fulfilled when they can know that they "abide in him."

Or, again, if there are others, whose thought turns less to the person of either the Father or the Son than to that Divine Paraclete proceeding from them both, which we have seen to be called by the New Testament the Spirit, as actually happens with some branches of the Church Universal, — then, provided only they will receive it in simplicity, our doctrine makes ready room for them also, offering no violence to their peculiar culture or affinities. And these will seize on those many passages that ascribe the work of renewal to the Holy Ghost, or refer the joy and peace of believing to His power.

By all these ways, in accommodation to all these shapings of devout belief, will the view we have opened, if it be reverentially studied and welcomed with a docile heart, yield confidence and guidance to true Christian disciples, of whatever name or fold.

Nor is it an incidental, but an essential and inherent, operation of our doctrine, that it exalts our conceptions of the personal work of the Messiah, as the Head of the Church and the Divine Agent of man's regeneration. Crucified at Calvary, he lives throughout the world. Slain as our Passover, he survives as our Advocate. Ascended from our sight, he blesses us still by the Spirit. Before Abraham, in the bosom of the Father, he reigns till he has put all enemies under his feet. In that he died, he died unto sin once; but in that he liveth, he liveth unto God, and dieth no more.

It remains that we turn our thoughts to those immediate offices of the Spirit towards our own personal experience, which serve to bring the doctrine practically home to the religious affections and life.

Do we feel a consciousness of mortal weakness, which quite disables us from originating, out of our own virtue, the regeneration of the soul, and cleansing the heart from all the defilements of sin? The Holy Spirit comes to meet that very incapacity: freely, without money or price, the offered and waiting bounty of God's infinite affection comes, only asking that we accept it. So it came, with a mighty wind and tongues of fire, at Pentecost; so it will come, with reviving breath and burning zeal, to every heart in us that will believe. What said Jesus of the new birth to Nicodemus, but that every man so renewed is "born of the Spirit"? and Paul, but that "the washing of regeneration" is "the renewing of the Holy Ghost, which God sheds on us abundantly through Jesus Christ our Saviour"?

Are we overtaken with a solitary sense sometimes of our need of *guidance* through this tangled labyrinth of life and its temptations? The strong voice of an Apostle answers to that need: "As many as will be led by the Spirit of God, they are the sons of God." Or does your mind stand, dark and perplexed, when some fiendish enemy from within or without — a sneer, a passion, a provocation — bewilders your judgment and agitates your temper? Behold, says your Lord, "the Holy Spirit shall teach you in the same hour what ye ought to say." With him who could fight with wild beasts at Ephesus, and sing anthems in prisons, and terrify pompous magistrates with his inbred dignity, we can "speak, not in the words which man's wisdom teacheth, but which the Holy Ghost teacheth." And so we find the Spirit not only a guide, but an instructor; not only leading us to the truth, but educating us to receive it.

When you want encouragement under failure, or peace in bereavement, he is your "Comforter"; which is the very signification of "Paraclete"; and in the same breath where he promised that guide and teacher, Christ promised "peace" also, — his own peace, given "not as the world giveth." And if you inquire how this comforting comes, Scripture is ready with a reply: "Because the *love of God* is shed abroad in our hearts by the Holy Ghost which is given unto us."

And then, when the mood makes transition from penitence, despondency, or grief, to courage, and your necessity is that you be restrained rather than pardoned, stimulated, or soothed, you are taught that the same Spirit exercises a power of forbidding, as well as of impelling, and are reminded that even a purpose which seemed so right as preaching the Gospel in Asia was forbidden to an Apostle by the Holy Ghost, because the Heavenly Wisdom foresaw results hidden from the best man's eyes.

And, finally, that highest and crowning grace of Christian character, sanctification, is declared, in the Epistle to the Romans, to be the work of the Spirit, — Renewer, Guide, Comforter, Restrainer, Sanctifier! Witness the beneficent and celestial offices which we either reject with worldly unbelief, or entertain with devout thanksgiving.

Nor can there be any evasion under the apology that there is partiality in the invitation. For we listen to the earliest inspiration of the Church, and hear Peter indignantly questioning, " Can any man forbid water that these should not be baptized, which have received the Holy Ghost as well as we ? And they of the circumcision were astonished, because that on the Gentiles also was poured out the gift of the Holy Ghost." I am not at liberty to judge of its reality by any outward manifestations; for I am uniformly taught to look for that gift as a secret messenger to the soul. I turn with veneration to the noblest and holiest saints, like Stephen the protomartyr, and the first companions of his unspeakable tribulation, and find it repeatedly said of them, that the richness, and grace, and stability of their manhood was, that they were " filled with the Holy Ghost." Nay, I must contemplate with a new feeling of solemnity and Christian awe my own poor frame, when I read, " Know ye not that your body is the temple of the Holy Spirit? Whosoever defileth the temple of God, him shall God destroy; which temple ye are."

It becomes us to remember the great law of the gift; that *condition* with which we must implicitly comply, if we would have our souls enlightened and expanded by the indwelling Spirit of our Father and our Redeemer. Hearken to it, as it is uttered from Divine lips: " Your Heavenly Father shall give the Holy Spirit"—to whom? To them that seek it not, and prize it not, captives to their traffic, bondmen to their ambition, satisfied with what they eat and drink, and with the shapes and colors wherewithal they shall be clothed? No; but " to them that ask him."

May not the Spirit be resisted, and scorned, and insulted, then, and even fatally and finally forfeited,—sorrowfully withdrawing, at last,—yet with intercessions and yearnings of tender pity that cannot be uttered? The answer is not ours. It is the warning of One greater than you or me: "Grieve not the Holy Spirit of God." "Quench not the Spirit." "Whosoever blasphemeth against the Holy Ghost, it shall not be forgiven him."

And now, what are the fruits of this Spirit in the hearts and lives of men? Will not our own reason, our conscience, nay, our very eyesight, as we read the characters of those we know, make the same answer with revelation? "The fruit of the Spirit is in all goodness, and righteousness, and truth, — love, joy, peace, — long-suffering, gentleness, temperance." "If we live in the Spirit, let us also walk in the Spirit." Let the doctrine find its unanswerable testimonies in the greater purity, nobleness, and devotedness of the Christian's life before men.

We do greatly want a fresher and deeper doctrine of the Holy Spirit. We want it individually, to give vitality to our professions, and energy to our effort, and sanctity to our faith, and unconquerable constancy to our will. Christendom wants it, to heal the waste places of its foreign and its domestic heathenism, to repair the desolations of bigotry and formality, to advance the flagging march of its principles, to animate the languid piety of its churches, to invigorate pure and undefiled religion, to gather unrepenting but homesick prodigals in, to enlarge, and build up, and strengthen the enclosures of the Saviour's everlasting fold.

Come, then, thou Holy Spirit, the Renewer, to replenish our wasting lamps, and revive thy work, in the midst of the years! Come, Guide and Teacher, to take our hands in thine, and pour light on our way and on our mind! Come, as the Comforter, to heal bleeding hearts, and bind up the bruises of uncharitableness, and every sorrow! Come, Restrainer, to keep our feet, and all our hidden desires and imaginations, from evil! Come, thou Sanctifier, to purify and perfect us, — unto the worship of the Father, and obedience to the Son, — till we are a true and accepted branch of the immortal Vine, — a people patient and believing, and zealous of good works!

SERMON XX.

THE SOUL'S DEPENDENCE ON CHRIST, AND VICTORY BY HIM.*

WITHOUT ME YE CAN DO NOTHING. — John xv. 5.
I CAN DO ALL THINGS THROUGH CHRIST WHICH STRENGTHENETH ME. — Phil. iv. 13.

In the two members of this double text are affirmations of both the weakness and the power belonging to us. " Without me ye can do nothing," from the lips of the Redeemer, signifies our complete dependence. " I can do all things through Christ strengthening me," the exulting claim of an Apostle, exposes the breadth of our liberty. And inasmuch as they who *can* do all things ought to do greatly, this sinless boast of Paul challenges us with a grand ideal. It utters a stimulating call to our spiritual energies.

In this twofold bearing, the text is only true to the profound facts of our nature and our position. We are — experience and analysis equally confirm it — we are both weak and strong, both dependent and free. Our probation is balanced between these conflicting conditions.

* Preached before the " Autumnal Convention " at Worcester, Mass., October 20, 1853.

There precisely is the problem we are to work out, and there is the sharp strain of our discipline. God knew that just these conditions were the most fruitful for producing moral maturity. Looking at our duty from one side, it would seem as if all we have to do is to put forth our moral energies,—to act. Looking at it from another side, it would seem as if our chief business is to appreciate what Christ does for us,—to realize that we belong to him. To learn how to adjust these elements,—how to combine and manage both our large birthright of free-will and its humbling limitations,—how to use our ability nobly, and at the same time to draw the grace of submission out of our insignificance, not suffering the one to engender impiety, nor the other to dishearten us into indolence,—this is perhaps the choicest secret in religious wisdom. We have to discover that our frailty is in fact a minister to our progress, in first making us feel that we can do nothing of ourselves, and afterwards drawing us to Him in whom the soul gains its perfection; and, on the other hand, that our native capacity is the spur that keeps our muscles from palsy. Our dependence is the needed check on vanity; and our power puts us to work in the Master's vineyard, after we have entered it under that lowly door of self-renunciation.

Let me say, that, in my present treatment, I recognize no distinction between the Messiah speaking and the God who speaks by his lips. "The Father who dwelleth in me," he says, "he doeth the works." "As the Father hath given me commandment, even so I speak." Raising no question, therefore, of the interior relations of their nature, nor touching the dogmatic aspect of the case in any way, I find that, for all the practical interests of the subject, what is declared by Christ of himself is declared of God. Understand me, then, as taking for granted this oneness between them, by which each speaks for the other, and as waiving from the discussion any possible notion of a conflict of their dignities.

My method will be, first, to offer you some illustrations of the beautiful law, inwoven into our spiritual constitution, that it is looking upward to a Power above us which works the largest effects in both animating and purifying the soul, rather than any introspection, peeping about for ever among our own petty attainments or defects; then, to observe how this essential want is met in Christ Jesus, and how he becomes the elevating Presence and informing Power which lends to every true life its order, its constancy, its peace.

Undoubtedly, the chief and most urgent sense of our need of Divine help comes by the conviction of our sins. Dependent for all inspiration and furtherance on the Father's Well-Beloved, we depend on him most of all for the reconciliation that brings forgiveness, and so we *feel* this dependence most completely, when smitten by the consciousness of our alienation. The perfect but violated law, with no lax nor exceptional clause; the bright immaculate standard; the unqualified "Thou shalt" from the mouth of the Judge, insulted by our constant transgression; the faithful and rebuking memory that will not sleep, but fixes on us the guilt and the dread of offenders; — these are what wring from the dependent breast the heartiest cry, "Lord, save us, or we perish!"

Apart from this, however, and in a more general view, it is by one of the most signal spiritual laws that human hearts are made to receive their chief impulses from a being exalted over them; as child from parent, —

scholar from teacher, — the soldier from his leader, — the citizen from the majesty of government embodied in the ruler. So in the Church, which is the nursery, the school, the camp, the kingdom, of religious training and growth. There is no principle so wondrously efficient for the production of holiness as faith in that eternal play of the Spirit into our common life, promised by Jesus, as the perpetuation of his own mediatorial office, under the names of Comforter, Paraclete, Holy Spirit, Spirit of Truth. When our lives lose this transfiguring faith, the celestial splendor has faded from them. It is this that establishes that affecting commerce between humanity and the heavens, which brings down the help of the Almighty to renew, from hour to hour, our wasting devotions. This is that doctrine of the Spirit, — wakening, encouraging, sanctifying, — which the modern Church seems often so stupidly bent on denying, as if it would bereave the earth of its only celestial light. And it is indispensable to the doctrine, as a faithful study of John's Gospel will interpret it to us, that we understand by the Spirit something more, something nearer, something warmer and more efficacious, than the inarticulate influences of nature; namely, that peculiar and personal energy which Christ referred to as in fact the continuation of his own life in his Church, and declared to be inaugurated on his going away, and which is clearly separated from the domain of natural law. The Saviour uttered no syllables more full of tenderness, than when he besought his followers to feel that without him they could do nothing. He furnished man no uplifting nor propelling impulse so august or so benignant as when he cried, "No man cometh unto the Father but by me." Study deeply enough, and we shall see that God nowhere gives such final honor, or such immortal blessing, to the names of his separate sons and daughters, as when he exalts his Only-begotten over them all, and gives him a name that is *above* every name, that so their faith might look up to him, and climb after him.

I think you will agree with me, that there is some secret provision in our nature which makes this act of *looking upward* the grandest exercise of our faculties. It is shadowed forth by the fact, that, in the common consent of all languages, what is noblest and best is placed over us. Heaven is arched above our heads. Excellence is a height. When we improve, we ascend. Greatness is figured as an elevation. Virtues in character are measured according to their loftiness. The divinest motions of the human spirit are aspiration and veneration,—both looking upward. Prayer, we say, goes up. The more a man sees above him to reverence, the humbler he is; and "he that humbleth himself is in due time exalted." The finest symbols of all generous attainment are mountains and the sky. And just as to a true and thoughtful mind the largest satisfaction found in the society of great hills is in looking up toward them from beneath, and letting the kindled and devout imagination travel up their glorious peaks into the infinitude and mystery whither the summits point, rather than in putting the foot on their crown and sending the eye arrogantly down into the conquered plains,—so always, if our spiritual state is right, what is grandest on earth most impels us to look beyond it.

This conviction of a constant dependence on what God does for us, by his Spirit and his Son, as the great spring and motive of what we are to do for ourselves, stands in intimate connection with other dispositions, besides humility, equally necessary to the higher types of character, — such as self-denial, gratitude, penitence, love, — all heroic traits. Is not self-denial a part of magnanimity? But strike away its divine impersonation in Him who died that we might live, and, if we could no longer gaze up to that standard of sacrifice, how soon would the glory of such virtue grow dim! Penitence is the sorrow that haunts a guilty breast for having rejected that condescension, and so it is the child of Christianity. Gratitude is the answer of nature to the Being who so lent himself to the world's malice, and to the forgiveness that blesses penitence with pardon. And if you speak of love, — was there ever a feeling worthy to be called by that holy name that did not see in the person beloved something superior to self? By all these bonds of better feeling does Christ fasten us to the way of life, when he makes us realize that without him we can do nothing. The idea that man is the originator and autocrat of his religious life, by severing us from our Head, robs us of these radiant graces. Submission to self is no submission. A hard, bold, conceited, and finally a disappointed and recanting temper, is engendered, and because the soul would not lean on its Lord, piety perishes.

It may be pretended, I know, that this doctrine of dependence on what is done for them may indispose men to act for themselves, and, by locating the main work above them, turn redemption into a temptation to idleness, leaving Christian believers only passive recipients of salvation, instead of energetic doers, working it out. But whatever color of plausibility such an objection may have taken from extravagant or one-sided representations, the view, as it opens from the New Testament, offers no practical room for the charge, and the best philosophy takes sides with Revelation. Let any heart *really feel* that a great sacrifice of love has been undergone for it, and must it not, by a mighty necessity, give back the service of love in return? To maintain the opposite is the worst libel human nature has ever suffered yet. On the contrary, it presents human nature on its more attractive side, I think, that it is found to be striving for generous achievements quite as effectually out of the grateful sense of what has been done for it, as out of the more ambitious and Pharisaic hope to do everything for itself. There is no nobler order of souls than those that know how to owe their best wealth to a Hand above them, without servility or sloth. The secret of beautiful manners, in society, is social reverence, or that tacit subordination of selfish convenience to the whole, which is like a perpetual offer of free and dignified service to others. The most refined of all courtesy is that by which a man makes the most of himself, only for the sake of making, in himself, the worthiest offering to his kind. Hence the ancient loyalty was often self-ennobling simply because it was unselfish. Christianity, transferring the homage from all accidental principalities to a Prince of perfection and peace, sustains the principle with a better application. It is clearly declared, in the spiritual code of the Gospel, "Whosoever is willing to give his life away for his Master, shall save it."

It is not a mere conceit of speculation, I think, to seek, in this way, a confirmation for the Christian doctrine of dependence, in the natural facts and constitution of the mind, — in the rule of manners and in every-day emotions. For, however complete our deference to the authority of Revelation, there are capricious moods in the most believing minds, when intellectual curiosity will be prying into the realm of ordinary reason for some echoes to the vast witness in the Bible. In such furtive licenses of doubt, it is no light comfort to faith to find that even all along the highways of nature, in the public paths of custom and of reflection, there are scattered consenting monuments to the insufficiency of our mortal ability, to the power of the Divine redemption.

Accordingly, it is interesting to see that the history of the higher speculations in philosophy scarcely shows a period when the idea of man's belonging to a Superior was not embraced by some of the leaders of thought. Ever since the morning of science, the foremost danger of intellectual activity has been audacity, or that self-confident unbelief which thinks to dispense with God; this danger the instincts of the deeper-sighted thinkers have not failed to apprehend. Standing in the Grecian twilight, hear Plutarch, as he looked still farther back into what was antiquity to him, bewailing the departure of an earlier faith. "The ancients," he says, "directed their attention simply to the divine in phenomena, as God is the centre and beginning of all, and from him all things proceed. But the moderns turned themselves wholly away from that ground of things, and supposed everything could be explained from natural causes,"—the identical presumption of our nineteenth century scepticism. The great modern master of that philosophy which affects to be most independent of Revelation introduces into his system a principle which, if you only allow it to play into personal as well as abstract relations, does really suspend everything on God's will; namely, that in all human minds the sense of an Infinite is the necessary condition and counterpart of a finite consciousness. And while European culture in its last and most subtile elaboration thus leaves in its splendid edifice a virtual confession of the fundamental axiom of religion, we find the solitary thinker of the Western Continent, Jonathan Edwards, in his Berkshire study, by reasonings not less original and independent, nor less influential on the world's ideas, maintaining the much plainer and more evangelical proposition, that the whole universe, in every part of it, is supported by a continual succession of acts of the Divine Will, not different from that which at first created the world, "just as an image is upheld in a mirror by a continual flow of rays of light, each succeeding pencil of which does not differ from that by which the image was at first produced." So do the extremes of human theories, in the diverse voices of genius, through all the periods of which letters inform us, unite in rendering their testimonials — from the most vague and reluctant, to the most articulate, cordial, and clear — to the simple truth which Paul put better than any of them, — that in God we live and move and have our being. And without him as he is manifest in his Christ, spiritually we can do nothing.

You will hardly need an argument, I think, my friends, to satisfy you that the active forces of our time are working in a direction that is very liable to drift men's thoughts and affections away from this humble upward-looking faith and religious submission. The very enterprise that builds the gorgeous structure of our civilization, threatens to undermine the vastly more needful shelter of the Church; because, by so many triumphs over the resistance of matter, the brain grows self-assured, and comes to deem itself almighty and all-sufficient. As we go on making the earth more convenient, there is less feeling of the need of that other heritage, lying all glorious and serene beyond it. Ships, factories, railways, mills, aqueducts, instead of being made the consecrated instruments of a *holier* society, *may* be only the boasted badges of a *richer* one, and beget a shallow and ungodly impudence. In the piety now fashionable, we miss, how often! the simple, childlike character that waits every hour for the beckoning hand of God. At church even, the preaching encroaches upon the prayers, and wins the livelier interest. At our business, the swift eagerness of motion puts life at awful hazards; the great channels of public travel planting and peopling graveyards at every bend of the road. All is persistent will, valiant energy, pushing and victorious worldliness. How little of meek, persistent communion with the everlasting Lord! How little dependence on the Spirit! How little of that deeper meditation which sees that, without religion, all this fretting action will be but a noisy ruin after all, and that without Christ it can do nothing! We are impatient for results. We measure the spiritual life by the wealth or size of parishes and the ostentation of philanthropy. We are willing to pay liberal prices for that piety which yields a handsome return of self-complacency. No sooner does some sect get a little faith, than, instead of modestly crying, "Lord, I believe: help thou mine unbelief!" it goes about to challenge admiration, and expects applause, and sets up a competition with its neighbors, — too sure evidence that what it got was not faith. The old Puritan habit of connecting every change in place or venture in business with God's providence, and hallowing it by a prayer, is praised perhaps in the eloquence of Pilgrim anniversaries; but is it practised in State Street and the State-House? Commerce crowds upon the closet. The school-house gets jealous and impatient of the Bible. Universities talk of closing their chapels. An upstart learning, idolizing knowledge, but only half wise, screams its smart sneers at the Revelation which will be true after it is dead, as it was before it was born. The sin of the brain has always been audacity. And the hardest and least relenting of all unbeliefs is that of a bitter intellectual pride. In the Hebrew allegory, the fallen angels of *Love* regained the celestial light, because they confessed their weakness, and crept back, through the dark, dependently begging to find again what they had lost. But the fallen angels of *Knowledge*, confident in their vain boast of self-emanating lustre, plunged obstinately on, till they sunk, obscure and lost for ever, into the pit. "Without me," — it needs to be written out over all your warehouses, and wharves, and banks, and barns, and starting-points of travel, and ships' decks, and places of amusement, — it needs to be brought into the souls, and so into the labor and life, of the people, — "Without me ye can do nothing, — without the principles of my religion, — without the purity and justice and charity of the beatitudes, — without faith in my person, — without the spirit of my life, and the sacrifice of my cross!"

Believe it, brethren, man needs a more generous motive than his own promotion. To be satisfying, or serene, or strong, his life must link itself through a mediator to God, and breathe by his inspiration. When I can begin every day, or undertaking, with the feeling, "I do it not of myself, so much as the Spirit through me," then I labor with more than my poor mortal ingenuity; the cunning of my fingers is the simple desire to be about my Father's business; and I *can* do all things through Christ strengthening me. Consciously, distinctly, resolutely, habitually, we need to give ourselves, our business, our interests, our families, our affections, into the Spirit's hands, to lead and fashion us as he will. When we work *with* the current of that Divine Will, all is vital, efficient, fruitful; for, leaning back against the Omnipotent arm, this human frame attracts strength into all its sinews. But when we strive *against* that current, some secret flaw vitiates even what we call our successes; and how do we know but our proudest successes then are only failures in disguise? You have seen the rower's strength put vigorously against the tide; and, judging from his own narrow point on the water, the dash of his oars *seemed* to be dividing the waves, and sending him up the channel. But when the mist lifts, let him send his glance away to some stable land-mark on the shore, and he finds the triumphant stream has all the time been drifting him backward and downward. So with the moral issue of our plans. By our conceited standards, we seem to compass our ends; but transfer the scale of measurement to eternity, and behold! we have been losers of the soul while we gained the world, because the Spirit was not invited to befriend our toil! After the bolts are all driven, and the shrouds are set, we must still wait for the breath of heaven to fill the sail. Nothing, literally nothing, in the final reckoning, without our Lord!

An illustration, how we never comprehend the facts of experience in their Christian meaning, nor look on our duties rightly, till we project the centre of our interest and love out of ourselves, and fix it in God, may be found in the progress of astronomy. The little planet we stand on was once reckoned the centre of the material universe. But when Copernicus supplanted Ptolemy, the earth, retiring into the humility of a satellite, waited on the silent lordship of the sun. So in the false computations of a short-sighted worldliness, self is central; self-will is sovereign; man is deified. But when Christianity brings in her grander "calculus of faith," the supremacy is removed from man to God; the moral universe is no longer anarchical, but heliocentric again; the earth depends from the heaven over it. The true order of piety, worship, life, is restored, because all the events of life gravitate about the Eternal Providence; the heart obeys a heavenly control; the affections are swayed by the attractions of the Spirit. Without our Lord we can do nothing.

Turn, now, to the wonderful way whereby all these necessities and cravings of the soul for help from beyond and above itself are met in Jesus of Nazareth. Ponder it, and you will exclaim, with Paul, "I can do all things through Christ strengthening me." By his wide and mighty heart, he strengthens you, embracing all the possibilities of experience, and covering all the moral emergencies of life; reaching up to heaven, in the exaltation of his nature, and having his home in the bosom of God, but stooping down to the earth also in his mercy, writing on its sand, kneeling on its sod, breathing its air, touching its saddest trials with his miracles. Tender enough to soothe the sorrow of the gentlest child by his pity, he is regal enough in his power to command into his service twelve legions of angels. Praying to his Father, he lends the ardor and steadfastness of his fidelity to our dull, irregular affections. Lifting special petitions when he had special wonders to work, or special agonies to bear, he brightens every midnight of our perplexity by his midnight supplications in the mountain, aids our hesitations by his cry at the grave of Lazarus, supports our faith by his thrice-repeated entreaties in the garden. When reviled, reviling not again, and forgiving his murderers, he furnishes a heavenly peace to every one in your houses that is wronged or betrayed, — the child that is feeling the first pang of faithless friendship, the merchant defrauded by his partner, the woman defamed by her rival. Thus, tempted himself like as we are, he is able to succor them that are tempted.

By every incident in his earthly history, every office in his ministry of humiliation, he strengthens us. So marvellously did virtue go out of him, the spots where his feet lingered but a moment became shrines of homage, where all centuries and nations kneel, — Galilee, Nazareth, Bethlehem, the Well of Samaria, the Mount of Olives: what strengthening names! The bed of every new-born babe in Christendom is safer, because his was made in a manger. All the shores of countries on to which Christian discovery has leaped, are more sacred for his walking the beach of Tiberias. His reading in the synagogue at Capernaum has added a holier dedication to every sanctuary and pulpit. When he paid the tithe of his people, he sanctioned every righteous claim of the civil government on the citizen. And when he sat down with the affectionate circle at the home in Bethany, the kind securities of family and kindred received a more than mortal benediction. So was every step in his Judæan journey radiant with the eternal Light, lightening thenceforth every man born into a Christian world, and strengthening him.

By the benevolence and the power of his miracles, he strengthens us. Not only by breaking the monotony of nature, and attesting with supernatural proofs that the

Almighty *must* be with him, but also by the lasting lessons of compassion and consolation which those miracles have left for us. We see the Saviour standing once with his gracious hand on the dead girl's heart; and lo! that image multiplies itself in a thousand weeping homes, through all the dying race. *Once* he spoke the word of resurrection to Lazarus; and the voice echoes and re-echoes in endless reverberations from all the walls of Christian sepulchres and graves that will ever be hollowed out on the globe. He healed a few sick; and all sickness and pain are more endurable. He hushed the storms at sea; and every sailor knows more surely that the waves are curbed by a heavenly control. He opened the ears of the deaf; and all his disciples listen more gratefully to his instruction.

For, again, by his true teachings he strengthens us. The Sermon on the Mount kindles virtue to-day, as gloriously as when its unequalled sentences fell on the multitude at his feet. When crime seems to be grinning in horrid triumphs over innocence, when vice grows riotous, or mammon cruel, in our New England cities, we turn back to the beatitudes, to the parables, to the conversation with Nicodemus, declaring that, except a man be born again, he cannot see God's kingdom; to the rebuke of those ambitious politicians, the sons of Zebedee, seeking high offices in the new administration; to the stern rebuke that bade the prosperous young worldling go sell all he had and give to the poor, and so crush by violence the idolatry in the heart; and in these rare discourses, reaching down, plain, piercing, and practical, to us, as to the publicans and statesmen and mechanics of eighteen hundred years ago, we feel that every word from the Saviour's lips is bread of life, coming down from heaven, strengthening us.

By his cross and death, above all, he strengthens us, — strengthens us to fight afresh with the sin that he there vanquished, to buffet the temptations that he there conquered, to hope for the forgiveness which he there pledged and sealed. No soul among you that has ever known what remorse is, — a convicted conscience, — a yearning for reconciliation with a broken commandment and a forsaken Father, — needs to be told how the cross strengthens. There are passages in human experience when all else is weakness, and confidence rises over no other spot in the dark field of sight but Calvary.

By his surviving spirit, too, — by what he still is to the world, — he strengthens us. Dispensing secret gifts to his true followers, as the living and present Head over all things to his Church, he remains the divine friend that opens his heart to the simple communion of the humblest believer. Ages do not outgrow him. Libraries cannot supplant him. All our science casts no ray that dims his transcendent glory; for the solar beam never pales before a torch. He is with *us*, if we seek him, as much as with Peter, and John, and Mary, and Thomas. "Lo, I am with you alway, even unto the end of the world."

And just here we discover light on the ecclesiastical difficulty that has so long vexed theology, namely, how to attain unity in the Church. You are met here to-night, a company of Christian students, with breasts full of aspiration for that grand consummation of history, — one fold and one Shepherd. How else shall the body be one, my brethren, except by abiding in its Head, its heart, its life, and beholding his presence? How else shall disciples see eye to eye, but by all ranging themselves in the divine circle of affectionate reverence about the central Master, sitting at his feet, and looking into his countenance, and doing his works? Christ did more than stand apart, and lay the corner-stone of the Church with his hand, and then retire into distant heavens. He pours his own heart's life, which is the Spirit, into it daily. Realize this, and you will no longer have to complain of churches that are not vital, or churches that hate and devour each other. Communion will be a fact. Society will be beautiful. Justice and love will crown commerce and government.

By his intercessions as advocate before the throne, seconding our prayers, and prevailing with the Father, he strengthens our devotion as greatly as his doctrine strengthens our work. Still, as we hearken, in the midst of our secret supplication we hear him saying, "Without me ye can do nothing," and, "Whatsoever ye shall ask the Father in my name, I will give it you."

And finally, by his resurrection, bringing immortality to light, he strengthens us, — strengthens us just where faith was feeblest and most likely to fail, — among the fears and sorrows of death. As fast as experience deepens with you, friends, it will sway the soul, if you do not unbelievingly resist it, more and more to the only Interpreter of its mystery, the only Deliverer from its bondage. Processions that halt each moment at opening cemeteries; tears that are falling, falling for ever, and baptizing burial acres; the wails of grief that moan through desolated households,—they all articulate, in some undertone, the old cry of Peter, so tender, so grateful: "Lord, to whom shall we go? Thou alone hast the words that comfort mourners, open tombs, and give us back our dead, — even words of everlasting life." And then, is there any heart beating here this evening which has not its own secret accusation, or strife, or fear, — its hidden cross of fire clinging to the inmost sensitive cords of life, — not to be outrun by travel, not to be dispelled by gayety, not to be drugged by anodynes, nor outwitted by philosophy, nor rejected by any restless artifice of fashion, — shown to no mortal eyes, but only whispered in the petitions that besiege the mercy of Heaven? It is as if God kept our secret soul opening in, on one of its many sides, only towards that one Friend that is closer than brother, or wife, or lover, — a perpetual memorial that without him we can do nothing!

As I bring this meditation towards an end, let me ask you to advert to two of the most common usurpers that we irreligiously thrust in to displace the Redeemer as the source of spiritual power, — denying his own word, that without him we can do nothing. I mean, first, material nature, with its laws of order and its aspect of beauty; and secondly, self, — self as independent of a Master.

Of the first, it will be generally agreed, I suppose, that the places where the grandeur of the visible creation is most magnificently shaped to the eye are high mountains. Our fatal mistake is in presuming they have, or could have, any really efficacious influence on character, whether by way of incitement to holiness or restraint from sin, — anything in fact beyond a certain vague, æsthetic, and transient stimulus of the finer sentiments, apart from that faith in Christ and his religion, with the hallowing associations that surround them, which we carry, or may not carry, with us to their impressive, august ritual. When I have stood on the loftiest peak of our Northern ridge, and looked off alone on the vast billows of rock and forest that stretched like a stiffened sea below, or up into the sky, which seemed no nearer, but more immeasurable there, I confess one of my first involuntary recollections went away from the sublime scene about me to the tides of human life rolling far off their dark elements of remorse for sin, of pain, and grief, and penitence, and hopeless love, and sighing of slaves, and baffled aspiration. They sent no sound up into that cold solitude; but the mortal breast I had brought up with me told me they were all living, and chafing, and surging on. And so my next thought was of that Christ by whom this hardened humanity, waiting so many generations, must be redeemed. The upheaved and tangled rifts of rock, ploughed only by volcanic revolutions and the wearing weather, reminded me how the whole creation groaneth together for the manifestation of the sons of God; the broken pillars of the hills became prophets of the second coming of the Son of Man; and from the jagged monuments of ancient change, Christian hope ran forward to "Christ's new heavens and the new earth, wherein dwelleth righteousness."

Or, finally, will you seek the original fountains of goodness in your own breast? Blind and disappointing search! That is a short sight that can trace any righteous impulse which gleams across your soul only to yourself. It has a diviner parentage, and a supernatural history. Its birth was in the Spirit of the Most High. The gracious influences set playing through Christendom by the Holy One of Nazareth have nurtured it. Whenever, after years of ignoble and selfish indolence, a sudden conviction of uselessness has smitten your conscience, and then a resolve to be a benefactor to some human lot has scattered this dismal suspicion that you might be living to no purpose, brightening and refreshing your whole heart, — it was the gift of his Spirit, more than your own invention, and the glory should be his. The noble host of reformers, that have stood between old abuses and their victims, are his army. The conquerors of oppression, of crime, of poverty, of superstition, of oceans that lay this side of heathenism, have all conquered in the name of Him who came to open prison-doors, and set the bruised at liberty. The valiant priests of labor have been but servants of that great High-Priest, passed into the heavens, who sanctified all lawful industry when he said, "My Father worketh hitherto, and I work." The successful vindicators of sinning outcasts have all watched and prayed through Him who came not to call the righteous, but sinners, to repentance. And all the lengthening train of redeeming charities and philanthropies lift their accordant anthem to the one Redeemer, "Not unto us, not unto us, but unto thy name give glory!"

Brethren, we have raised, I know, but a corner of the fold which veils the strengthening offices of Jesus to the world. With such animating, but all inadequate glimpses, we must retire from the unexhausted theme. The spiritual power in Christ is without limits. We call the celestial spaces, where the planets swing, infinite; but not as the quickening life in our Lord is infinite; for that is deeper than the sky, holier than its mystery, brighter than its effulgence, more inexhaustible than its variety. In the discoveries of astronomy, it is as if one star after another, like drops of flame, fell into the field of our vision from some supreme and inexhaustible stellar sea, and gave themselves into the hand of Science. So, as we study, with spiritual eyes, into the Saviour's divinity, one after another new points of light, new traits of love, new features of blended majesty and tenderness, gleam out upon our gratitude. We have only to look to find The heart's matchless telescope is simple, childlike faith

And every spot of common life where Providence plants our feet is an observatory, — if we will but stand in it looking upward, devoutly upward, — lofty enough for the whole sweep of that condescending heaven.

As we go, and wherever we stand, let us remember, that, for truths revealed from above, duties are to be practised on earth; for gifts of the Spirit granted, works of the heart and hand are enjoined. What remains, then, but that we go to Him without whom we can do nothing? Go with resolute obedience; go with grateful trust, — the inspiring trust that you can do all things through Christ strengthening you!

SERMON XXI.

THE HIDDEN LIFE.

YOUR LIFE IS HID WITH CHRIST IN GOD. — Col. iii. 3.

WHAT gives the doctrine of Christ's mediatorship its practical dignity, is not only its unspeakable display of Divine mercy in the redemption from sin by the cross, but also its wonderful fitness to invigorate and encourage a spiritual life in the believer. It is a striking fact of our inward economy, and is one of the proofs that we are attempered for spiritual uses, that, the loftier the exaltation we ascribe to the Saviour in his divineness, the more intimately always we find him related to the sympathies of our humanity. It is they that most elevate him in honor, who find him nearest to the affections, and most efficient as a helper to familiar duties. This is where a superficial criticism, founded on a shallow experience, constantly stumbles. When we have received a Redeemer whose being reaches back into the fellowships of the Father's bosom and glory, we have also received one who abides, with mighty ministries, in the fellowship of the Church, and in the disciple's breast, to this day. The most reverential view of God manifest in the flesh is the largest producer of daily holiness, as well as the dearest to the heart. And thus it is proved, as in many instances besides, that those truths which most rouse a religious veneration are best adapted to inspire simple goodness of character; and what is most profoundly spiritual is also most directly practical.

"The life that is hid with Christ in God." This is one of those illimitable utterances of the mind of the Spirit, which suggest so much to faith through the imagination, that we feel as soon as we repeat them how utterly impossible it is to fathom or exhaust their meaning. Deep opens below deep. But for the condescending guidance of the same Spirit, we might well retire, discouraged and dumb, from a theme so august. May the Divine pity forgive our errors and lighten our darkness!

After the appearance of the Son of God in his personal ministry, eighteen centuries and a half ago, in Bethlehem, the first fact we encounter, in the historic consciousness of the Church, is his invisible supremacy as its Head and Lord, not less in the private hearts of disciples than in their public organization and missionary activity. No sooner was Jesus lifted up from the earth, than we find his Apostles, with the widest personal diversities of habits and tastes, singularly united in that one common bond of a *hidden life*, — hidden as to its spring, but open as the day in its generous and beneficent effects. Journey where they will, their eyes turn always to one transcendent image, ascended, indeed, into the heavens, but still giving gifts unto men. Their hearts cling devoutly to one invisible Master. Their lips bear always upon them one all-prevailing name. Their prayers are all breathed through one intercessor. Their thanksgivings and songs of triumph end with one ascription, "To Him who died, yea, rather, who is risen again." At every step in those fearful perils, — from solitary wildernesses where they flew with the standard of the cross, from crowded cities and old temples, on the sea in storms at midnight, amidst the brilliant enchantments of Corinth, in the Athenian Agora, before the judgment-seats of tyranny, under the shadows of the Parthenon or of a Libyan palm-tree in a sultry noon, with the barbarians at Melita, in prisons, in love-feasts, — everywhere, they felt their hands to be laid in one sure and mighty hand, leading, blessing, delivering, serving them. One Divine form walked ever, in brightness, among the "seven golden candlesticks" whereon they had lighted church fires. Descend into the Roman Catacombs that modern curiosity has opened, and there, where they used to hide from persecution, and spread the Lord's Supper on the sepulchral tablets of their dead, every inscription, symbol, monogram, points to one incorruptible Shepherd. The constant confession of each of them was, "Of mine own self I can do nothing"; but the great assurance followed instantly, "I can do all things through Christ strengthening me."

And so it has been in the true line of spiritual descent ever since. Personal fellowship with Christ has been the hereditary blood in the veins of the Church. Wherever genuine piety has burned, there this Apostolic sentiment and power, the love of Jesus, has been the animating force, — distinct from nature-worship, from moral science, from the religion of prudence, from the culture of proprieties. And this inward life, "hid with Christ in God," is the life we have now to interpret. I propose to ask what it is founded in, what it is in itself, and what are the fruits it yields, — or as to its necessity, its nature, and its results.

I. The necessity for sharing the Mediator's life is

within the soul itself. It is implicated in the essential conditions of our spiritual being. We are not obliged to search for it in any mystical or strange region of speculation, but in the most natural and obvious of our feelings. The simplest analysis of humanity discovers it, lying evident among the elemental facts of life. For the wisest philosophy is not more sure to recognize, at last, this cry for the Son of God, among the profound and primitive prophecies of our inward constitution, than the most unsophisticated common sense is to confess it, amidst the daily discipline of the heart.

It springs out of both of the two sides of an earnest experience in human nature, the consciousness of spiritual deficiency, and the notion of perfection, — our discontent with what we are, and our desire for what we were meant to be.

We all feel, — at least if our life amounts to anything that deserves to be called an experience, — that we are not what we ought to be; that we are terribly otherwise. Let us not try to get around the fact. These hearts — our own hearts — have taken in other guests than purity and honor, devotion and disinterested love. These lips, — have they never displaced the honest words of charity and prayer for bitterness and mockery? These hands have been about other than the Father's business, — those royal services of justice and mercy. Has there been no jealousy in our dispositions, or overreaching in our dealings, or conceit in our self-esteem, or arrogance in our social intercourse, indolence in our habits, extravagance in our luxuries, slander and equivocation in our talk, vanity in the appointments of persons and households, intolerance in our judgments, hypocrisy in our professions, — none of the radically impious love of the world with which the love of the Father makes no compromise? Now, if we were under the government of abstract laws, — as Materialism says we are, and as the Pantheist will say, whenever he is both logical and honest, — then this sense of deficiency would remain only a moderate, intellectual, and inoperative discontent; for it would show us to have fallen short only of an ideal standard; it would trouble us only with the negative feeling of having failed of something which we might have achieved, and of having abused the possibilities of our capacity; so that we should be but offenders against our own ambition, — not sinners, but only mistaken or undeveloped specimens. On the contrary, we are under the government of a God who has both personality and consciousness, who is the very essence and source of all personal consciousness, and whose hourly dealings with us are direct and intimate. Our goings astray, the Gospel says, are not mistakes, but sins, — not abstractions, but concrete crimes, — not merely dwarfings of our manhood's stature, but affronts against an affectionate Father. They disturb the harmony and benefit and beauty of a gracious intercourse between the parent and the child. God has spoken; we have heard. God has commanded; you and I have disobeyed. He commands every day afresh, — publishing a new apocalypse of our duty with every sunrise. But every day afresh we are selfish, and petulant, and censorious, and proud, and not quite sincere; our purity is not white; some duplicity creeps into our conversation; some bodily sacrilege profanes God's temple. The law is holy, just, and good. Our lives are not holy, nor just, nor good. It is nowhere written that we may partly keep that law and partly break it, and yet go acquitted. But we break it still. Suppose the past score settled by our repentance; even if the integrity of the Divine government were left unimpaired, we have no reason to think we shall be perfect men or blameless women in the future. We are rather painfully and shamefully certain that, after all our endeavors, we shall sin again and again. What then were our life, without a Mediator reconciling it? What, if Christ, coming in from above its broken strength, did not touch it with his inspiration, renew it by his grace, sanctify it by his love? What if he, who alone is competent, uniting both the estranged elements in his own redeeming person, did not come and take this fallen life, and quicken it by the breathing of his spirit, and revive its torpor by his truth, and warm its frost in his bosom, and restore its deadness by his intercession, — and thus hide it again, with himself, in God? What would it be, except it were thus animated by his indwelling power, were forgiven by the pardon which no other voice on earth but his ever promised, and no other seal but his death could ever accredit? Past offences are then blotted out. The penitent passes into the disciple. Memories of transgression torment no more. So that thenceforth, Christ being formed within him, the believer might say, "This life that I live in the flesh, I live by faith in the Son of God, who gave himself for me." It is a life hid with Christ in God.

On the other side, there is the native notion of perfection. That trace of glory past, and pledge of immortality yet to be, lingers, in most minds, a witness of Heaven among so many tokens of shame. The soul will not be content with degradation. The prodigal refuses to eat husks with the swine. The sensualist has better moments, when he loathes the companionships, and the kennel, of his appetites. The hard idolater of money relents, and has a brief vision of something better worth his striving than dividends and profits. The scholar is kindled by momentary glances of an ambition that aspires beyond office or reputation, or any of the praises of earthly emulation. Nicodemus dreams of a character saintlier than a Pharisee, and wakes and feels his way to Christ by night. Woman is wretched among her ornaments and accomplishments and admirations, and feels insulted when your compliments imply that these emptinesses are the stateliest honors her heart knows how to worship. Even the woman that *was* vile, in some penitential moment is irresistibly attracted to the Saviour. Tears from the spring that has been so long dry, to wash those blessed feet; the hair that a meretricious vanity had often braided, more eagerly loosened to wipe them; kisses of purified passion; the ointment, not too costly if it impoverishes her for ever, — what signals of an indestructible longing for holiness deep down in the breast of sin! The young man comes to Jesus with that mournful confession and question, — the pathos of it sadder, I think, than anything to be read in any tragedy, — "The heights of legal virtue gained, what lack I yet?"

Here, again, if there were no personal God to whom these aspirations reach up, — if they did not culminate, at last, in the supreme desire for harmony with the infinite and infinitely holy Father, — then we should need no personal Mediator. These notions of a more perfect state, visions of a spotless virtue, would be only floating and transient visitants to the soul, — passing and leaving no permanent effect, like the luminous forms that tremble across the night sky, transfigure the darkness for an instant, and vanish. They would not consolidate into principles. They would be only the "haunting oracles that stir our clay," which heathen souls knew, and heathen genius has celebrated. But the moment our eyes are opened on our true relations to God, we see that there is no such thing as a satisfactory striving after ideal standards, but only after reconciliation with him. We see that the restless heart gets peace, the moment it gets the conviction that God is its friend, — or rather, that it and God are at one, having one will and one love. Whatever else the world can give us, it gives us chaff and the east wind, till it gives us that. Perfection of character is not to be gained except by that inspiration. A peaceful progress in goodness comes only by that faith. And now, again, the only way unto the Father is by his Son. For in Christ every ideal of spiritual excellence is realized. We have no longer to aim at the vague phantom of a dream, nor after the cloudy excellence of imagination. Christ is before us. Those that place their hands in his he leads to the Father. "All mine," he says, "are thine, and thine are mine." To be Christ-like is to be perfect, — and to have faith in Christ is to be brought nigh to God. Here is the spiritual bond which unites our loftiest aspirings with Heaven, no less than our lowliest self-accusings. In the Mediator our hope as well as our penitence is satisfied. We are not only restored from what we have been, — we are helped forward to what we would be. If our sin finds pardon, our love of excellence finds a pattern. Both sides of our twofold nature are relieved and blessed. Our whole humanity is redeemed. No thought or affection, but Christ leads, and trains, and unfolds it. And so our life at its best estate, — whether that be its humiliation or its triumph, — whether in the valley of dejection or on the delectable mountains where the city of God beckons us, is "hid with Christ in God."

Here, then, lies the unchangeable necessity of the mediation in Christ, in these two primary and inevitable wants of every human heart, — to be restored from sin, and to ascend to God, — to obtain forgiveness for the past, and to go on unto perfection. In each we should be helpless, and could do nothing of ourselves. In both we can do all things through Christ strengthening us.

II. What, then, as the next step, is this life, as to its nature; or in what special *kinds* of force do its power and its peace and its charm consist?

First of all in this, — that being received into our faith in just these two characters in which we have seen that our spiritual exigencies need him, Christ both creates within the disciple the freedom that comes of the consciousness of being forgiven for the past, and directs his practical energies to a model that is divine. If you have ever known, in some early experience of filial confidence, what it is, after going burdened and stifled with the sense of alienation from your parent, then to have the whole look and feeling of the world simplified and brightened by a reconciling explanation, you need no other key to the satisfaction of a conscience liberated from guilt by confession and forgiveness. That is the beginning of all healthful obedience. What was dismal compulsion before becomes a spontaneous and free-will offering now. Life seems to start from another point, to proceed by another principle, to tend to another issue. Its spring is gratitude, not law; its principle is love, not fear; its end is the Divine glory and the good of man, not a selfish salvation. And just in proportion to the joy of being set free from the frightful phantom of the old terror of judgment will be the personal and confidential intimacy with Him by whom that deliverance comes. The life is hid, thankfully and joyously, "in God"; but it is "with Christ" that it is hid. For, expunge from history the ministry and cross of Jesus, and tell me in what other Gospel, in all the literatures of the tribes of men, you will look for the glad tidings to penitence, — "Thy sins are forgiven thee"? Every ascription of gratitude will be a conscious recognition of what Christ has done, and will interweave the believer's life more closely with his.

But again, the spiritual life depends on Christ in that he becomes a Divine Pattern for the energies that form character. At every stage of growth, under all the phases of conflict, in the development of each proportion and feature, the soul finds an original in the spiritual symmetry of its tempted, suffering, sinless Lord. But this doctrine of Jesus as our example seems to me to lose its grandest inspiration, when we contemplate him as standing apart from his followers, raised on the pedestal of mere historic honors, a being of a distant age, and thus maintaining towards them only the cold and mechanical relation of a model to the artist. We need to bring him into the sphere of our personal contact and sympathy. The example is not a statue outside of us, but a vital force working within us. To have our life hid with him, we must, in the Apostle's significant language, have "Christ formed within us." And when we look to him for a pattern, it must not be the Christ of Judæa and of Cæsar's time, so much as the Christ of our own indwelling humanity and of to-day, — not the Hebrew Messiah, but the ever-living Immanuel. Paul had that fellowship so palpably, that he said, "It is not I that live, but Christ that liveth in me."

So it is that, in order to have our inward life in the profoundest sense hid with him, we must become conscious of some present and personal relations to him. I do not speak of a mystical or visionary fellowship. Like other spiritual attainments, this conviction, that the Saviour who died for your soul must still know its weakness, and visit it in its danger, and comfort it in its sorrow, and chasten it in its wilfulness, must be made strong by exercise. It will be a palpable and refreshing reality only to those who have cultivated it, and prayed for it: in different degrees distinct, according to the measure of the desire, and possible at all only to those who have got so far clear of the tyranny of the sensuous understanding, as to give free play to the faith, that things which are impossible to men are possible with God. Let that beautiful confidence once secure a lodgement, however frail, in the soul, and it opens into ever-enlarging and cheering demonstrations; the Christian conflict becomes a more animating struggle under the eye of that heavenly Leader; he that mediated for Peter and John mediates, not by a presumptuous metaphor, but literally and veritably, for me; "Lo, I am with you alway," becomes a universal promise to the Church; the bread and cup are more than memorials of an absent Saviour, — they are the symbols of a friendship abiding and inseparable. Whatever accommodated meanings our hard and rationalizing interpretations may put into the apostolic language now that it is written, — would Paul and his companions have ever said anything to us, think you, of such transcendent realities as the "life that is hid with Christ in God," if they had imagined Christ to be a departed benefactor, whom the Church was to know only through its memory? Nay, neither the imagination nor the memory was a faculty they had any use for, in expounding the doctrine of Jesus. They *knew* in whom they believed, and they knew that He was with them always.

Again, " the life that is hid with Christ in God " is a life that is perpetually reinvigorated from a conviction that Christ imparts to the soul what is more than his teachings, and more than his example, — even the direct quickening of his inward spirit. It is as if God had said: " This world of mankind has gone infatuated and stupid. Its very capacity of spiritual apprehension is stultified. Lo, I will breathe into it another breath. I will clothe my only-begotten Son in a mortal shape; by that incarnation, all humanity shall be informed with a new vitality." And this animating force, reviving the race, is received by faith. It is another world we live in since that incarnation. A new quality was poured into all the channels of human thought and feeling. The paralytic frame was touched by a heavenly energy from within, and started into a nobler attitude. Nor is the gift limited or partial. Wherever any soul leans its affections on the breast of Jesus, returning, homesick, from whatever wandering or sorrow, there, as once to the beloved disciple, the Master tells his secret, and thenceforth — O joy that passeth knowledge! — the " life is hid with Christ in God."

But furthermore, this doctrine of spiritual union, through Christ, with God, affects devotion. He who is conscious of that internal fellowship knows it by the richer interest, and the intenser relish, given to his prayers. For it reveals Christ as what the New Testament so often represents him, our " advocate with the Father." How *can* he intercede for us, but by a present acquaintance with our needs? Praying "in the name of Christ" is something more, my friends, than repeating the syllables of a proposition at the end of our petitions. No form of words like that can wing any supplication in a stronger flight heavenwards, nor return us spiritual gifts. Praying in the name of Christ must be praying from the feeling that he knows the substance of our prayer, that he knows the heart it confesses, and that he aids it now by his prevailing sympathies, as much as he aided it when he stood in Judæa, and taught his followers how to say "Our Father." But this will be confidently affirmed by those whose experience has ever ascended from the prayer of nature to the prayer through an interceding Christ, — that the latter gains as immeasurably on the former, in its claim and its satisfaction, as the religion of the New Testament is dearer and more consoling than the religion of sunset skies, of cabinets, and observatories, and regularities of nature. "Whatsoever ye shall ask in my name, that shall ye receive." If you need the Master in the sharp temptations of the market-place, the cares of the household, the bewilderments of business, and the seductions of society, you surely cannot bear to part with him in the closet. And if you have walked with him, to catch his celestial wisdom, among the ships on the shore of the sea, you will not forget how he goes, at nightfall, to the mountain, to pray for the world.

How strikingly it unfolds the plans of the Eternal Spirit in our behalf, that even in those relations and duties which lie most directly between our souls and the Father, — duties and relations in which we might therefore seem to be most independent of a mediator, — practically even there the highest style of piety is rarely found without a lively sense of Christ. That central and comforting faith, for instance, that every concern in our lives, from those that our fallible estimates pronounce the most momentous to the most minute, are directly contrived for us by an interested and sympathizing God, whose hand is for ever shaping and guiding and bending every little force and event in our discipline towards a definite and special end, — a faith which embosoms us in a care so immediate and so fatherly, that we almost want some warmer word than Providence to express it, — that is not found, in its most radiant and effective exercise, I think, except in hearts that are most alive with the personal love for Christ. Our life seems never, in any way, to be really hid in God, except with and through his Son, — and because that is the divinely ordered way.

III. What, then, is this life as to its results? I answer, first of all, it is the life of love. If it is hid "with Christ," it is penetrated with the spirit of Him who loved as man never loved. If it is hid "in God," it is suffused by the affections of Him whose name is Love. No man hating his brother can abide in that fellowship, — no unmerciful despiser of the poor, — no bigot, whether in the creed of church, or science, or fashion, — no self-avenger, — no cherisher of vindictive passions or ancient grudges, — no oppressor, whether on a throne, a plantation, in a family, a factory, a parlor, or a shop, — no conceited Pharisee, whose dress publishes the pride of rank by fabric or by phylactery, whose manners boast perpetually, "I am holier than thou." Jesus is charity, — charity conscious and living. To live in him is to live mercifully, fraternally, liberally. When the world's inmost life is hid with him, its outward life will be humane and beautiful. The members of his body will cease to be fratricidal. The bloodshed and aggressions of nations, the overreachings of commerce, the unequal administration of governments, the barbarous contrasts in Christian cities, the private hatreds that disfigure households, will yield to a constructing and benignant principle of heavenly order. The indwelling affections of a brotherhood will break forth into fresh and fairer forms of fellow-service every hour, colonizing the planet with apostles of generosity. "I in them, and thou in me, that they may be one." The social life of the disciples hid with Christ in God!

This life, therefore, fast as it is admitted to dominion in the soul, solves the old theological contradiction between works and faith. For it gets down below the roots of that barren quarrel, and shows that all rich and noble works must spring out of a faithful heart. No true, strong Christian character was ever fashioned by disconnected impulses. There must be an organizing force. Christian character is not a mosaic of moralities, nor a compilation of merits, nor a succession of acts, nor an aggregate of amiabilities. It is a growth. And that principle of interior vitality out of which it unfolds branches and foliage and flowers, is the life of God planted through Christ in the soul. We confound the whole philosophy of our being, when we think to attain to goodness, which is salvation, by beginning on the surface and working down. What we have to do is to receive Christ inwardly, and then the fruits of daily righteousness will spring forth, as naturally as leaves on a tree or streams from a fountain. We cannot keep them back, except we crush out and crucify this Christ within. They need no forcing. Believing and doing will not be separate processes, of which you may take one away and leave the other. That mistake grew up in the creeds only when faith degenerated from this living and spiritual power into a dogmatic and ecclesiastical letter. But in whatever heart Christ really dwells by faith, there holiness in all forms of manly uprightness, womanly serenity, conscientious citizenship, intellectual sincerity, truthful talk, honest trade, beneficent industry, will be the inevitable harvest, and the reapers of a nobler civilization shall come singing, bringing these sheaves with them.

Thus the doctrine gives the world truth as well as love, — truth, the absolute and immortal treasure that the soul of humanity has been searching for from the beginning, — truth, the pure and colorless element, that is to the mind what light is to the eye, and reveals the scenery of the inward world, as the sun shows the headlands and offing and hill-tops of the globe, — truth in all its uncompromising rigor and concrete applications; — not the conventional veracity of the warehouse and the drawing-room, that is satisfied if it equivocates with lying labels upon merchandise, and evasions in the bargain, and artifices in courts of law, or, in general society, with silly falsehoods of flattery, or cowardly falsehoods to avoid offence, or malicious falsehoods to breed alienation and give jealousy its disgusting triumph; — but an altogether stricter, holier thing. For if you once suppose Jesus to be admitted, in all the purity of his transparent soul, as a visible witness among these traffickings and assemblies, who would dare to confront with such deceptions the look of his divine rebuke? Christ, then, hid in the heart, is the test and guardian of truth.

And of justice, no less; not that formal honesty which is only a moral name for the selfish policy that is just as radically unrighteous under one name as another; not the legal integrity that has no higher sanction than the letter of a statute-book, and so cheats the helpless, or defrauds by indirection, or steals a competitor's reputation; but rather that spiritual justice which treats every human heart uprightly because it is a child of God, — and is honest, with the genuine and thorough honesty that goes unbent through all temptations, needs no certificates, hides behind no corporation privileges, — and stands as much in awe of the divine law of right in a servant or office-boy, as in any board of trade or missions, and would as soon be a defaulter to the most merciless creditor of the exchange, as to a mechanic or a slave; — a Christian justice. "For if any man have not the spirit of Christ, he is none of his."

The hiding of our life with Christ corrects the theological error of these modern times, which treats religion as a product of humanity, a discovery of mortal ingenuity, rather than as a help let down from Heaven. Christianity is not an invention of the ages, but a revelation from on high. Our common religious notions are vitiated by the idea that we are to *make ourselves* acceptable. A few conquests over matter, a few surprises of science, have flattered us into the conceit that the Infinite One must look with vast complacency on our attainments, and so we come to substitute decorum for piety. A simpler and heartier reception of Christ within would expel this eternal self-reference, self-measurement, self-inspection. There was a grand thought in that saying of a believer of the primitive stamp, — "I do not want to possess a faith; I want a faith that shall possess me." The safest strength of the heart is the feeling of complete dependence. Paul was no sentimentalist, and no mystic. Such common sense and such bravery have hardly got into the Church's brain and sinews since; but he said, knowing what he said, "When I am weak, then am I strong." There is something in this self-renouncing and trusting temper that makes piety fragrant with the air of Gethsemane. You find it only where you find the life hid with Christ in God.

The subject completes its circle, and so it comes close home. This inner life in Christ, with all its power and peace, is offered to the soul, because otherwise the soul is weak and dark. We long, occasionally at least, — do we not? — for reconciliation with the Almighty Spirit that lives and breathes on every side of us, in these skies and shores, these heart-beats in our breasts, and these pulses of the ocean on the beach. Which one of these hearts is satisfied with what it is? Which of you is content — deeply, thoroughly content — with a decorous and prosperous and cultured career? Is there no crying out, from within, for the living God? Does not the infinite and solemn mystery challenge us from the hours of suffering, and of silence, and even of gladness itself? Does not the very beauty of the earth and the sea and the sky awaken an awful sense of the "light that never was on sea or shore"; and does not society sometimes leave you weary and hungry and cold, and is not the fulness of joy attended by an emptiness that the world with its largest promise cannot fill? Have you not spiritual sensibility enough to feel yet that you are poor and blind and miserable and sinful, before God?

These, then, are all inner voices beseeching for the life that is hid with Christ in God. And so these blind and beggared aspirations that the Spirit planted in us, lying helpless by the way-side before, so soon as some startling sound of Providence, or admonition of pain, informs them that Jesus of Nazareth is passing by, lift their supplications, like Bartimeus, and cry, "Jesus, thou Son of David, have mercy on me." Everything in us that is truest and tenderest in some sense asks for the Christ. Our intellects entreat for him who knew all that was in man. Our affections yearn toward him who so loved us as to give himself for us. Our sympathies supplicate him who took our infirmities and bare our sicknesses. Our household love winds itself about the gentle form that left Jerusalem and its pomps, at nightfall, for the retirement of Bethany, where were Mary and Martha and Lazarus. Our tears cry out for Him who wept at his friend's grave. Our pain demands Him who through suffering is made perfect, and bore the nameless agonies of the Garden. Our more generous affections lay hold on the disinterested Lord that died, "the just for the unjust," bringing many sons into glory. Our joy takes a loftier freedom and a holier tranquillity, when it rises after Him who rejoiced in spirit, and said, "Now is the Son of Man glorified." Our energies are braced to new labors when we are with Him who affirmed, "My Father worketh hitherto, and I work." Our fainting hopes for another life cling to the ascended Master who is the resurrection. But more than all does our penitence beseech, with groanings that cannot be uttered, for the healing of his cross. Thus, through all its deepest organs, the soul is kept mercifully restless, till it tastes of the life that is hid with Christ in God. At the last, if never before, amidst its final intellectual victories, humanity takes up the words of one of its own imperial children, and says, with Michel Angelo, writing, in his old age, to Vasari:

"Well-nigh the voyage now is overpast,
And my frail bark, through troubled seas and rude,
Draws near that common haven where, at last,

the Apostle of their salvation, lo! he turns to the Gentiles. As if purposely to break up confidence in mere ecclesiasticism, and clear the Gospel of bondage, the visible Church is scarcely at any epoch suffered to enfold the Church spiritual with a clean circumference. And the instant any majority begins to be at ease in Zion, some terrible prophet, fed on locusts and wild honey, with iron hands and lightning on his lips, comes crying out of the wilderness, "Repent!" shows what "the circumcision" is, and turns the world of the Rabbins upside down. But always, observe, the old faith goes into the living body.

So at the present moment the indications seem to foreshow that the old order is to be much broken; — scepticism says, to be finally dissolved, — faith says, to make room for a new and fairer order, descending like a bride out of heaven.

Thinking men seem more and more to agree, that unless a fresh dispensation does set in, acting by new affinities, yet bringing on the old spiritual powers, the kingdom of Christ must become a kingdom of this world. For this fatal issue may accrue, not only by the ever-present solicitations of worldliness, but by the voluntary flinging off of our hereditary relations, seeking by some mortal contrivance, and outside of the Christian family, the blessing that can fall only under the parental nurture of a Divine Past.

I shall be meeting an existing case, therefore, if I introduce to you the question, *What is the inheritable blood? What are the conditions*, so far as we can discern them, *of that heirship in the spiritual fold? Who are "the circumcision"?*

It urges the subject into more importance, that Christendom, at present, offers proofs of so mischievous a disregard for anything like an organic unity of believers; that we are so much more committed to a habit of contemplating the Church as plural than as one; that we have so far lost the conception of the majesty of a universal co-operation for regenerating and saving ends; in short, that we are so careless whether we are of "the circumcision," or not.

In opening an answer to the inquiry proposed, I shall not need to travel out of the method so satisfactorily furnished by the text: "We are the circumcision, which worship God in the spirit, and rejoice in Christ Jesus, and have no confidence in the flesh."

I. "Which worship God in the spirit." The first proof of spirituality is prayer; and the most subtle disorder invades our religion when it waives an act of belief so primary. Among the sophistries that drug our interior sense is this, — that the children need not even ask their Father for salvation. "Under the Infinite Pity that softens the skies," it says, — "watched by a kindness so indiscriminate and so universal as God's must be, if he is Love, — indulged by a fond Deity, that revolts at anguish, and never *waits* to bless, — we have only to build our headstrong civilization up, and ply our petty industries among the vineyards here, unanxious about our intercourse with Heaven." The fallacy lies in the very posture of the heart that can tolerate itself in such a plea. Unless the worship of the Father is a privilege that the soul cannot refuse itself and live, then the devices of an institutional religion are only an imposition on ourselves; and the prayer that does not breathe itself forth by an impulse so spontaneous that it cannot be kept back, is nothing but a barren form of mechanical friction, where the galvanizing of the sensibility exhausts the strength on which sensibility depends. The moment we come to think of apologizing for a prayerless piety, our faces are already turned aloof from God. When we compose that apology of a reliance on God's compassion, we are lying against His Witness, and the grand old Puritanic element in all valiant piety, — awe at God's sovereignty, — has vanished from our flaccid sinews.

Of substitutes for "worship in spirit," our tendencies specially encourage two. The first is a notion which, in popular speech, gets no more definite expression than that *forms* of devotion are absolute hinderances, and that God can be adored more simply in his own works than in man's temples; but which rises under a more refined nurture, through different channels, — of artistic ecstasy, mystical contemplation, or philosophical abstraction, — into the sombre dignity of Pantheism. The impatient youth, bewitched by the conceits engendered in him under crude studies, sallies into the fields on Sunday morning, elate with the discovery that the sky is larger than the meeting-house; and because his mother had the holy instinct to tell him, among her lullabies, what Christianity had the grace to whisper down through the ages to her, — that God built and keeps and loves his world, — he illustrates his gratitude by ignoring his dependence. The artistic devotee sees divinity enough in the majesty moulded under the hands of the old masters; why bend before God seeing in secret, when color and form manifest him, — and what need of a better Intercessor than Raphael? The Mystic lifts a venerating glance at the Infinite; what wonder that his worship of the Mighty Inane should be inanity? The Peripatetic tells you to follow hard after your ideals of perfection, and not be tormented by verbal petitions to a Jehovah that after all is only the varying reflection of a human conception, and therefore his immutability a logical impossibility. And the latest apology of all for prayerless worshippers is that of a sentimentalist, who announces that, when we are nearest to God, we are too near him to speak to him!

The mischief is not shut up to the schools. It oozes out from the few scholarly circles that hold it with a kind of scholastic innocence, and drips down upon the masses of society, — trickling its popular poison even where the formulas that should define it would not be accepted, nor quite understood. Now and then it gets a pulpit for its receptacle, and some ordained Platonist for its vender. Perhaps most of us have known what it is to be so far borne up from the common level of emotions, when we have stood in the presence of some sublimity or loveliness in nature, as to have half suspected in ourselves some new-born religious consecration; and yet, on returning to the old routine of business vexations, political compromises, and domestic trials, have found the impression fleeting, and no permanent contribution lodged in character. You have mistaken the mythological influences of a starlighted sky for lessons of faith; and it is not till you stand under them, stripped of hope, shelterless as Lear, or solitary like Shelley, or bereaved like Burke, that you see how the blazing canopy that animated your poetic reverie is cold as the marble dome it looked to childish wonder, — that the forehead of midnight droops with no answer to your sighs, — that its splendor is not the warm light of Home, — that among its constellated diagrams shines no promise of a Resurrection.

Or will you try the experiment for a different relief? Come, then, to a scene universally acknowledged to be one of the most impressive outwardly, — some shore of the sounding ocean. But come there when conscience is laying its scourge upon your heart; when remorse chases you with inexorable fury; when the agonizing conviction of a violated faith and an offended God so pierces and haunts you, that no ingenuity can toss it off, no gayety disarm it, no inebriety narcotize it, — and all that you have you would give for a quiet spirit. It is no unfamiliar emergency. What, then, says the steady beat of the waters to you, as they break against their barrier? There, *if anywhere*, you might cast yourself, prayerless, on those orderly appointments of Nature that have perverted your homage; for there the stability of Nature, matching her rule of resistance against her ficklest element, daily solving the beautiful equation of a swinging globe with its tides balanced against a shelving beach of pebbles, plants the finest symbol of her regularity. What hope, then, do the winds that have been wrestling so mightily with the sea, from continent to continent, bear in upon your bosom, from this wide search upon the deep? You might as well listen at the perished shrine of a Delphic oracle; you might as well spell out some chance response from the withered leaves of the Sibyl's cave. No rest from the waves; no pardon from the breeze! But, come back to the Saviour that once stilled the sea, and the tenderness that taught us to pray, saying "Our Father," tells us of the joy in heaven over every sinner that repenteth. The magdalen is accepted. The prodigal is welcome.

But man is something more than a sufferer to be consoled, or a penitent to be restored. He is a workman that must work out his salvation, and needeth not to be ashamed; he is a soldier under the Tempter's siege, and his summons is to "come off more than conqueror." Consider the fundamental mistake, if he persuades himself the earth he works on does not depend from Heaven; his dismal profligacy, if, instead of confronting his daily engagement in the armor of a lowly prayer, he spends his energies in laboriously forgetting the Almighty, and, with the price of a crippled manhood, buys himself orphanage. Boasting our noonday light, some of us, scarcely visited by that beam of truth that gleamed even on the Stoic twilight of Aratus and Cleanthes, deny that we are God's offspring.

And so a distinct form of naturalism is propagated among us, under the doctrine that the highest aim of man is self-culture, — or the development of the natural faculties. "Man is here on earth," says a careful statement of an able anti-supernaturalist, "to unfold and perfect himself, as far as possible, in body and spirit; that is the purpose, the end, the scope and final cause of individual life on earth." "The chief end of man," says another religious philosophy, "is to glorify God and keep his commandments."

Under the legitimate and logical ultimate results of a theology of self-development, worship would be impossible; though it may survive in its modified and mixed degrees, just as virtue survives in Antinomianism.

Or if some tender feeling remains, asking a God to worship, still its worship cannot be to the personal, objective God, manifest in Christ. Nor can it amount to anything more than a pious thrift, adoring God for the sake of a profitable reaction on our own interest, subsidizing Heaven into an instrument for private elevation.

The malady that ails the virtue of our people is, that it seeks to multiply noble means, misconceiving the means for the end. Not sunk to sottish Mammonism, it yet thinks to get signally through life, and comfortably out of it, with no direct recognition, confession, worship, of a personal God, — Witness, Judge, Searcher of Hearts, Hearer of Prayer. It constructs, with or without philosophy, some specious system of abstract principles, maxims of prudential morality, rules of self-preservation, and, fancying it will stand all shocks, and meet all tests, bows itself in the house of Rimmon. But let rain and wind and flood beat upon it, — some fiercer onset of temper, — some secret occasion for a safer fraud in business, — some cooler infliction of bad faith in a debtor, — some bitterer buffeting of political scorn, — and it slides from its sandy foundation.

And if errors so disastrous creep in among the less besotted moods of men, because no "worship of the Father" forestalls them, what shall be in the lower debasements of selfishness and sensuality, — when foul appetites put God's descending angels to flight, — when the scramble for money, for social standing, for pioneering in fashion, stifles even the natural aspiration, and Belial drugs the conscience, only to kill it more securely in the dark? What shall hinder, when society comes to be an abandoned Ephraim, "let alone" for his idols, playing on to gain the world at every hazard, that he shall lay at last his very immortality down, a burnt sacrifice, on its pagan altar?

Brethren, there must be prayer to hallow labor. There must be faith to consecrate enterprise. There must be holiness to sanctify business. There must be a cordial "Thy will be done," uttered to a personal God, to interpret suffering. The most inward desires, the purest affections, the loftiest aspirings, that stir our blood, — all that is tender in us and all that is strong, all that is sacred and all that is enduring, — pain and loss, love and death, repentance and fear, — as each in turn through all this solemn discipline of life has its hour of trial or of triumph, — cry out for the living God, and bid us worship the Father in spirit.

Without a living worship of the living God, not only will these mortal multitudes be satisfied with nothing, and repose in nothing, but they will at last believe in nothing. The age of stark denial will return, on a wider theatre than ever, with the added armament of all the science and skill of the new era. And we shall see, — what some close observers think they begin to see portents of, in some quarters, already, — while much that is excellent and moral and just remains, devotion, devotion herself, — that single and unmistakable and untransmutable thing, — driven first from the bosom to the church, and then from the church into the fields, and there evaporated into something so like earthly air, as not to be inconsistent with profanity, nor preventive always of infamy. This is the atheism — sometimes taken for the Gospel — of to-day.

The materialistic views must probably be tried, both by the mind and the heart of Christendom; but unless human nature is reconstructed from what it was when the old saints lived, or when the old infidels died, they will be found wanting by both. The favorite result they propose is social liberation and progress. And so long as the traditional influence of supernaturalism should linger about their new economy, they would doubtless see fruits of their reformatory attempts. But the second generation, under their culture, would miss, and the third would quite forget, that ennobling sentiment of *reverence*, which is both the grace and the dignity of a lofty civilization.

There is a stage in the history of most communities, as there is in the lives of most persons, when they try the experiment of manufacturing a deity of their own. Sometimes the conceit takes the form of sordid worldliness, and sometimes of philosophical self-sufficiency. The one is as unsanctified as the other. I am as far from the kingdom of Heaven when I mistake the divinities of thought for the mind of God, as when I accept factories for missions, commerce for a church, and a luxurious equipage for heaven. Men are no more docile to Gospel truth when they have exchanged their New Testaments for Cobbett and Combe, than when they have sold their simplicity for dividends; and it is as discouraging to a spiritual man to see his friends going to the sanctuary having heads drunken with the pride of philosophy, as shoulders stooping under bales of merchandise. Regeneration is the casting away of both these soulless idolatries, to "worship God in the spirit."

II. "And rejoice in Christ Jesus." Coming next within the visible limits of the Church, all questions centralize more and more in the vital one concerning the office of Christ; whether he came as a great Master of the spiritual culture already discussed, a Teacher and an Example, — or, superadded to this, as the incarnation of God.

Not dishonoring the importance of great problems in church polity, in ecclesiastical fellowship, in the practical relations of Christianity to society, this transcends, or rather anticipates, them all.

About the principles of righteousness, the thought of the world is agreed. That goodness is good, and love is better than hatred, and purity and charity are blessed, is speculatively settled; and it only remains for the Church, in her practical dealing with men, to force home upon the heart truths that can never again be brought under controversy. But back of these lies an issue where philosophy and faith still claim to be heard in argument. Whether the Church itself is a human school or a heavenly; whether Christ's ministry is summed up in his representing a *perfect humanity*, or whether he *shows us the Father*, and brings from heaven a new element to plant in the affairs of the world, — so that his Gospel is special as well as absolute, and offers what moves upon men with a power wholly peculiar to itself, as not only originated, but *embodied* beyond the sphere of nature, — and so whether influences centre in his person and his death, quite different in kind from any other known to us; — this is a question that is yet to try the mind of Christendom with a stress of unparalleled intensity. It will need prayers for patience, as well as for wisdom.

Unless the Apostolic language transgresses, not only every rule of literal construction, but all parallels in the latitude of metaphor, it declares Jesus to be a Redeemer in some sense that no notion of instruction, or of exemplary character, satisfies. If the terms of the New Testament mean only that, they imply a nomenclature so anomalous that any expectation of positive knowledge from them is unreasonable. And, judging by its working on the necessities of experience, the theory is as inadequate to the permanent wants of the soul as to the Biblical statements. When naturalism, weary of its long ramble through the sciences, and neology, faint with stumbling on dark mountains, and poetic self-reliance, homesick with its comfortless solitude, shall come kneeling, to lean again with John on the bosom of Jesus, it will be an hour of more majestic triumph than when all royalties shall cast their crowns at his feet.

In two ways we may rob ourselves of the plenitude of Christ's redemptive power.

First, by severing our internal life, in its daily changes, from a familiar converse with his person. Coupled with a formal recognition of Christ's historical reality, there is a frigid distance kept up between his Church and his personality. A proposition that the headship of this mighty system, reaching through ages, revolutionizing kingdoms, and itself a sovereign surviving revolutions, is all vested in a Judæan peasant, whose personal relations to it ceased before he was thirty-five years old, — is thus made to cut off the friendly arteries by which the life should stream from the heart into the members. Faith petitions, on the other hand, that it may have leave to sit at the Saviour's feet, now; and, with a clearer trust than hers who sat there at Bethany, to say, not, "Lord, if thou hadst been here, my brother had not died," but, "Lo, thou art with us always." Humanity will realize its complete proportions only by conscious membership with a Head who fills all the chambers in his Church with the glory of his presence, and all its veins with his blood, and all its body with his breath, to-day. What less can these strong sayings signify? — "He that hath the Son hath life"; "Except ye eat the flesh of the Son of Man, and drink his blood, ye have no life in you"; "Your life is hid with Christ in God"; "God forbid that I should glory, save in the cross of our Lord Jesus Christ."

It is no unusual spectacle, I think, to see young persons among us — for these sore conflicts of aspiration with attainment are always most tragical and affecting in the young — yearning for some effectual doctrine of reconciliation, as the desert implores the sky for rain; and probing, with pain unspeakable, into their own diseased spirits, — intellectually analyzing their restless state, counting their prayers, chiding their sluggishness, — looking in distress from their imperfect lives to the perfect standard, and back from the standard to their short-comings. They wonder religion is made so stern a mistress; they ask, almost in despair, "Is there no rest to the heart from this endless strife?" You tell them they must outgrow the imperfection, add virtue to virtue, toil away at the wheel, and when they are pure enough, they will be happy. But, O short-sighted counsellor, mocking their grief! do you not see that the very want they are wrestling and gasping under, is a want of peace *before* they are perfect, — on the way, and under the sun and dust of the struggle? And is it not possible that *that* is what the Gospel of forgiveness and redemption brings them?

Reconciliation they want; and the moment they forget what they are and are not, or have and have not, to cast their burden on a Saviour, believing with the heart that by that act alone they are already justified and free, then they are taken up out of themselves and their heart-aches into heavenly harmony with God, and know the joy of adoption. There are states of the soul, when, after his long perplexities and morbid introspections, instead of dwelling with ascetic self-maceration on his experience, the disciple's first need is to forget it altogether, — to let the thoughts, jaded with this eternal chafing in the prison-house of consciousness, spring away into healthful liberty, — from deploring what self has left undone, to centre a grateful praise on what Christ has done. Faith bids these groaning hearts not to toil for ever to loose the knot, by the intellect, *in* the dungeon; but, throwing the tangled problem of good and evil down, to swing the door wide open, and let the light of the Father's face shine down into the breast. For, as a searching writer has said, " After we are in peace and power, self-analysis is instructive, humbling, and bracing; but while we are cold and dead, it is a poisonous thing, like a draft of quinine while the ague fit is on."

Others there are, who try to come near to Christ by studying, intellectually again, with busier industry, the incidents of his life, as if bare erudition, even in the writing of Evangelists, could tranquillize remorse; another, by integrity, — and he exhibits an uprightness magnanimous enough to shame Aristides, — but yet he does not feel the breath of his Master; another, by philanthropy, ardent enough to outburn Howard's or Sarah Martin's, but not constant with the constancy of Him who, having loved his own, loved them unto the end.

Now, under the fatigues of this mortal struggle, the flesh lusting against the spirit, we want an *instant* relief, as well as a future rest, — a Christ who can say to our affections, " Lo! I *am* with you even before the end of the world"; while he also says to our hope, " I am the resurrection." We need the presence, as well as the promise. We want to know that Christ *has* overcome the world, and that we are, this hour, joint heirs with him in the conquered heritage.

And thus opens the second deviation from a right Christology, in an attempt at self-salvation.

For the more earnestly a man asks himself whether his life is worthy of God's acceptance, the more utterly hopeless of acceptance, on the score of worthiness, he must become. The only standard given him, out of the cross, by which to measure himself, is the perfect one, and contains no provision for short-comings. Held under it by requirements he never can fulfil, — subject to a law he never can keep, — conscious that self creeps into his best aims, and sin defiles his purest services, — and yet nowhere told that he may partly violate the commandment, — where does he stand? On the platform of the Pharisee. His piety is hard, barren, Jewish. He cannot ask to be saved, till he has hardihood enough to claim salvation for his merits. When shall we learn that we are never to be saved by our own deeds, nor in our own way, but by the heart full of faith in what our Lord has done, — in God's way, by his Christ? To attempt a retreat from this central Gospel hope to the Jew's salvation in payment for good works, is as futile as Julian's was, when he sought to rebuild the Hebrew temple at Jerusalem, to falsify the prophecy of the Son of Man.

We may baptize the interesting displays of an intermittent virtue with a Christian name, but they may yet contain no scintilla of Christ's distinctive light. They may leave the life all untouched by its unrivalled aurora, however resplendent their own beauty. Their sterile justice is not the justice that treats men honestly because they are God's children, — which was the law of Christ's great honesty. Their kindness is not redolent of the beatitudes. Their moderation is not guarded by those mighty warders, reverence for God and the Saviour's love. Their liberty is not that "where the Spirit of the Lord is." Nor is their wonder devout with the fervor of Olivet and Gethsemane.

It is common with some writers to abandon the ground of salvation by merits, rhetorically, even admitting its opposite, by a sort of parenetic license, for spiritual utility; but still to reserve it as defensible by philosophy. Now it is precisely the philosophical element in religion that most emphatically rejects the idea of a spiritual salvation by merit; because, the moment the whole aim and energy are concentrated on self, that moment the noblest grace of piety is gone. A profound science of human nature discovers nothing more clearly than that faith in objective Help is a principle of action overmastering all aims that conclude in personal results, and more in harmony with all the higher laws of the soul. When Paul simply said, "Believe on the Lord Jesus Christ, and thou shalt be saved," he struck a deeper vein in man's inward economy than all the stirring champions of education. He announced a law of spiritual growth, eternal, practical, and by some of its relations omnipresent to our experience. Till we adjust our beliefs to it, and conform our lives as well, we are not clear-sighted, nor strong-handed, nor is our tent pitched within the encampments of the Christian "circumcision."

When one of our preachers puts it to himself, whether a morbid, excessive religiousness is one of the chief enemies to the salvation of his people, he is struck at finding how much of the preaching that reaches the ears of one denomination is only an oblique rebound from the short-comings of another, and so, where it lights, less nourishing than the east wind. Enthusiasm is not our peril. We want righteousness much, but faith first, the root, the quickener, the *animus* and inspiration of the other.

We may call these humiliating doctrines; but are

they half so humiliating as those ever-present facts in life, — sorrow and shame? Does not the law run through all our being, that we must find peace by sacrifice, — must go to rest through struggle? Every field of heroic strife; martyrs' stakes and scaffolds; fastings and pilgrimages; blood running in rivers; the songs of dying patriots; strains like those that rung from Madame Roland's dungeon the night before her execution; the Puritans' privations; prophets wet with dews, or walking through furnaces of fire; — all stand as grand historic monuments of the law, No pain, no progress. Yet what we allow to the earthly triumphs of liberty or country, we grudge for the victory of eternal life.

Christ humiliates us by showing us our unworthiness, that he may exalt us in due time, and glorify us with seats at his right hand. He bends us in something of David's prostration, that we may rise on the wings of Isaiah's rapture. Have we not served idols? And so we must be mourning captives in Babylon, hanging our harps on weeping willows, before we can return with joy. The cross *is* an offence; we must be content to come after a Man of sorrows, — him whose visage was marred more than the countenance of any man, — must take that cross of offence up, before he will come with his Father to take up his abode in our hearts.

In the striking paradox of one of the mightiest builders of empire the world ever bore, "There is no force so overwhelming, as that whose strength lies in its very weakness." And so the most wilful spirit, arriving at its new birth, feels that there is no conquest so absolute as when all the heart *submits*, and no self-possession so sure as when self is utterly renounced.

In the very midst of the deep waters of that wondrous

passage, whereby discipline proves and purifies the disciple, it must have been an obdurate spirit that was not ready sometimes to cry, "O blessed violence of Love, that quells, even with penitential grief, this wild revolt of passions! — O merciful Cross, that cools this cruel fever of ambition! —O healing Hand, that doubles my agony for an hour, that I might have heavenly health for ever!"

Imagine even our noblest achievements, the churches, and benevolent brotherhoods, and missionary societies, assembled to lift an anthem of united praise; the refrain of their thanksgiving must ever be, "Not unto us, not unto us, O Lord, but unto thy name, be the glory."

We want a life hid with Christ in God. And herein the religion revealed in Christ meets us. Holding up to our aspirations an object beyond ourselves, it makes faith in Him a surer test of acceptance than any outward works, and stimulates our affections by showing us a Mediator. Something without us to lay hold of; an arm from above to lean upon; a Saviour to go to, and walk by; a Father to trust in and forget our little selves in glorifying;—this is the "circumcision," both "worshipping the Father in spirit," and "rejoicing in Christ Jesus."

III. "No confidence in the flesh." At this point the text's definition of "the circumcision" changes from a positive form to a negative. I shall follow this variation; adverting to some of the more comprehensive and more instant obstacles both to the spiritual reviving of the Church and to the unity which can never come without its reviving.

Christendom shows a general expectancy of some fresh dispensation of the Spirit. I ask you to glance, in what remains, at those chief stumbling-blocks which Christendom itself — and our portion of it along with the rest — is most tempted to cast in the way of such an outpouring of the Holy Ghost, and such a gathering of the Christian clans; — unteachableness in the doctrine of sin; intellectual dogmatism, whether as abstract from images of life or imperious over the emotions; a confounding of virtue with religion; ceremonialism; a provincial species of ecclesiasticism; and denominational intolerance.

Is it true, or is it not, that in most of our congregations family prayer steadily declines? Is it true, that the very naming of such a test of spiritual security shocks some liberal judgments? Is it true, that, of the young persons nurtured in our Sunday schools, so few distinctly recognize in themselves a Christian aim, or join the visible Christian body, — that in many cases the Church is a lean minority of the congregation, composed chiefly of females and aged men, drawn to it by a rare temperament, or driven in by some stress of sorrow? Is it true, that even strong spiritual impressions and impulses fail constantly to be consolidated into a consistent character, for want of a deep and definite faith to crystallize upon and abide by? Is it quite general, that a superior righteousness of life atones for the latitude of speculation, — and is it not true, that conventionalism and formality come into our assemblies, in an average proportion, as the wealthy and fashionable classes come, and that, while we propose a spiritual walk, through some excess of hospitality worldliness clings tenaciously to our skirts?

One almost shudders to consider how terrible an opening might be made into the religion of the times, if its nominal friends were to make candid answer to this question: Suppose a permanent personal immunity from pain could be guaranteed without religion, how many of them would feel it rather a relief to be rid of religion altogether?

I have laid it down as the distinctive office of Christ in the world, and in the individual heart, to introduce a new element of religious life, and to furnish a special relief from sin. The whole appeal, then, of his Gospel is to the felt need of this heart. The old system is right in laying so urgent a stress on conviction of sin. The grand significance of the Gospel is help. The measure of man's eagerness to receive help, — is it not his feeling of helplessness? It is no secret, probably, that in most of the persons we meet in the streets, and even in our meeting-houses, it would be difficult to find any such thing as a vital consciousness of sin, at all.

Go to a successful worldling, comfortably cushioned among his flourishing fortunes, his selfish habits, and his fashionable family, and tell him of his sin. You speak of a difficulty, a discontent, an empty heart. What difficulty, what discontent, what emptiness? Have not his notes good securities? Did he not sleep well last night? Will not the choice selections of the market smoke upon his table to-morrow? Sin? He has found a way of disposing of all that annoyance as conveniently as of some doubtful mortgage. Your praying publican was a poor fanatic, and his penitence a piece of wild extravagance, putting the case far worse than it really was. This abasing doctrine of conviction and confession, for a gentleman, a man of quality, a master of half a million of money, — it is an impertinence.

A specious answer, I know, may be made, — that an active life, busy with profitable work, is doing something better than deploring its short-comings. But answer, again, how profitable, or permanent, that work is, which does not begin and end in a sense of submission to God, — or how noble work can be, not dignified by the spiritual meditation that must so often terminate in a confession of utter unworthiness. Clarkson's brilliant retort, to the inquiry about his soul, that he had no time so much as to consider whether he had a soul, has been much worn by quotation, and never quoted, as I am aware, but to be admired. The earnest witticism is justified, perhaps, as it leaped from Clarkson's lips; but converted from the impromptu extravagance it was, into the deliberate maxim of conduct it was never meant to be, it is as mischievous as it is shallow. Modern Philosophy has followed in that line a little; and to her loss. The unspiritualizing of moral enterprises comes of it; the self-unchurching of noble reforms comes of it; the dislocation of Christian symmetry, the divorce of labor and prayer, the orphanage of Human Charity herself, comes of it.

Again, the understanding may plan and rear a house; but only the heart can warm it with sunny friendships, and twine the grace of sweet charities about its door-posts, and dispose throughout its rooms the benignant charm that makes the meaning of a home. And so a dogmatic intellect may pile the structure of a creed; but it needs a tenderer confidence to domesticate the soul in the temple.

It would seem as if some rarefying intellectualism, by insinuating itself into our modern religious speech, unrealized the objects of faith, and emasculated faith itself. A truly comprehensive study of God, and of the real conditions under which he must be revealed, makes it more than doubtful whether we have gained a more accurate, or even a more spiritual conception of God, by discarding what is called the anthropopathic imagery of the Old Testament, — representing God as feeling emotions, joy, grief, pity, like ourselves. The straining after literal accuracy dilutes the vigorous conception. Our God sometimes seems farther off than the Jewish Jehovah was, and what we gain to exactness, in our attempts to eliminate these material configurations of Deity, is worse than lost to trust, in the dissipating of the personality. So, by the application of a similar process to the idea of heaven, representing heaven as nowhere in particular, we fail to present it at all, and hope is bereaved of heaven; and by diffusing hell over all of life and the world, we take it in such minute particles that it grows familiar and tolerable. When you have made all the amiable and correct dispositions to constitute and complete membership in the Christian Church, your Church has vanished; and the moment you have persuaded my reason that prayer consists in nothing but want, or aspiring to an ideal, and wishing well to my neighbors, I am no longer of the disciples that their Lord has taught how to pray.

And in this, the New Testament language suits itself, by a perfect adaptation, to the nature it addresses and would relieve. No ideas charge their symbols, words, with such subtile and hidden correspondences as the religious, the use made of a single theological term often condensing the entire character of a creed. It is the spiritual laws that fit and sanction the rhetorical. A theologian may refuse from his studied treatises the sacrificial phraseology of the Epistles, as scornfully as a Lollard would spurn a picture of the Virgin; but he will take it all back into his prayers, as the iconoclast, after the havoc was over, lifting his eyes to the lofty arches of the cathedral, uncovered his head and knelt.

For the rocks of offence that men put out of their path, when they walk forth in the pride of controversy, they seldom stumble at in the closet. The devotee leans his bosom on the stone that the system-builders rejected.

It is a noble thing to abide by a piety so natural, sincere, and true, that it never spoils the rich terms of the Bible by perverting them into cant. But it is just as noble for a piety that is natural, sincere, and true, to hold them fast, and choose them for its speech, even though Cant has tampered with them,—ignoring her presumption.

Doubts about prayer are not answered by argument, but by showing the heart how it needs its God. Probably no man ever adopted prayer by finding a philosophic basis for it, but by beginning to cry, "My God, my God!" and thus, tempted on by a single taste of the holy privilege, the heart takes up the cheerful task of persuasion for itself, and the suppliant thenceforth prays, because the restraining of prayer would be the refusal of his chief desire. And whereas he once thought it brave to doubt, he now knows it is blessed to believe.

At first, perhaps, his petitions are the broken entreaties of that sad contrition that cried: "Slay me, O God, if thou wilt, but leave me not sinful thus. I am miserable; and cannot heal myself. Put me to shame; I am shameful. Behold, I hide nothing; Thou art Light, expose my darkness. I will palliate nothing; I am worse than I know; show me all that I am. If I must die, let me die in thy light!" But afterwads, when mercy has reassured him, he is able to take a more exultant tone, and sing:—

"'T is Love! 't is Love! — Thou diedst for me;
I hear thy whisper in my heart:
The morning breaks; the shadows flee:
Pure, universal Love thou art.

"My prayer hath power with God! the grace
Unspeakable I now receive:
In vain I have not wept and strove:
Thy nature and thy name is Love!"

Piety is not always ready to go before the court of reason, defensible against every rigorous indictment of consistency. Like the poor Scotchwoman, rejected from communion with her Lord by her catechising priest, because her answers stammered, it breaks into tears as it goes disappointed away, crying, "Though I cannot speak for my Saviour, I could die for him." "No confidence in the flesh."

There can be no serious difficulty in adjusting the relations of this new and renewing element in character, Faith, to general goodness, piety, benevolence, and integrity.

As the expression — no more than that — of an originating and creative faith, the moral decencies bear much the same relation to religion that manners bear to morals. You will never have the morals without their fruit in the manners; but you will often get the manners quite out of company with the morals. Byron said that by far the mildest manners he ever met were those of the bloodthirsty and remorseless Ali Pacha, and that the most civil gentleman he had conversed with picked his purse from his pocket. You might as well propound George Brummell and Lord Chesterfield for standards in pure ethics, as go about to inaugurate a Church of God in the world, by recommending dry rules of behavior. That is not the New Testament method. Christ poises the scales of character implicitly on the heart, and the first word of his Apostles everywhere is, "Believe."

It is because the whole soul is not thus concentrated on the love of Christ which constraineth men, putting away all "confidence in the flesh," that some branches of the Church so invert the relations of the form to the substance. Instead of cherishing the inward spirit which vitalizes every tabernacle it inhabits, they insist on pressing to their bosoms the moulds it dwelt in once, putting antiquarianism for righteousness. Because the cistern held the living waters in ancient times, it must stand shrinking and warped in the sun, an unsightly encumbrance, after the waters have sought other courses. The mind, instead of ascending freely from the altar to rest in God, and be purified for active effort, is led off by scholastic fancies, idly busy with the painted windows that catch the rays of earthly sunlight.

It is because we undervalue the religious heart, and attach an exclusive importance to religious opinions, that we commit so many unprofitable mistakes in our attempts to increase our ecclesiastical bodies, or denominations. For, in answering the question, Who are "the circumcision"? and bidding us put "no confidence in the flesh," our doctrine decides inferentially how we are to propagate our faith. It bids the Church take up every child of her loins, born within her house, before the sorceries of the world have wrought their deadly spell upon him, and, baptizing him into holy affections, bear him straight on into full communion with her Lord. In speaking to the prodigals that would wander, it sets regeneration before tuition. It shows us that association, organization, machinery, are dead, till a living piety burns in the hearts of its masters. Bureaus may stand ready, and boards, and officers, and even funds, — though these last, being more dependent on zeal, and less attainable by cold blood, are not so likely to abound; but when the whole apparatus waits complete, it is only the system of wheels within wheels; what is still wanting is the spirit of the living creatures descending into them like lamps of fire, lifting them up and driving them on. Without this, we shall only tax, and exhort, and mortify ourselves, in vain, — perplexed that the seed-wheat does not grow, amazed at our own impotence, scarcely suspecting that the real difficulty is, that we are sacrificing all the while to our own sectarian net, or burning incense to our denominational drag, instead of "worshipping the Father, and rejoicing in Christ Jesus." Do this, and ye will no longer need to say to one another, "Know the Lord. For the Lord will create in every dwelling-place in Mount Zion, and upon her assemblies, a cloud and smoke by day, and the shining of a flaming fire by night."

Under the normal nurture of Faith, the outward institution and the informing life will grow together; so that in the Church, as in the body,

> "Nature, crescent, does not grow alone
> In thews and bulk; but, as this temple waxes,
> The inward service of the mind and soul
> Grows wide withal."

Nothing will be done for ostentation, — for a really devout man will no more parade his piety for exhibition, than he will throw his heart into the street; but the earnest piety will spontaneously fit to itself a dress and demonstrative apparatus becoming its dignity. The world would not be disgusted with imposing ecclesiastical arrangements, mocking an empty house, but the expanding force will make its way constitutionally, pushing its structure no faster than its family.

You complain that the people are concerned too much with the talents — or the want of them — in the minister; and justly. But can you abate that poor ambition, that "confidence in the flesh," till you have supplied a loftier passion? Parishes that have no God to worship will naturally, out of certain traditional associations that confound the official functionary with the religion, make an idol of their preacher; and it will not be strange if, in the end, the incense so works upon his manhood, that he becomes literally *their* preacher, and not Christ's.

Or if he should not happen to be of substance sufficient to make an idol of, the people go mourning for lack of what they call religion, — the first suspicion some societies have that they are godless, arising when they lack a minister to stand as a substitute. Plant a diviner ground of trust; plant a living love for Christ, that Head of the Church who never fails any of its branches; and the prosperity of a parish will no longer swell and shrink, nor its zeal rise and fall from fever-heat to freezing-point, by the favor of its servants.

Hence, too, finally, by this personal power and life of piety, in the heart, comes the only hope of Catholicity,— the "One Fold" predicted so long. Out of heirship comes kinsmanship, and the rule of the one defines the other.

All direct labor for a mere marrying of creeds, a blending of sects, and mortising of platforms, is false; for it turns off the mind from the ineffable glory of Divine Love, and from the honors of sainthood, to petty adjustments of opinion and mortal measurements by one another. The Church for the present may have statement and counter-statement, indoctrination and recantation, systems and system-destroyers, kingdom against kingdom, — cries of, "Lo! he is in the desert," and, "Lo! he is in the secret chambers," — only because the hour of unity is not yet. Ours are analysis, thesis, and antithesis; the grand synthesis is of God.

Any unity that councils shall consolidate will lack the harmonizing principle. Honest good-will may compact some comely covenant, but it will prove too bounded for the purposes of Providence. No preadjusted mould can coerce the elastic growths of that future Church for which no past can legislate and even the present can only watch and pray. In the freehold of the Christian inheritance, my friends, we do not hold by adverse title. Let us learn it, even before we see ourselves to be externally and formally one; and then the visible unity shall be ushered in.

Meantime, brethren of all encampments in the Church Militant, — for militant she still is by destiny as against the world, but militant, if our hearts are right, she should no longer be as against herself, diverting toil from the perishing harvests to fratricidal strife, and beating sickles into swords, — what do we? On the margin of that land of promise which eighteen centuries of providential history have been shaping for our heritage, we fall to hurling poisoned javelins into our allies' enclosures. The strength that helpless humanity yearns to feel lifting up its wounded limbs, we waste in this fiendish folly.

A truce! a truce of God! Slaves, sensualists, atheists, wait for redemption. Reluctant want, staggering under its unrighteous load, — rich idleness, sick with its slow consumption, — filth grovelling and generosity despairing, — woman, wronged and bewildered, straining her patient ear to catch her Redeemer's consolation, — and we, the strong, the free, the wielders of opportunities, the openers and closers of gates, — we, that believing mothers have sung songs of Bethlehem to in our infancy, — we, that schools and universities have fostered in their bosoms, only that they might hand us on, in greater plenitude of grace, to the service of Christ and his Church, — we are tossing our petulant gauntlets from tent to tent; not watchmen on the walls of Zion, yearning to see eye to eye, but eaves-droppers at our neighbors' doors, eager to hear the jarring controversies of the sects, rather than the hymns of seraphs!

"Worshipping the Father in spirit; rejoicing in Christ Jesus; having no confidence in the flesh," — we are all "the circumcision."

If you would find a church that is true, and alive from on high, you must seek one whose members serve each other by first serving Christ, whose law and motive and bond of concord are in their looking up into the same divine countenance, listening to the same heavenly voice, leaning together on the breast of the same Son of God.

The unity begotten among sects by this looking to one undivided Lord will be spiritual, not mechanical. It will come, not by any sly foisting in among the sects of each other's phraseology, or any imitation of each other's measures, — not by cunning nor concealment; but by a candor that is transparent precisely because it is above partisanship and selfishness, — by a speech whose mightiest power lies in its sincerity, its unction, its evangelic necessity; not, in short, by the will of man at all, but by so making the Saviour of our souls the centre, substance, and inspiration of the doctrine, that love for him sends every smaller passion out, and there is oneness only because there is One.

And so it has appeared how, in order to heirship in the fold, there is needed a doctrine of God, a doctrine of Christ, and a doctrine of the Spirit; of worship, of redemption, of the Church; of piety, of discipleship, of fraternity in the spiritual house.

Over against these pillars of safety stand the besetting spiritual perils of the time, — all represented at last in that anti-Christian trinity, self-worship, self-deliverance, self-love.

Let us be steadfast on the Corner-stone, and we will not suffer solicitude for our heritage. We shall realize the infinite endearment of that condescending promise, " Fear not, little flock; it is your Father's good pleasure to give you the kingdom." We shall hold in our veins the blood of Israel. The conditions are unencumbered, and the title will belong as much to us as to the oldest hierarchy in the world.

" For he is not a Jew that is one outwardly; neither is that circumcision which is outward in the flesh; but he is a Jew that is one inwardly; and circumcision is of the heart, in the spirit, and not in the letter; whose praise is not of men, but of God. And we are the circumcision, which worship the Father in spirit, and rejoice in Christ Jesus, and have no confidence in the flesh."

SERMON XXIII.

THE RELIGION THAT IS NATURAL.*

TO BE SPIRITUALLY-MINDED IS LIFE AND PEACE. — Rom. viii. 6.

THE association called the "BOSTON YOUNG MEN'S CHRISTIAN UNION" has already explained itself to the public. The causes that created it seem to have been both positive and negative. It was felt by the persons whose desires originated and whose thoughts shaped it, that there were young men enough in this city, seeking to guide their lives by Christian principles, to constitute an organized body, with the functions and furniture for united action in many ways. On the other hand, it was felt, with equal force, that the moral exposures besetting a business life in a centralized community, with metropolitan habits, required some systematic protection; and especially that the young who come here, with no large experience of the peculiarly crafty and beguiling forms that iniquity assumes in such a place, fortified as iniquity often is in these attacks by homesickness on one side, and social proclivities on the other, might well impose some special painstaking on the right-minded, to surround the strangers with something like the warmth

* Addressed to the "Boston Young Men's Christian Union," December 12, 1852.

of a Christian household, or at least with the fellowships of a moral brotherhood. For there appeared to be no good reason why sin should come into these men's characters under the cheerful guise of virtue, when virtue itself might be equally welcome in its own. And then, when the time came for determining of what materials so broad and noble a design should compose its structure, generous spirits could, of course, decide the question but one way: it must be equally open to all men sincerely claiming a Christian belief and purpose, whatever other name they might superadd to the grand primitive one; and so the society became a "Christian Union."

At different points in the progress of its history thus far, these feelings that led to its formation have been laid open, in meetings and through the press, — sufficiently, I should think, to have secured a general understanding of their scope and object. In discharging the office assigned me by the government of the association to-night, therefore, if I might find a subject which, while it should touch and cover those salient features of this plan that it is most desirable to notice, would also possess some inherent unity and independent interest of its own, I should probably serve your wishes by nandling it, more effectually than by limiting my discourse within the specific details of your movement.

Such a subject has offered itself, I conceive, under the form of an inquiry into the characteristics and the power of a religion, which, in a better sense than the technical, theological one, is natural. A better sense, I say, meaning a simpler and more grateful one; because, while the Natural Religion of theology signifies a scheme distinct from express revelation, and bereaved of Scripture supports, this *religion that is truly natural*, of which I am to speak, is the gift of revelation, and rests its whole law, promise, and authority on the Bible. It will be for you to judge, as I attempt to identify it and describe its traits, whether its common reception into faith would not do more to satisfy the wants that young men are conscious of, more to strengthen and beautify their characters, more to save them from every species of danger, than any agency beside.

It would be a poor affectation, however, to ignore that other view of the relation between nature and religion, which has written itself out into a distinct philosophy under the name of Naturalism. Denying the operation of any other causes than those that lie within the full grasp of the understanding, and are capable of being subjected to the definitions and analysis of science, in those grand religious facts, the inspiration of the Scriptures, the redemption of man by Christ, and the renewal of the soul into spiritual life, Naturalism, so called, opposes itself in direct issue against all the positions I intend to take, and all the Christianity I should wish to expound. It lies directly on my way into my theme, and is required by the terms I employ, to remark of this scheme, that its fundamental fallacy is in a radical misconception of the first fact in the case, religion. By its primal suggestion, in the first step it takes with us, religion carries us over into contact with *super*-natural realities. Locating its objects in a sphere beyond nature,— the infinite,—all its revelations, to be authoritative, must, of course, proceed from a supernatural source, authenticating themselves by supernatural signs. To claim for a revelation pertaining to religion, therefore, that it be judged exclusively by the canons and criticisms of secular science, is in effect to begin by denying the premise,—

denying that there is any such thing as religion. To proceed further, to argue that, since supernatural facts, the incarnation, and divine offices of the Spirit, are impossible, or contrary to reason, the claim for them discredits Christianity, is to introduce such confusion of reasoning as amounts to impertinence. This is the logical offence of pure Rationalism, and, being irrational, is an offence against itself. It mistakes one science for another; and, what is worse, turns the necessary condition on which man can have religion at all, into an argument against the only possible way of his getting it. Religion, by derivation, signifies what binds the human soul back to God, — finite to Infinite. Of course, supernaturalism inheres in it by *its* nature. In short, not to extend this introductory train of observation, it is no paradox to say, that a supernatural religion is the only natural one. So far from the fact that revelation involves mysteries acting as an embarrassment to it, it would be the blankest refutation of its pretences, and a destruction of its object, if it did not. Christianity comes to bridge the gulf between the creature, who is also a sinning creature, and the perfect God. That mediation, and the Mediator embodying it, must then of necessity contain elements, not human, but divine; and the only interpretation of the New Testament that is natural, I contend, is that which accepts this truth, and commends it to the world's faith.

Leaving this point, I shall go on to lay before you, in a direct form, what appear to me the chief characteristics and offices by which we shall recognize the religion that is at once natural and supernatural, thus bearing the brightest marks of truth and divinity; supernatural, that is, in its design and introduction, but *natural, or accord-*

ing to what we know of natural, in its manifestations in character, and its working in the world.

What connects the subject with this occasion, is the circumstance that it seems to meet two of the commonest obstacles to a cordial adoption of the Christian standing-place on the part of young men: one of these being disgust at the *un*-natural phases that religion is often made to assume, in formal manners and unhuman affectations; the other being a tendency to lax speculations, which flatter the pride of immature students, or those that only repeat the catchwords of such, so slipping into cant of another species, but which are finally found to cheat the soul under any real experience of life, and dissatisfy the heart.

I. The first mark I shall mention of the religion that in this high sense is natural, is this, — that it unites the culture of those qualities which men esteem for their manliness, with those that God requires for their sanctity, and so harmonizes nobleness of spirit with strictness of doctrine.

Harmonizes them, — does not confound them. Honor, frankness, magnanimity, make no man a Christian disciple. But then Christianity suffers no disciple to be treacherous, cunning, or mean. Honor, frankness, magnanimity, and the whole of that royal family, are the vigorous and graceful stock on which Christianity ingrafts its new and divine principle. Whatever moral beauty it does not create, Christianity claims and makes its own by adoption. These well-born virtues are orphans in the world, till Christ shows them the Father. Something is greatly wanting in them, till they learn from Jesus a filial submission and a holy trust. Honor, frankness, magnanimity, may all consist with pride, or prayerless self-will, — that pride which Christianity prostrates with its first word, when it cries, "Repent and be converted." Under that vicious alliance, they can never carry the soul forward into its ripest maturity. They stop at a half-way stage of the possible stature of humanity. But separate them from that self-confidence, and you liberate them for a boundless progress. Hallow them by a Gospel penitence, and they rise into a new and an infinite dignity. They root themselves, then, in a firmer soil. They take a new guaranty of perseverance from Him who is the same yesterday, to-day, and for ever. They put on the attribute of stability, borrowing it from the unshaken throne where they are now centred and balanced. That cluster of radiant traits, which gain a uniform approval in the worldliest companies, which conform to the highest secular standard, and which are required in the code of gentlemen, never reach their loftiest growth till Faith crowns them with her unrivalled glory. On their own ground, then, and for their ultimate perfecting, these traits that men everywhere admire for their manliness must confess the sway of Religion, and be sanctified by her doctrines.

There is no looser nor less philosophical heresy, than that Christianity does not bring into the world, and put into character, something peculiar to itself, — a charm unborrowed and inimitable. No instinctive amiabilities, nor generous propensities, can rival it; no combination of Pagan merits can counterfeit it. A character truly touched with the Christian consecration carries upon it a certain spiritual sign, which even eyes of flesh take knowledge of. The real disciple, spite of his modesty, and all the more infallibly because of his modesty, has the seal written on his forehead, to be known unmistakably, and read of all men.

On the other hand, there is no brighter token that the Gospel came from the Builder of the worlds, than that it takes up into the scope of its own design, and makes a part of its own honor, whatever goodness has come to light in the world, outside of its conscious kingdom. The moment this all-comprehending and catholic law of life was revealed on earth in Jesus, all pre-existing morality seemed at once, by a natural necessity, to become an element in its strength. All foreign loveliness merged itself in that transcendent beauty. Name whatsoever virtue or aspiration you might, it had its niche provided for it in this Christian Pantheon of the new worship. By this wonderful assimilative energy, Christianity instantly appropriated to itself all the lawful forces of nature. It enthroned itself as the sovereign of the world's experience, claiming the universal empire of life by divine right. That reverential attempt of Christian art to represent the Saviour as the centre of original light, by encompassing his head with a glory radiating in every direction, might have its meaning inverted, and still be a true symbol; for all the rays of moral splendor, playing before like irregular lightning along the horizon of history, suddenly converged, to shine with a concentrated and steady beam in the face of Jesus Christ. Some critic has said: "Paul, the Hebrew, had as fine theories of art as he had of society, if he had only had a chance of working them out." And this may be only a concrete way of saying, that Christianity, holding in itself the law of every human interest, is capable of blessing the science of universal beauty or order, as much as the actings of the will. So manifest has this been, that some writers have been led by it to exhibit Christianity as being nothing else than a compilation, or systematic compendium, of all the natural religions; the rules of the common moral sense of mankind codified; the *residuum* of all heathen instructions; a kind of pantheological eclecticism. The fallacy of that notion lies in overlooking those distinctive and attested supernatural facts, of the divine incarnation and the cross, with the doctrines they embody, — reconciliation and forgiveness, — which, while they separate the Christian from some religions, as the complete from the partial, or the absolute from the relative, distinguish it from others as the redemptive from the educational. Other faiths propose to benefit man by advising him as to his behavior; Christianity, by first saving him from his sins. Other teachers help the race; Christ redeems it. But what was plausible in this theory was the fact, that Christianity does adopt, and welcome, and embrace, every trait that the intuition of right minds follows with its admiration. It asks no man to be a whit less manly, — less cordial in his fellowships, less cheerful in his temper, less companionable and genial in his relations to society, less penetrating in his sagacity, less noble in his manners, or less punctual in his industry. Does it not say, "Not slothful in business," as well as "fervent in spirit"? You speak of sincerity, downrightness, or transparency: were not the sharpest rebukes that the Prophet of Nazareth ever pronounced — those awful "woes" that almost darken the page, and must have sounded like the fore-peals of the trumpet of eternal judgment — levelled at Pharisees and pretenders? Did not Christ declare it the direct, uncompromising function of his truth to uncover what is hid? and is it not expressly made a condition of that "wisdom which cometh from above," that it be without insincerity? Or you speak of knowledge, culture, science, as something worthy of man's esteem. What is Christianity but the fundamental science, — the science of man himself? Christianity knows men. Is it not written, and believed by you, of Christ himself, — whose person embodied Christianity, in whose thought it was organized, and in whose heart its blood throbbed, — that he "needed not that any should testify of man," and that "the Father showeth him all things that himself doeth"? You say there is another kind of intelligence that men lawfully respect, which is called shrewdness, or practical acquaintance with affairs. But is not that, too, provided for in the New Testament? Do you suppose it was irrespective of their practical experience among men, that Christ chose his first disciples, the foremost representatives of his truth, from among tax-gatherers, fishermen, tent-makers, and physicians? Or will you look through literature or biography, or the marts of commerce, or the boards of the exchange, for a shrewder insight into all the ways and windings of human nature, than lurked in the sharp eye and wakeful perception of that leading Apostle, who turned the world upside down with his calm hand, carried his points with the dignitaries of provinces, foiled Felix and Agrippa, foresaw and forearmed himself against all that men could do to him, and in his Epistles tears open the cunningest wrappages of self-deception with his holy satire, — conquering Greek sophists and Roman disciplinarians with weapons out of their own quiver? You instance courage; and is there not enough of that in that pioneering rank of the "noble army of martyrs," whom there was no dungeon dark enough to terrify, from Jerusalem to Rome, and who would not blench, nor even revile nor murmur, under all the scourges of Jewry, the whips of dainty Philippi, or the lion's teeth in the Roman amphitheatre? Generosity, you say, is manly; but who will so disown his own reason, as to confess he finds no generosity in that faith whose primal lesson is self-sacrifice, whose chosen badge and emblem is a cross, and which was taught and sealed by Him who gave his very life for the life of his followers? You mention hospitality; and is not hospitality enjoined, with repetition and emphasis, by both Paul and Peter, as the attribute of saints, the grace of bishops, and the duty of all believers? Of patriotism; and who was he that cried, weeping, "O Jerusalem! Jerusalem! if thou hadst known how often I would have gathered thy children"? Of the taste and love for the beautiful; but whose finger was that which pointed most admiringly, as he discoursed, to the summer glories, the waving wheat and nodding lilies, the trees and lakes and gorgeous skies of Palestine? — whose eye, that rested with sweetest satisfaction on that affluent and varied scenery? — whose word, that blended the mystic openings of the sunrise with the light that lighteth every man that cometh into the world, and so taught us how the relish of all that is sublime or lovely should rise at last and culminate in the worship of the Father, even as every manly and heroic quality is perfected only in the soul that is united to the Son?

So it has been in history. The religion of Jesus has realized its own promise, — completing not only Judaism, but all good yearnings and beginnings everywhere. It did not come to destroy, but to fulfil. It had its kindly word at the outset, even for those that, having not the law, did by nature the things contained in the law. And ever since, it has spread the benignant arms of its adoption over every worthy purpose, and every pure aspiration that will acknowledge its guardianship. Wherever the germs of lofty action unfold themselves, there the fostering hand of its discipline is present to train them. The sublimity of all honorable achievements, the valor of pure-hearted patriots, disinterested sufferings, the patience and fortitude and constancy that come out so grandly in fearful emergencies, — they are all as much the Gospel's as they are humanity's. You always see how much they lack, till they take on the sanctity of a conscious communion with the Christ; till they are invested with the dignity of a regenerate devotion. But the instant they so submit themselves, they all render in their concordant homage to the Universal Lord; and he calls them his own. They bring their honor and praise, wisdom and power, to "Him that sitteth on the throne," "whose right it is to reign" over them. Manliness enters into the composition of piety. All that the unperverted judgment of the world approves, the Gospel invites. What lends their real lustre to the memorable spots on the globe, what attracts the companies of genial and innocent fellowship, what makes the joy of light-hearted children, the usefulness of labor, the benefits of civilization, the hardihood and enterprise of traffic and invention, colonies and arts, what binds families and blesses homes, — these all are, in the last sense, yours only when you are Christian souls. Over every field where real goodness starts into life, Christianity extends its benediction. So what the world holds as its best, the Messiah accepts as his tribute. His Church has arms wider than the charity of the world. Providence realizes prophecy. "The sons of strangers build up thy walls. Thy gates shall be open continually, that men may bring unto thee the forces of the Gentiles. The flocks of Kedar, — the dromedaries of

Midian and Ephah; these that fly as doves to their windows; all they from Sheba shall come, bringing gold and incense; the isles shall wait for thee; the sons of them that afflicted thee shall come bending unto thee, — for brass, gold; and for iron, silver; and for wood, brass; and for stones, iron. The glory of Lebanon shall come unto thee, — the fir-tree, the pine-tree, and the box together, — to beautify the place of the sanctuary."

No doubt, there is such a thing as manliness without faith. But its defects are patent enough, even to the eyes of the faithless themselves. You cannot live with it very long without seeing its weak places. God kindles fires to prove us, along our mortal discipline, in whose burning heat it falls to pieces like a flimsy fabric; such fires as require stuff of another tempering to come out refined, in vessels fit for immortal uses. Manliness without faith is not to be trusted; for on Christian faith depends Christian principle; and no other principle can stand all the solicitings of appetite and ambition. The other kind lurches away sometimes, leaving terrible chasms where some trusted pillar in the body politic, or body mercantile, went down. Manliness without devotion must ever want the highest attraction in character, which is self-renunciation, — the producer and ally of true simplicity. That comes only of a secret persuasion of infirmity; and that comes only of the Gospel, showing the commandment and the violation, — the perfect law and the alienated life, — and spanning the gulf between, by its blessed doctrine of reconciliation. Manliness without piety misses the profoundest and purest form of gratitude, because that exists only at the feeling of the Divine forgiveness for a sinful heart, — the gracious discharge from an infinite obligation producing the unspeakable peace. In short, manliness without faith, at its best estate, is all frailty; at its surest strength, it is unsteadfast; at its fairest promise, it is treacherous; at its fullest joy, it is empty. It may gain the world; but, like the young man of the Evangelist, it turns away from Jesus, and in its great possessions finds no rest.

And no doubt, on the other hand, there is such a thing as religion without manliness, — pietism, and not piety. This is as unnatural as the other. You not only rob religion, but you insult and betray it, if you present it, through your characters, implicated in narrow judgments, small sectarian manœuvres, a barren brain, frigid sympathies, or a petty style of manners. Religion without manliness whines and crouches. It acts as if Providence were a tyrant, the world a prison, and man a slave. Instead of holding its clear look up, with conscious and grateful dignity, to the light, and standing face to face with all the cheerful and solemn facts of life, and looking straight into the eyes of every creature, as faith gives it a supreme right to do, it goes to the church with a ghastly expression, or none, — creeps to the prayer-meeting abjectly, — is half afraid to own its cause, and shows its meagre mind by abusive and unillumined criticisms. It resorts to tricks for the building of a meeting-house, which the code of honor among unconverted men would reject from the shop, and settles a minister or equips a missionary with a management too tortuous for the broker's counter. It makes common-sense cry out in despair, Why cannot the disciples of Christ show the world specimens of human character, as broad in proportions, as free in outline, as magnanimous in temper, as sensible in practice, as appreciating in taste, as liberal in accomplish ments, as they are superior by their celestial calling?

It is an indirect confession, I think, how consistent the strictest and most earnest system of doctrine is with the inward testimony of the heart, that a majority of young men who are thoughtful enough to fill a stated place in *any* sanctuary, when they choose their church, choose one where the administration is most decidedly and simply religious. I have known young men, themselves perhaps not yet fulfilling the demands of a Christian vocation, and certainly not openly avowing their Christian purposes, to say this: "When we go to a house of worship, we wish to see the same engagedness and earnestness there, that we see expended on a different class of objects all the week. We are suspicious of a style of preaching that is merely genteel, rhetorical, or philosophical. On Sunday we want sincerity, fact, and substance, as much as in our business. We want life, — not bare intellectual life, but spiritual. There are books enough, lectures enough, science and poetry enough, elsewhere. When we go to church, we want to come into close contact with the very root and marrow of religion: otherwise it is no object. Once, the Sunday preaching was literature, poetry, art, lyceum, university, company, and all, to the New England people, — the grand intellectual stimulant and social facility: now, it is no such thing. We go to meeting to get glimpses of a Saviour, of heaven, and peace. Besides, we hate shams and half-beliefs in anything, — politics or prayers. If religion is what you pretend, give us the solid thing, no dilution nor fancy-work. We hold you to your honest word. We say, as the great English captain and disciplinarian, lately dead, said to the delicate young clergyman, who undertook to win from him an assent to some lax construction of the Gospel errand, 'Follow *your* orders.' We say, as another man, one of the broadest intellects of our Western continent, more lately gone, said, 'Let clergymen preach more to individuals, and less to the crowd; let them say, "The Judge standeth before the door"; make it a personal matter'; for, even when we do not obey, something in us makes us choose to hear the naked and wakening truth."

"Why do you go," it was asked of one of our merchants' clerks, "to a church where a creed is embraced in which you do not believe?" "Because," he replied, "I find religion there presented as a concern — a pressing, intimate, exigent concern — of the soul: repentance, faith, newness of life, and Christ crucified, are preached to me." It seems to me he was right. The religion that is really natural harmonizes nobleness and manliness of spirit with strictness of doctrine.

II. In the second place, the religion that is natural unites an open confession of faith with the hiding of its inward power, and so strikes a just balance between the two faulty extremes of reserve on the one side, and hypocrisy on the other.

We have in our community, first, a class that would supersede the anxiety to *be* Christians, by vigorously and continually saying that they are; a class that would rather let iniquity hide under the altar, than thin the crowd that bend decently before it; and that hold up no other sign to distinguish a disciple from an unbeliever, than the subscription to a covenant. Out of that class comes hypocrisy. Opposite to these are the timid minds that shrink honestly from all church ties, and, with hearts tender to holy impressions, miss both inward completeness and their outward efficiency, by keeping aloof from church-fellowship. Theirs is a wrong-headed reserve. But between both these stands a larger class than either, excusing their non-profession by the inconsistency of false professors, but taking license for a low standard of life from the same example; scoffing at the former, who profess without practice, and practising with the latter, only in not professing; telling you they can be just as holy men out of the Church as in, but evidently more careful to be out of the Church than to be holy men. Clear of these alien elements, it is the problem of Christianity to combine a Church of believers, who shall be both doers and professors of the word of life.

And to that end, Christianity insists, first of all, on a real faith. Whatever else it has or lacks, the soul, to be saved, must obey an honest purpose. Pretence and falsehood must be stripped off it. It must believe with the affections, heartily. With the *heart* man believeth unto salvation, before confession is made with the mouth. In all departments of life, sincerity is the salt that saves men from the disgrace of acted lies. Men of the world, legislating only for mutual convenience, cannot be mistaken in making downright and unpretending reality the foremost command in their statute-book. To get rid of the semblance of goodness where goodness is not, is as important to the purity of the Church, or the acceptance of a soul before the Judge of hearts, as to get rid of sin where sin is. In fact, the pretence *is* sin. Get the conviction, which is the fountain, and it will furrow out a channel, and fill it with a stream. Get the new life, the love of God, and it will shape a body as the juices in the germ shape the tree. Have something to say, and the Everlasting Mind will give you, as well as the Apostles, in that day and hour, how ye ought to say it. It is useless for a man to *tell* you "his heart is right with God, if you see his hand feeling in his neighbor's pocket," or clutching at unfair advantages in the market, or devouring widows' houses; subscribing to philanthropic projects and swindling contracts on alternate days; or reaching forth to the bread and wine of Christ's table to-day, and fingering some dishonest bribe in office to-morrow. You will hardly trust the tongue that swears an oath of divine allegiance when it is good-natured, but a profane one in a passion; nor the lips that repeat formal prayers in the pew, and babble scandal in the parlor. You will not be satisfied that men should declaim against iniquities which they happen never to be tempted by; nor that they should come, with late professions, limping, maimed, and sickly sacrifices, such as even Hebrew priests refused, after the fire in the blood of youth has cooled, and the indulged appetites have burnt out through satiety, to offer God a wreck wasted in the service of his enemies. For "some," says South, "hope to be saved by shedding a few insipid tears, and uttering a few hard words against those sins which they have no other controversy with, but that they were so unkind as to leave the sinner before he was willing to leave them." So that, after all, the fundamental test of profession is sincerity of faith, and the test of sincerity of faith is righteousness. To be natural, religion must be real. For "in all natural productions," from cedar to hyssop, from the sun shining in his strength to the dullest lump of clay, "there is no hypocrisy."

But then, Christianity as naturally requires confession. The excuses by which men, and none more than young men, apologize for not cordially espousing Church relations, are for the most part evasions, and so involve some obliquity, as uncandid, possibly, as the unworthy professor's. John Foster suggests that the religious loquacity of incompetent pretenders may be a kind of compensatory judgment on those believers who might honestly testify for the Gospel, but refuse. Is it not natural to show which side you are on? Is not that counted the way of fearlessness, of frankness, of independence, in your common relations, — in politics, in local questions, in measures of social change? There is a greater issue pending before you, nay, within you; and what makes neutrality especially respectable there? The world over, and pre-eminently in a city like this, two gigantic forces, under two leaders, claim your adhesion: these two are contrary, the one to the other, and there is no third. Christ and his Church are one; Mammon and worldly good are the other. You must choose which, in you, shall be supreme; it is a providential necessity laid upon you; nay, you have chosen, and do literally choose every hour, anew. To be uncommitted is to be on the side that is not God's.

We are not nearly enough in the habit of treating religion as a cause, and ourselves as soldiers, whose honor is bound up in it, our all at stake in it. Who is on the Lord's side? is a question that rings up and down our streets eternally, and in voices more solemn than brave Xavier's when he cried it through the cities of the East; for we are nominally Christians, and so in a position to do Christ more discredit infinitely than heathenism ever could. It is of the utmost consequence to every young man's singleness of heart, saying nothing of his future welfare, to have this choice settled. Till then he is perpetually compromised. We treat religion as if it were an isolated idea in every heart, and not a unity, a kingdom, a cause, which it certainly is if the New Testament is true. Our excessive individualism wrongs it. It is an organization, it is a church, it is something we have to enter into, and fight for, and abide by.

Nominally we are Christians, and thereby hangs an obligation. It may be that you, with all your contempt for insincerity, are wearing a false name, and acting a part as essentially Pharisaic as if you were at once a preacher and a sceptic, or a deacon and a miser. Religion does not ask to be complimented and bowed to, on occasions. It is not honored in its own spirit by any formal attention to its technical services, — its dress and ritual, — divorced from a hearty submission to its interior control; nor by any ball-room compliments paid to its respectability as an institution, unsupported by obedience to its personal behests. These things are both discourteous and dishonest. When we venture to speak approvingly of a system of science, integrity demands of us to shape our speech by its own definitions. We must take it for what it is, and not for something else that our wilful constructions might put instead of it. If you join in that universal and swelling confession which these eighteen centuries have been accumulating, you are held to a personal consistency. Christianity is afraid of no scrutiny. It invites the boldest handling. It wants no fine things said of it, out of etiquette. It throws its evidences into the light, and stands on the facts. Like the divine Person that embodies it, it says: "Come, reach hither thy finger, and thrust it into my hand; and reach hither thy hand, and thrust it into my side; be not faithless, but believing: and yet deny me, if you will, rather than heartlessly assent; for open foes are better than treacherous followers." In a thousand ways you all profess to be a Christian people: why not, then, profess it in the one plainest and directest way? If we will not own the kingdom of heaven, how is the kingdom of heaven to own us?

Another consideration ought not to be passed over. Society, in its inequalities and injustices, is constantly presenting a necessity for reforms. Private sins settle together, and get organized into gigantic forces. To resist the collective evil, a collective sanctity is wanting. That is a Church. Now, if the Church ever enacts the public shame of proving faithless to this sublime privilege, leaving the great moral reformations to be taken in hand by well-disposed persons standing outside of the Church, then, instead of forsaking or avoiding the Church, let your disapproval rather draw you into it; enlist your disinterested energies under its standard. Working according to that providential way, you will work with tenfold greater success. Put your reforming zeal, then, inside the Church, where it is too much wanted. Revive its ancient primitive martyr-spirit. Warm it with your prayers, expand it by your charity. Cast into it all of spiritual strength and hope you hold, and you shall both save yourself, and build up truth, liberty, and love, beating down intemperance, war, licentiousness, and slavery.

So in all other workings, where the Church of Christ has suffered foreign devices to outwit or outdo its appropriate business. This Young Men's Christian Union was not formed to compete with that divine body, nor to supersede it, nor to comfort any of its own members with the feeling that they need not belong to it. The right office of your association will be fulfilled only as it leads more and more of you to open recognitions of faith, and active participation in the parishes. Instead of carping at the faults you see there, enter and remedy them. If you find God's houses fenced about with an illiberal policy, — their pew-doors locked, literally with bolts, or virtually with exorbitant taxation, imposed to support luxurious appointments, and give worship a stylish equipage, — then do not stand complaining; but come into the active care of these parish economics, lifting them gradually to the level of your juster, equalizing ideas. Take the meeting-houses up in your arms, and do with them as you will. The body of men before me, consecrated and baptized with the Holy Spirit, might revolutionize the whole ecclesiastical fashion in twenty days. Only let it be done out of the propelling energy of faith, and not from an ambitious, conceited, or sectarian policy.

We all have our creeds, and, in spite of ourselves, we profess them; — the creed of fashion; the creed of appetite; the creed of a selfish expediency; the creed of a sect; the creed of indifference, which is as irreligious and as bigoted in its way as any other; or the creed of eternal right and gospel faith. Conduct is the great profession. Behavior is the perpetual revealing of us. A man's doctrines flow from his fingers' ends, and stand out in his doings. What he may say is not his chief profession, but how he acts. Character lets out the secret of his belief; what he *does* tells what he *is*. He has "put on the Lord Jesus Christ," when he has "Christ formed within him." His profession is as natural as the pulse in his veins. The good man makes profession of his goodness, by simply being good; but the Christian man will not forget that he is not wholly good till he has joined himself to Christ's body. He publishes his adhesion as spontaneously as Nature publishes her laws, — as the sun its light, — as the rose its sweetness; — by being steadfast; by shining; by fragrant charities. It costs a graceful elm no spasm to paint a graceful image on our eye, and the sea spreads its mysterious arms around the hemispheres without vanity. They make their nature known by silently keeping its laws. And because the Christian soul is made to be a conscious member in a living organism or church, it keeps its own high law only by being there. Religion belongs in the heart-beat of a man's affections, and the breath of his daily desire: till it has so possessed him, it is a small matter that he keeps its effigy as a connoisseur keeps his marble Apollo, — on the outskirts of his practical fortunes. The true hospitality takes it to the heart. But when the heart has taken it in, it will not lock it there, and make it a prisoner. It must go abroad again, for the blessing of man and the praise of God. It will put its owner into the Church, not to show himself, but that he may the better become one with his brethren, and their common head. So does the religion that is natural unite the public confession of it with the hiding of its inward power.

As has been wisely remarked by Morell, "The proper profession of Christianity is its practice; and, were that practice based upon an elevated idea of Christian duty, the inquiry as to a man's profession would be as much out of place as the inquiry respecting a Howard, whether he *professed* a love for humanity!"

III. Thirdly, the religion that is natural unites the exercise of a scrupulous conscience with the sentiments of devotion; so reconciling morality and piety. Indeed, the divorce of these two is so *un*natural, that we can account for it only on the score of some terrible infirmity, either in the heart or the will, — the affectional or the executive part of us. How else could that twofold command, wedded by the word of Christ, summing up the ethics and the worship of earth and heaven, — Love God and love man, — ever have been wrenched apart? Morality loses its finest quality, its inspiration, its aroma, its constancy, its divine peace, for want of prayer; and piety misses its effective force as a producer of righteousness, because the link is lost between the closet and the market.

In one of the bright books of the day, I find a courageous and impulsive young English fox-hunter saying to a clerical Oxford cousin: "I feel that the exercise of freedom, activity, foresight, daring, independent self-determination, even in a few minutes' burst across country, strengthens me in mind as well as in body. It sweeps away the web of self-consciousness. As for bad company, when those that have renounced the world give up speculating in the stocks, you may quote pious people's opinions. We fox-hunters see that the 'religious world' is much like the 'great world,' and the 'sporting world,' and the 'literary world'; and that, because this happens to be a money-making country, and money-making is an effeminate pursuit, therefore all sedentary sins, like covetousness, slander, bigotry, and self-conceit, are to be plastered over, while the more masculine vices are hunted down by your cold-blooded religionists. Be sure that, as long as you make piety a synonyme for this weak morality, you will never convert me, nor any other good sportsman."

Now, Christianity ought not to be afraid to hear the thoughts that are working in young men's brains speak out with just this candor. True Christianity will not be afraid, though she may regret the narrow premises, the dim reasoning, and the superficial conclusions, which make the selfishness of unscrupulous worshippers an excuse for despising the religion of the New Testament. Her advocates and ministers may learn something from it, and be able to take a more intelligent and forcible attitude for it. They may learn from it that any religious ardors are, in the long run, maniacal and delusive, which do not work themselves out straightway into all parts of life. They may learn that the proud friends and self-styled elect of the Church may be its most ruinous traitors. They may learn that precisely the religious administration which the world needs now is one that never ceases to insist on a consistent manifestation of faith, through works that bless and ennoble humanity.

If I might venture to define what is the great mischief of the merely moral or conscience-system of life, I should say that it excludes the most powerful principle of disinterested action, which is a grateful trust in a love flowing infinitely from God, through Christ and his cross. Instead of this, it takes the iron rule of law or command. Of course, on that ground, its only standard and hope of acceptance or success is in the more or less merit which comes of more or less obedience to that law. But, at this point, the soul, looking at the law, is awe-struck to find it a perfect law, coming from a perfect author, allowing for no sin, and nowhere offering the least encouragement to a half-obedience. At the same moment, it discovers, with dismay, that, owing to inherent propensities and passions, this obedience never was nor is likely to be perfect. Where is it, then? Merit is out of the question. The utmost duty falls short, and the servant is unprofitable at best. One of two things follows: this man must either deny to God his perfection of purity, and to the law its binding authority, so as to make room for his short-comings; or else he must sink into utter despair, because they do nothing but condemn him. This would seem to be the result of the conscience system alone, without the mediatorship, and its doctrines of reconciliation, in Christ. It leaves man either without reverence or without peace, or both.

Then it engenders a poor habit of continual self-reference, self-measurement, and self-centralization, instead of taking the soul up above itself, giving it an object there to live for, in gratitude and love. It diseases us with "that morbid self-consciousness and lust of praise," so common among our Christians even; of which it has been wisely said, "that God prepares for it," in his own way and time, "with all his truly elect, a bitter cure." It sets consciousness above revelation, as a light to the mysteries of our inner life; and that "consciousness is a dim candle over a deep mine." The aspiration after the Perfect, in all noble natures, is the mightiest hunger of the heart. But if no blessed promise of forgiveness is to come by faith, and comfort its failures, all its yearnings are tortures, and it is only the mightiest tormentor of the heart. What is needful but the prayers of faith, seconding the intercessions of a Church and a Mediator, to bear it up above these sad distractions, and rest it in the peace of God?

But, then, just there you see how the same habit, in another stage, invades the domain of prayer itself, and enfeebles its peculiar energy, with the strange theory, never gained from Scripture certainly, that prayer is, after all, another name for work, or behaving morally, — that there is no veritable asking and receiving in it, as Jesus plainly declares, but that we are to go through the ceremony of praying to God just as if there were a God hearing us and answering, only because, by imposing on ourselves that trick, we excite our own resolution, climb into a purer mood, and gain some favors from the natural laws; — this, instead of praying such honest prayers as children bring to their parents, doubting nothing, and as real believers have known to be answered ever since belief was, — such prayers as the Bible prays for us. What faith asks, again, therefore, is that our very prayers themselves shall be re-christianized, and a literal communion between earth and heaven be re-opened.

Inverting now the direction of our search, we look for morality. James, with his Epistle for godly conduct, must follow Paul with his fervent enthusiasms of devotion. Life is a vineyard. Its business is a task. We are set down in a field white already to harvest. Humanity has wrongs to be righted, and oppressions to be lifted off. Bargains are to be made immaculate. Lusts are to be quenched. Selfishness is to be softened. In a word, faith is to bear fruit an hundred-fold, and piety to lead a moral life. Otherwise, the whole head of faith is sick, and the whole heart of piety is faint.

This every-day, familiar, working religion, the religion of little things, is Christianity. To Jesus, the lily growing in the shadow of Gerizim was as sacred as the temple blazing in the splendor of Mount Moriah, and the widow's mite and humility worthy as Joseph's courage and fortune. You have heard of the Turkish piety that will carefully put aside all fragments of paper, lest the name of God, written on them by chance, should be trodden on and profaned. Christian reverence will gather up the scraps of time and opportunity, because on them all is certainly stamped the law of religious accountability. The dyer's hand, they say, is subdued to the thing it works in; but so, morally, is every man's. Suppose you tell a friend, who comes to be your guest, that you will set apart one house that shall hold him locked up, where you will meet him one hour in the week, and there pay him professions of extravagant esteem; but you will not allow him in your home, your shop, or your recreations. That is the hospitality which many of us show to religion. Neither devotion nor conscience will reach its natural growth so. Character — joint fruit of piety and morality, prayer and work — is the glory of the world; and only that holiness has immortality.

IV. My fourth and final position is this: — The religion that is natural unites a supreme zeal for evangelical belief with the largest Christian catholicity, and so blends fidelity with charity.

My meaning is, that religious toleration ought not to stand indebted for its prevalence to religious indifference. A part of the "Christian liberty" of which our modern age boasts, may be merely a liberty, or license, not to be Christian. Some of our powers, both civil and ecclesiastical, care too little, possibly, about any faith, to oppress any. The reign of true charity can never be inaugurated on earth by discrowning zeal.

Zeal any vital and conquering system must have. It is one of the manliest and mightiest attributes of our nature. To Christian character it is what heat is to the sun. Now, zeal implies convictions; not loose, vague, slippery notions, so carelessly held as to breed unconcern, or so falsely spiritual as to melt away before the eye, into thin, vapory generalities; but convictions, — definite, decided, special. These are the things that beget an honest zeal. Men do not toil, and sweat, and lay down fortune and fame for the sake of cloudy abstractions; nor do martyrs go to the axe and fire for the sake of being "a pretty good sort of men for the most part," or doing about right in general. I have already spoken of the relish strong minds have for strong doctrine. When you go to church only to hear it preached to you, that self-cultivation is all you want; that sin is an old-fashioned, obsolete phantom; that, having got rid of the notion of a devil, theology has now only to get rid of the anxiety about his works; that the difference between converted and unconverted is only the difference between more and less of manhood, or personal distinction; that retribution is soft or a nullity, and divine justice a figure of speech, and intuition the grand guide, and passion the voice of Divinity, or dying penitence an atonement for a vile life, or the redemptive work an easy acquittal and substitute for our own, — then you feel, I have no doubt, that you have been debauched by the preaching. If you are a dissipated and profligate man yourself, you will yet despise the minister for flattery and falsehood, who tells you the dissipated and profligate man is nothing but an immature style of man, a little behind his regenerate neighbor on the same road. You know that Christianity divides the world into two sorts of men. If you are a sinner, of any shape, something in you will extort your consent when you are told that God hates sin. You know that, after a sinful life, the religion that cries, "Be born again," is the most natural religion, — that guilt involves the peril of perdition, — that repentance is the only rescue, faith in Christ Jesus the only blessedness, and righteousness, springing therefrom, the only salvation.

It is a striking etymological confirmation of the tie that connects strict believing with strict living, that in the history of language the term "libertine" was first applied to lax or sceptical speculations, but came, in process of time, to signify corrupt morals. It will be only an irreligious liberality that argues for charity by striking out the pillars of faith; which would be to the contentious sects in the Church much like producing harmony among the angry inmates of a house by tearing away the foundation.

And yet, that these contentious sects be pacified, the growing Christian consciousness of the age feels to be one of the very foremost wants of the Church. The time has come, and is coming more perfectly each day, when the extinction of sectarian bigotry and intolerance is made necessary, not only to the practical power and consistency of the Christian religion itself, but to the satisfaction of Christian men as they are. Your own title and schedule as an association give an intimation that you have caught the foreshining of that day-spring; and, as if you recognized this as among the chief desiderata in rational piety, you have called yourselves a Christian Union.

The pressing question, now, therefore, respects the mode of this Union, or how a better state of mutual forbearance is to be brought about. Not, in the name of all that is natural, in the first place, by any sacrifice of convictions. We must not think to heal our quarrels by crucifying our Lord. Obtain uniformity by the least abandonment of doctrines which you really believe, and it is a uniformity not worth having; it is a league of death; you have destroyed the greater for the less. The truth as it is in Jesus, first; then the "seeing eye to eye." The Unitarian cannot say to the Trinitarian, "Give up your faith in Christ's absolute Deity, and I will give up my faith in man's natural purity; and then come, and let us agree." The Protestant cannot say to the Romanist, "Try to stretch your belief so as to embrace a half of the doctrine of justification by faith, and I will try to stretch mine so as to take in half of your absolution by sacraments; and so we will be brethren." All this, in every degree of it, is artificial, false, infidel. It is paltering with the most sacred verities, and a denial of the everlasting fact. Systems of theology are not to be patched and accommodated, like blocks of wood, by paring off here, and adding on there; raising one side, and lowering another. Every honest spirit revolts instantly at the bare conception, and there is no need to argue upon it. If unity could come only in that compromising way, every believing man would cry out, "Then, in Christ's name, let the Church stand split to the end of days, and the Saviour's prayer, 'that they all may be one,' be unfulfilled for ever."

At the extreme opposite to this mistake is the more common one, held by each of the sects, that, whenever the present religious hostilities cease, that event will be due to the perfect and universal triumph of its own creed; the world swinging round exactly on to its own platform. This notion seems as contracted as the other one was lax. It is undoubtedly true, that to himself every man's convictions must for the present appear to be right; otherwise they are no longer convictions. The moment he ceases to have faith in his views, he must dismiss them, or hold them in suspense; and in his efforts to spread or propagate the Gospel, he must seek to propagate his own view of what the Gospel is, and not another man's; that is, what is truth to him. So, in shaping to himself an idea of the perfect doctrine that will organize a united church, he cannot distinctly conceive what other it shall be than the one he now believes to be true. All these are plain propositions. But this, surely, is not the same as his saying that God cannot, or will not, disclose to another age what he has hidden from this. You can be sincere and consistent in your own belief, without denying human progression. You can suppose the faith of the future will, in many things, differ from your own, and yet be true, though you cannot distinctly conceive how. Of course, nothing is plainer than that this hope, on the part of the sects, each one by itself, that its own precise creed shall finally prevail, to the total overthrow of all the rest, must be futile; for, of fifty different things, each one cannot be substituted for all the rest at the same time. Ought not the absurdity of this expectation to teach us denominational modesty, — teach us to be less confident and dogmatical as to those tenets wherein we differ, — teach us to hold a less repellent attitude towards each other, as to all the less essential peculiarities of form, polity, and mere intellectual opinions?

Essential, — that is the word on which all hinges. Something is essential. Suppose now that, ceasing to look at one another, to compare themselves with one another, to criticise one another, and to contend with one another, the sects turn and look only to Him who is the acknowledged Head of all. Suppose they should become so intent in their personal affection and devotion to him, as to pass over their various interpretations of terms without dispute; so devoutly grateful to see the Father thus manifested in the flesh, as to lose their interest in wordy controversies; so ardent in their worship, as to be raised out of concern for sectarian numbers; so absorbed in the deep conviction of unworthiness, while they look on the moving spectacle of the cross, and see a pure Redeemer suffering to reconcile them to the Heaven they have deserted, as to forget the poor interests of party pride, — then would it not begin to be clear as noon to them all, just as far as they should do this, what the *essential* is? "Be ye reconciled to God": that is the essential. Put this state of coldness, of indifference, of spiritual torpor and carelessness, or of positive alienation between yourself and him, — put it to an end. Come into a free and peaceful harmony of will with him. Let penitence win his forgiveness; let confession secure his favor; let prayers — such prayers as swell and move the whole heart — scatter your doubts; let faith give you constancy, and practical righteousness place your feet on solid rock. All this is of the heart, not of the brain. It comes by way of the conscience and affections, not by outward form or creed. It is a personal experience, and not a sectarian calculation. Believers will be reconciled to one another just so fast and so far as they will heed Paul's entreaty, beseeching them in Christ's stead to be first reconciled to God.

You will see, from this exposition, that I look for the Christian concord, of which I have spoken as an object very precious to good men's hopes, not as coming by the neglect of Christ's doctrine, nor by dogmatic obstinacy; not by paring down creeds to make them fit, nor by one sect overriding and swallowing all others; but by going down so deep into all the affecting and powerful realities belonging to the soul's reconciliation to God in Christ Jesus, that every earnest believer's heart shall be found meeting its fellow there, all beating in friendly unison, and all resting in the Divine Love. Or, to vary the image, Christian unity is to come, not by attempts to concoct a mental conformity with ingenious contrivance, working on a human level; but by letting the soul be taken up into that lofty region of warm devotion, of holy trust, of heavenly communion, where it loses sight of the little boundary lines that mark off sect from sect; and where it forgets alienations by ascending far above them towards the peace of God. "If ye then," says the grand exhortation of the Apostle, — "if ye then be risen with Christ, seek those things which are above, where Christ sitteth on the right hand of God. For your life is hid with Christ in God."

Nothing is plainer in prophecy, than that each of the existing sects has, in its form of faith, some element to contribute to that Perfect Church, or visible Body of Christ, which the future is to realize. It is very impressive, and it ought to inspire us with reverence for the methods of the Divine Providence, to see how every separate denomination is thus put out to school by itself, fashioned into a peculiar form, nurtured to a peculiar life, qualified for a peculiar task; and then, when their several ideas are developed, how they are to be brought together by the attractions of the Spirit, and their distinctive qualities melted into one homogeneous whole. We stand at the preparatory or transition point, in this process. Protestantism has broken up the old false and formal unity, where the letter had overborne the spirit, and has installed the new state of divided parties, — a necessary stage on the way to final peace and purity. For, remember, purity is as precious to God as peace. There is a false kind of peace; such as was before Luther, — the peace of absolutism and tyranny; such as may be again, — the peace of worldly stagnation and religious unconcern. The only union that can satisfy the Almighty, or bless mankind, is where peace stands in agreement with wholesome activity of mind, a ruling love of truth, and holiness of life. It is to accomplish that, that we are passed through all this stir of inquiry and agitation of opinions, incidental to a Protestant age. What it most concerns us to observe, while in it, is not to let difference pass into hostility, variety run into sectarianism, individuality shrivel into dogmatism, and comparisons of doctrine be deformed by a dishonorable proselytism, or a wicked intolerance. And equally does it concern us not to continue divided after the time has fairly come for us to be one, nor maintain opposing organizations when their providential function has ceased, and their historical significance been taken up into a more comprehensive order. This will be our danger, just as far as we scorn any indications of a growing religious harmony, or persist in pushing party projects when it is plain we can render God better service by acting just as if parties were abolished, or had never been.

You all know that, a few years ago, certain patriotic venerators of the majestic character of Washington devised a new offering to his greatness, in a national monument, to be composed, in part, of stones contributed by the several States of the Union which his wisdom and heroism founded. These several communities have brought their blocks to that grand pile, each carving some inscription befitting its own history or genius, or expressing the dominant local sentiment. On the faces of these tablets, products of quarries scattered over a country so broad, the eye of the future will read the characters of those ideas which the discipline of American history has wrought into the minds of the people, their copy stamped on these durable pages, dedicated to the common founder and leader. But the best monument of our divine deliverance is the body of living disciples. Ages are its builders. Faith is its corner-stone. Love is the artist that shapes its symmetry, and forms the unity of the design. For that "growing temple," as the Apostle fitly calls it, every sincere and thoughtful sect brings in its hands some needed contribution, the result of its own single experience, carved with a thought which nothing but the wisdom born of its own special life could have inspired. And, as even the savage Indian hordes, whose only blessing from this new civilization has been exile, oppression, and temptation, with a touching forgiveness quite redeeming in their barbarian natures, have added in their votive stone to commemorate the political father of the nation; so, I cannot help believing, those persecuted and outcast tribes of heathens, whom Pharisaic judgments now rank as beyond the pale of the circumcision, will be found at last to deliver in some tribute, more acceptable than that of the Pharisees themselves, to the Building of the impartial Lord, in whom there is neither circumcision nor uncircumcision, barbarian nor Scythian, bond nor free.

America was not discovered to be merely a magnificent workshop for enterprise, nor a camp for political parties, nor even a theatre for the play of civil liberty. God meant it for a nursery of believing and valiant souls, — the home of a sacred brotherhood, — a church of his living praise. It becomes us to see to it, so far as our individual life and confession will achieve or further it, that here his pure word and will shall have free course, run, and be glorified.

There is a deeper wisdom awaiting the unfolding of God's plans than has yet got itself taught in our universities; a more perfect social order than is commanded by any statute-book, or enforced by any government; a truer theology than is written in any creed or catechism. It is well to live and labor under these cheerful expectations; for we shall live more effectually, and labor more faithfully. But, after all, for each single soul the work of life lies not on any public sphere, nor amid great public problems, but in a smaller lot. To stand diligent and trustful in that lot, is what God asks. To work out the salvation of one penitent and fallible spirit, is our appointed task. And the only way whereby we can render any worthy service to the Church, or the world, is by first yielding to the entreaty of the Gospel, and being personally reconciled to God.

Here, then, would seem to be the outlines of a religion, which, being revealed from above nature, as nature looks to us, is yet perfectly and beautifully accordant with nature in its workings among men, divinely suited to the sphere where it is to win its triumphs; — a religion natural in these essential attributes of nature: 1. That it harmonizes with all the lofty and pure natural sentiments of humanity, — as love, gratitude, zeal, decision, tenderness, courage, self-denial; 2. That it is consistent in its manifestations; 3. That it acts from within outward, — that is, from an inward force or faith into visible fruits, or righteousness; and 4. That it fits the facts of experience, from sin and its misery up to reconciliation and its peace; — a religion at once profound and practical, contemplative and enterprising; affectionate as a mother, and inflexible as justice; tender as John, and bold as

Paul; solemn as the stars, and cheerful as the sunrise; awful as the midnight, and frank as the day; one with the innocent joy of children, stretching their arms to the future; one with the sober conflicts of manhood, wrestling with the present; one with the calm rest of age, waiting between its little yesterday and its infinite to-morrow; — a religion at once beneficent and prayerful, watching at Gethsemane, feeding the famished in Galilee.

Come, then, men of a strong heart, in the power of a religion like this, come to the healing and purifying of our social state! Begin here, and set this city of Puritan piety once more on a hill, a flaming beacon of holy light. Let not sloth, cowardice, compliance with the effeminate fashions of the world, and inconstancy, too ready to falter and look back, lay waste the vineyard of the Lord, and, while New England, the American Israel, peoples the continent, make her heart sick!

More than this, make your Christianity aggressive; crowd it up into the seats of spiritual wickedness in high places, the encampments of the *rulers* of the world's darkness; press it down into the kennels of sottish degradation. Cast yourselves into these exhilarating tasks of Christian renewal. Unless our Christianity does this, it is death-struck at the core. The Church that stands still, forfeits its right to be called a church. "It is a maxim of the military art," said the great modern master of that art, "that the army which remains in its intrenchments is beaten." If that is orthodoxy among the armies of empires, it is truer yet of the armies of the cross. If we stand still, we stagnate. New outlays of Christian heroism must widen the enclosures of the new kingdom. This needs men such as your Association ought to marshal and multiply, not to be shaken by a crude speculation or a sceptic's sneer.

My companions and fellow-subjects under the discipline of life, I have said nothing to you in detail of those manifold solicitings to sin, those trials of fire, besetting your steps in the city, — that raining shot of temptation, filling all our city air, through which your virtue must pass and be proved, and out of which it is a chief office of this Christian Union to help you to be delivered, with your purity unspotted. Those warnings are familiar to you. You know every one of these siren seducers as well at least as I. You know what prayers mothers, sisters, loving kindred, and believing friends, raise for you in quiet homes. You know what the choice is, and on which side of it all peace and strength, all order and grandeur, all present and eternal welfare, all honor and heaven, stand. I have attempted to show you the more positive doctrine; to exhibit that place of strength, where the soul, once fixed, is almost beyond the reach of danger, disarming evil by the breadth and intensity of its convictions; and to trace before you, too feebly and faintly I know, some outlines of that religion, at once evangelical and rational, devout and practical, zealous and manly, centring in the Gospel, but spreading itself over the life of all men, all cities, all countries, all ages, binding them into the unity of one mighty Church, — which is truly natural, insomuch as it comes from the God whose nature has suited it to ours. This might rather anticipate temptation, and, working within your souls, a living and honest faith, prove indeed "the victory which overcometh the world."

SERMON XXIV.

FOUNDATIONS OF A CHRISTIAN CITY.

A CITIZEN OF NO MEAN CITY. — Acts xxi. 39.
A CITY WHICH HATH FOUNDATIONS. — Heb. xi. 10.

BY the first of these phrases, Paul vindicates the dignity of his origin, against the contempt of the most contemptuous of races, challenging a hearing before a Jewish mob. The second is a serene prophecy of that immortal and equal society, the commonwealth of justified spirits, gathered by the Redeemer "out of every kindred, and tongue, and people, and nation." In the one, we have an instance of honorable municipal pride, taking the sanction of an Apostle, whose heart, though flaming with zeal for the cross, and supremely consecrated to preaching Christ and the resurrection, could yet make room for a human passion so pure. In the other, we find a type of that perfect economy, whose citizenship is heavenly, whose charter is the infinite grace, whose title and right of freedom is a faith like the Patriarch's, whose Builder and Maker is God.

To bring the first of these into unity with the last; to make our patriotism, or local attachment, consist with a divine hope; to conform our civil state here to the celestial pattern, — is at once the highest scope of our civilization, and the unyielding demand of our religion.

That religion does not scorn the sentiment of loyalty. Paul — who was no one-sided enthusiast, but had proportions broad enough in the structure of his manhood to take in all manly affections, blending genial emotions with inflexible principles, and who could harmonize the sagacity that knows how to deal with nature, on its practical side, with the loftiest spirituality — recognized the advantages of having been born in "no mean city." He was ready to assert that lawful claim, and, while a stranger at Jerusalem, arrested under religious jealousy, and led off to prison by a rough police, charged by false accusations, was resolved to have his share in the good repute of his native town. He told the chief captain, or city marshal, that he was by no means the seditious Egyptian he had been taken for, — making an uproar, a ringleader of murderers, — but a Hebrew himself, of Tarsus, a city of Cilicia, "a citizen of no mean city," and so entitled to an audience with the people. His plea of citizenship served him; and, standing on the castle-stairs for his pulpit, he snatched an occasion for his Master out of the very teeth of this ferocious, persecuting Judaism, and opened the whole doctrine of his ministry.

It becomes a distinct motive, then, for elevating the character of any community, or state, that, as in this instance, such character proves a protection to the individual citizen. Each contribution of uprightness, purity, fortitude, or devotion, made to the public stock, returns back benefits to the social stockholders, in their private emergencies. Nor is that consideration wholly self-interested; for it is as natural to regard it as affecting your fellow-subjects, as your own convenience. Every day, all over the world, it is happening that travellers and voyagers are rescued from restrictions on personal liberty, or other detriment, by the political virtue of the national flag; and the moral virtue of a local reputation is hardly less, in furnishing exemption, furtherance, or some species of facility, quite independent on the personal worth of the recipient. The character of your birthplace and residence is a shield of slow construction, but ponderous when it is once wrought; and every man who derives safety from its shelter should help compact its strength. It is only meanness and cowardice that will draw out of a common treasury, putting nothing in.

It is, in fact, on this principle — the law of personal relations to the public weal — that all national judgments come to be held as penalties to be warded off possibly by private penitence, fidelity, and prayers. A sharper perception of this connection, a certain lively sense of religious responsibility running into all collective action, which their children have partly lost, was what instigated our fathers to isolate special occasions for really deploring social sins, and supplicating political salvation.

But apart from the bare motive of immediate utility, every right-minded man is bound to the loyal duties of Christian citizenship by a constraint, which, if held to be less efficient by the estimate of a low expediency, because it is less involved in our outward security, is none the less sacred in its authority, and of a loftier nature. I mean the obligation laid on us to build our public morality up, according to our inbred conception of what a Christian community ought to be, — and *because we have* that conception, — the dowry of the Christian ages; our obligation to shape our actual society, and its institutions, by the configurations of that ideal, whose outlines and plan are drawn in the Gospel, — to fashion our own earthly city into the nearest possible resemblance to that city that hath foundations, not built with hands.

My subject, therefore, is the Foundations of a Christian City. It will be natural if, in treating it, I shall make special reference to this city of Boston we are in.

I. I speak, you will see, of foundations that are moral, — not material, not commercial, nor industrial. The first of these moral foundations is Domestic Purity; and the institution representing it is the Family. Two reflecting persons were asked to give extempore definitions of the idea of family. One called it "an item of a poor nation's wealth, and of a rich nation's poverty." The other called it "matrimony doing penance." Both answers suggest how far our best communities are from realizing, at large, the exalted conception of what a Christian home should be. It is sad to think how few steps we should need to take in any street, to find some dreary confirmation of that witty satire on heartless marriage, — "Going home by daylight, after courtship's masquerade." Men and women do not enter into wedlock as if they were entering a sanctuary; yet no temple is so sacred.

Outside of cities, the idea of family has external supports, — separated domiciles, — some space put between every household and the next. Neighborhood does not there mean contact and attrition. The awful sublimity of an infinite sky comes down between the dwellings. The local distinctness is a symbol of the social. Families come to have more marked characteristics, and grow into more decided forms of character. The storm and the winter, binding them together in a more vivid sense of segregation from the rest of the world, render them conscious of mutual dependence. But the city huddles individualities as it does houses. It ranges buildings into blocks, and characters into ranks of imitators, and disperses kindred into a crowd. There are advantages in this, and disadvantages. But it does not tend to nourish souls of strong personal will, nor independence of judgment, nor that equipoise of original faculties, careless of the verdict of surrounding fashions, which, in town and village alike, is an attribute of every valiant and effective mind.

The danger suggests the caution. As fast as we lose the reserve and retirement of a true domestic habit, we lose purity and power; and so we weaken the foundations of the city. How much affectionate preference for the evening circle over the excitement abroad,—so much inward strength. How much choice of that calmer and familiar communion between brothers and sisters, — so much inalienable resource and satisfaction that will survive the fever of youth. How much reciprocal affection and veneration between children that hasten home eagerly from all the fascinations of company, and parents that go reluctantly out from a charm in-doors which overmasters every foreign pleasure,—so much barrier built up against all the breaches of misfortune, — so much prepared soil for the culture of public and private morality. Parents that forego mature tastes for the thoughtful wisdom that condescends to bind these amulets of home delight about their children's necks, are as much saviours of the city as they are providers of their own honor and joy against age. Parents that teach their offspring to look on home as only a dressing-room for mixed society, — a point of convenient sallying forth to catch the afflatus of frivolous assemblies; or who turn their table-talk into recitations of the scandals engendered in some vacant brain, or their parlors into a rendezvous of those falsely assorted platoons that somebody has described as "the sexes' school of mutual misinstruction," a "camp of modern Amazons," — these are sowing for a harvest of private heart-aches and general decay.

There are other thoughts. Home is a foundation of Christian cities, because, if it is what it was meant to be, it opposes the surest and Heaven-appointed resistance to the vices that dense populations encourage. It cools the inflammation of competitory hatred. It heals the disorders of prodigals. It forestalls crimes that the law is helpless to forbid. It opens Bibles and books that the Bible has written. It gives the key-note to refining music, and from song the transition is often spontaneous to prayers. It bolts out a thousand tempting imaginations, and wards off, by its chaste employments, the wanton possibilities of shame, as if they were ugly fables of some antipodal tribe. Build up one Christian home, — Christian in no forced nomenclature of courtesy, but one that Jesus himself might enter with the blessing that visited Bethany, — and you lay a new support under the foundations of a Christian city.

II. The next great pillar of these supports is Education, and the institution that represents it is the School. At this point the city frequently takes its turn in superiority over the village. Bring the stimulus of interacting intellects to bear on an organized system of culture, and you obtain a development of mental activity that is more intense, if not so well balanced. If the ambition and hurry of the teacher for immediate results do not esteem the compass of his scholar's attainments out of proportion to the depth; if rapidity does not displace care; if the mere projecting of ill-assorted and ill-combined information into the memory does not create oblivion of that assimilating process by which knowledge is taken up into the circulations of the heart's blood, and so converted into wisdom; above all, if the head does not overbear the heart, so that science displaces religion, and so that the central, indwelling, and all-encompassing God is forgotten in a study of the surface of his creation, — then the school is indeed a nursery of the commonwealth. Emphatically is it true that the hearts of children — so tender to impression, yet so mighty in the germination of their energies — are foundations of the city. Misdirect *them*, and, as with the godless earth in the Psalmist's picture, all those foundations are shaken out of their course.

I learn from authoritative documents, that during the last year,* in this city, eleven hundred and ten juvenile criminals — offenders under age, of both sexes — were arrested for punishment, — a number more than a third larger than that of the year before, — and distributed to their several scenes of legal correction, many of which ought in simpler truth to be called seminaries of hardening and seduction. It is such statistics as these that make the yearly reports of the chief of our police sound like the gloomy bulletins of a helpless physician, chronicling the decline of a constitution he cannot save. Why should our system of education be confined for ever to prescribed methods, and to the better provided classes? Why should not new emergencies and advancing thought strike out new and nobler plans? Why should not facts so terrible as these — crying out to us like the very trumpets of judgment — create schools for the vicious as well as schools for the respectable, — for the vagrant as well

* A. D. 1851.

as the domesticated, — the ragged as well as the clad? Tuition *costs* less than imprisonment; but a civilized city should be ashamed to wait for that discovery. Every thieving boy and mendicant girl has a soul for which Christ died. Do not mock the Father of lights by putting them into sunless dungeons. The head of the municipal government said, not long ago, "At the rate with which violence and crime have recently increased, our jails, like our almshouses, however capacious, will be scarcely adequate to the imperious requirements of society." What will be adequate? Education will. Pour in light, — Heaven's inexhaustible and ultimately effectual medicine for depravity. Depose Ignorance, — the high-priest in the idolatrous temple of sin; lead in Truth, — the royal minister of righteousness, and "heir apparent of all the world." Seven hundred thousand pupils, the missionary reports tell us, are under the tuition of the Gospel, in heathen countries. What an incongruity that there should be a thousand Pagans in Boston! That word Pagan reverses now its original Latin meaning. First it signified the rude dwellers in villages. But in the process of centralization that goes on in older nations, it finds a fitter application in the neglected hordes that wallow and prowl about the purlieus of great centres. Say nothing of the impossibility, or the hopelessness, of tuition for the degraded. That doubt has been settled by practical demonstrations in our favor, in the lowest extremities of the largest cities. For you and me, the evening schools in yonder chapel ought to have settled it. The testimony of the faithful men that have toiled in domestic missions, ever since their foremost leader in Boston, Dr. Tuckerman, twenty-five years ago, wrote down the now fulfilled prophecy, —

that, with every successive year, each minister serving "in the true spirit of that ministry would find his soul bound to it by stronger ties," — all that testimony unites to prove that the vilest iniquity and the completest wretchedness beget no despair of human nature. After Wordsworth — with his delicate sensibility revolting at the slightest stain on purity, — a soul of almost childlike refinement and innocence — had returned to the quiet of Rydal Mount, from a visit to the enormities and abuses, the sufferings and the crimes of London, he recorded this just conclusion of his unmoved confidence in God, and in man as God's child: —

> "Neither vice nor guilt,
> Debasement undergone by body or mind,
> Nor all the misery forced upon my sight,
> . . . . . could overthrow my trust
> In what we *may* become."
> "What one is,
> Why may not millions be? What bars are thrown
> By nature in the way of such a hope?
> Our animal appetites and daily wants, —
> Are these obstructions insurmountable?
> If not, then others vanish into air."

Of knowledge comes industry; of the interpretation of the divine laws, written all over a radiant universe, from the Old Red-Sandstone to Sirius, — on rock and grass-blade and shelving sea-shores, — on soils, and the structure of plants, and the anatomy of animals, and the motion of stars, — comes a wiser life. Except science regulates brute instincts, organizes industry, and so casts up the highway of the Son of Man into the Jerusalem of faith, the social foundations rot. Where there is no vision of truth, the people perish. Stringent legislation will not save them, nor an imperious constabulary, nor a standing army. Generate an explosive agent, like a

Parisian rabble's madness, inside a vessel, and clamps on the exterior avail little to hold it together. The human will, perverted by an unreasoning fury, is mightier than all statute-books, as is proved by the outbreak of what Mazzini calls "the great electric currents of revolution." In the end, there will be no law but truth. Truth is to be learned; and that learning is the just creation of the School.

III. From the School, on to the Church,—from Education to Religion, the third and chief foundation of the Christian city. But, observe, I do not mean by the Church any inert or Pharisaic body, looking on the wastes of virtual atheism among us with folded hands, contenting herself with a few handsome decencies of temple-worship, or a genteel routine of professions and ceremonies that will not soil effeminate fingers. I mean a Church of God and his Son; and that means a Church of sacrifice and self-renunciation,—a Church whose first law is spiritual labor, whose function is conversion, and whose most irresistible impulse is aggression on the empire of Satan. I mean a Church whose members take Apostles for their examples, as well in bold regenerating incursions into the Macedonia of unbelief, as in quiet communings at Olivet and the upper chamber.

Surely our great seats of population ought to be also seats of the vitality and energy of such a living Church. We want it in America, and all sects ought to be enrolled in one militant army to push its peaceful conquests on,—their jealousies melted down in the common heat of a purpose so holy, and their suspicions scattered to the winds by their enterprise in reclaiming the lost, gathering outcasts into the fold, clothing the destitute, and preaching the Gospel to the poor. It was of such a Church that Jesus announced himself the Head, when he stood up to read from Isaiah's prophecy in the synagogue of Nazareth. Yet, in most of the larger cities of Christendom itself, only a fraction of the citizens ever come within reach of the Church's voice. She needs, herself, a fresh baptism of the spirit of consecration from on high, fresh oil to refill her wasted lamps, fresh conversions to swell her ranks, and fresh love to make her *whole.* And, "inasmuch as the apostates of Chorazin are more incorrigible than the impenitent of Tyre," she needs these new supplies even more for making Christianity evangelical and operative among the wayward captives of Mammon and sense in our prosperous capitals, than in Burmah or Koordistan.

At one extreme of our vulgar competitors for comfort stand the besotted rich, as far from the kingdom of Heaven as the needle's eye from stretching to the compass of the camel, neither entering it themselves, nor suffering those that are entering to go in. At the other end, the *victims* of this pride, or of their own sottish passions, or of malicious and radical despair, chafing at all that is wholesome, and defiling all that is holy. At both extremes riot those identical sins that bind the rich profligate and the poor in a degrading kinsmanship, — intemperance, lust, and sloth. One street alone in this city, last year, yielded to your grand jury two hundred and five complaints, for violations of peace, for Sabbath disorders, for the dissipation of lewd cellars and tippling-shops, and the whole brood of petty and aggravated crimes that nestle in these kennels of filth and guilt. Why has not Christ's Church a missionary for every hovel, — a patient compassion to lead every child, clothed and loved, to worship? Modern sanitary ideas wisely forbid burials of the dead within municipal limits, excluding that corruption. Looking as God looks, it is a far more fatal forbearance that leaves the pestilent breath of this moral death, with vents at every corner, to poison the living.

While we lay the foundations of religion deeper, in filled and faithful churches of the better-provided, in consistent lives and a reverential habit of devotion, let some missionary ardor reclaim, if possible, — and God has made it possible, — the perishing aliens. By our established institutions, needing only the infusion of warmer zeal from our personal will, — our Provident Associations, and Ministry at Large, and Children's Mission, — let us make our convictions more aggressive, our sincerity more unquestionable. If we were to name the man who, in the conditions of modern society, more expressly and literally reproduces the outward work of Christ and his first disciples than any other, would it not be the missionary to the poor in our cities? How shall he go, except he is sent, or work, unless he is fed? If you shrink from his tasks, has all your due been given to sustain his willingness? Your municipal government and your police-officers save dollars. The religion of Christ saves two wherever these save one; but it also saves what dollars cannot buy; for it casts into the world's sick life that spiritual medicament that cleanses its leprosy. It is an alchemy that impoverishes by comparison all the mines and money-mints of the nations. It holds open the door of access into heaven. It nourishes the communion between all burdened and penitent spirits and the Father, through the Mediator. It lays the easy yoke and the light burden on the grateful disciple.

It brings down beams of forgiveness, to brighten the lot of suffering, to bow the pride of station, to soften stony avarice. It makes mankind one, in their Lord. And so the Church is the mightiest and the deepest of all foundations of the Christian city.

The continual sophistry of our metropolitan habits, my friends, is to arrest the gaze of self-examination, to stop all insight with the surface, to cheat us out of all profounder spiritual meditation, and to bend every fact to the standard of immediate and outward effects. There are things in the city, solemn verities and a spiritual Presence, that no census can reckon. So many objects arrest the eye close at hand, so many voices call, and bribes clink, and flatteries dazzle, so many prizes of fortune glitter on all the way-sides, that we cannot afford time to go up into the still watch-towers, and take the telescope of faith, and hold commerce with the everlasting lights and oceans! O how well for us, immortal spirits, if we would! How else shall we ever comprehend our heirship in the kingdom of Heaven? To adopt a paradox of the Apostle, we need to look more at what we cannot see. We want a stronger faith in things that lie out of the range of our touch, and deeper than the plane of our frivolity. We want an affection, — not merely a fanciful sentiment, but a hearty and constraining affection, for those lowly traits of humanity, and those invisible fellowships with the divinity, which are the under-currents of all our better lives, and are the arteries that join us to Christ, making us one in the body of his Church.

You have, traversing all the streets and squares of your metropolis, in dark passages under ground, the conduits that bring in country waters, to cool your thirst and purify your dwellings. These streams are silent and hidden; but they flow none the less constantly, in obedience to the skill of science, and the bubbling supply is a manifest, daily benediction upspringing in your houses. These hollow pipes beneath lie among the "foundations" of the city's welfare. So ought to run, in many secret channels, noiseless to the ear, but mighty in their final good, the benignant currents of love and faith. "There is a river, the streams whereof shall make glad the city of our God"; and *these* are its streams, — the love and faith of Christ; give them access from the fountain of his heart, as you do the lake's tribute, and they shall make this your city, every city, glad, — cities of our God, — make them whole. You know them by the glory of their result. Their testimony is in the excellent lives they nourish. Their fruit is in a polluted sensuality redeemed, and a barren worldliness refreshed.

So have you those winding conductors, also laid among the foundations, which spread the airy fuel that feeds so many thousand lamps. All their course is hid, and never so much forgotten as at noonday; but when night falls, the dull rods are tipped with innumerable tongues of flame, and the city blazes with a radiance that almost counterfeits the sun. The years will come, I think, when we shall lay as carefully, and at as cheerful a cost, those trains of beneficent design that shall illumine benighted minds, and cheer the whole air with hope.

I was shown, a few days since, that complicated contrivance of mechanism and genius, the municipal electric telegraph, applying the grand wonder-working agency of our time to the communication of alarms of fire. This wirework woven over our heads, like a dry organization of pure nerves, without body, blood, or bones, intercepting no light or rain, or splendor of the sky, the talking appa-

35*

ratus of a few distant watchmen for the safety of life and treasure to a careless or sleeping city, with the hammers of church-bells for its tongues, and a thousand men to start at its summons, and a common clock to tell, with its hourly stroke, the entire order of the circuit, — all seems to a half-initiated spectator as a sort of demiurgic miracle, or wizard's spell. But it all has its match — and more, has it not? — in that spiritual marvel, which we will not marvel at, — the fine sympathy that knits human classes into a brotherhood. Not less quick than the flash of the fluid is the thrill of pity, or trust, or gratitude, that vibrates from one end of the social scale to the other. Ignore it as we will, to our injury, — deny it if we will, in some selfish mood of treachery to the Messiah, — God has put the same blood into the veins of all his children. He has wrought our structures of one fibre, under all housings, clothings, and complexions. For a millennium, or else for a universal death-dance and reign of terrorism, as we choose, we are all, my brothers, each other's keepers. In this *our city*, whether one member suffer, all the members suffer with it; or one member rejoice, all the members rejoice with it. Dismiss from their posts the blessed guardians that keep the vigils of Christian charity, and the whole moral order would explode, like a city on fire, with no concert for alarm and action. We cannot be wholly segregated, or isolated, or self-containing, if we would. God has made us of another kind; and Christ has died for no such race. East end or west end, north or south, can no more rot in atheistic sloth, and the rest not sooner or later be convulsed and agonized, than one limb of the body can mortify, and the rest leap with healthy circulations. Let us respect this magnetic law of our life.

Tarsus, the Cilician city, standing by the banks of the

Cydnus, a river only two hundred feet broad, could hardly have looked to the eye of our admiration so impressive as it seemed to its patriotic son. For it is said of it that the luxurious monarch Sardanapalus built it, and another city besides, in a single day. Only its ghost remains. But even there, the superiority of ideas over materials was already illustrated. It was the learning of the inhabitants that made it the rival of Athens and Alexandria. It was the thoughts that had it for their birthplace, that shed their lustre across to Judæa, arrested the violence of the Hebrew persecutor, put a safeguard round Paul's threatened breast, and raised it to the honor of being "no mean city." Its "foundation" was its wisdom, and its glories were its schools.

Boston, subscribing fifty millions of dollars for its own investment, grasps the termini of three thousand miles of railway. Is it a question of no solemnity, whether the pupils it dismisses every evening from the great school of its calculations and competitions, to the number of not less than forty-two thousand souls, pouring them along these radiating avenues, and dropping them at the doors of all New England, are really better souls, or baser souls, for their learning? It exports, annually, ten millions of value. If true to the ideas that founded it, and faithful to the trusts of Providence, it ought to despatch from its bosom, under all those out-bound sails, an influence on the world's life not to be reckoned by mathematics, but by the moral measurements of eternity. It taxes property to the amount of one hundred and eighty-seven millions of dollars. Let that all be held by the New Testament estimate of stewardship; let it be used as the lending of Almighty love, to be reckoned for, every farthing, to Almighty justice; and would not some greater benefactions from its bounty bless heathendom and want, in its own borders, and to the utmost islands of the sea? It numbers a population of one hundred and thirty-eight thousand. What reason can you bring, other than the perversity of human passions, and our unbelief in Christ, why these should not be a hundred and thirty-eight thousand consistent witnesses to Christian righteousness? If a third of that number crawl yearly out of immigrant ships, with an imported superstition, and an indolence bred in their bones, ought not the chief city of the Puritans, with the vantage-ground of a clean continent and two centuries of providential history, to have created such an atmosphere of republican light and virtue, that the immersion of Old-World barbarism itself should be like a cleansing baptism into the renewing spirit of the Gospel?

The true foundations of the city — those that most resemble it to its pattern in the skies — are not its breadth of acres, or the costliness of its square feet; not the firm pavements of stone, worn smooth with the everlasting beat of travel; not the solid walls that bear up its ambitious roofs; not the lengthening wharves that welcome the merchandise of all coasts, and grasp the commerce of all waters; not the entries of its custom-house, nor the splendor of its mansions, nor the sum of its capital; not any nor all of these, though they all may be the tokens of a righteous prosperity.

Those foundations are rather in the mind and temper of the people. They are in the virtuous order, and the self-controlled moderation, and the refined dignity, of your families. They are in the patient thoroughness, the regular discipline, the wise forecast, and the religious reverence, of all your systems of education. They are in the zeal, the punctuality, the strict devotion, and the generous toleration, of your worship. They are in the abundance of your charities, the cordiality of your courtesies, the sobriety of your hospitalities, the modesty of your manners, the steady march of your industry, the integrity of your traffic, the nobleness of your policy, the liberality of your government, — the graces that adorn your manhood. Plant such foundations as these; lay them deeper and surer every day; and you shall be "citizens of no mean city."

And though the humiliating conclusion of all our proudest and most loyal meditations must be, to confess that we are pilgrims and strangers, and have here no continuing city, not even the venerated tabernacles of the fathers, our Isaac and Jacob; yet, lifting our eyes heavenward, we confidently seek one to come, — a city that hath eternal foundations, — the type of these our fairest cities on earth, — the Jerusalem that is above and free, — the city of the living God.

SERMON XXV.

NATIONAL RETRIBUTION, AND THE NATIONAL SIN.*

BECAUSE SENTENCE AGAINST AN EVIL WORK IS NOT EXECUTED SPEEDILY, THEREFORE THE HEART OF THE SONS OF MEN IS FULLY SET IN THEM TO DO EVIL. — Eccl. viii. 11.

THIS annual Fast is rather a relic of a past age, than a natural and vital expression of the present one. For better or for worse, — some among us say for the better, but I am disposed to think rather for the worse, — the ideas and associations, the forms of thought and life, which gave such an anniversary its birth, have either drifted away, or been essentially changed. It is evident that the stated proclamation from the Executive for "a day of public fasting, humiliation, and prayer," is a document extorted by a decent respect for ancient usage, or by a deference to official routine easier to follow than to break through, rather than a cordial utterance, or even echo, of a strong and spontaneous impulse from the heart of the whole people. And, on the other hand, as we might expect, that degree of reluctant, languid, and interrupted observance which the occasion gets, is more like a hesitating acquiescence on the part of a few in a

* Preached on Fast Day, 1851, soon after the passage, in Congress, of the bill known as the "Fugitive Slave Law."

custom to which the consent of good men has lent first a religious and then a prescriptive sanction, than it is like the eager and general homage of a lively conviction, or a constraining emotion. Our Fast serves as a sort of spiritual high-water mark, to show how far the stanch, self-denying sincerity of our Puritan ancestors once rose, and how far the same tide, from one cause or another, has ebbed out in the children. It stands as a monument, graphic but awkward and funereal, of a state of things and a set of feelings gone by, looking very much as some surviving memorial of the monastic or ascetic period of the Church would look in the midst of the easy manners and luxurious indulgences of times that came after, — a hair shirt, or hermit's girdle, or spiked shoe, re-appearing in the wardrobe of a modern bishop's palace, or an anchorite's skull for a *memento mori* in the voluptuous oratory of a fashionable devotee.

But the observance, heartless or hearty, common or exceptional, does call to mind the honest, sterling virtues of a race of men that really believed in God. There is something refreshing in the remembrance that such men have lived, — men that planted themselves on the everlasting foundations, and stood there cheerfully, come blandishments or come tortures, harvest or famine, peace or a sword; men that, being surrounded by hollow artifices and hypocritical shams, could yet be simple and pure; men that saw down through sophistry to the lie at the bottom which the sophistry was put over, to hide and recommend; men who, in every kind of perplexity, threw themselves back on the oracles of Scripture as if they were walls of rock; men that dared to take all manner of sin that came in their path by the throat without fear of being thrown, and could march up to look at death face to face, without so much as a thought of running, if conscience only went with them; men that, so far from doubting that God's original law is more perfect and binding than any legislation of his fallible creature, man, saw plainly — what men of deep moral discernment have, in fact, never failed to see — that this very allegiance to a superior law is the only bond and safeguard of governments or constitutions which are human; men that held no parley with corruption, made no compromise with wrong, took no price for right; men that had reasons to give for serving the Almighty, but would take none for serving the Devil; that might be killed, but never could be seduced; and for every threatening question, from throne or judge's bench, in the teeth of raging prelate or mighty monarch, inquisition or scaffold, answered with a valiant "Thus saith the Lord." If it is refreshing to remember that such men *were*, what a joyful inspiration to know that they were our fathers! What a motive, tightening every sinew in our frame, to prove ourselves not utterly unworthy, by cowardice, corruptibility, and practical atheism, to be called their children!

These invigorating recollections, still clustering about the faded and decaying observance which they ordained in earnest, fitly lay open my subject, the doctrine of which is this: that the slowness of God's public retributions never embarrasses their certainty; that while, "because sentence against an evil work is not executed speedily, the heart of the sons of men is fully set in them to do evil," that sentence is only gathering force, to strike down with more unerring aim and heavier penalties, at last. Let us endeavor, my friends, like fearless and candid inquirers, discharging ourselves of the transient passions which only becloud the moral vision, and rising above the narrow issues which agitate, but do not strengthen, the judgment, to lay calm hold of a principle which reaches beyond passing interests, embraces many special examples, comprehends the whole history of human society.

For, in fact, the simple conviction that men need now most of all, condensing as it does all the lessons of instructive experience, is this: that God governs the world. Plans are ours, but their prospering or overthrow is with God. Beginnings are ours; but not the end. Courses of life and systems of policy that run on, under human guidance, many years, are brought up at last by a Providential catastrophe. Just as they get strong, and begin to feel domesticated, a subtile element, interfused, — no diplomatist could tell how or when, — works up and down to vitiate their organization, rots their fibre, and disorders them to death. Governments, founded by the fresh energies of a colony, or the solemn earnestness of revolution, grow prosperous only to grow weak, take up the seeds of decline along with the juices of health, and, finding their destiny means their doom, die the death of suicides. So that at last we are driven to doubt whether even plans, beginnings, and undertakings are ours, except by permission. The little that mortals can do, in building or governing, is hedged about by the checks and limitations of Omnipotence; and, if not otherwise, at least by sheer inability to account for history by what we know, we are driven to believe that the nations are judged by God, and the earth dependent on Heaven.

The grand perversity of society and politics, from the first, has been in their ingenious devices for obscuring this fundamental religious law; a law which in itself, by its infallible accuracy and its inevitable execution, sufficiently proves the superiority of a Divine over every human law. From Assyria to Spain, from Babylon to Mexico, from Hebrew sedition to British bankruptcy, this has been the inevitable, mathematical demonstration, which national ambition has set itself to deny. Sometimes by commerce and sometimes by war; now by a better disciplined defence, or a more savage military drill, and then by a faculty of financial accumulation, more peaceful perhaps, but equally crafty, selfish, and unscrupulous; now by comforts singing of security like Sirens, and then by aggressions formidable for prowess, — the nations have each promised themselves insurance against judgment, and played their several games of self-perpetuation, — relied on an immunity from evil, because sentence against evil was not executed speedily. Find one amongst them all, — one tribe, or country, or dynasty, or empire, — that has not travelled to ruin as men travel to their graves, or else allow that the rule is beyond dispute.

It is in the nature of every public or political sin, that it must have a double retribution; first, that which falls on the individual who commits it, or is a party to it; and second, that which undermines and destroys the commonwealth itself. There is a private judgment, and a public judgment. The soul of ruler or citizen, lawmaker and law-keeper or law-breaker, must render up the account of its personal stewardship; and likewise, the collective body called the nation, whose great organized sin is made up of these personal contributions, has to be reckoned with, according to the laws of the Eternal Providence, by its loss or its progress, its ruin or its glory. And how fearfully does it augment the responsibility of public conduct, that the downfall of a nation drags with it into the common wreck such hosts of sufferers, the guiltless with the guilty!

The law of the Divine economy seeks out the personal offender and hauls him to the tribunal, in whatever alliances, social combinations, and political fashions he may screen himself, — showing that accountability is not to be put on and taken off as we go in and out of legislative halls, primary meetings, corporations, or parties of pleasure; that though the sinner may say WE, God's law says THOU; that, "though hand join in hand, the wicked shall not be unpunished." Now, just as certain as this is, so certain is the slow preparation of righteous chastisement for nations. If the fraudulent dealer must answer for his deceptions; if he who kindles in himself the foul fires of lust must afterwards be steeped in the fetid fumes of sensuality; if the unprincipled worldling must come abashed before the blaze of Christ's spiritual glory; so must every country and government that persists in oppression, in cruelty, in injustice, in venality, in refusing to hear the cry of them that have no helper, and in clutching at extorted riches, stand at last before the judgment-seat, and be weighed in those bright balances that never rust, nor swerve, nor break. "The hire of the laborers that have reaped down its fields crieth, and its cry enters into the ears of the God of Sabaoth."

What an eminent patriot of the Old World, himself almost a martyr to liberty, has said, deserves to be considered, that "religious principle has presided over two thirds of the revolutions of single nations, and over all the great revolutions of humanity." What higher proof than this fact need we, that nations always stand before the bar of Christian rectitude, and that, though the sentence be not executed speedily, yet equity, mercy, and freedom shall finally press down their immutable measure on every government under the sun?

The mistake is, that they who exercise the trusts and enjoy the emoluments of government are too ready to forget the primal law in the vast mechanism and complicated distribution of power. In something of the impious spirit, though without the frank presumption, of that arch-prince of godless rulers, Frederick the Great of Prussia, they are ready to say, politically, "Religion of some kind is necessary to the well-being of a state, and he is not a wise king who allows his subjects to abuse it"; but they also add, with him, "Nevertheless, he is not a wise king who allows himself to have any religion at all." Now, in a republic, those persons who exercise the trusts of government, and share the temptations of rulers, are the citizens. It is they, therefore, who are here tempted to great peril if they forget the law of natural retribution,—they that need to be girded up, as Christian men, with the faith that the delay of that retribution is never, and cannot be, because God's justice sleeps.

We commit a radical error, if we imagine that national retributions are always attested by outward calamity. They are often most actively at work where no visible disasters darken the sky. Many a nation has gone to destruction with a sound exchequer and regiments full; because the surest perdition that can overtake a people is the deadening of its spiritual sensibility, the blinding of its sight for discerning between the true and the false, the darkening of its inward light; and "if the light that is in thee be darkness, how great is that darkness."

This fearful process may be going on, at the core, while all externally is fair and flourishing. Conquest may be stretching out its arms to grasp unrighteous gains; enterprise may be heaping up its treasures and strengthening its stakes at home; fortune may be filling its coffers and multiplying its bank-vaults; traffic may be sliding its merchantmen from every port into all navigable waters; the eyes of voluptuous complacency may stand out with fatness; and yet, beneath all this prosperous show of life, there shall be the daily inroads of death. The land may be full of the finest of the wheat; and yet consumption is on those faculties which are the vitals of the soul. Herein is another working of the everlasting law. With every wanton denial of our purer aspirations, those aspirations themselves grow faint. Resistance to our better angels drives those angels away. If we cast insults on our power of moral discrimination, the power itself will perish. No nation can smother, whether in the legislative council, the fashions of society, the iniquities of trade, or the oppressive enactments of the statute-book, those eternal sentiments which rise up to bear their melancholy witness, even in debauched and degraded souls, without realizing in the very act a punishment infinitely more dismal than any defeat of its armies or any damage to the credit of its treasury.

This, I suppose, is the real significance of those many passages in Scripture where a disobedient people, rejecting the guidance of the Almighty and quenching the lamps he has lighted in the soul, is said to have its heart hardened, — to have grievous delusions sent upon it that it should believe a lie, — to be "let alone," like Ephraim, because it is joined to idols, — to be forsaken of the heavenly compassion. Just in proportion to the intensity of that accumulated light on which we obstinately shut our eyes for the wages of injustice, is the depth of the damnation already preparing for us. The cup is at our lips; and though we do not taste its bitterness, it is none the less poison in our blood. If we cover up some avaricious appetite under a plausible pretence of seeking the public good; if we plead for private profit under the sacred name of general concord; if we apply handsome names to unseemly plots, and baptize a bargain with oppression as a reconciliation with alienated friends; if we make ourselves parties to a systematic policy which is the essence of all vices and the sum of all crimes, because we love an unobstructed market better than the rights of humanity or the favor of God; or if we plead an unrighteous promise given once as a justification for perpetual fraud, then are we ourselves sold and bound slaves under sin, and though the wheels of retribution seem to tarry, and sentence against the evil work is not executed speedily, we might as well doubt our Maker's eternity as the prophecy of our own perdition.

Why will not men see this intelligible law, blazoned forth as it is in characters of light in every chapter of all the chronicles of our race? Why will not citizens and rulers alike understand, that force is not persuasion, coercion is not conviction, conscience is not teachable by chains and bayonets, nor amenable to the prudential maxims of political economy? The ever-accumulating burden of experimental wisdom is against us. The irresistible flight of time, the very revolution of the earth, and the hastening of the hours, are against us. The voice of rebuke from the ages, the deep thunder that has been drawing its awful *crescendo* from the first human tradition, gathers volume and intensity against us every instant. We may build barricades for our prison-houses, and plant guns and staves and chains about our victims; we may stigmatize or crucify the prophets that tell us the truth; we may rejoice in every fresh success of cruel usurpations over human freedom; but we cannot thereby stay the advancing steps of retribution. We cannot, by police or militia, by conventions or statute-books, by certificates of bondage or judicial forms, press down behind the eastern horizon that ascending sun which shall bring in the day of our judgment.

God forbid that I should say these things, or utter these warnings, save with a sorrowful mind and reluctant lips. The times are not bright enough, the prospects around us not cheerful enough, to suffer conscious levity of thought or inconsiderate speech. Questions too perplexing and too intricate disturb and divide the best intelligence amongst us, to be passed upon with hasty or over-confident opinions. One of the very transgressions we have to deplore, as well as to reckon for, is that very violence of language which irritates and provokes passion, instead of convincing the understanding, and that bitterness of partisan feeling which first robs itself of the faculty of seizing any other than a one-sided and prejudiced view of the great question at issue, and then goes on to create discord between brethren, to open and widen breaches in social intercourse, to spoil the amenities of hospitality, and to insult the sacred charities of religion.

This, among others, seems to me one of the gravest errors into which the present posture of the public mind in reference to the recent legislation on slavery has conducted us, — that so many who speak and write on the subject, both in public journals and in private conversation, refuse to recognize the existence of any other than two broadly distinguished classes; namely, unqualified advocates of the law as it stands, and traitors to the government. I cannot think that the self-possession of this community has been so completely unsettled, nor its intellect so stultified, that it is necessary to resort to this sweeping classification in order to guard against an alleged incipient rebellion. It not only exasperates well-disposed persons by its presumption, but it inflicts a positive wound on the truth. *There is a third class* of men in the country, — how numerous cannot be told till they are counted, but not very inconsiderable in numbers nor contemptible in character. It is composed of those who are, always have been, and resolutely propose to be, loyal subjects to the general government under which they live, unwavering friends of the union of these States, and obedient observers of the laws. They do not assort with disorganizers, nor take counsel of fanaticism. Their daily associations are with such as rely most securely on the settled order of society, and their liveliest sympathies lie on the side of submission, good faith, and good feeling throughout all sections and classes of the country. But they have been led, by processes within their own minds as uncontrollable as the winds of heaven, and which they honestly trace to the workings of that spirit which Christ compared to the wind that bloweth where it listeth, to contemplate every possible enslavement, or re-enslavement, of any human being, under any supposable array of circumstances, in this age of the world and within the great American republic, as a terrible offence against the plain will and word of God, and against that humanity which he has made and called his child. They believe the system of negro slavery as it exists in the United States to be explicitly at variance with the Almighty's will and law, and with all the duty, integrity, purity, and innocent happiness of man. They regard it as the special and overshadowing affront of this nation against the Father of eternal justice, truth, liberty, love. They know that it is an anomaly in our national institutions, an abnegation of our history, a plague in our politics, a gigantic curse upon industry, a foul insult to morality, a blight upon learning, science, and the arts, the annihilation of God's ordinance in the family, the prostitution of woman, the scourge of innocence, the violation, direct or indirect, of each of the commandments, and the denial of the Gospel, the intensest meanness and the foulest filthiness and the most profane impiety, the consummation of crimes, the comprehensive antagonist of the kingdom of Heaven, constituting, in the whole and in each of its parts, "the abomination of desolation," "standing where it ought not." They deliberately and assuredly believe, that every man so convinced and so seeing ought in every place, by every means, in street and house and shop and office and caucus and legislature and pulpit, to bear his most earnest, express, unmistakable, consistent witness against it, — against all its spirit, rules, methods, actings, devices, excuses, — but most of all, against its aggressions and extensions. They believe that such aggressions are forbidden by the civil constitution, while the very continuance of the wrong, in any shape, is rebuked by the entire spirit of that venerated instrument, and by the designs and convictions of the men that formed it. I ask you if it is more than just, that these men should stand exempt from being ranked with rebels and revolutionists, — if it is more than reasonable, that enlightened legislation should show some respect for such citizens, — if it is more than right, that *they* should dispassionately labor and pray for some relief from a requirement which would render their active obedience to the magistrate, by the re-enslavement of a fugitive, in their eyes as direct and impious an affront towards Almighty God, as falsehood, blasphemy, or robbery ? Let us consider these things in the temper of brethren, learning thereby forbearance, moderation, and charity,—excellent graces of the Christian life always, and never more needed to save us from disgraceful inconsistencies than now.

It was well said by a wise old writer, that " to trouble and unsettle many things is not to do much ; but, being unsettled, to compose them, more ; to keep them from being unsettled, most of all." Respecting this maxim, it is the duty of high-principled statesmen and legislators to heed, not only the loftiest and single suggestions of their own nature, but the consciences of the people whose will they profess to administer. There is no measure, especially in a republic, so radical, as that which arrays what is most Christian in a nation against the magisterial authority; no publication so inflammatory, as a law that commands a moral people to do that which a large majority of them believe to be unjust ; no document so incendiary, as one that sets on fire the quenchless instinct that abhors oppression, or wakes from sleep that unmanageable instinct which has shaken so many thrones, — that " resistance to tyrants is obedience to God." And if, on the other hand, the conscientious opponents of this law will apply to their determined and unflinching efforts for its repeal the same purity of principle that makes its provisions offensive, and calmly rely on that serene Providence which is sure to work out a final success to them if they do not forsake its guidance, then who knows but we may avert, by action and by prayer, the impending judgment?

This faith let us all hold fast, parting with it no sooner than we will part with life,—that there is no true patriotism without faith in God,—no artifice of selfishness, or partisanship, or ambition, which can hide us from those retributions that search out all the secrets of the universe; that though sentence against an evil work be not executed speedily, it will descend at last.

Could some penetrating apprehension of this unbending law seize on the mind of the people, then, dropping all our childish exultations in American progress, restraining our idle boasts of growing territory, prosperity, and wealth, we should turn to some manly regulation of the advantages we enjoy. Instead of avariciously clutching at the promise of larger gains, we should soberly bethink ourselves how we may most honorably *devote* the advantage already committed to our hands. What we are to do, will rise into a question of far more imposing magnitude, than what we have done. How to be true to the lofty and stern demands of Justice, of Freedom, of Truth, of God, as these are so clearly and emphatically proclaimed through the facts of our history, the intimations of Providence, and the wondrous exigencies of the times,—will be a problem taxing the intelligence and the energy of the people far more urgently than any schemes of political ambition. The formation of a true national character, broad in its moral foundations, firm in its supports, and symmetrical in its proportions,—combining together the religious faith of the old Puritans and the enterprise of the young West, the warmth of Southern impulse balanced and directed by Northern steadfastness, — beating with the blood of Raleigh and of Penn, of Carver and Eliot, of Roger Williams and Henry Vane, — blending Norman chivalry with Saxon industry, and the reverence of the Elder World with the hope of the New, — this should become a nobler stimulus to our hopes than any accumulations of perishable glory. All extension of empire would look poor, beside the fulfilment of the aspirations of Christianity in our life, — all the splendors of outward fortune turn dim, before the upright doing of God's Eternal Will.

SERMON XXVI.

THE WORD OF LIFE: A LIVING MINISTRY AND A LIVING CHURCH.*

HOLDING FORTH THE WORD OF LIFE; TO WIT, THAT GOD WAS IN CHRIST, RECONCILING THE WORLD UNTO HIMSELF. — Phil. ii. 16, and 2 Cor. v. 19.

It will not be travelling out of the path of thought naturally set open by the introduction of ministers to their office, if I seek to represent the preaching of Christ as a means of communicating life.

Vitality is a test of any system of doctrine, as it is of any teacher's qualification. If you would find the value of any message, ask of it, Does it live? Do vital pulses leap through it? Does it reproduce its life? Does it help men to live? Does it leave them more alive or more dead than they were without it? Get an answer to these questions, and you will find whether the given ministry is of heaven, or of a private self-interest, — whether it comes out of the all-quickening and all-comprehending God, or out of some dreamer's brain.

Nothing goes with much momentum, in the long trial, that does not carry life with it. Accumulate the learning

* Preached July 30, 1853, before the Graduating Class of the Meadville Theological School.

of a thousand Melancthons; pile together the erudition of ancient schools and modern universities; what does it contribute to the real treasure of men, if it does not create life in them? The alcoves of libraries may be but the chambers of a mausoleum, — sepulchres of thought, instead of its nurseries, — and meeting-houses, spiritual dormitories. Eloquence, burning as Peter the Hermit's, is wasted breath, unless the succeeding life of men shows that it reached the springs from which that life was fed. So in all communication of man with man. Nothing *tells*, nothing does execution, nothing survives very long, but what makes men feel and will and act, — nothing but the "word of life." Find me a book, a speech, a preacher, a gospel, that is not life-giving, and I know there is no *true message*, no inspiration, no revelation from God, there.

We meet, gentlemen, for your anniversary, at the season when the forces of creation are most exuberant and exultant; when the early summer is sending its swift pulses into every shrub, its moist breath across the clover, and affluent Nature encompasses us everywhere with her wealth of beauty.

We are thus reminded, that every manifestation of God in the body of his works is a new beat of his heart. His successive creations are the puttings forth, in forms of matter, of an unchangeable life behind and within, — a life never exhausted by expressing itself. The worlds, thrown out into their chiming revolutions; solar systems, set playing in the shining cycles of a universe; races of animals, whose skeletons, bedded in rocks, become the illustrations on those leaves of God's great history, the strata of the globe; the spring sunshine that unveils the fragile beauty of the wind-flower; the autumnal chemistry that paints the woods; the majestic elm that stands a graceful goblet brimmed with streaming life from root to leaf, and the frail weed that springs under its shade, and the moss that clings to its bark,— these are only so many orderly utterances of God's vital being, so many words of his life.

But we must add, instantly, that for the spiritual being, man, the only real life is in goodness. Can it not be proved so? If the fountain of all the life that flows through the fields of the universe is God, God is but another name for goodness. All the life that proceeds from him, therefore, must be according to goodness, or love; whether it beats in the bosom of a sinless child, or nerves the arm of a hero-saint; whether he rounds a planet, or tints a rose-leaf; whether he balances the Pleiades in their spheres, or adjusts the microscopic machinery of an insect's wing; whether the afflatus of his Spirit bears up the "seraph that adores and burns" before the throne, or lights the lamp of a feebler reason in these vessels of clay. Only so far as we share in the Father's goodness, then, are we partakers in *his* life. The measure of our being, as living souls, is precisely the measure of our excellence. In proportion as our actions are in harmony with divine laws, and our familiar frame of feeling with God's will, we live. Herein is the Apostolic saying true, "To be spiritually-minded is life." Every rising up of pure aspiration; every clinging to principle when you are tempted; every choice of abstract right above politic selfishness; every putting down of sensual passion by prayer; every preference of a truth which inherits a cross, over the lie that flatters you with a promise of prosperity,— is a palpable motion of God's life within you. Indeed, this is the most intimate subjective knowledge you have of God. God, out of his express revelation, never speaks to us so audibly as when his spirit prompts us to struggle, or braces us for a sacrifice. A generous impulse is the plainest pledge of his presence; a devout trust in him, the mightiest demonstration of his Fatherhood. Superseding all our painstaking, traditionary beliefs in a God that was alive once, this makes us believe in a God that kept his vigils over our last night's slumbers, tinged the east with purple at this morning's dawn, and opened a new apocalypse of his glory in its sunrise; — a God who is as busy in the drops of this season's early rain as when he gathered the waters out of chaos; whose voice comes as clear from the rustling of every way-side shrub, as when the first man heard it among the cedars in Eden; who revives the glorious pageant of his ancient wonders and splendors in every year's seed-time and fruitage; who is as close to the sorrowing heart that bends over the new-made grave to-day, as to Hagar in the wilderness; and who is as faithful to the good man's prayer now, as to David's harp, or the songs of Paul and Silas at midnight in the prison.

Let these general thoughts serve at once to introduce, and to project into its widest relations, the particular theme of my discourse.

The order in which the subject will most naturally exhibit itself requires me first to state, as briefly as I can, the essential doctrine of that "word of life" which Christian preaching is to hold forth; not the gospel of to-day, but of all days, — the same yesterday, to-day, and for ever. It is of vastly more moment to any preacher that he should have definite and realizing notions of *what he is to preach*, than any set of rules or formal furnishings for the manner of preaching it. After considering, in this way, what the "word of life" itself is, that is, the living and life-giving doctrine, we shall proceed to the characteristics of the living ministry of that Word; and then of the living Church, embodying and obeying it.

I. First, in order to apprehend what the life of the Christian Church, or of the Christian soul, is, we must apprehend the life of its Head. He is "that word" made flesh.

Now, inasmuch as the true vitality of the Church consists in the fact that its chief functions are reconciling functions, and as the Church's complete consummation will be the complete reconciliation of human society, — so it finds its supreme sanction in the reconciling, or literally the *atoning*, character of its Head. "God is in Christ, reconciling the world unto himself." Those words are the key to all the Gospel, to all Christian history, to all Christian experience. They hold in them the power of that life which has so far energized Christendom, and is to redeem and sanctify the world.

Stated in its theological relations, I hold this truth to stand thus. For reconciliation between finite and infinite, there must be a reconciler combining both in his own person. Here, precisely, is the grand, redemptive synthesis, effected in Christ. Bridging over, by the mystery of his nature, — a mystery whose very claim on our faith consists in its transcending the definitions of science, since faith, of course, never properly begins till we have got to the limit of science, — bridging over the gulf that yawned between the perpetual frailty of man and the perfection of God, — he is the *vinculum* that binds up the spiritual organism of the world, dislocated and bruised by sin. If Christ were only man, he could not mediate between man and God. If he were only God, he could not mediate between God and man. Here is the eternal, inherent necessity of the mystery of the Incarnation, reaching back before Abraham was, into the bosom of the Everlasting Father; and there deriving the purchase-power to lift humanity to heaven. The vital point of the whole Christian system is the inspiring contact it establishes between the life of God and the life of man, by a mediating Christ; a Christ qualified to mediate, by bringing over the forces of the Almighty Spirit to reinvigorate the wasted spirituality of the race, to restore and comfort the individual soul that will receive him. Here is the only corner-stone for a Church, — a personal, divine Christ. Any plan of theology that misses this is defective at the core. Pride of speculation, ambitious will-worships, theories of self-culture, philosophies of intuitions, moral respectabilities, never reach the disordered spot, nor meet the practical want of souls in earnest. Under the real stress and strain of life, what the penitent soul cries out for is that heavenly mediation that unites and reconciles the two opposing elements of utter imperfection in the performances of human nature, and the immaculate holiness of the Judge of all.

If you ask whence comes the need of this reconciliation, I answer, it comes from the need every man is under of passing over from the mere natural life, which is the life he is born with, into the spiritual life, which is simply the inward reception of Christ by faith, and which saves him, that is, makes a Christian of him. Of that new birth, Jesus himself explicitly asserts the universal necessity. The natural life has for its ruling principle selfishness; and, however decent or even lovely to the eye, it is never holy. Being mixed as to its good and evil elements, it has no security against perdition. The regenerate or holy life may begin so early as to open along with the powers of consciousness, and grow up with the growing faculties, thus blending with and sanctifying the natural; but it is a distinct process. It cannot begin too early nor too suddenly: to create its beginning, in accordance with the laws and promised help of the Holy Spirit, is the office of preaching. But it is a new life when it comes; it is the reception, into a sinning and enfeebled humanity, of the quickening and supernatural life of Christ the Reconciler, who comes into the world quite as much to impart to us of God, as to be the perfect pattern of a man. In accordance with this view, sin being a universal taint, error, guilt, of the race, the renewed life must begin with a Prodigal's confession, and be baptized with a Magdalen's tears. Saintship always rears its most beautiful proportions on the lowly ground of that humility. The full burst of rapture from the lips of the redeemed is an august *crescendo* from the sobs of the penitent; and every *Gloria in Excelsis*, from the Church Triumphant, swells up from a heart-broken *Miserere*.

There are two theories of salvation; or rather, one is a theory of self-propelling; the other is God's plan of salvation. I mean, human development, and divine deliverance or redemption. One says: "Save yourselves; nature gave you noble capacities; put them forth. Apply your mind to self-culture. Unfold your own faculties. Inspect your own attainments. Instinct and intuition are your only Messiah. Study the Constitution of Man. Read Combe and the 'Vestiges.' Respect the natural laws: they are your only religion. Genesis is a myth. Man is no such creature as the Bible says. The first animated being was an animated atom, and then slowly expanded into a mollusk, which afterwards grew into a fish; and this, after many attempts, struggled on to dry land, and converted its fins into legs (the only kind of conversion, by the way, that this philosophy recognizes), and so became a reptile; and then the reptile shot out wings and became a bird; and the bird dropped its wings downward one day, and so, by reconversion, got two more legs, and became a beast; and the beast, after a while, rose erect, and became a man"! You are aware that this, called by courtesy a philosophy, is no caricature of a theory put against the Bible by some of the thinkers of the nineteenth century, like Lamarck and Demaillet, who have remained outside of insane asylums. The theological notion which makes the chief end of man to be self-culture—if that can be called a *theo*logy which leaves the Θεός quite out of the account—is only a legitimate induction from these postulates in science.

I think you will not suspect me of standing up in the middle of the nineteenth century, in the face of a theological school, to discredit human culture; but I say, that, under the *logical* action of a theology of self-development, worship would ultimately be exploded. It may survive awhile by virtue of old associations, but it survives illogically. Self-culture is limited solely to the human consciousness, and there it must spend its energies, groping in its own twilight, pulling at its own feet, supplicating its own will,—an endless series of moral contradictions. It is godless, for the simple reason that it has no God. It makes of Messiah nothing more than a Hebrew youth, who managed his propensities more skilfully than other men. Faith is dwarfed down to confidence in our own power to accomplish what we undertake. Remorse is only the natural regret for an Epicurean, or at best a Stoic, miscalculation. Not satisfied with the fine reaction of Channing's thesis, that human nature is a glorious product of God, — against the ultra-Genevan hyperbole, frozen into a dogma, that human nature is utterly devilish, — it goes on to boast the individual self to be a glorious creature. Man is much hampered for the present, it says, by his circumstances, but only needing fair play to outdo the archangels; and his only responsibility is to his own organization. As to sin, it is only the bugbear of Calvinistic nurseries and Scriptural legends. There is no such thing. Imperfect culture, crude impulses, half-way development, — these are what old wives call sin. One of the latest foreign bulletins of this mad materialism proclaims, with a *frankness* which some of our domestic deniers, who have really reached the same pitch of irreverent negation, might well emulate, — "The true road to liberty, equality, and happiness is atheism. Let us teach man that there is no God but himself." And another ridicules "poor, timid Voltaire and Diderot," as not half-infidel enough in their infidelity. Why? Because "they were never quite ready to look on man as the culminating point of existence."

Of course, then, prayer can be nothing else but a poor mock-device, whose real function is self-excitation. Asking and receiving, prayer and answer to prayer, are out of the question. If we pretend to pray at all, like politic bargainers we bring our modicum of homage, not as the spontaneous tribute of a glad soul, that cannot keep its praise and glory back, but to say, "Lord," or rather, "Great Impersonal Inane, O All, Pan! here is my petition; give me the value for which it pays the price." Even Schiller candidly declares, that with him piety is not the *end* of life, but only a *means* of attaining to the highest culture through the calmest repose, or balance, of the mind,—the frigid ultimatum of Pantheism! Paul declares, peremptorily, "Ye are not your own: glorify God in your body and your spirit, which are God's."

Turn, then, to the other system, — Deliverance, or supernatural Redemption. That says, God in Christ reaches down to help, save us; only asking that we, by love and faith to the Saviour, and corresponding or outflowing faithful moral effort, will let ourselves be saved. The Gospel is an offer from above us. It is a divine interposition of deliverance, embodied in a Divine Redeemer. Christ comes forth to men from above, according to the whole plain doctrine of John's Proem to his Gospel, and the New Testament everywhere. And why? Because man is in a dilemma. He is tainted. Disobedience has forfeited his safety, under a perfect and inviolable law. He knows he is beset with proclivities to sin. Mortal infirmities encompass him on every side. The integrity of his moral power is broken. His part now is, like that of a traveller fallen into a pit, to lay hold, and keep hold. Do you say that is *doing* nothing, and gives no room for work or the muscles? Try it, and see if it is not work. Believing gives up the heart. Do you fear this heart of love and faith will not produce righteousness of life? But did you ever know a person to refuse or grudge service to the being he supremely loved? To keep it back is harder work than to give it, then. The heart's affections originate and *compel* work. The heart wrought upon, and then given, an inexhaustible fountain is opened, out of which all spiritual action must proceed. In that thought lies my whole philosophy of salvation ; and it is far enough from being mine in any sense of property. If I understand him, it is precisely Paul's doctrine of justification by faith. It is the inspired and inspiring doctrine. It is the doctrine of "God in Christ, reconciling the world unto himself."

We are able, now, to contrast the two, as to their results or fruits. The habit of the one is introversion; that of the other is aspiration. The emotion of success in the one is self-complacency ; in the other, devout gratitude. One yields a virtue that is steadfast, a character permanent, because its roots clasp the Rock of ages; the other, a virtue fitful and uncertain, snapped like tow in the fire of temptation, — a zone of moral restraint more dissolute than the Corinthian, and principles looser than the Spartan's ; and in society, by this time, through the accumulating pressure of an unchristianized barbarism, we should have worse than Punic honesty, and the veracity of Arabs, — a civil anarchy like what might convulse a world full of Cuban buccaneers, and a commerce that would disgrace the market-place of Circassians. The one would show us, at fairest, a few instances of moral beauty, finite, artistic, and mortal. The other would pour its gushing devotions out in some musical aspiration of the closet or the conventicle, surpassing, in its heartiness, all the cool deductions of the brain. Its chosen lessons are lyrics, not demonstrations. It feeds on the rhythmic contemplations of a John. It kindles at the songs from David's harp. It weeps over Thomas à Kempis's prose. It soars to heaven on the contagious ecstasies of a Moravian hymn.

Christ, then, is more than the Founder of the Church, as he is so often called. He pours his own life into it.

It is his body. He did not stand apart, and, by a mere manual exercise, lay its corner-stone, and rear its structure outside of himself. He rather threw it forth from himself; and, informing it with his Spirit, the Comforter, took up a constant abode on earth, in the life of his followers. Laying down his Hebrew body, his soul emancipated itself from all national restrictions, and went forth to make its dwelling in every believing heart.

His advent was the inauguration of the Divine Life on the earth. Hence the saying, half mystical but all true, reported by the Evangelist, " The bread of God is he who cometh down from heaven, and giveth life unto the world." So intimate is the union between the disciple and Jesus. " I am the vine, ye are the branches"; " *I in you*, and you in me."

According to this doctrine, it begins to be plain enough where, and where only, you may expect to find a Church that is alive. It is only where the reconciling office of Christ is felt as a reality, and where the immediate gifts of his divine Spirit, in the communion of love, are a part of the soul's experience. Without this, you have very interesting associations, no doubt, and social combinations, — civil, political, scientific, philanthropic, ethical, and even religious; but unless they are religious according to the way of Jesus of Nazareth, you have not got a Church. The only idea that will organize that, is the idea of the Cross, and Reconciliation by it. Morality, or the virtues, — Philanthropy, or the humanities, — Naturalism, or self-culture, — they are all taken up, embraced, guaranteed, in the Christ and him crucified; for then they rest on an authority that at once transcends and supports them. Without him they have lost their root; and, though originally started from the living vine, if they persist in their ungrateful will not to abide in him, nothing can prevent that they be cast forth as withered branches.

Precisely here, my friends, may be found a deep defect in much of the current theology. Christ is too much regarded as having *introduced* Christianity, and then retiring to let it work its way. It has been a mistake to dwell exclusively on the benefits wrought by Jesus Christ's coming on past conditions of society. The infusion of that fresh and living stream into the stagnating current of human history, when the world by its own wisdom knew not God, or had forgotten him, and the garden he had made beautiful by his own planting, and radiant with his miracles, was turning into a dry desert of heathenism, did not end with the ascension, nor with the apostolic age. The life that was then poured into the world's empty channels, through the quickening words and the yet more inspiring works of the Redeemer, has a faint and feeble symbol only in the reviving of a thirsty and dusty city, when the cup of a country lake's cool waters is made by the careful hand of science to run over, and their gracious wave sets in, a regulated blessing through its streets; — a faint and feeble symbol, I say; for Jesus said, " Whosoever drinketh of this water " — deep as the well is, cold as the spring may be — " shall thirst again," — thirst in fever and in toil, and in the burning sorrows of mortality; " but whosoever shall drink of the water that I shall give him, it shall be in him a well of water, springing up into everlasting life."

What we need to comprehend, then, is that Christ, in all the power of his Spirit, and all the sanction of his promises, and all the searching application of his precepts, is introduced a spring of reconciling life into the affairs and the heart of the present world; life into the very organic structure of human society; life into the operations of commerce; life into the legislation of governments; life into the order and training of families; life into the responsibility of individuals; and consequently, that he is as much a gift of life to this generation and to this community as to the primitive brotherhood, or to the cottage at Bethany. If Christianity is what it pretends to be, or anything kindred to it; if Christ himself uttered one word to be believed in all his claims to the Messiahship, then every man, woman, and youth in this house may have as real and close a union with him as John who leaned upon his bosom, or Mary who washed his feet with tears, or the children that were privileged to be taken into his arms and blessed. For he is a Spirit, and not a form; a vital presence, and not a bygone story; an energy in the heart, and not a soulless echo of tradition. The infant, whose brow felt the breath of our American air for the first time yesterday, enters as much into the inheritance of that life, as the Judæan fishermen that he called to leave their nets and follow him. The young man who to-morrow consecrates the enterprise of his manhood to purity and justice, making his character a steadfast column in the framework of an upright society, — to be trusted always, and believed in everywhere, — is as much an heir to that life, as the brothers that were told they should drink of Christ's cup, and be baptized with his baptism; and every patient soul, self-sacrificing amidst this week's trials, as those immediate partakers of his cross that he pledged to seat on the twelve thrones in his kingdom.

I speak to you as thinking men, not less than as feeling and sometimes suffering men, when I ask you, if you have never felt a meaning in that comparison of the Lord, expressing a union the most entire between himself and those that thus accept him, — "As the branch cannot bear fruit of itself, except it abide in the vine, no more can ye, except ye abide in me."

Does it not begin to appear, then, how the Church depends on the characters of those who fill its ranks, and execute its tasks? The life given it is given on such conditions, that if the Church is not filled, from time to time, with believing, earnest, holy hearts, its past renown will not save it. The Church of to-day depends on the souls living to-day. The Church here depends on the souls living, and about to live, here. Salvation is still a voluntary matter, and must be worked out. Christ does not abrogate free agency. The Church universal, or any branch of it, must receive ever fresh accessions of life, interest, power, through individual hearts, or else must sink inevitably to death. It lives only as they that are of it live. It is vital only with their vitality. It is a live body only as they are live Christians. "Now, then, we are ambassadors for Christ, as though God did persuade you by us: be ye reconciled to God."

II. Here enters, then, the office of the ministry. It is to produce this Life, — to take up and carry forward, in man's behalf, Christ's reconciling work; by whatever methods, according to whatever theory; by communication and by incitement; by rousing and kindling the dormant capacities of the soul, and by taking the things of the Spirit, and showing them; life, at all events, and at all cost, — life as opposed to stupor, half-belief, spiritual indifference, or a heart split between God's worship and mammon-worship, — life, not death.

1. A Living Ministry; what constitutes that? The first condition it requires is confidence, on the part of the men that exercise it, in the office and work itself. Whoever harbors a settled scepticism as to the truthfulness, the high Christian legitimacy of his calling, carries a virtual treachery in his own heart. Unless a candid and penetrating reflection will scatter it, he should abdicate. It will vitiate all his action, and unnerve the right hand of his resolution. No work can be done right thoroughly, and handsomely, about which there is a perpetual doubt, querying of the hearer's mind whether it is worth doing. Believe in it or fail in it, is a maxim that will hold of any vocation, preaching or ploughing, statesmanship or masonry. But it holds especially of work spiritual in its nature, or dealing with humanity and truth. To go on there, after a fair facing of the doubt, and a failure to overmaster it, is a trespass. It leads to a thousand mischiefs, not the least of which is the ruin of the workman's simplicity. Service under the loss of integrity is not only falsehood, but it is slavery, which is also death. Whoever would be a freeman, or even a living man, must believe in what he does. Otherwise, sow broadcast as he will, a certain subtle poison flies out with all the seed he throws, that cheats him of a harvest. It is in vain that he goes forth against sin, with lightning like Chrysostom's on his tongue, arms stout as bars of iron, and thunderbolts in his hands, if he cannot lift, out of a fervent and believing heart, the old watchword of the Crusaders, "God wills it."

2. Another condition, indispensable to a life-giving style of ministry, is distinctness of purpose. There is such a thing as ascending a pulpit from a vague feeling that the institution of the ministry is a very becoming

appendage to good society, — ought to be kept up as one of the props of respectability, without any clear conception of the object to be accomplished, or any definite aim, directing every exercise connected with it. Double-mindedness creates confusion, and confusion begets uneasiness, and uneasiness irritates to disease, and disease brings death, or that indifferent stupidity which differs from death principally in the doubtful distinction of not being buried. That labor is always most satisfactory which cuts off the loose shreds and entanglements of side-aims, and possesses a clean, rounded unity. There is no employment in the world that contemplates a more precise and clear result than preaching, — the forming, religiously, of the character of the hearer, renewing in him a spiritual life. There is always a charm and a power in sharpness of drawing, whether in an outline of Raphael, a process of logic, the progress of a profession, or the plan of life.

3. Another means of life to a living ministry is the constant presence, in the administration, of a quick and profound sense of the nature and the dignity of the souls it speaks to. It is one thing to foist human nature into the throne of God, but quite another to honor it as God's child. Every religious teacher knows, that the sanctity of the subjects he is familiar with does not secure him against belittling impressions, any more than their native vitality secures him against a lifeless utterance. Even in pleading for salvation, the august appeal to the spirit, in behalf of its eternal peace and freedom, loses half its unction and its power, because we forget, even while the burning message is on our lips, what that spirit is in its origin, in its destination, in its immortality. Could every preacher come before his people, each

time he meets them, penetrated with a living conviction of the grandeur, the infinitude, the preciousness of the soul of every hearer; could he escape from all the benumbing influence of habit, and the constant tendency of details to fritter away reverence, and tame wonder down; could he keep his realizing perception of what a soul is, as vivid as if the revelation of it were made each instant afresh to his own mind,—it is safe to say, not merely that harvests, richer than his most venturous hope dared dream of, would crown his toil, — an unprecedented intensity touching his Christ-like lips with inspiration, and clothing every word with wings of fire, — but also that a zeal for the task would seize on his own heart, sending him to it with an impulse that he could not keep back, and would make his every message like a chapter from the gospel of life. What was a task before would be a task no longer; and he would be raised so far above all lust for an outward recompense, that the thought of waiting for it would be like that of asking a premium for giving the fatherless their due, or being hired to love one's mother.

Regard man as only a creature to be got decently through the ceremony of life, or only as a lay figure to be dressed in the trappings of a prosperous civilization for purposes of art, or as an actor to be trained to a skilful part among the decorations and appointments in the histrionic genuflexions and tergiversations, the etiquette and the bargaining of a great conventional and commercial play-house of a world,— nay, further, regard him only as a mind to be filled with knowledge, or as a memory to be stuffed with information, — and it will not be strange, if, so far as all the purposes of a Christian discipline are concerned, a ministry followed under such estimates were lifeless, and should yield a lifeless product.

4. The living ministry is a ministry that never loses sight of its original and spiritual purposes, in the dull round of a mechanical or perfunctory discharge of the external duty; never sacrifices the spirit that giveth life to the letter that killeth, sense to sound, truthfulness to propriety, honesty to expediency, simplicity to exhibition, nor, what is more common than all, heartiness to sheer habit. There is a kind of preaching, and it is not confined to any one school of theology, which, if it spoke itself out, would say on Sunday morning to the congregation, after this fashion: "Well, dearly beloved brethren, I have come into your pulpit to-day, because I have agreed to come. It is in the terms of an old contract between us; a contract that was formed, to be sure, when I was disposed to take a somewhat more fanatical view of the matter than I am at present. But I respect the bargain: worship is a social decency, and a graceful adjunct to civilization. Established usage looks in this direction, and religious institutions are a politer kind of constabulary. I am here in my place, as the bell rings, therefore, and I take occasion to remark to you, as I think I have done before, that it is proper you should be saved. The Bible is pronounced authentic by competent antiquarians, and has uncommon literary merit; the laws of good-breeding have settled it that virtue is a desirable accomplishment, besides being a safe protection against unpleasant penalties invented by magistrates; and Christian faith I will recommend as a prudent specific against disagreeable consequences generally reported to follow wicked courses. Amen." In this quarter lie a peril and a wrong, which at present

comprehend in their bearings more mischief to genuine Christianity, and more disasters to the prevalence of a Christian manhood, of the heroic stamp, than all other perils and wrongs combined. I mean the tendency to a continual decay of vital sincerity in the routine of the business, the dissolution of all earnestness under the slow paralysis of the custom. The biographer of De Maistre discloses the estimate put on preaching in the seventeenth century, by observing that, in early life, he had an intention of becoming a preacher, but, happening to *become religious* on the way, he gave it up! Are there not some in our own day who reverse the process, and, having begun to preach religion, persist in preaching after they have ceased to be religious? It is this heartless routine that is fatal to both parties: it is the death of the function, and the damnation of the functionary. Rather than have its life eaten out by it, a Christian society would do well to be disbanded. Better that the formalities of such a ministry should be brushed away, as a stumbling-block before the gate of Heaven.

5. A Living Ministry: its engagedness will be a natural engagedness, and its methods natural methods; not a spasmodic, not a fitful, not an artificial activity. It will not attempt to excite a warmth of the moral parts by friction, nor to promote a galvanic action of principle by the apparatus of an ecclesiastical battery, nor to extort gushes of pietistic sentiment by the forcing-pump of strained exhortation. It will throw itself back on the laws of the soul, and use no other dynamics than the spiritual. It will do nothing for stage effect, which is the essence of cant; using speech out of which all meaning has withered. The life it will seek first to possess in its own inmost heart, and then to transmit and diffuse, is

that sustained, regular life, having its springs among the pillars under the oracles of God, beating with the even pulse of health, revealing its transcendent beauty in daily purity and justice, as conspicuous in the household, the market-place, and the counting-room as in the sanctuary. This life will *tell* on the open and yielding heart of the world, with a benignity of influence, of such holy and regenerative power, as no reach of vision, save that prophetic eye that looks into the immortal ages, can measure.

6. A living ministry will cast off the spirit of formalism, or rather that dead body of formalism that has no spirit; it will forsake paths that have no better recommendation than that they are beaten and dusty, out of allegiance to every behest that comes direct from the bosom of reality; it will be in itself, on its practical side, an example of its doctrine; it will set that doctrine forth in a spirit at once transparent and fearless, unpretending and scholarlike; despising all guilty servility to the overbearing few or the popular many, it will refuse to be hemmed in by any arbitrary geography of its province, or to be imposed upon by politic sophistry; it will have its frank and independent word on every matter that affects the hopes or the integrity of mankind, without the boyish folly of perpetually running about to proclaim its independence, and saying bold things only to show that it dares to; it will free itself from all prejudices that impair its single-mindedness; it will place itself among men, as a genuine helper of humanity, in all its garbs and all its trials, brave as a prophet, devoted as an apostle, tender as John, fearless as Paul, ardent as Peter, blameless as James, a learner of the Christ, a workman whose errand is from Heaven, to persuade and lead

men's souls thither. When such a ministry is realized, be sure not only that it will not have to dispute its title to honor, will not have to plead for a hearing, will not complain of a decline of its prestige; be sure not only that the eager heart of the community will reverence it, will leap to listen to it, but be sure also that the reign of irreligious worldliness will be broken up, and the fairer kingdom of spiritual truth and life will be established on its ruins.

This sort of ministry, too, proceeding out of an endearing faith in the Lord of life, will extinguish the vile ambition among preachers to turn sermons into orations, and the pulpit into an ethical or literary lecture-stand, substituting smartness for sanctity,—the bitter root of so much clerical impotence. Preaching that runs from any man's brain downward is very likely to run thin and run out, as so much preaching does. Only that unction is mighty, which, being poured through a mind at once cultivated and consecrated, draws its original inspiration from Him who spake as man never spake. Overmastering all his anxieties about his position, foreclosing the query what he shall preach *about*, a query that always reveals a relaxed conviction and an empty covenant, this sweeps all his energies one way, in spite of indifference or opposition, in spite of worldly complaisance and flattery.

I have said enough already of the substance of doctrine to be preached, to forestall any occasion for enlarging upon it as one of the qualifications of the ministry here. One or two warnings, however, lie so much across the line of our liberal tendencies, that I cannot forbear an allusion to them.

7. A ministry of the word of life, as follows from our

doctrine thus far, is one that preaches more than moral decency, — preaches piety, regeneration, and faith. Enthusiasm is not a danger that the modern Church has much to fear from. We want righteousness much; but a vital faith first, as the quickener, the inspiration of that. In the Pilgrim's Progress, Bunyan tells us of a Mr. *Legality*, "a very judicious man, and a man of very good name"; and of his having "a pretty young man to his son, whose name is Civility"; and of their both boasting great skill to take off the burden from Christian's shoulders; and of their dwelling in the village of Morality, where provision is always cheap and good, and one may live with honest neighbors in credit and good fashion. But Evangelist shows that Mr. Legality is a spiritual cheat, and that his son Civility is a hypocrite, and that the village of Morality has no church in it for the preaching of any but the doctrine of this world, because "by the deeds of the law shall no man living be justified." We must go, brethren, beyond Sinai to Calvary, — beyond the deeds of the law to the pardon of the cross.

> "Talk they of morals?
> The grand morality, thou bleeding Lamb,
> Is love of thee."

8. The ministry that holds forth the "word of life" must not be afraid to assert sometimes, on the authority of Scripture, what passes its own reason. Every great spiritual doctrine terminates in mystery, by the very necessity of spirit. Bound religion by the geography of the understanding, and it ceases to be religion. Faith is sacrificed to science. There is more in our religion than dictionaries can define, or syntax state, or logic prove. The very essence of faith is a reverential confession of

the limitations of sight. In one of the temples at Memphis, there was a statue of Isis, with the face veiled. A son of the priest, curious to unlock this marble secret, and to see what hidden beauty might glorify the features beneath, hacked off the stone veil with a hammer. He found, of course, only the ragged gashes of his own mischief. An impious inquisitiveness, prying too far, had spoilt the divine symmetry of the image. So is it with us all, too often,—foolish children, that would subject the mysteries of revelation to the inspection of sense, and, despising faith, rudely insist on vision. We leave only a deformity to admire, and a ruin to adore. Not yet, not yet, can we behold face to face! Few eyes, I think, have seen deeper into God's majestic disclosures than those piercing ones that looked out from under the dark Hebrew brow of the Christian historian, Neander. But this was the motto that he kept inscribed on his study-wall, making his library to open upward into heaven,—"Now we see through a glass darkly, but *then* face to face."

9. A living ministry is one that not only speaks with directness and simplicity, addressing itself, with a tone of manly earnestness, straight to the matter in hand, as if dealing with ponderous realities that need no circumlocution, but it avoids abstruse terms for the most part, and, in preference, chooses language that is concrete and personal. The individual or the sect, for instance, that speaks habitually of Christianity, however reverentially and gratefully, will be found to exercise a feeble command over the affections of men, compared with the one which, when it means the same thing, says, *Christ Jesus, the Saviour*. So the preaching that enumerates the doctrines which cluster about the crucifixion, and presents

them, however eloquently, as only an abstract scheme of truths, will often glide languidly over the unroused conscience; while enthusiasm takes fire, and zeal stretches every nerve, at each thrilling mention of that central figure, the cross, or those dear scenes, so vivid to the sense,—Calvary and the Garden. Napoleon's celebrated maxim, "There are but two powers in the world, kindness and the sword," is but a feeble paraphrase of the fiery-hearted Loyola's,—"Two kingdoms divide the world, Immanuel's and Satan's." It was never the utterance of smooth abstractions, that wrought with drastic energy on the dead in trespasses and sins;—brought three thousand converts into the Church, by a single sermon at Pentecost; fascinated the young Florentine artists, ând drew them away from their models and galleries to catch the pictures that were unrolled in the sentences of Savonarola, the author of the "Triumphus Crucis"; moved back an audience of French noblesse in a perceptible bodily recoil from the cathedral altar, when the fingers of Massillon's imagination opened the covers of the blazing pit; cast down thousands of sturdy English yeomen upon their knees to pray, when Wesley ordered the visible array of heaven and earth into the service of his oratory; bore the gracious blessing of Bunyan's enchanting dream on its world-wide errand of holy delight,—a charming evangel; made the stout-hearted New England Puritans at Northampton clutch the railings of their pews when Edwards told them of the "due time," as if their feet were that instant veritably sliding; and extorted from a brave but sensual soldier the confession, that he would rather storm the bridge of Lodi than hear a chapter of the Epistles to the Corinthians. *Dying* men, you have observed, speak little of Christianity, and less of the system of truth, or laws of nature. They say *Christ.* Last breaths are too short for abstractions, and can only articulate the one dear and all-prevailing name. The fading sight loses all images but the cross. And so a whole body of hard divinity has sometimes been melted down by one hour of pain; and, on the stammering lips of death, a dainty philosophy has burst into that strong cry of praise, — " I know that my Redeemer liveth."

Revelation is never abstruse. The New Testament says nothing of " Christianity." The word is not there. But when God would save the world, he sends the Saviour, with a throbbing heart and a living voice. The first teachers said nothing about Christianity; and, for an abstract Christianity, it is doubtful if they would ever have faced martyrdom. But "Christ crucified" and "the resurrection" they could preach in jails and synagogues, turn the world upside down for and die for, counting it all joy. And so effectually were some of the strong concrete words they used,—though borrowed from a Hebrew economy swept clean out of the world almost while they were writing, — yet lodged in the undying affections of men, that you can no more extract their power by age, than you can dry their odors out of the cedars of Lebanon.

Is it said that such representations of the profession as I have here given, by presenting a standard that is impracticably high, are a discouragement to those that might be induced to enter it? Heaven forbid that anything should be said, here or anywhere, dissuasive of assuming the ministerial office; the reluctance is deplorable enough already. But I do not suppose that a stringent standard is one of the things likely to repel any laborer true-minded and stout-hearted enough to make the Church desire him. On the contrary, I believe a lofty standard, to every man whose nerve is not flaccid, — any brave, resolute, aspiring man, — is one of the most fascinating things under the sun. It will even tighten slackened sinews.

And just here I find a new argument for a living ministry, in the fact that it would be the speediest antidote to that dearth of efficient ministers that is now, in all Protestant sects, so generally lamented. Various remedies are proposed. But let it be thoroughly understood and felt in a community, that its religious teachers were a body not merely reputably alive, but crowded and instinct at every point with life, absorbed with interest, aglow with enthusiasm, and nothing in the compass of human attainments would be so commanding over the inclinations of young men. Possibly some, whom other callings tempt by a louder promise of wealth or reputation, might be found willing to forego fame and luxury, for the sake of contributing their share to the sanctification of the coming age. Let the nucleus formed be in Christian earnest, — be full of living, burning heat; and, like the molten jet of volcanic lava we sometimes see shooting up through the inert strata of rock and soil about it, it would fuse all the surrounding mass into a state homogeneous with its own.

So of the want of sympathy complained of in the profession. How can sympathy exist where there is no consentaneous spiritual life? What is sympathy, indeed, except that, — *σὺν πάθος*, — a feeling together? A lifeless sympathy is a contradiction in terms. Fellow-feeling in death, — harmony between corpses, — is an absurdity. Bring in vitality of purpose, and vitality of action, and you break down all barriers of suspicion.

Raise the head-waters of spiritual life, and all the separate fountains become so full and leaping in their motion, that they gush spontaneously over, and mingle together. When the new life is begotten, even the tongue of dumbness becomes vocal, — like the healed man's in Decapolis.

III. But it is time to turn, and contemplate the living Church, — the whole body of Christian disciples, ministered to by this living ministry, nourished by a vital communion with Christ the Source, and putting forth the energy of its inner life, in a practical piety on the one hand, and a spiritual righteousness on the other.

See how such a state of the Church would furnish the best possible safeguard against the evils that, in these times, most threaten its purity and its peace. One of these is dogmatism. Once possess a man, no matter whether he is a Puritan or a Bishop, a Quaker or a Cardinal, with a quickened and renewed spiritual life, and to him dogmatism becomes impossible. He may be a controversialist or an enthusiast, but never an acrimonious dogmatist. A principle animates him, which, just so far as it actuates him, saves him from that particular sin. It marks the distinction between that cordial attachment to believed doctrine which is commendable, and that complacent assumption of infallibility in the creed which is condemnable. It gives him a touchstone, by which he instinctively shrinks from bigotry, as from a partnership in disgrace, and arms him against being victimized by the idol-speculations of his own brain. Whatever names the boasting sects may chronicle in their calendars of saints, none that deserved canonization ever lived who worshipped the abstractions of dogma more than the Lord of life. It is with denominations as with persons: in proportion as they are quick with spiritual purpose, they are free from the shame of dogmatism.

Another danger is formalism. Formalism crept into the Church from two sources, Judaism and Paganism,—one of which completely wrapped up and hid its life in ceremony, till it suffered consumption; and the other had not life enough under its ritual to keep its pomp and pageantry even outwardly decent. Once in, formalism found material enough to foster it in human indolence and human pride; and so it kept on growing by the help of every idle Christian's sluggishness, and every bad system's misleading, and every ecclesiastical despot's ambition, till finally it swelled into the vast, stately, hollow, tinselled, and draperied fabric of the Popedom. When religious forms have first been devised, a certain freshness of conviction has gone into them, that has made them vital. But presently the life has refused to stand and stagnate in these cisterns, and so ebbed away and sought out new channels. The mistake has been, that the forms have insisted on standing, after the life within was gone; and accordingly their figure has been that of wooden vessels shrunk and dried in the sun. It was so with the forms of the Romish Church, of the Church of Henry the Eighth and the Bishops, of Presbyterianism and of Quakerism, for the Quaker is in his way a formalist. But indolence and pride are as much opposed by *spiritual life* now, as the Judaism and Heathenism of eighteen hundred years ago. Where there is that life, how can ceremonies be put before virtues,—the husk and shell before the kernel and substance,—broad phylacteries for a generous character,—religious usages as substitutes for righteousness and faith,—mint, anise, and cumin, for self-sacrifice, charity, and truth? In a consecration to the substance of piety; in a nearer fellowship with Jesus, and a more palpable and inwrought experience of his regenerating and transforming truth,— in this, and this only, shall the Church, or any of its societies, find escape from formalism. Form is body. A living doctrine never need advertise for a body, nor go carefully about to invent one, any more than a young oak needs to advertise for a trunk and branches. God giveth it a body as it hath pleased him. Get the faith, and it will shape a form of its own. Have a heart full of prayer; or else a liturgy, a gradation of priestly offices, postures, wax-candles burning in the day-time, bowing to the east, priestly manipulations, will never so conciliate the Holy Ghost as to matriculate you in the arms of the holy Jerusalem which is above and free, the mother of us all.

Another embarrassment to the modern Church is in the suspicion, if not the open enmity, of those companies of men associated for the special reform of specific social abuses, whose young ardor for the favorite cause makes the Church seem lumbering and superannuated. Is it not clear that the Church will best discharge herself of blame, reconcile her sometimes unfilial child, Philanthropy, to her bosom, escape all compromise of dignity, and at the same time be realizing her own destiny, by addressing herself to the most earnest unfolding of the divine life within her, out of which all humanities must be supplied, and becoming altogether alive with Christ?

Another bad tendency is to partisanship. Malicious as the temper of religious parties and partisans is, *direct* efforts to allay it will always be less effective than that consecrated fervor in the life of godliness, which crowds it out of breath, and grows over it. It is hardly to be supposed, that an Antichrist that has lodged under the shelter of the nominal fold so many centuries can be eliminated by a single struggle. He is too hospitably entertained, and too assiduously courted, even by those that in their better moments venture to hint that he is unwelcome, to make such hints effective. The Church has never enjoyed an entire exemption from civil war. The moment men agreeing in theology have been denominated, as if their name had wrought a malignant spell upon them, they have begun to commit denominational sin. Sectarian ambition springs up; sectarian pride sets in; sectarian animosity is engendered; sectarian officiousness goes out capturing proselytes; sectarian jealousy rankles; and finally, with all its fury, wrath, and strategy, its bloodhound passions, and its musketry of accusation, and its small arms of malignant slander, open sectarian battle rages. Christendom slips back into practical Paganism, while Christians sit picking motes out of one another's eyes. One would think an intelligent reading of experience would show, that, if any other possible agency than a higher tone of spiritual life were to accomplish unity or concord, it would have been attained before this. That is the only experiment that has not been fairly and fully tried. When it is tried fairly and fully, it will solve the difficulty that theology has been spending ingenious abstractions upon ever since the days of Constantine. Ecclesiastical councils will drop into matters of history. Trent, and Dort, and Nice will be only landmarks of a completed pilgrimage across a desert, — the grass-covered battle-fields of a finished crusade, — ending, not in a holy sepulchre, but in a holy life. Tests and bulls of excommunication will be respectfully hung up with other antiquarian relics, and it will be seen and felt that a Church is nothing less than a vital body of cordial believers in Christ, partakers of his spirit, and workers for his truth. A faith so quick and ample will one day realize the wondrous reconciliations of the Prophet's vision in the holy mountain, — where the lion lies down with the lamb, and none hurt nor destroy; it will lay Calvin's hand in Channing's, — put the band of one magic name, even the common Master's, round the lives of the philanthropic Clarkson and the mystical devotees of Port Royal, — draw a Protestant veneration to the Catholic Fénelon, — and canonize the practical, road-building Oberlin of Waldbach into companionship with the quietistic saints of the Romish Calendar.

Thus we come, finally, in our subject, — as God grant we may come veritably and visibly in the age that he is preparing, — to the *Living Church.* It is a body, whose life, in all the possible strictness and signification of the word, is the life of Christ in the soul. Of the accomplishments, the amenities, the graces of intellect that adorn our worldly relations, modern civilization leaves no deficiency. What we most deeply and pressingly need is the life of religious sensibility, — the faith that leans on God, the hope that reaches up to immortality, the love that seizes things invisible. This we need, superadded to our civilization, — our educational and commercial privileges, — or rather, laid as the basis of them. Life itself, the true or inward life, is overlaid and crushed by the mere appendages of living. Buying and selling, getting gain and getting knowledge, are made to limit the energies of our immortality, and dwarf God's image in us. Science as well as traffic, literature and the schools as well as business, wait for the ennobling influence of faith, the purifying breath of devotion, the sanctification of prayer. I have heard of an honest clergyman, a preacher to sailors, in one of the floating Bethels that are seen at some of our Eastern seaports, whose controversial reading hardly kept pace with his zeal, and who was asked one day, whether his chapel was "high church" or "low church." Supposing, in his simplicity, that the question referred to the position of his Bethel, he answered, that it depended entirely on the tide! Now, fashionable worldliness is the tide that graduates the standing of too many of our churches; and the higher it keeps their taxes and social reputation, the lower it keeps the tone of their piety.

Never so accommodate religion, gentlemen, in your preaching, to the fraudulent practices of the business world, that you will fall into the same class with the Gypsy mother mentioned by Borrow the traveller, who said to her children in the morning, "Now, children, say your prayers; and then go, steal your breakfast."

Spiritual indolence is, in these times, the worst enemy the Church has to encounter. It is not that men openly reject and make war upon her, but that they drowsily sleep around her altar. It is that men are content with such paltry satisfactions and tinsel comforts as the senses can bribe them with, heedless of the inward instincts that claim communion with the skies. It is that eternity has no awfulness to them, life no depth of meaning, enjoyment no obligations, bereavement no solemnity, suffering and sorrow no prophetic suggestions of an hereafter, the soul no aspirations, conscience no echo of God, Christ no enrapturing beauty in his holiness, the resurrection no pledge of heaven. It is that men can stretch themselves on their couches of ease, and slumber, amidst the sublimest mysteries and most stirring revelations of Providence. What we need, then, to bring back the Church to her life, is to awake and arise; to hearken and watch; to wait on the Holy Spirit; to snatch the film from our eyeballs; to lift our waiting souls to God, like flowers parched with drought to the rain; to breathe in his blessed life; to be regenerated and consecrated by his inspiration of love, communicated through Jesus Christ our Lord.

There is a life that is fitful and spasmodic, lively in the conference and enthusiastic at a revival, but which falls into a dreary eclipse at the merchant's desk, or the lobbies of a State-house, or the political caucus, or the round of a housekeeper's vexations. But the life of a Christlike soul is as steadfast as it is earnest, as firm in the scoffs of the judgment-hall, or under the crown of thorns, as in the meditations of Mount Olivet and the solemn stillness of the temple. It stands with as serene a forehead before the scorn of fashion, as before the flatteries of partisans. It lifts itself with as majestic port against the sly seductions of Fortune, when she bids a higher and higher price for the soul, as when the way is safe, and all perils are swept out of its path. Where the Church *lives*, — where it holds its Master's spirit and truth, not as the mortuary of a deceased and buried benefactor, but as the inbreathing of a present inspiration, — it will never suffer its members to sit idly with folded hands, looking lazily out on the white fields of harvest, where no reaper's sickle rings against the wheat; but it will send them forth to work, nerved with an impulse that no disappointment can palsy, no misgivings keep back. You may burn temples; you may pulverize rituals; you may absorb creeds; you may strangle missionaries; but the eternally reproductive energy of such a Church as that lives on.

If the Church will go forth, then, to win new victories, she needs only to take fearlessly up the supremacy with which her God has dowered her, namely, the reconciling life of her indwelling Lord. Shutting up all internal questions that make her militant against herself, she is to move on in her own absolute, sublime majesty, militant only against every form of sin, to enthrone the kingdom of God. She must cease to beg favors of worldly policy. She must stop her infamous coquetry with Mammon. She must not be bowing on Sundays to sectarian prejudice, nor on week-days to social respectability, nor ever whisper guilty flatteries to popular sins, nor wait till great public vices are manifestly dying out of themselves, and feeble with approaching dissolution, before she dares strike at them. The stanch, uncompromising sincerity of old Puritans and Confessors must be in her muscles. An awful zeal must gird up her loins. Purity, freedom, equity, are to be more to her than costly churches; the prayers of saintly men and women, and children too, her patronage; and her daily speech, the benediction of charity. She must hold forth, through her ministers, the word of life; to wit, that God is in Christ, reconciling the world unto himself.

You, my brothers, members of the Graduating Class, are henceforth permitted the unrivalled privilege of entering into these grand enterprises of amelioration, furnished by wise instruction for your lofty office.

I bid you move into your sacred calling with such joyous hopes as the Puritan army had, who marched to the fight at Naseby chanting praise. Go, charged with something of the brave temper of that devoted missionary,

Gordon Hall, so ardent to reach the heathen with his message, that he offered to work his passage to the field; with the faith of those valiant discoverers that burnt their boats behind them when they touched the shore; with the self-scrutiny of Paul, who agonized, lest, having preached to others, though woe was on him if he preached not, he himself might be cast away. Without these, all the machinery of Funds and Theological Schools will be like expecting to make sand deserts fruitful by drainage.

See that no needed reforms are unchurched, because the Church would not nurture them, through your lifelessness or cowardice. Be independent, and not mere movable articles of church furniture. Scorn all measures of self-promotion, and renounce ambition before you cross this threshold to-night.

Lean only on the Spirit of Infinite Pity and Help. Keep the simplicity of childlike trust. Never measure your fidelity by the poor signals of man's applause. Be willing to share your Master's glory, made perfect through suffering. Nowhere be ashamed of the Gospel of Redemption. Be sure your real success, in the last awards, will be found in the exact measure of the fervor and constancy of your communion with your Lord. Let it be enough if his strength is manifest through your weakness. Hold forth "the word of life." Preach "God in Christ, reconciling the world unto himself." And

"May the hour
Soon come, when, all false gods, false creeds, false prophets
Demolished, the round world shall be at last
The mercy-seat of God, the heritage
Of Christ, and the possession of the Spirit!"

THE END.

www.ingramcontent.com/pod-product-compliance
Lightning Source LLC
LaVergne TN
LVHW020933110826
845150LV00004B/845

* 9 7 8 1 4 2 5 5 5 3 3 1 9 *